D0309063

TYRONE GUTHRIE

TYRONE GUTHRIE

A BIOGRAPHY

✦

JAMES FORSYTH

HAMISH HAMILTON
LONDON

First published in Great Britain 1976
by Hamish Hamilton Ltd
90 Great Russell Street London WC1B 3PT

Copyright © 1976 by James Forsyth

SBN 241 89471 9

Printed in Great Britain by
Ebenezer Baylis & Son Limited
The Trinity Press, Worcester, and London

CONTENTS

	Prologue	ix
1	'Do Well—Doubt Not' (1900–1914)	1
2	Wellington and War (1914–1918)	20
3	Oxford and Acting (1919–1924)	34
4	Belfast and 'The Wireless' (1924–1926)	52
5	Glasgow and Theatre on a Shoestring (1926–1928)	68
6	London and The Microphone Play (1928–1929)	80
7	Cambridge—The Festival Theatre (1929–1930)	85
8	Montreal and 'The Romance of Canada' (1930–1931)	98
9	Marriage and the Westminster (1931–1932)	107
10	Over the Waterloo Bridge to the Old Vic (1933–1934)	127
11	West End and Broadway (1934–1935)	139
12	Back to 'The People's Theatre' (1936–1939)	145
13	War Again (1939–1946)	172
14	Here There and Everywhere (1946–1948)	197
15	Festival (1948–1952)	203
16	Canada, Triumph and a Tent (1952–1953)	221
17	From Shakespeare to Sophocles (1953–1956)	248
18	The U.S. Repertory Campaign (1956–1963)	260
19	Money for Jam (1963–1969)	284
20	Trip to the Antipodes (1970)	307
21	All's Well That Ends Well (1971)	328
	Epilogue: In Memoriam, Judith Guthrie	345
	Appendix: A Very Irish Sort of Will	347
	List of Theatrical Productions	349
	Tyrone Guthrie's Honours and Awards	354
	Published Works	355
	Index	357

ILLUSTRATIONS

Between pages 36 and 37

1a   The Festival Theatre, Stratford, Ontario.

1b   The tented theatre founded by Guthrie—from which the above grew.

2 and 3   Family Scrapbook: Annagh-ma-Kerrig, the Power and Guthrie family home; Norah Power; Dr. Thomas Clement Guthrie; Tyrone Guthrie with the Annagh-ma-Kerrig lake and house in the background; Peggie Guthrie and Judith Brereton; Aunt Sue Power; Tony and Peggie.

4a   Guthrie as actor: Arcadian Shepherd, Oxford U.D.S. production of *Le Bourgeois Gentilhomme*.

4b   Guthrie as pioneer radio producer, Belfast BBC studio, 1926.

Between pages 164 and 165

5a   On tour with the Scottish National Players.

5b   Flora Robson in the Guthrie production of *Iphigenia in Tauris*, the Cambridge Festival Theatre, 1929.

6a   Tony with his mother, soon after her blindness, at the front door of Annagh-ma-Kerrig.

6b   'Prayer session' by the honeymoon tent: Tony and Judy.

6c   Picnic pairs: Hubert, Peggy, Judy, Tony.

7a   With Charles Laughton, during Guthrie's first season with the Old Vic.

7b   With Vivien Leigh and Laurence Olivier at rehearsal of the Olivier *Hamlet* in the courtyard of Kronberg Castle, Elsinore, 1937.

8a   The Guthries with the Old Vic group during wartime evacuation at Burley.

8b   *The Three Estates*, the Assembly Hall, Edinburgh.

Between pages 292 and 293

9a   Tanya Moiseiwitch and Cecil Clarke with the model of the stage, Stratford, Ontario, 1953.

9b   With Tanya Moiseiwitch in rehearsal, by the tent pole.

10a   *Oedipus Rex*, the Stratford Theatre Company at the Edinburgh Festival, 1956.

10b   With T. Edward Hambleton in the Phoenix Theatre, New York, 1960.

11a   *Uncle Vanya*, the Guthrie Theatre, Minneapolis, 1969.

11b   By the Newbliss Signal Cabin office of the jam factory.

12a   *The House of Atreus*, the Guthrie Theatre, Minneapolis, 1967. Agamemnon returns from the Trojan war with Cassandra.

12b   *The House of Atreus*. Orestes suppliant.

12c   Tony and Judith Guthrie.

Illustration numbers 1a and 1b are reproduced by permission of Herb Nott & Co.; 5b by permission of Scott & Wilkinson; 7b by permission of the London News Agency Photos Ltd.; 9b and 12c by permission of Walter Curtin; and 11a, 12a and 12b by permission of the Guthrie Theatre, Minneapolis.

PROLOGUE

Anti-Broadway, anti-West End, anti everything implied in the term 'Legitimate Theatre', he ended up with a legitimate claim to the title of 'most important, British-born theatre director of his time'.

Tony Guthrie came in with the century—he was born in 1900. In person he was at least three things: a formidable, remote, giant of a public figure, very, very English in manner; a rather shy, boyish, private Irishman, of great wit and companionability; and —emerging between these paradoxical poles—the electrifino professional figure of an indefatigable *worker* in Theatre. He sweated more on the job, and had more sheer fun out of it, than most of the devoted subjects of his inspired—or his catastrophic— tyrannies. To be tyrannized into a Guthrie failure could be as thrilling as to be involved in somebody else's success. The benefit of his commanding presence, and the loss of it, affected not hundreds in the Theatre but thousands in and out of it. From these may I specially mention a few who greatly went out of their way to help me with this book:

Mr. and Mrs. Hubert Butler, Miss Tanya Moiseiwitsch, Dame Flora Robson, Professor Christopher Scaife, Mrs. Dora Mavor Moore, Mr. Alfred and Mrs. Dama Bell, Mrs. Annette Chamberlain, Sir Alec Guinness, Mr. Barrie Stavis, Mr. T. Edward Hambleton, Miss Mildred Stock, Mr. Kenneth Rae, Dr. Robertson Davies, Mr. Tom Patterson, Mr. and Mrs. John Goetz, Mr. John Boyd, Professor Fred Alexander, Mr. John Sumner.

It is impossible to give a 'curtain call' to all who deserve it. Therefore, in accordance with Guthrie's contention that in a production there are no 'extras', just some players playing smaller parts than others—all equal in human importance—let it be equal tribute to the following:

Mr. Henry Adler, Mr. James R. Aikens, Mr. Louis Appelbaum, Mr. Dominic Argento, Mr. Charles Baker, Mr. Paul Ballentyne,

Dr. Arthur Ballet, Mr. Freddie Bennett, Mr. John Boyd, Mr. Philip Von Blon, Mr. Martin Bretherton, Mr. Tom Brown and Tammy, Mrs. Mary and Mr. Robert Burns, Miss Zoe Caldwell, Mr. James Cairncross, Mr. Douglas Campbell, Mr. Cecil Clarke, Miss Elspeth Cochrane, Dr. Sherwood Collins, Miss Patricia Conolly, Mr. James Cowan, Mr. John Coulter, Mr. John Cowles, Jr., Mrs. Julia Crampton, Mr. Jon Cranney, Mr. Michael Curtis, Miss Margaret D'Arcy, Mrs. John Drinkwater, Mr. Robert Eddison, Mr. Robert Fairfield, Mr. Simon Finkel, Colonel O'Connell FitzSimon, Mr. Christopher FitzSimon, Miss Kaye Flanagan, Mr. Tom Fleming, Mr. Norman Freeman, Mr. Brian Friel, Miss Annette Garceau, Mr. Jean Gascon, Mrs. Ravina Gelfand, Mr. Colin George, the late Mr. John Gibson, Sir John Gielgud, Miss Rosamund Gilder, Mr. Norman Ginsbury, Professor Rodney Green, Mrs. Jonathan Griffin, Miss Charlotte Guindon, Miss Amelia Hall, Mr. Donald Harron, Mr. John Haynes, Miss Eileen Herlie, Mrs. Joan Hodge, Mr. Joseph Hone, Mr. Ronald Horner, Dr. Norris Houghton, Mr. Eric House, Mr. H. S. P. Hughes, Mr. William Hutt, Miss Frances Hyland, Mr. Brian Jackson, Miss Patricia Kennedy, the late Miss Norah Kesteven, Mr. John V. Killer, Mr. Michael Langham, Mr. Alan K. Lathrop, Mr. Bill Lavender, Mr. John Mabbott, Mr. Fulton Mackay, Mr. Herbert Marshall, Mr. Elliott Martin, Mr. Joseph Martin, Mr. Ronald Mason, Mr. Jack Merigold, M Peter Mews, Mr. John Moody, Mr. Mavor Moore, Dr. Robert Moulton, Mr. Eugene McCabe, Mr. Seamus McGorman, Lord Olivier, Mr. Richard Pasco, Miss Joan Peterson, Mr. Vic Polley, Mr. Anthony Quayle, Mrs. Mary Quinlan, Mr. Oliver Rea, Mr. Llewellyn Rees, Miss Barbara Reid, Mr. Ken Ruta, Mr. Al Rossi, Madame Suria Saint-Denis, Mr. Max Schaffner, Mr. Alan Schneider, Mr. Don Schoenbaum, Miss Molly Sole, Miss Pauline Spender, Mr. Roger L. Stevens, Miss Elizabeth Sweeting, Miss Jean Taylor-Smith, Dame Sybil Thorndike, Mr. Powys Thomas, Mr. Neil Vipond, Mr. Michael Wager, Mr. James Wallace, Mr. Herbert Whittaker, Miss Joan White, Dr. Jean Wilhelm, Mrs. Margaret E. Wilson, Miss Elizabeth Wood, Mr. Peter Zeisler, Mr. Louis Zelle.

My task was made much lighter by the generous cooperation of:

The Phoenix Trust of The Society of Authors (grant towards the considerable travelling expenses necessary for a subject of such international coverage); The Old Vic; The Stratford

(Ontario) Festival Theatre; The Guthrie Theatre, Minneapolis; and the BBC, London and Belfast, for access to archival material; The Guthrie Estate, through the Irish Ministry of Finance, in giving access to and use of Guthrie papers; and, for the three years of the book's preparation, the valuable help of my wife Louise as research assistant and secretary-general to the project.

As for the subject of the book himself I shall always remain deeply grateful to him, and it remains to be seen if it was a wise bit of 'casting' by which—not many days before his death—he cast me in the part of The Biographer.

JAMES FORSYTH,
Grainloft, Ansty,
Sussex
29th April 1976

CHAPTER ONE

'DO WELL — DOUBT NOT'*
(1900–1914)

In the first summer of the twentieth century on July 2, 1900, William Tyrone Guthrie was born. The event took place in Tunbridge Wells, county of Kent, 'Garden of England'. The royal spa still drew a fair number of Victorian gentlefolk to take the medicinal waters. Bath-chairs could be hired from polite, bowler-hatted, strong men, so that one might come and go at a more convalescent pace than by horse-cab. In current social values the baby was certainly well born; having a general's daughter for mother and a successful young Scottish doctor for father. In early years there were assuring signs for his adoring mother that Willie Tyrone would decidedly be a bright boy and that, in some chosen sphere, he would probably grow to be among the successes of the new century. He was in fact to outstrip expectation in both success and growth. He grew to be quite a giant of a man physically. But even giants begin as small boys, and one of the discoveries of the century with which he grew is how much of the Man is already determined in the Boy.

At the age of one the alert infant, gifted as he was with the eyes of an eagle, might have seen an awful lot of black crêpe ebb and flow on things a-move in the vicinity of his high perambulator. Nobody could tell the congenitally loyal little subject that he had just become an Edwardian. Nobody could immediately be certain what that would mean (it being unpredictable just how much of a royal folly King Edward might turn out to be). But the great Queen Victoria, of Great Britain and her great Empire, had gone to join her beloved Albert in Heaven.

By the time he was four and noticeably handsome, the Theatre began, mildly, to have an influence on him. The influence came from his mother's side. Theatre, as we shall see, was in Norah Guthrie's family tree and she was a keen theatre-goer. Up in London, ladies like her would be well aware that the daring

* Motto of the royal spa of Tunbridge Wells.

plays of Henrik Ibsen were now being referred to as 'The Ibscene Theatre'. However, at the same time, a new play by J. M. Barrie was proving to be the best of theatrical news for her and all literate mothers of adorable sons. Peter Pan had just flown in through a stage window for the first time, and had begun to subject the nation to a new, and not undangerous, nursery mythology.

At the age of five the adored boy was subjected to the shock of a new arrival in his nursery—and not through the window: a little sister. Susan Margaret was called Peggy, and was to be the only other child in the archetypal Guthrie family of Father, Mother, Son and Daughter. At the age of seven he was taken by his mother to his first theatre. There he was bemused by all the stage necromancy of Peter Pan, Wendy, Tinker Bell and the whole adept bag of Barrie theatrical tricks. Through his mother's theatre-going he was being moved into the fringes of Stage society; one of the regular companions of Norah Guthrie—and one to whom she served as bridesmaid—was Katie Gielgud. Mrs. Gielgud was one of the great Terry family and it was very few years later that she took *her* small son, John, to his first play: *Peter Pan*.

The Guthrie nursery at 'Belmont', Church Road, was smaller but of a class with the Barrie stage nursery. But though the Theatre may have invaded the boy's nursery to haunt him with the coy possibility of nightly visitation through window by boy who would never grow up, it was by looking out of that high window in the day that young Guthrie caught sight of Drama which immediately fascinated him; a more public drama. Pretentious academics of our day would call what the boy saw Ritual Street Theatre. It was in fact scenes from weddings and funerals. They took place in porch, on steps and pavements of the church opposite—Trinity Church of Church Road. It stood slap opposite the Guthrie semi-detached. The nursery window gave a 'gallery seat' view and somebody encouragingly enjoying the show was his young Irish nurse, Tia (Christina Moore). She adored the boy. But the boy adored organizing his little sister and by the age of eight he would arrange things so that the right stool or chair would ensure that Peggy joined him as audience. Outward-looking and enormously observant as he always was, he could observe that the spectacle of a wedding was a kind of comedy—a funeral a sort of tragic mystery. Both fascinatingly had to do with people dressing up and acting strange. For a wedding the

bells would ring happily and everything would go at a jolly pace;
flowers would feature in both; but the lady of the principal pair of
players at the wedding would make a spectacular entry in pure
white, accompanied by girls and ladies in gay silks; coloured
confetti would be thrown—sometimes, by some strange ritual,
rice; tableaux would be struck to let all the people in the street
(and windows) get a good look at the cast; then organized dis-
persal would take place in an atmosphere of fun. Funerals were an
utterly different affair; moved at a slow pace with everyone in
black; ladies with black-veiled faces and the bell tolling slowly;
then, by the church door, the little crowd would fall silent; every
man out in the street at the time would take off his hat or cap,
and, out of the church, men in black would move as one, like a
many-legged black beetle whose body was the coffin, its back
sometimes banked with flowers. The two keen pairs of juvenile
eyes would watch in awe from their eyrie as it moved towards the
glass-walled hearse where the patient, black-plumed, black
horses nodded and waited. When it moved off it would go as slow
as men walked. There could then be a real procession of horse
carriages; with maybe a motor-car to follow (trying as hard not to
backfire as he had tried not to hiccup at morning Family Prayers).

Those two small but potentially tall figures at the Guthrie
window were to remain very close throughout much of life; were
to continue to make acute observations on 'Them'—the world of
others out there—from the secure vantage point of 'Us'. The
little Guthrie family of tall people with distinguished ancestors
was a very secure base from which to observe 'people'.

The adult Guthrie, in his autobiography, said that he was first
smitten with Theatre when, at the age of eight, his mother took
him to see *The Yeomen of the Guard*. The critical point of catching
the bug was reportedly when Henry Lytton, as Jack Point,
swooned away and fell with a final clatter of cap-and-bells to die
on-stage; all 'for love of a lady'. All the evidence, however, sug-
gests that he had become seriously—as they said of his mother's
grandfather—'inoculated with the dramatic fever' much closer
home. The infection seems to have come at him from two
directions: the public rituals across the street and the private
theatricals on the drawing-room carpet, in the area adjacent to
his mother's piano; both 'open stages'. Norah Guthrie's love of
both the Theatre and the boy made her his household Muse of
Drama. This was a home-loving household, in a day when family

entertainment gave a bright and exhibitionist boy ample opportunity both to perform and to invent performance. His mother
being the great love of his life, it was therefore quite natural that
Guthrie should be drawn again and again throughout his life
towards these basic factors of the apparently inconsequential
productions created within range of her piano: (a) no physical
barrier between audience and players; (b) a company as familiar
with each other's gifts as a family; (c) an audience of friends
or neighbours and (d) an occasion for celebration or festival. Over the childhood years the occasion for such theatricals
was Christmas, when the family came together.

His mother, Norah Guthrie, was the middle one of the three
big, attractive and eminently eligible daughters of General Sir
William Power, K.C.B. As a widower retired after a very distinguished military career, he lived on the fashionable heights of
this Kent spa in the quiet tree-lined avenue of Broadwater Down.
His house had a greystone, pillared, Ionic portico; monumental
to the boy. Inside was a beautiful billiard room where Grandfather let him play (not billiards but his own games). The rear
quarters were run by friendly Irish servants. Later he would learn
why people had affectionately called his kindly and dignified
grandfather 'Potato Power'; but it had something to do with
these Irish folk. Much later he would discover how 'a general'
could come to be born almost like young Jack Gielgud's grand-
aunt, Ellen Terry—off-stage in a theatre hamper.

Of the other two Power girls, Ann—the beautiful one—married
a successful solicitor, moved to Sevenoaks, grew rich and little
influenced the Guthrie story. The other and eldest, 'Aunt Sue',
stayed by Father, never married, became a militant feminist (first
woman town councillor in Tunbridge Wells), and kept a commanding eye on the growing boy whom, she was sure, Norah was
spoiling.

The Spaland of Tunbridge Wells was natural territory to which
a general should retire. It was also natural hunting ground for a
gifted young Scottish doctor with a growing practice and need of
a wife. Dr. Thomas Clement Guthrie was as reticent as he was
reputable, but the warmth of the love Norah Power had for him
gave him courage to claim her hand in marriage. This is a scene by
James Barrie (who was then also well on the way to total success).
When young Dr. Guthrie took his new wife down to the semi-
detached in Church Road, she kept his accounts, kept house and

encouraged him like a Barrie heroine; and she had brought with her from 'Kilmore', up on Broadwater Down, two Irish servants, Tia Moore and her sister Bella, from Newbliss, County Monaghan. Tony Guthrie therefore grew up attended by Irish 'nannies'. They were one of the joys of his young life, and a lasting influence too. Tia Moore was too beautiful to stay single long, got married, wept over separation from Master Tony and went back to Ireland. Then there was Becky Daly. Becky was more the age of his mother, had the same statuesque build and was no servile servant. She was very much a proud and independent lady who wrote a lovely hand and stayed long with the Guthries, even when she married their mild little English gardener. There was no spoiling of the boy from her. Surgery was Dr. Guthrie's speciality. In the other half of the semi-detached his partner, and brother-in-law, was the physician. In a sense it was a very Scottish household, for Dr. Wilson was also, like Dr. Guthrie, from Edinburgh. It was a very busy, a very happy home; until Education set in.

It would be Irish Tia who would be most distressed for her handsome and bright little charge when he first started out for school and got into educational distress. The first stage in education, for Guthrie, W. T., was the normal one for such a boy—daily Dame School. Miss Slann's establishment can claim to have established a world-famous theatrical phenomenon: the Tyrone Guthrie hand-clap. Anyone who has attended a Guthrie rehearsal will know what is meant. In conducting a class Miss Mabel Slann was strict and was wont to command instant silence. Tyrone Guthrie was a strict disciplinarian too when he was conducting a rehearsal. The difference was that he was a lot more fun. Both clapped their hands for silence in the same way. Martin Bretherton, who for a time also suffered the Slann tyranny, described it as 'a sharp and resounding meeting of the palms as they whipped past each other travelling opposite ways'. Guthrie only improved the pattern, raised the height of delivery and increased the range; so that it should span not a schoolroom but an entire auditorium.

The school was no great daily journey from home. He later described its architecture as 'a crestfallen mid-Victorian villa, which had a brass plate on the gate, and into which pupils entered by a little door in the basement'. His mother would mostly deliver him to the day's incommunicable fate.

'Do Well—Doubt Not' was the town motto. And Guthrie,

W. T., did want to do well. It was just that he did not have it in
him to 'doubt not'.

'Dreaming, sir?'

'No, Miss Mabel, I was thinking—Miss Mabel, please, why *are*
seven nines sixty-three?'

'Continue, *sir*, and don't argue.'

'But, Miss Mabel, *why* are—'

Crack! Down would come the ruler on some part of the small
person not supposed to be critically vulnerable. And the utterly
vulnerable party in all parts would 'continue'—through bitter
tears; half of whose anguish would be the sheer frustration of
having to recite, *unquestioningly*, 'Tables'—which were 'Maths'—
and 'Dates'—which were 'History', or 'Towns-On-Rivers'—
which were 'Jography'. He was already as alert, as he was to be
all his life, in making detailed observations of how people acted
and dressed; for dress, he always had an especially quick eye. He
noted that the French Mistress was small, dark, and costume-
conscious. Her elaborate, white, crocheted collars would simply
be a concession to fashion. But on Mademoiselle's bosom there
would always lie one large satin bow: scarlet mostly; occasionally
gold. But one Holy Week Mademoiselle went right over the edge
in exercise of the religious arts related to Costume. Using her
bosom as a sort of heaving altar, there was, resting there—right
through Monday, Tuesday, Wednesday and Thursday—a black
satin bow; on Good Friday a violet one. Black came back on
Saturday. And, on Easter Sunday, the satin bow was pure
shining white! Guthrie remembered this right into manhood.

At the age of eleven came two significant changes in his life.
In accordance with the education of 'leaders of men'—and there
would be little doubt outside his own shy heart that he would be
one—he was sent from home to board away in a prep school. He
was first sent to the local 'Hurstleigh', then soon after to 'Templegrove', Eastbourne. The other change took place at home.
Another little girl joined Peggy in the nursery. Each day she came
from about five minutes' walk away to be taught under the
Guthrie roof by the same governess who taught his Peggy. That
little girl was Judith Bretherton. And he really did not like it at
all; that, while he was exiled from home, a stranger should be
usurping the place he so loved to occupy beside his beloved
sister. This had to stop. But it did not: it went on—for years.

The Brethertons were in fact no strangers. Mrs. (Nellie)

Bretherton was a friend and neighbour of Norah Guthrie's and though they were utterly different both were supremely strong, and highly intelligent characters. They shared one passion—a love of flowers. The Mrs. Beaton of gardening, Bentham and Hooker, in its two green leather-bound volumes, stood ready to hand in both households and was a bible of Botany beyond which there was no appeal. About the Bible itself—that black-bound book—Nellie had reservations. She was reputedly an atheist and had the sort of free-thinking children—Judith and Martin—who actually addressed their mother, in these Edwardian days, as 'Nellie'. She came of a family of Channel Island shipowners, the Lacheurs. Mr. Bretherton (Gordon) was a small, friendly solicitor who had to wear a spinal brace and was a keen amateur actor. He shared with Norah Guthrie the organization of the Christmas home theatricals and occasionally wrote them a little play. The Brethertons lived what the Guthries would call a somewhat 'physical', somewhat 'bohemian' existence in a red-brick villa of confused architectural design which Tony and Peggy christened 'Peacemeal'. It was from this Bohemia that Judith came daily to be schooled exactly to the same pattern as Peggy, by 'Ino' or 'Peglerino' (Miss Pegler, their governess). Neither of the girls ever went out to school.

There is little evidence to show that prep school was any great misery to young Guthrie. But when the novelty wore off he began to see dormitory life as an intolerable substitute for the home life he so loved. He was bright, he did well and here he was allowed some leave to doubt. 'Works excellently . . . quick to learn' were typical reports. It was a boyish competitive life and he was a competitive creature. 'Competition in our class is just *fearful*' he wrote home; and with relish. 'Top again!—by one mark!!'

As a deeply faithful character he was faithful to the social norms of any such superior young gentleman: 'Matron is not bad. I don't think she's a lady, though she speaks like one.' And it is notable that as yet he was rather more pleased than embarrassed by the surprising height to which he was beginning to grow. 'Most of the boys are about 11 or 12 but I am rather bigger than most of my age.'

As far as school theatrical experience was concerned, this, together with singing in the choir, was no more than a normal activity for a boy with a promising voice and good looks. 'We have great fun rehearsing . . . "Olympus Up-To-Date" and "Pygmalion and Galatea"—Galatea—that's me.' One thing which was standard prep school discipline was the weekly letter home. In Guthrie's case, it was the start of a more or less life-long correspondence which, with weekly regularity, spanned the separation whenever he and his mother were parted. It was a private journalism, to become quite brilliant as it went on. There were to be very special reasons later why it should be vitally important to her. But one letter to his mother at this time is quite prophetic in its precocious journalism. It would certainly have disturbed the family Mrs. Pankhurst, Aunt Sue. She was just about to join Sir Edward Carson's Ulstermen, and to march under the banner of 'ULSTER WILL FIGHT AND ULSTER WILL BE RIGHT'.

> I enclose [*wrote young Tony*] the proportions of R.C. to Protestants in the counties of Ulster per 1,000 of total population. [*And he added*]: Rather startling considering that they represent *Ulster*.

	Prot.	R.C.
Antrim	60	20
Down	68	32

Then he got down to the county next to where the Power family had their Irish estate, and the exclamation marks came out:

Cavan	19	81 !!

And the county his own mother was born in:

Monaghan ...	25	75

Ireland even then, when he was still in the heart of an English society whose politics were very Gilbert and Sullivan, had a powerful influence on him. His home roots were loosened by this uprooting sort of exile to boarding school. He began to talk, like Tia Moore, Becky Daly and the other Irish servants of 'home' and to mean, not 'Belmont', Church Road, Tunbridge Wells at all, but 'Annagh-ma-Kerrig',* Monaghan, Ireland. After all, apart from some Christmas holidays, Ireland was the holiday place and holidays now meant home. Therefore a big stone house in the Irish country parish of Aghabog, his mother's Irish family home,

---

* Even the best of Irish scholarship cannot confirm what Tony Guthrie made of the name: 'Bog of The Boat'. Other locals say it is 'The Rock of The River'. *Annagh* means 'a water passage' and *ma-Kerrig* could be a corruption of a proper name.

became the standard of values for everything. So that, from prep
school he could write:

> . . . the schoolroom is about as large as Aghabog Church . . .
> there are only 4½ weeks more then A-Kerrig—won't it be just
> heavenly!! . . . I am already hungry for the eggs and bacon on
> the Dundalk train—I think it is the most delicious meal
> possible, don't you?

And here one must pause to see why General Sir William Power
had Irish folk for servants and how Annagh-ma-Kerrig became
the Guthrie ancestral home. Because, without a knowledge of
what that Irish place and the Irish folk meant to the Guthrie boy,
one cannot understand the man.

His Becky, his Tia and all the Power servants up in 'Kilmore'
were a sort of colony of Irish exiles in English Tunbridge Wells.
But they were not just from anywhere in Ireland, they were Power
servants and estate employees from over the other side of the
Irish Sea. They were 'our people', where 'us' was the Guthrie/
Power family. It was from these—the only people 'of a lower class'
that he was able to get anywhere close to—that Tony Guthrie
acquired a life-long respect for original and native intelligence. It
was a respect which made him totally impatient of pretentious
urbanity—at whatever level he found it, be it with railway cleaner
or royalty.

These were for him the real People, and for six whole summer
weeks of the year the Tunbridge Wells servants went 'home' from
their exile in England; and he went 'home' with them—from *his*
'exile', at school. This was a bond. Not only did they go home,
but in Grandfather Power's day the whole Power/Guthrie
caravanserai—including the horses and carriage—migrated, too,
to Monaghan. In a military, or gypsy, sense one can see Tunbridge Wells as just 'winter quarters'.

It was a blissful escape for any boy, to this Summer Place: a
biggish greystone house amid forests, above a lake and beyond a
bog, in Monaghan, that area of remote countryside which is now
within a northward bulge in the border of the Southern Republic
with Northern Ireland. There, the whole operation of life was
delightfully tangible to a boy: wood cut from our forests, or
'turf' from our bog, to feed our fires; fish from our lake, milk
from our cows and home-baked scones and bread coming out of
our kitchen ovens to be food for us all. There were the great

conifer woods to walk in; and to smell—the resinous pines; the mossy little old oaks round the lake, as if they had lived half their life under water; and the rowing boat. All this to look forward to. Utter bliss to bundle into a steam train and start on that fabulous journey to the Summer Place:

Tunbridge Wells to London (1st Class). Cabs across London, then chuffing away from London, Euston, by the boat train, all the way across England to Holyhead (3rd Class, for economy); the steam boat (S.S. *Leinster* maybe) for Kingston, Dublin—now Dun Laoghaire (1st Class in cabins with red plush upholstery). And after some hours of the year's variety of storm or calm, the churning arrival alongside; creaking, dripping hawsers, oily smells, and the clanging of the ship's telegraph bells; the screaming of seagulls and the calls of 'Old Davy' the newspaper man, who always came aboard with a clean, folded copy of the *Irish Times* for General Sir William. From the wharves of Kingston by horse cab across cobbled Dublin, clippity-clop, to Amiens Street; to catch the morning train going north up the east coast-line, as far as Dundalk. Here was the journey to freedom that gave young Guthrie a lifelong love of trains—gave him too 'the most delicious meal possible', Irish eggs and bacon on the train to Dundalk. There the travellers turned inland on a branch line where the train chuffed into Ireland's mid-west, a green territory of little hillocks, small fields, small haystacks; and all the soft summer country that lay round the little lakes. The sound of a lone farm dog, the lonelier bray of a donkey, it was all out there in the air: where the smell of turf, burning on a small farm's big fire, now mingled with the train smoke. The end of the railway journey would be the little country station with the small square signal-box which had signalled them to a clanking halt. There would be an exciting escape of steam. 'NEW—BLISS!'—that would be the call of the stationmaster—NEWBLISS, that was the name on the signal-box.

Out of the train would come the whole party of the gentry, plus Johnny Beggan, the butler, Mary Ellen, Mary Ann Corrigan (Kilmore housemaids), Mickie Corrigan (coachman in transition to becoming chauffeur) and Willie Dunn, the footman; all of them slamming carriage doors and sniffing the scents of their own homeland. Standing there, ready for the invasion, would be old Frank McDermott. He would be holding the head of the horse that stood in the shafts of 'the outside car'. This would be to get the General's party the three miles to the house. A farm cart would follow the jaunting car, as it wound its way home, with the baggage and the servants. Sometimes it would be in view and sometimes hidden by the turns of the roads and the high banks each side of them. Finally came the forests of the General's land and the long lake with the wild swans, and the white-painted cast-iron gates which gave into the long, long gravel drive by the lake; and on through rhododendron bushes all the way to the greystone house standing up above the lake—'home'.

There would be a clean-scrubbed 'reception committee' waiting there, including a man with the corporeal substance of a Hindenburg (and with his Teutonic moustachios too)—James Dane, a cousin of Sir William, who managed the estate and made the magical 'bog garden'—and Eddie Thompson (steward at Annagh-ma-Kerrig).

Up the steps the travellers would go, and straight into the big stone-flagged hall, where an unusual stag's head stared sadly down (it had a gold cross stuck between its antlers); first left into the big bay-windowed drawing-room for home-bake and tea. The farm cart with all the baggage and its gaggle of Tunbridge exiles would lumber into the yard and soon the backstairs would be full of the talk of winter and who married whom, who died and was born on both sides of the Irish Sea. If there was daylight left, and time, it would be off with the Norfolk jacket, Eton collar and tweed cap, and straight into old thick sweaters for all Guthries, then out for the first breath of Annagh-ma-Kerrig air; or else it would be decent dress and hair plastered to sit down with the General to dinner—in a dining-room where the brass candelabra over his head had eighteen candles and his own ancestrs in leathery oil-paintings looked down, their faces reflecting the candles' light. A candle too lit him and Peggy up to bed. Tunbridge Wells and the tyrannies of school were very far away when Becky tucked him in and his mother said good night. Ten years later, when Guthrie was one of the Oxford bright sparks of the Gay Twenties, he wrote:

I wake up every morning feeling homesick for Annagh-ma-Kerrig and lie in bed picturing my favourite views. The White Walk and the big trees from the hall door; the view over the country from Mullenagraw—the lake from the gap in the planting on Macullan's land . . . With a very little effort I can feel the feel in the air and the smell of the grass and the feeling of brushing against spruce and fir branches after rain—and the smell of a turf fire—and the silence and the little, birdy noises down by the lake when it's nearly dark. Oh! if only we could be there!

Well 'we'—all four of them—were there. But how did 'we' get there? Why was it the Power home? And who were his ancestors who looked down on him as he dined in the candle-lit room? Who, for instance, was the Tyrone Power from whom his own name came?

He had seen signs of this Tyrone Power in several rooms. In the study—at the back of the stone-flagged hall—there were some framed theatre bills on the walls. They were so old you could think they had been dipped in the tea. And Mr. Tyrone Power's name was on some of them. There was also an exciting picture of a ship in a storm: a steam-ship that had sails as well, the S.S. *President*. It sank—so it said below—in 1841. The family said that it had something to do with Tyrone Power. And, in a painting in the drawing-room, this was him, sitting by a cottage table, looking delightfully wicked, and—so they said, for it was too high up for him to see—playing Connor O'Gorman in *The Groves of Blarney*.

Tyrone Power was the General's father. He had a mysterious start to life and a pretty mysterious end too. And between the start and the end of it he was one of the most successful, most wealthy actors who had trod the boards of the English-speaking stage. His story must have sounded to the boy like a tale of Romance. It started around 1795. A Maria Maxwell, daughter of some officer in the Waterford militia, was encouraged to leave home and Ireland. And she did, too, possessed of substantial travelling funds, and a very, very young son. In Dublin, *en route* for England, Miss Maxwell was relieved of her funds by some robbers but not of her infant boy. On the way to England she was shipwrecked, some say on the coast of Wales by Haverfordwest. At any rate, the bastard babe and Maria struggled on, to Cardiff. There—maybe with something still sewn into her bodice—she rented lodgings in the house of one Bird, a bookseller and publisher to the Cardiff Theatre. Through this Bird, it is said, the boy 'became inoculated with the dramatic fever'. It was one way forward. But it needed learning and money was needed and his name

was Tyrone. So the mother stormed at 'the Waterford Powers'—
who had title to the lands of County Tyrone too. She demanded
the due means to educate the child; and whether those she
stormed at were really the Le Poers, who of Waterford were, or
just the 'powers that be' in Waterford, we just do not honestly
know. Nor did young Ty, for he soon left his dear mother and
ran away with a company of travelling players.

This was the start of a hard but, in the end, a highly successful
career, at the height of which his mother reputedly said to him,
'You are now, my son, a proud man but if you knew who your
father was you'd be prouder still.' Then—as if to provide her son
with a splendid curtain to act one, but little means of completing
act three—she dropped dead.

Who the distinguished father of Tyrone Power was, Tyrone
Guthrie later desperately wanted to know. But if Tyrone Power
ever found out he never said, and—such was his character—he
never flaunted nor tried to make use of any blue blood in his
veins. Though he longed to be a great heroic actor (in Dublin he
made an awful mess of Romeo), he found his success in playing
Irish 'character parts'. In this the quality of the man came
through; for he would never stoop to lampooning the parts or
burlesquing the Irish character. The greatest success of his life—
and he played it year after year—was Paudeen O Rafferty, in a
play whose title he changed from *Tilly the Tiler* to *Born to Good
Luck*. And so he was—till his dying day, which was not so lucky
as dramatic.

Mr. Power had conquered London from the Haymarket and
Covent Garden stages, also Dublin from the Theatre Royal, but
he had also at least twice triumphed throughout America. In 1841
he had just done it again. He was in New York, about to sail
home. It is a mark of the status given this man that on another
Atlantic voyage home a passenger who sought out his company—
even read to the actor when he was ill in his bunk—was none
other than the eventual Napoleon III.

Before he embarked on this present trip he had invested a large
lump of his takings in the purchase of a plot of land in New York.
This, it seems, was the soil and rock on which Madison Square
Gardens now stands. The deeds, as far as anyone knows, were in
his baggage. His bags were packed. His homeward passage was
already booked. But, some days before his own sailing, he went
down with a friend to the ticket office. His friend was confirming

his own booking on a ship leaving next day. This was a 'transition' ship (sail *and* steam); the pride of the fleet, the S.S. *President*. Power scanned the passenger list. He saw that his good friend Lord Fitzroy Lennox was on it. He regretted then that he had not booked on the *President*. He had also seen that another friend, Joseph Wood (husband of Miss Paton the opera singer), was on the list. As luck would have it he met Joe Wood on his way back to his hotel. And, as luck still seemed to have it, he said, 'Hello, Joe, I see you've got a berth on the *President*.' 'Yes,' said Joe, 'and I'm wishing I could find somebody who'd take it off my hands now.' 'You have,' said Tyrone Power.

The *President* sailed on March 11, with much waving of high-quality handkerchiefs. Here is the story the Dublin papers finally printed:

THE LAST VOYAGE

On the 11th day of March 1841, the *President*, one of the finest trans-Atlantic boats of the time, steamed down the river from New York. Accompanying her was a small vessel, *The Orpheus*, a craft that was dwarfed by the big, blustering proportions of the larger ship . . .

On board was the Lord Frederick Lennox and his old and close friend, Tyrone Power, prince of Irish actors. Fair shone the sun, the weather promised finely, and all on board were merry as marriage bells.

But weatherwise old salts shook their heads, and talked of the equinox most learnedly, and held out that dirty weather was ahead. The old salts were right.

Two days and two nights passed, and then the storm arose, throwing up the waters into angry mountains and sweeping the decks of the ill-fated ship. The little *Orpheus* stuck pluckily to its big brother.

DARKNESS CLOSED AROUND THE SHIPS beating against the terrible storm on that night of the 12th March. Dawn of the 13th, but only one ship there, battling, plunging, sinking, rising again, climbing the dark water. It was *The Orpheus*.

From that day unto this not a trace, not a bit of wreckage, not a bale of the cotton cargo of the *President* have ever been found.

The body of poor Power, light-hearted, laughter-loving, the darling of Dublin audiences, was sea-washed ten thousand fathoms deep.

So was all claim by Power's descendants to Madison Square Gardens.*

So much for the man who put the Tyrone in young William Tyrone Guthrie's name. The William, of course, came not from the Stage but the Army—from his grandfather. General Sir William was the eldest of the six surviving children of Tyrone Power. Two sons tried, with no great success, to emulate Father, and took to the stage. Of these, Harold was notable in retrospect: as the grandfather of Tyrone Power, the film star. Frederick, the engineer of the family, achieved cast-iron distinction. He built, for a grateful Tzar, the Trans-Caucasian Railroad.

Tony's grandfather William was twenty-two when his father died. He chose the Army as his career and rose, by steady promotion, from junior officer in Whitehall, via distinguished service abroad, to be Commissary-General-in-Chief of the British Army. He had the same genius as his grandson—a gift for organization. And this is how he came to be the owner of Annagh-ma-Kerrig, its lands and its bog. (Owning a bog was as profitable once as owning a mine: for the fuel that was in it—the 'turf'). It is also the story of how he earned the nickname 'Potato Power'.

He first appeared on the Annagh-ma-Kerrig bog in 1849, when he was a very handsome young officer, brilliantly organizing Famine Relief in the wake of the disastrous Irish Potato Famine. After the years of failure in their staple food crop the people of Ireland were in a desperate state. Those who had the means to emigrate did so—at the rate of 75,000 a year. Of those who could not, or would not, flee around a million had died by 1851. The British Army was sent out into the countryside to organize paid relief work. It was a land-improvement scheme that brought the young officer to Annagh-ma-Kerrig, to supervise the digging of what is still called The Drain: a ditch as big as a small canal, draining the fields at the head of the lake. Owning Annagh-ma-Kerrig at that time was Dr. Moorhead, a local doctor who must have had almost as much American success as Tyrone Power, for he had returned home with a rich wife from Cincinnati and, when one of his patients amid the landed gentry hit such hard times he could not pay the doctor's bill, the doctor put him in funds by buying him out of his house—Annagh-ma-Kerrig. It was the doctor's daughter, Martha Moorhead, who fell in love with

* For much of this information I am greatly indebted to Mildred Stock.

William Power, when he appeared on duty down by The Drain.
So, William married Martha—who was half-Irish, half-American.
Martha finally inherited the place and through her William came
into the land and the property. In 1911 General Power, much
mourned, and much missed by his one grandson, died and was
buried beside his beloved wife in the family grave up on the hill
by the tiny Aghabog Church, about one winding, green mile
away from the house.

It was here, in Ireland, as a boy, that Tony Guthrie began to be
the non-establishment creature he continued to be as an adult.
Annagh-ma-Kerrig had this importance to him, too, that it was
the one place where he could be sure of his father's company. In
Tunbridge Wells the devoted—and ambitious—doctor could
never tear himself away from what his son later referred to, in the
anger of frustration, as the 'sickaneedy'.

To a degree he was a deprived child in relation to his father's
company. Not only the practice took his father away at all hours
of the day and night, but Doctor Tom Guthrie was a reticent man
who tended to withdraw into his shell on the social occasion.
There was no harshness about the man, but he had the calm
austerity of a crack shot and a fine surgeon. The personal crest on
his library of books was a dagger held aloft in a firm hand surrounded by the motto, STO PRO VERITATE (*I stand for the truth*).
The boy could not yet be expected to know that, in his Scottish
soul, his father was as much in love with Annagh-ma-Kerrig and
as much in revolt against Spaland society as he was now. So, at
prep school he sent out this heart-cry. 'You simply *must*,' he wrote
Mother, 'make Dad play in the fathers' matches, you must tell
him that if he doesn't I'll duck him in the baths when I get home!!
. . . *Make* Pop come for the week-end, or at least S/day. He's a
heartless father if he doesn't, in spite of what the patients will
think.' Senior House Surgeon of the Tunbridge Wells Hospital
and Hon. Surgeon of Dr. Barnardo's Home for Crippled Children,
he was a father worth claiming. And it's not fun to a small boy at
school if no father shows up. It was Mother who came. It was
Mother who, in the Mothers' Match, actually scored 94 not out!

In a quite serious way he turned more and more to his mother
for all responses, emotional and intellectual too. But at Annagh-
ma-Kerrig it was different: Father shared with his son the love of
the open, of old-clothes days doing rough jobs, cutting and saw-
ing logs together, clearing the rhododendron jungle between the

house and the lake, fishing and walking out into squelching wild
weather together. To the doctor this had echoes of his own
Scottish childhood. He was a hunter too—a good shot with a
gun. Definitely an all-weathers open-air man; so was his son. And
that takes us back to the sad stag's head staring down from the
wall in the stone-flagged hall of the house, with that little gold
cross stuck between its antlers.

The notepaper at Annagh-ma-Kerrig had on it the crest of the
Power family: a royal stag's head and, set between its antlers on
the animal's brow, a little cross. It had a very Christian motto
below—'Per Crucem ad Coronam'—'By the Cross to the Crown'.
'Per Crucem ad Coronam' could also have served as a motto for
Tony Guthrie's great ancestor on his father's side, for there was
also fame there. And the greatness of his forebears had much to
do with Tyrone Guthrie's natural air of authority. This time the
fame was historic too, but from the Pulpit, not the Stage.

The bronze statue of Tony Guthrie's Scottish great-grandfather stands high on a plinth that sits among the flower beds in
Edinburgh's Princes Street Gardens, where he keeps monumental company with other great Scots like Sir Walter Scott.
There his Uncle Sandy Guthrie could take the boy by the hand to
read the large lettering on the plinth:

DR. THOMAS GUTHRIE, D.D.,
born 1803 died 1873
ELEGANT PREACHER OF THE GOSPEL . . .
FOUNDER OF
THE ORIGINAL RAGGED INDUSTRIAL SCHOOLS.
A FRIEND OF THE POOR AND THE OPPRESSED.

The figure the boy would look up to is a strong, gently-
smiling gentleman, not noticeably clerical. (In fact, though a
Doctor of Divinity, he went to Paris first and there studied
Medicine.) He has humour's wrinkles at the corners of his eyes
and one protective arm is about the shoulders of a 'ragged boy'.
Philanthropy, oratory and an imperishable fidelity to the Word
were the trumpet notes sounded by this famous Scottish great-
grandfather. And trumpet he did. 'The greatest preacher I ever
heard,' said Sir William Hamilton, the metaphysician.

If I 'take after' either of these ancestors [*Tony Guthrie says in his
autobiography*] . . . it is Dr. Guthrie . . . from whom I derive, I
suspect, a certain rotund eloquence, a certain Scottish candour

and a determination to face facts, even, and possibly especially, unpleasant facts, together with a voice which, if not rich and ringing, is remarkably 'carrying'.

He could pack Greyfriars Church and he was also known as 'the greatest pictorial preacher of his day'. But what pictures:

> I have seen one [*a sermon of his runs*], who had roughly reckoned up the cost of the gems, the rubies, pearls, emeralds, diamonds, that studded the golden arches of an *earthly* crown, stand astonished at its value . . . And yet . . . in point, either of *cost* or brilliancy, what is that to the crown any ransomed beggar or saved harlot wears in heaven? Imperial diamonds are *nothing* to the crown of glory! In the sanctuary balances, a saint weighs heavier than a sovereign. And there is more value in the crown of a redeemed infant—one of these little ones—than in all the glory of all the holy angels! . . . But to make a saint, He—who never left his throne to make or save an angel!—descended on our world in the form of a servant, and, more amazing still, hung on a cross in the form of a sinner. The price of our pardon was nothing less than what the apostle calls the *blood of God* . . . A spectator of the scenes, the dreadful, tragic scenes, amid which Judah's sun set in blood, tells that wood was wanting for crosses, and crosses were wanting for bodies. Yet— had Babylon's, Tyre's, Jerusalem's, all these crosses, been raised to save *you*! and on each cross of that forest, not a man, but a dying angel hung!—had all heaven been crucified!—here is greater love, a greater spectacle.

Awesome blood and thunder stuff. The Reverend Doctor became Moderator-General of the 'Kirk' of Scotland. His son, David, wore 'the cloth' too and married a lady with the appropriate name of Hannah Kirk. She came from Keady in Armagh and was the mother of Tony's father, the medical 'Doctor Guthrie'. Armagh being in Ulster and not so very far from Annagh-ma-Kerrig, Tony could say that *both* his grandmothers came from the same bit of Ireland. And it was these great ancestors that made of him a very Irish sort of Anglo-Scot.

As he approached fourteen the boy faced the regulation change of life proper to potential 'leaders of men' and for which prep school was a mere foretaste—public school. His junior educational record was good in Latin, French, Divinity, and Geography, and in English and History excellent. In Mathematics he was miserable and Greek remained Greek to him, except that he got some fun, and some drama too, out of studying the 'Myths of Hellas'. He was tall, he was handsome, he had looked fine (and much wanted Mother and Father to see him) in his cadet uniform. As a grandson of a Commissary-General-in-Chief of the British Army, Knight Commander of the Order of the Bath, what more appropriate school for such a boy to go to than that militarized educational memorial to the Duke of Wellington, Wellington College. There the sons of mainly military families were trained to be 'leaders of men'. It was 1914. Summer was coming, but the Guthries' attention was fixed not on Germany, but on Ireland. That country had been granted Home Rule. But this break from English government had been bitterly opposed by the Protestant Ulstermen. Annagh-ma-Kerrig was in Monaghan. Monaghan was in Ulster and there, in the papers, was a picture of Aunt Sue presenting a great banner to the army of Ulster volunteers, 80,000 of whom Sir Edward Carson had raised and trained to fight under British Army officers. On the embroidered banner in bold letters were the words, 'ULSTER IS RIGHT—ULSTER WILL FIGHT'.

Dublin's answer to this militancy was the formation of the Irish Volunteers. At a conference of both factions called together by George V at Buckingham Palace, no agreement could be reached. Both sides returned to Ireland to prepare for certain Civil War. And the Guthries were left with the question: Did they dare prepare for the summer migration to Annagh-ma-Kerrig this year?

Suddenly, in the Balkans, came the shot that killed the heir to the Austrian throne. By July Austria was at war with Serbia. By August 1 Kaiser Wilhelm's troops had marched into France and on the 4th England was at war with Germany. The Great War had begun, and fourteen-year-old Guthrie had his name on the rolls of the military college of Wellington.

Any adoring mother at that time would have said to herself that he was just a schoolboy and this war would be settled in months by the might of the British Army. The idea that it would last till he was eighteen, that schoolboys not even that age would be falsifying their date of birth, in order to be as patriotic as their teachers who had already left to face the Hell of Flanders all this was inconceivable in that summer.

CHAPTER TWO

WELLINGTON AND WAR
(*1914–1918*)

SEPTEMBER 1914 was an historic moment for any boy to enter this monumental Victorian school. Over one of its doorways it was possible for him to see the carved words put there by the first of its celebrated Masters, 'THE PATH OF DUTY IS THE WAY TO GLORY', in itself no way daunting to a naturally dutiful boy. But, within the first few months of this assumedly glorious war, there were 2,400 Old Wellingtonians in the armed forces, ten members of staff had sought commissions, twenty-three of the college employees had enlisted; and the Roll of Honour had begun. It grew with a frightening acceleration. Public school education was to be peculiar for young Guthrie, in that he knew Wellington only 'at war'.

Its grandiose buildings of brick and dressed stone stood on that bit of England known as Bagshot Sands, in an area that had been a heathland of gorse and heather. The school's open acres of playing fields, rhododendron drives, and its lake too, were bordered by the pinewoods of Berkshire. It still stands there a short distance from the military place names of Sandhurst, Bisley and Camberley. By any description it is an imposing edifice and young Guthrie, W. T., at fourteen must have had butterflies in his stomach as he approached its famous skyline. It had the same planned isolation from Life as a mental asylum. But the new boy's tenseness would have gone unnoticed, in this unusual year. The school reassembled in tense excitement on September 2nd, which was early, because, when war had been declared in August, the alert headmaster had immediately been in touch with Lord Derby, chairman of the governors. He wanted permission to hurry the pupils back ahead of time, in case Wellington should suffer the same fate as Christ's Hospital, and be earmarked for the housing of German prisoners.

The houses, into which the college community was divided, were named after notable commanders who had seen service under Wellington. The house he was assigned to was the Hardinge. This all sounds excessively military. In fact, long before young Guthrie's time, the intake of sons of the military had been limited to what an official history calls 'a nucleus . . . and not a predominating caste. . . . Thus there came into being that curious dualism, compound of two elements, the soldier and the civilian, each modifying the other—which is College.'

The whole nation now being at war, the distinction between these two categories had totally disappeared and in the first few months of Guthrie's time all and sundry felt themselves to be of the military. There were two drill parades a day, manoeuvres and 'field days' every Thursday, guard duties by day, and sometimes night too, on the local reservoir and railway bridges. And one had to keep a critical lookout all hours of the day and night for 'spies'. Therefore uncritical excitement coloured the days when the boy was getting used to the grey fact that in dormitory he was to live more like a stabled horse than a shy and not insensitive family boy. Dormitory had the indefinable smell of many young human animals corralled together under one roof and living within walls rubbed smooth by past generations. His 'stall' was one of about seven cubicles either side of a long, wooden-decked aisle, whose floor added to the indefinable smell a very definite aroma of Ronuk furniture polish. The carved, scored and tack-pitted walls of his cubicle were not much higher towards the rafters than his own height (already almost six feet). Filling most of the rest of the space not occupied by him, was a standard bed (whose bottom end was bound to terminate just about where his bare ankles began), a rudimentary desk, bookshelves and chair. There was no door. A dull red drape, with little sandbags sewn into its bottom hem, could be drawn between him and the draughty corridor. From this academic cell a window looked out from first-floor level to the nineteenth-century-baroque detail of the next bit of brick and stone. It had a windowsill where there would be, under the Guthrie tenancy, a defiant horticultural display of all sorts of flowers. But first days were indeed grim. A basin of tepid water pushed through the red curtain soon after dawn began a life more spartan than anything he had so far known; even at dear old Annagh-ma-Kerrig. Institutionally he started tough, and he took the toughness on with him through his life. Coal was restricted. There was, he wrote home, 'no heating in dormitory and no hope of it before mid-winter. We mostly sit in our coats, and skip from time to time.'

No games came into his early curriculum, because as the Year Book sombrely put it, at the end of his first year, 'We have come to understand, in the presence of the real thing, that games after all are only games, useful though they may be.' The 'real thing', which had previously been Waterloo and Mafeking, was now Flanders Fields. The names for the Roll of Honour came back with dutiful regularity. By 1916 the College 'scoreboard' read:

Killed	... ...	597
V.C.'s	... ...	5
D.S.O.'s	... ...	302
M.C.'s	... ...	336
Mentioned in Despatches	...	944

Grim news followed for even the most heroic parents at home; and the Guthries were not ones to cosset even an only son. The Master had asked for the authority to waive all notice in the case of boys who got 'unexpected opportunities' to get into the Army at once. Still, Guthrie had not yet reached a vulnerable age.

His loving parents in Tunbridge Wells had just moved up in the town, from the Church Road semi-detached to a villa called Warwick Lodge, which stood high in Roedean Road. They were now trimming this elegant new ship for their civilian service in war, flower beds were making room for vegetables and chickens were kept. At Wellington the Black Watch marched in, pitched their tents, watered their horses at the lake and, in the morning, sounded their bugles and marched on. Tony later wrote home that, beyond the gorse pinewoods on a calm clear day, he could hear the sound of the guns on the Somme. Week by week he got better at rolling on and rolling off his khaki puttees. Drills were done with a personal zest that had less to do with the bark of the officer/teacher in charge than with the nation's determination to be prepared at a call to cross the sea and stop spike-helmeted 'Kaiser Bill' and all his grey hordes dead in their tracks.

Despite all this, despite regular rotas of duty—digging, to help the nation grow more potatoes, and so on, War and Flanders Fields began to be simply a tragic backcloth to scenes of academic concentration. Even sports came back into the curriculum. In drill and on the field at football, hockey, rugger, even cricket—

which did not suit his impatient soul—he played with what was noted as 'zest'.

It might seem that there simply could not be much academic concentration at such a time. But there was. There were no idle moments at Wellington. The Master then was William Wyamar Vaughan, also a dynamo of 'zest'. '. . . a big clumsy figure with hair he grew too long . . . full, straggly moustache, bulging pockets.' This was no military martinet but neither was he any lover of the work-shy. 'I like him more and more each term,' the hard-working boy wrote. And anyone who knew the habits and attitudes of Guthrie in his prime, will see patterns for these in the attitudes of this man:

> His definition of 'Vulgarity' was, 'over-estimating the trivial things of life, and under-estimating the big things'. He had a loathing of 'sham', valued integrity, courage, enthusiasm and hard work above all else . . . slow to praise he remained strong in the belief that virtue was its own reward but he had eager sympathy at any time of stress or trouble . . . a great organizer . . . not a great scholar.*

It could have served as William Tyrone Guthrie's own obituary. If the boy had not his own father around as much as he needed, here was a father-figure that could not have been a better substitute or more in accord with his eager young soul. And maybe 'not a great scholar', but it was Vaughan who first got Shakespeare off the page for him and made the plays vital. 'Send my Shakespeare. We're doing *Hamlet* with Vaughan. I'm simply adoring it *now*.' He added that he was almost pleased he had found it such dull stuff before. Here was where he took to heart his first great, and 'family', play.

'Fagging' was no more than an excess of dutifulness in a dutiful boy. However, being beaten for breaking a host of new rules he could not keep up with at a time when he could hardly keep up with the wearying growth of his own body, that was stupid. His House Master noted his characteristic 'zest' being qualified by a difficulty in 'pulling himself together'. This was on account of being 'so overgrown'. Here was the beginning of a lifelong impatience with and embarrassment about a very awkwardly long frame. And there was that short bed. One thing he positively hated about school was 'dorm' life. It was such a synthetic

* *A History of Wellington College*, D. H. Newsome. John Murray, 1959.

substitute for family life. At home the social group was full of
meaningful relationships which went deep. In dorm, he said—as a
botanically minded boy—'like five or six bulbs in a pot' boys
were planted with friends not of their choice and forbidden to
make others. It was not that he was a boy afraid of or averse to
what was a very competitive life; but to his Irish/Scottish soul
dorm and house rivalry was sham tribalism. However the point
should be made that in later years he made his school life sound
much more miserable than it was, by the evidence available. He
was a regular success in his class-work, also on the sports field
(football, rugger, hockey); he finished up as a proud Corporal in
the Corps, captain of his house rugger fifteen and head boy of the
Hardinge.

One thing which gave him immediate success was the Voice.
Here 'zest' had full play. With pride he wrote home that so strong
was his soprano that the choirmaster had to balance it by not one
treble but *three*! Singing was fun. 'I was sitting next the altos who
were rather powerful so I found I was singing sopralto.' It also
had its solemn and moving moments.

The Old Wellingtonian who had led his Black Watch companies
off, towards the sound of the guns, was long dead, and the gift of
the Voice had often brought the boy to be 'on parade' in Chapel.
There he would witness (on its 'open stage') solemn ceremonials
which were to be memorable pictures: 'We are practising a short
anthem about "the departed" for a service to the memory of the
soldiers who have fallen in the war. I am one of the soloists . . .'
And the processional ceremonials took place in a sacred playing
area or pitch not too different in architecture from that area on
which he finally made his revolutionary stage, in Edinburgh, in
the Kirk's Assembly Hall. The pews in Sir Giles Gilbert Scott's
Victorian chapel at Wellington were tiered up and rose away
either side from a wide central aisle. As a theatre director he was
to have an appetite for processions.

Not only was the Voice developing; so was his capacity to
write letters which would span the chasm of the intolerable
separation from home. They were letters to his mother. Father
would be too busy with the 'sickaneedy', of whom some would
now be the wounded.

However much she was the General's daughter, she must have
worried constantly about the narrowing gap between War Service
and her only son. He had boasted that he had got himself passed

A.1 through an Army medical check, by suppressing the fact that he had a bad knee. She wrote: '. . . I suppose, darling, I am glad you passed A.1. I *am* because *you* are glad but otherwise it is all a horror to me and just does not bear thinking of but, Oh, please God we are firmly victors before you are a full-blown soldier, my own precious . . .'

The war had crept nearer home. Dr. Thomas's youngest brother suffered the final penalty of being heroic and six foot seven. He stood up in a first line trench and stopped a Boche bullet. God help the tall zestful Tony if the moment came. He continued between academic sessions to roll his puttees on and off. Norah Guthrie rolled bandages for the Front, found homes for Belgian refugees, attended the 'wounded's canteen', helped Aunt Sue with her 'work house', kept hens, grew vegetables and tried to keep some shape, by late lamplight, in the busy doctor's accounts.

One of the casualties of war, for Tony, was the summer escape to Annagh-ma-Kerrig. With German submarines sinking sufficient shipping to raise the serious possibility of Britain being starved into surrender, crossings to Ireland were inadvisable. Anyway, boys were expected to volunteer to spend holidays working in summer harvesting camps. He and a pal and two bicycles spent a hand-blistering, and hilarious, summer in Wales. But he did get home to Tunbridge Wells.

He found that 'home' was now a considerable height up in the social scale: an architect-designed villa with its own tennis court, and a more spacious 'schoolroom' where his sister Peggy and Judy Bretherton were still taught by 'Peglerino'. He had had weekly accounts from his mother's letters of how his sister and the 'Peacemeal' girl kept up an academic competition week by week; a competition which became amazingly intense when it came to the botanical. They quickly collected specimens of wild flowers from their weekly walks on the downs, hurried home to check them against Bentham and Hooker, and anxiously took the score:

> . . . on to Dunton Green [*wrote his mother*] and in both places got 50 flowers—wild delphiniums and bella donnas among them. We hope we have now passed the Brethertons. We could not bear them to be ahead. Pea [*Peggy*] has 304 all told.

These two girls, Peggy five years behind him and Judy three, were becoming as close as actual sisters. But to Tony the family was sacrosanct. She was not of 'Us' but of 'Them' and, to Peggy's surprise, when he came home for holidays now the Bretherton girl was banned firmly from Warwick Lodge. She adored him but he would not have her around at any price.

To the observant boy, Mother was now weary and over-worked. Father was not his old self at all. She was unsparing of herself in a war effort which was to earn for her the Médaille de la Reine Elizabeth from the King of the Belgians. This was for service to Belgian soldiers and civilian refugees. The Doctor was struggling not just with his hugely increased medical duties but with a deadly enemy now attacking him but never then talked about, even in a medical home—cancer.

The big boy, now fully six feet plus, went back to school with-out any hope of Irish holidays. He had a letter from his former housemaster, now in uniform, Mr. Stocken: 'I am here [*in Belfast*] trying to keep your wild Hibernians in order . . . We took the Stranraer–Larne passage, with an escort consisting of 2 airships, 2 submarine-chasers and a destroyer . . .'

Tony had occasion to think of Ireland again. Sadly he shared his distress with his mother, and with the wonderful journeys to Ireland in mind:

> Wasn't the Leinster affair [*the sinking of an Irish ferry boat*] hideous? I did not know any of those lost even by name except Lady Abercorn's daughter: even so the business seems more horrible than others of the same kind simply knowing the ship so well—and all the circumstances of the voyage.

The war was getting worse, not better, and he was into his eighteenth year. Close to the Annagh-ma-Kerrig woods was Dartrey. The news of the death in France of Lord Dartrey's son came in: 'It is awfully sad for them poor things. I wonder when the war will be over . . .'

She must have wondered more than he when he wrote again: 'Major Blacker's son has been on the wounded list for some time but today his name was followed by an asterisk which means "Died of his wounds". I *am* sorry for his parents. Isn't it ghastly . . .'

In the late summer of 1918 a letter reached her from him. His very enthusiasm must have chilled the hearts of both war-weary parents:

Dearest Mum,

The prodigal son—literally as you'll see!—has returned after a strenuous but glorious excursion to 'the little village on the Thames'. Bryant (O/c the OTC) expressly arranged my leave so as to give us time to see a matinee. . . . That awful old Vaughan would only let me stay till a 4.55 train. However, Bryo said he didn't mind me seeing the play if I left in time to catch the train!

Self and youth named Wentworth set forth early this morning at 8.30 in our best attire and with our whole fortune in our pockets.

We caught our train quite easily at Wokingham and arrived safely at Waterloo. Then we made direct by Underground to 'The Adjutant, Irish Guards, Buckingham Gate', which was all we had to go on. Well we managed to get to Buck. Pal. Rd. and after asking innumerable policemen discovered that *Wellington Barracks* was the most likely lair of the elusive adjutant. . . . We wandered, or rather hastened to the Well. barracks and I accosted a *sentry* and demanded to be taken to the adj. I. Gds. He referred us to another—and this one to a third who sent us back to the first again!!! . . . Finding us too persistent to be got rid of our first friend took us through divers passages and places to an office where after parleyings (all done by me) with a sort of clerk person we were shown the dread adjutant.

He was in a small office—an old, very tall man with a stoop and a high cracked voice. With him was another officer—about 45–50—very handsome and pleasant looking. We were shown in separately. I went first. He asked me a few questions about myself—where I came from etc., then handed me over to the younger man, who took down:

Guthrie, William Tyrone.

Guthrie, Thomas Clement (Doctor)

   Warwick Lodge,   T.W.

   at Well. Coll.

and it was arranged that I should join at *Bushey*, all being well, in January . . .

It was significant that the new play he and Wentworth saw in London that day was the first production of J. M. Barrie's *Dear Brutus*—

PURDIE: The fault, dear Brutus, is not in our stars, but in ourselves, that we are underlings.
JOANNA: For 'Dear Brutus' we are to read 'dear audience', I suppose.
PURDIE: You have it.
JOANNA: Meaning that we have the power to shape ourselves.
PURDIE: We have the power right enough.
JOANNA: But isn't that rather splendid?
PURDIE: For those who have the grit in them, yes. And they are not the dismal chappies; they are the ones with the thin bright faces.

They stayed in their seats till the last possible moment, then slipped out and ran like mad for the Underground to Westminster, hared up out of it and over the bridge. Not far from where the Old Vic, at 2*d*. a seat, was catering for a very different clientele, they came into collision with another audience pouring out of a South Bank cinema. They cut through into Waterloo Station, and as the whistle blew and the guard waved his green flag they bundled into the shuddering train. So—breathless—back, by steam, to Berkshire, Wellington and Hardinge, to dream ... of ... being in the Irish Guards ... come January ...

But, come November, it was peace. The Armistice, and bells ringing, people in the streets, flags waving everywhere. And at Wellington, in January, peace brought with it one of the big days of his life.

Sad Mother had written not so long before ...

I am always regretting too that you and *all* the youngsters of your age are missing so many of the good times that used to be taken for granted. It is one of the large minor tragedies of the War ... therefore ... I do so easily understand your feelings about the 'big' days at College now which just pass over like the ordinary ones.

On Monday, January 11, 1919 he was in full command of the total production resources of the Hardinge, stage director at the start of a career he did not yet know he had.

My Dearest Dad,
    ... a perfectly delirious day here ... Vaughan standing up on a bench in the middle of the Quad led 3 cheers for the armistice himself, throwing his cap and yelling with the best.

A general rag in the front quad culminated in the decoration of Wellington's bust [*on the Museum*] with a bowler hat and a neckerchief and the twining of 3 separate fire hoses on the helpless bursar!

The various dormitories vied with each other in 'decorations' which in default of flags took the shape of chains of silk handkerchiefs, tablecloths or sheets, etc.

The Hardinge created a sensation by flying my counterpane (ruined anyway in the wash) on the end of a broomstick—on it in vast characters traced in red ink by my nimble white [*fingers*] was inscribed 'PEACE'! Later on we had an illumination—each window, by an ingenious arrangement of brown paper and cloth hanging, displaying one letter each of 'glorious victory'—also my idea and a crowning success!

There was another big event at Wellington while he was there: though not so much a 'big day' as days on end of it. But it had the bigness of the great event. The occasion was the arrival at the College of the Black Death—at least that was what schoolboys with a sense of history and a taste for drama whispered in the corridors. In fact it was the much-publicized Great Flu Epidemic of 1918. And it did sweep the war-weary nation like a plague—leaving many new graves, not war graves. Already in the College one of the servants at the lodge was dead and other cases critical. This, on top of all the strain there had been in keeping the muddy maw of Flanders fed by a tragic supply of his beloved pupils, nearly broke the heart of Vaughan. So, volunteers, from both pupils and parents, leapt to the call; young Guthrie in the van. And he outdid his overworked father, in the care of the 'sicka-needy':

> We have had a day of utter chaos . . . By Thursday there were 80 cases and the Combermere was turned out to provide a sanitorium overflow. Today I should say there will be well over *150 cases*! Hardinge received orders to pack up and move out this morning . . . The Murray is being converted into nurses' quarters . . .

And the communiqués go on:

> There are now about 350 cases, so that when one is ill one just lies down in one's room telling one of the nurses who are hovering about. Directly after breakfast this morning I, and a

2*

lad called Holdsworth Hunt [who are the only two feeling really fit], set to and made all the beds, emptied baths, etc. Nurses are short. Masters' wives are being splendid and a lot of mothers are here for Confirmation class whose boys are laid up. The nice ones are helping but some are being odious and simply getting in the way . . . Hunt and I have to do *everything* under the nurses. It's rather fun and an excellent preventive for Flu' I'm sure—but tiring and not conducive to exam work. [*He was still working hard on History.*] Having set the rooms to right we had to keep the nurses supplied with hot water for washing the patients; bring tea round and biscuits. Then the patients' rooms had to be swept and garnished. Then the tea things washed up. By now lunch was on the tapis: we had to fetch all the food up from the kitchens (up 61 steps) 3 journeys. Collect spoons, etc., then help with the food and take it round, finally wash up just in time for our lunch. Now Mrs. Cott (the Mamma in charge) is away for her lunch so I am in charge. Having straightened beds got drinks seen patients properly covered up, etc. etc. I'm snatching a well-earned rest in my room.

He was in his element. He loved organizing. He loved looking after people.

The war was over. He had a future and the path of duty, whatever it might be, would not lead to a 'glory' that the whole muddy and bloody business had put in doubt. He wrote to his father: 'I haven't the faintest desire to serve in the Army in *peace time*, what shall I do? Oxford? . . . Let me know what you think about my "feutchah".' And in fact he did head for Oxford.

But before Wellington is left behind, one thing should be noted. He came out of this exile from home, as afflicted in the foot as Oedipus; and this was the basic reason why all through his life he would, if he could, appear in loose tennis shoes, gym shoes, sneakers, sandals or such. It was not, as was often thought, mere anti-establishment affectation. The reason was a lost toe. Throughout his second year at Wellington he had persistent pain with a toe. With typical stoicism and no self-pity whatsoever he wrote home,

Please to tell the 'Dear Doctor' that Master Guthrie's second toe from the right on the left foot (as you face Trinity Steeple, sitting in the day nursery at Belmont, putting on your stockings

next the fireguard) has been 'really quite a bore'—I have
painted it with iodine, but wonder if there is any other sort of
nostrum that I could apply . . .

Then, what was obviously transmission of mechanical strain to
the leg itself resulted in collapse of knee. He wrote again: 'Playing hockey it just gave way and I came down like any poor ole
cab horse.'

Knee and toe, the trouble went on for another year till the toe
became referred to in his letters as a sort of parasitic pet animal.
He called it 'Toekin', or 'Tankynne'. 'Tankynne is better, but
still inclined to grumble . . .' But, finally in the middle of 1917, he
wrote,

I can't account for the relapse as all my shoes are comfy and
I'd been doing nothing strenuous. Of course the swelling has
always remained—quite a good lump . . . Do you think it
would be better to have the brute off? And if so do let me have
it done *at once* and not cut into next term . . . when I am head of
Dormitory.

And his father, the surgeon, reluctantly had the boy home to his
hospital. 'Tankynne' was cut off.

The departure from Wellington was total triumph.

During the last year at school, when he was getting used to
being a nine-toed adolescent, he had sudden success in the field of
writing. Earlier his writings had been dismissed by his tutor as
'always a bit of a journalist—too much given to phrase and
gesture'. Now the news came through that he had won the
coveted Williams Essay prize. This was followed by better news
still. A visit to Oxford, armed with self-filling fountain pen,
resulted in the award to Guthrie, W. T., of a History Scholarship
to St. John's.

It was an *honorary* scholarship, because he had written to
Oxford, before the scholarships came through to the effect that,
as to the financial side, he would not need the money, so perhaps
it could be diverted to someone more needy. It was a rather grand
gesture of a relatively rich young man going home in triumph.
He made the gesture first and informed his father afterwards.

He was on top of the world. And this is the world he thought it
to be, when that big day of The Armistice came:

Certainly we live in the most marvellous times since the Reformation—if not since Christ. I do not know whether we are 'lucky' or the reverse. I think for the older generation who see all things they have known and loved crumbling to dust its *too appalling*: but for the young, who will live to see the wounds heal and help in the reform and reconstruction to come, it's an opportunity such as the world has never known before.

Eighteen, and certainly speaking out now like 'a leader of men'.

There was a gap of many months before he could start at Oxford at the required time, Michaelmas Term in the autumn of 1919. What History at Oxford was going to lead him to he had no idea. Vaughan advised the Law. He himself had a hankering for Science. Meantime he did something which Great-grandfather Guthrie had done before he went full steam ahead in Divinity— a year's study of Medicine, at London University.

Something else was studied in this year, and it had more effect on his final choice of career than Medicine: Singing. In those months of dreams of a 'feutchah' so suddenly switched away from war, one legitimate dream he had was of taking to the Stage, as a singer. During most of a year, in which he commuted back and forth from London to Tunbridge Wells, he attended regular singing lessons. These were given in Maida Vale by a little old maestro in black velvet jacket and flaming *Bohème* bow. He was the last of a famous line of Spanish and Italian singing teachers— Gustave Garcia. The maestro, in the beginning, said, 'The voice is very *large*, you can sing at parties. People will ask you out'; and at the end, the maestro said positively, 'A voice, yes. You will not be much of a singer. But you will make a good listener, a good audience. Stick to that.' It was not an easy crash of hopes for a highly emotional, ambitious and awkwardly tall young man, whose public zest was often a cloak for real shyness and a tendency to private tears.

But the Gay Twenties were on their way. One can see evidence of this in the behaviour of two young commuters (himself and Judith Bretherton's brother, Martin). While Tony attended classes in his father's Medicine, Martin attended an office practis- ing *his* father's Law. These two bright sparks used to be the despair of the bowler-hatted sombre-minded, City commuters. To the annoyance of gentlemen trying to read *The Times*, they loudly talked their heads off, giggled at private jokes and carried on conversations in assumed characters. They could even be seen at the end of one wet day pushing imperiously through lesser mortals in the London railway terminus. As they moved towards the ticket barrier, Bretherton, with marked servility, would be playing the part of royal equerry. The tall prince of a figure over whose high head he strained to keep the royal umbrella open—despite being under the lofty glass and cast-iron roof of the Southern Railway—was played by Guthrie. When they reached the barrier Guthrie would announce in the loudest and most imperial tones of The Voice—so that all commoner commuters should hear, 'You may now take down our umbrella, Captain Jenkinson.' Imperiously they would sweep on to the platform, all heads turned their way, as they stifled giggles and strode on to a forward carriage. Oxford was going to be fun. But Oxford—unlike Guthrie—had not escaped the war.

CHAPTER THREE

OXFORD AND ACTING
(1919–1924)

DURING THE war Oxford had been a city drained of its young men. Now, in the late summer of 1919, young Guthrie found it full to the brim, with a log-jam of undergraduates on a frantic hunt for places to lodge. He was fortunate enough to be accommodated within St. John's. Yet there the ancient oak-panelled rooms, in which Charles I had found space enough, were partitioned and very nearly reduced to dormitory conditions. For the first year therefore he lodged, in a somewhat cramped quartet, with three other undergraduates; one of whom was Weekly, the son of D. H. Lawrence's Frieda, by her first husband. The 'gossip column' Guthrie letters started to flow towards Warwick Lodge, reporting conditions and 'playmates'.

As to conditions, it was a lovely place to lodge—in a building whose greatest ghost was Archbishop Laud; a building of stone and oak, all ancient grace and simplicity. The utter peace and high horticultural order within its walls were in immediate contrast to the Oxford bustle on the busy highway immediately below its windows to the North; an unorganized traffic laced through with agile independent bicyclists.

As to 'playmates', it was noticed that Guthrie immediately took Weekly's side and extravagantly championed him, when there was a certain consensus of criticism of his being an awkward card. (Till his dying day, Guthrie acted like a latter-day Dr. Thomas Guthrie, D.D., in the championing of the unfortunate.) In his opinion Weekly—whose mother had run off with that unethical novelist—was unfortunate, and he stubbornly stood by him. As to the college's opinion of Guthrie—with his skill in tennis, taste for theatre, a penchant for any good prank, and the piercing ability to sing a buffoon performance of 'Because' at any old piano —he was accepted as a social eccentric bridging the gap between the beer-drinking sporty set and the arty intellectuals. Things were definitely set for happy days.

Two undergraduates of St. John's are worthy of special note. Butler was a gentle, quiet-spoken and gifted scholar, who became Guthrie's close friend, in college; also in vacation time; for Hubert Butler shared his affinity with Ireland and the Irish. He came to Oxford after being head boy at Charterhouse and his home was in Kilkenny. His father was of the great Butler clan and related to the Ormondes of Kilkenny Castle. The other undergraduate of note was Robert Graves. And he brings into stark contrast the two sorts of student in Oxford then. Between their two camps there was, psychologically, an almost unbridgeable chasm. Graves belonged to the camp of those who had had painful and personal experience of the Western Front. They were the scarred and shaken survivors of a lost generation of young Englishmen, which in the end amounted to more than one million. Many of those lost would have been the cream of the nation's intellect; would normally have been on their way to Oxford or Cambridge when war broke out. Robert Graves had actually been on the way to Oxford in 1914. His public school had been Charterhouse, and he too had family roots in Ireland (Limerick). But unlike young Butler and Guthrie he was a mature man. He talked a different language. He was married. He lived out; on Boar's Hill in a cottage lent to him and his wife by Mr. and Mrs. John Masefield. And the few times he entered the mellow quads of St. John's was simply to collect his government allowance.

One thing the undergraduates at St. John's had to be grateful to those war veterans for was that they formed what they called a 'soviet'. It sounds like the revolution, but in fact its political purpose was limited to a simple domestic protest: College dinners might be taken in the most ancient and distinguished of all the halls in University and the plate, etc., splendid, but the food just was not good enough for those who had got quality out of bully beef and a billy-can. They wanted—and they got—an undergraduate representative to sit on the Kitchen Committee. To a nineteen-year-old with his heroics unsoured, and his most serious social satirists still Messrs. Gilbert and Sullivan, men like Graves were sad, unaccountable, awesome. One could not even be sure that Mrs. Graves was actually married to him; and they were socialists!

Guthrie's most serious attack at this time on the social norms of the establishment was to play tennis in what he called 'Japanese style'—that is, in bare feet. This shocked some. It was probably a matter of pure comfort to him.

Warwick Lodge had a tennis court of its own. With that reach, and his natural alertness, he played well. He played for the college and spent more time on the tennis court, or out on the river in a punt, than in serious study. These were the days of floppy 'flannel bags' and flowing mufflers for the men; short hair and shortened skirts for the girls, and 'ciggies' for both.

So as not to commit himself to too much book work he stuck to History and argued his way out of the tyranny of reading Law. He was a good arguer; a bad debater. When he was persuaded to join the college's Sophists Debating Society they soon found out that he was good for a five-minute impromptu speech, and no good at all for prolonged formal debate. He was too impatient.

He settled in, kept a careful budget—he always did—and, as far as the cash would allow, saw everything that came Oxford's way to the old Playhouse. Besides Gilbert and Sullivan this was still Barrie's day, but beginning to come into fashion was the cynicism of Maugham, the cutting edge of early Coward and the socially conscious drama of Galsworthy and Shaw. Despite Fun, the flowing blue muffler, 'anyone for tennis', and love of a good tune, ascetic Guthrie would draw the line at Ivor Novello. He was no highbrow but he took in all that the University Societies could provide, from the annual O.U.D.S. Shakespeare to the French Club's production of Beaumarchais's *Barbier de Séville*. He auditioned for the O.U.D.S. and wrote home very critically of their poor organization. They had done the unforgivable thing for Guthrie, at any time, in any production—kept people hanging around idle; including him. He filled a gap in a concert of the college Musical Society (singing 'Come, Phyllis, Come', 'Green Grow the Rushes O' and 'Barbara Allen'). And, because he was seen to sing, he was offered a singing part in a play. It was Ibsen's *The Pretenders*, and the director was the Shakespearean authority, Bridges Adams.

It was the custom of the Oxford University Dramatic Society to engage a notable professional director for the major production of the year. This was the first time Guthrie had seen a professional director at work. What impressed him with Bridges Adams, was the time and care he spent in the mere movement and placing of players. Vaughan had brought Shakespeare off the page for him but he had never before seen speech meaningfully on the move on

The Festival Theatre, Stratford, Ontario (1957)

The tented theatre (1953) founded by Guthrie—from which
the above grew

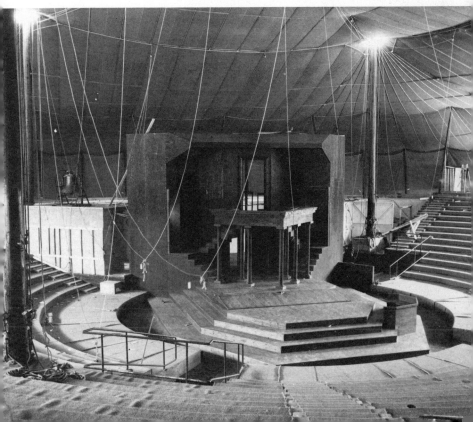

Annagh-ma-Kerrig, the Power and Guthrie family home, Monaghan, Ireland

Norah Power (mother)

Dr Thomas Clement Guthrie (father)

Aunt Sue Pow

Tyrone Guthrie (1927) with the Annagh-ma-Kerrig lake and house in the background

gy Guthrie and Judith Bretherton

nting colours to Carson's Ulster volunteers

Tony and Peggy, 1910

Guthrie as actor: Arcadian
Shepherd, Oxford U.D.S.
production of
Le Bourgeois Gentilhomme

Guthrie as pioneer radio
producer, Belfast BBC
studio 1926

stage. Other offers of parts followed. He was still more interested
in music, but fate faced him with a very peculiar part to play, his
next step in Greek drama beyond being a schoolboy Galatea. He
wrote home,

> I have been asked to play in *The Rhesus* of Euripides IN
> GREEK. They want me to play the Muse. She—She!—sud-
> denly appears upon a New College wall at the end of the play—
> holding a dead che-ild in the arms, sings a lament and says two
> and a half pages of solid Greek. The idea of doing a lady muse
> with pigtails and a dead che-ild amused me so much I said I
> would do it.

Time flew. Parents visited; tall Peggy too. He showed them his
Oxford, his friends, lodgings, and the day ended with a D'Oyly
Carte *Iolanthe* at the Playhouse, followed by a mad rush to get the
family on the 5.45 train. There were no sad partings now.
Annagh-ma-Kerrig vacations began again but his mother wrote
about news from Ireland which troubled her. It also made him
somewhat of a junior prophet in that letter he wrote as a prep
school boy; about the proportions of Protestant to Roman
Catholic in the Ulster counties. Southern Ireland was to be given
self-rule. The three predominantly Roman Catholic counties of
Ulster would now become a part of the new Irish Free State:
Donegal, Cavan, and Monaghan! Journeys to Annagh-ma-
Kerrig would no longer be journeys to Ulster and the border
would be north of, not south of their land and people now. His
mother was angered by the over-pleased attitude of some of 'our
labourers' on the estate.

Also at this time a cutting from the Irish press came to him
from Annagh-ma-Kerrig. It shows that the tragic pattern has not
changed to this day:

'Tragedy at Aghabog'

> . . . About 4 o'clock in the morning armed and masked men
> called at the house of a young man . . . They took him away
> with them and in a lane about a mile distant shot him dead.
> . . . [*he*] is the young man who was chained to the gate of
> Aghabog chapel with the word 'spy' painted on his coat . . .

The same isolated little chapel where Grandfather Power lay
buried; and where young Tony attended church when at Annagh-
ma-Kerrig.

But in gracious St. John's, little short of another world war could dampen the spirits. He continued the weekly 'gossip column' to Warwick Lodge:

Fashion note from Oxford: *Grey* flannels are *quite* out—the jeunesse dorée being now seen in voluminous creations of lavender, buff or biscuit tints.

I remain your constant
and entirely devoted friend,
Aristedes Phobbs.

It is an indication of the atmosphere of these irresponsible days that he would sign his letters as anything from General Sir Roger Bultitude to Ignatius P. Oliphant. Which brings one to Oedipus Biggs, his pen name in very undergraduate bits of authorship. When, in the fine days of a Trinity term, he would take all his books and push off in a punt, study was often secondary to his own reading and writing. He read a lot. He was a rapid reader; a rapid writer, too. In fact a rather rapid man. He was writing both an operetta and a play. He also had pieces published—in *The Oxford Outlook, A Literary Review. Edited by Undergraduates* (Editor, C. H. O. Scaife, Sub-Editor, Graham Greene).

And here is where, in his second year, an extraordinary character of immense influence crossed his path, or rather took a path parallel to and close to his for the rest of his life. C. H. O. Scaife and W. T. Guthrie were joint authors of an undergraduate take-off of the Sitwell cult. Two poems from this satirical exercise survive in *The Oxford Outlook*: '*Lines Written On Looking Into My Brother Aethelston's Jewel-Box*', signed 'Oedipus Biggs'; and '*Liquorice and Loose Hair*', signed 'Aethelston Biggs'. The 'Aethelston' was Scaife and the 'Oedipus' was Guthrie. This was totally un-serious. Yet, at a deeply serious level, both these young undergraduates were giants in talent and both were complete in their qualifications for a profound Oedipus complex. Both had impressively firm fathers and overwhelmingly magnificent mothers; and for most of the Oxford years they shared lodgings in and out of college. It was through Scaife, and his theatrical family, that Tony Guthrie was given his first two great opportunities as a producer. This was also the friend to whom he turned again and again in his life to measure how far he had travelled on his way, and how he stood. He gave the name Xtopher—which sounds a legendary name; and within the Guthrie coterie Christopher Scaife *was* 'a legend'. In the autobiography, Guthrie says of him 'I have never met anyone, who could [*better*] conduct his life in the way which suited him, with such an aristocratic disregard of conventional ideas.'

He could write to his own mother, in the tone of the times, about Scaife's mother: '. . . Ma Scaife? . . . she will come to tea in a pith helmet trimmed with humming birds and wax raspberries and will just adore being told how wonderful Chris is!' But Mrs. Scaife's attachment to her son was based on a personal tragedy out of which her son rose from being a boy actor in the halls to winner of the Newdigate Prize and President of the Oxford Union.

The facts read like the programme synopsis of a Victorian Melodrama.

One: Lovely young lady marries splendid gentleman in The Turkey Trade (Banking, Constantinople); finds his passion for procreation positively alarming and, after delivery of two daughters, two sons and a final boy, she conceives—while sojourning in Kensington—a passion for amateur acting, takes to The Stage and changes her name from Mrs. Scaife to Miss Saint-Eve.

Two: Her children are forbidden to have anything to do with the Fallen Woman. Sadly for her, Miss Saint-Eve on-stage is a searing flop, goes to pieces; is committed to an institution for the insane. Mercifully, she soon struggles free of this asylum; into lone theatrical lodgings in London.

Three: One night, when stern Father is at local suburban Ball, young Christopher is aided by his brothers to steal away; takes the appropriate steam train, and joins his adored Mother in her snug urban shrine; theatrical lodgings, Cathedral Mansions, Vauxhall Bridge Road, London.

Four: Education is now reduced to what the boy can pick up from the 1st Westminster Troop of Boy Scouts. *But*, through Steadman's Theatrical Agency and God's gift of a golden voice he becomes the breadwinner of the devoted two. He becomes a boy actor.

Five: A theatrical gent in same lodgings says that he can 'do something' for the boy. He does. He writes a vaudeville 'sketch' in which the boy and he can some day top the bill, somewhere. 'PHIL AND THE OFFICE BOY'. And they did —at the Putney Empire.

It goes like this:—Phil, a theatrical agent is down on his luck, faces ruin and the closure of his office. No 'artistes' now come to his door; so—sad to say—the Office Boy must go. Exit Office Boy. *But* in hardly no time at all the suicidal Phil hears a gentle knock. The glass door of his office lettered TNEGA YTEIRAV—SPPIHP LIHP opens to admit a smashing young blonde—with a golden voice! Phil signs her on. Phil's fortune soars as never before.

And the actual theatre orchestra, at the Putney Empire, at this point struck up and the blonde launched into 'The Rosary'. The audience wept, applauded and roared for more. Then the 'pay-off'—the dénouement—came 'she' whipped off her blonde wig. And who stood there?—The Office Boy!—Master Scaife.

Six: SUCCESS! for son, mother, and theatrical gent. But no— The Authorities point out that the boy soprano is under age. Surely that could be got round but, The Kaiser starts a World War; Father rescues disappointed boy from Shame; and from Mother.

Seven: In retreat from Education and Misery, the boy offers his services to Lord Kitchener and the nation. One year's Army training turns him into a very young batman about to go to the Armageddon of Flanders Fields. But fiercely the family tragedienne steps in. His Mother points out to Whitehall that her boy has nobly falsified his age.

Eight and Finale: Education is resumed but Great War ends before boy has gained the requisite years to face the furies of The Front. *And*—on the basis of 'one-year's war service', assisted by high level influence plus high-pressure from a good crammer, Scaife C.O. gets a Kitchener Scholarship to St. John's College, Oxford!

This highly original student differed from Guthrie in being active politically. He was a radical Liberal and advocate of the new League of Nations, but even in this Guthrie joined him for a time on the speakers' platform. And—besides lodgings in college and afterwards out—these two formidable and lively young giants of the student scene shared almost everything for the next four years. They shared a love of music; both shared literary tastes and wrote poetry; they shared an enthusiasm for then-fashionable Folk Art (folk songs and folk dancing), and they shared a taste for under-grad fun and downright provocative devilment; but what they did not share at all was the same attitude to sex. And cynics subject to contemporary sexual bigotries may not find it easy to accept the plain fact that, except intellectually, Tony Guthrie was personally just not interested in sex. And it continued to be so throughout most of his life. This did not mean he could not and did not love men, and women, passionately. But Sex, to Guthrie was the god-peculiar copulation essential to the mystery of pro-creation; and the Family and the Child (both sacrosanct concepts to him) could never be left out of what his era made into so technical and selfish, so abstracted an exercise. To put it posit-ively, his love of Family, Mother and the whole mystery of Creation saved him from believing in the twentieth-century fiction of Sex Per Se. He was therefore saved from much of the psy-chological obsessions and anxieties attendant, though of course not from frustration. But frustration has often been a potent gen-erative source of creation in the Arts and, putting it more fash-ionably and negatively, he was not just 'Oedipus Biggs' but Oedipus Tyrannos Guthrie, and his tendency to tyranny was part product of a sexual frustration that he would consider quite sec-ondary in importance to the two great things: love of fellow creature and the passionate game of discovery in getting 'the Work' done; 'the Work' being some form of performing art.

He often displayed the mannerisms—and mocked them in him-self too—of an over-energetic aunt; and in his hazy young days he was surrounded by giant female figures from whom he acquired the world's presumedly proper gestures. He was not, however, a homosexual. Perhaps it was because his partners in work often were, that he had such sympathy for the human pro-blems raised, and never in this sphere—except in unsophisticated youth—stood in judgment. To use the term in its most simple and unspecial way, his long friendship with Xtopher was lovely; and, characteristically, non-sexual. In his mother's birthday month, in the second year of the friendship, he wrote home:

22nd May 1922
11, St. John Street.

. . . the next expedition was in honour of May-day, yester. We joined the crowd that went to hear the May Day Morning Anthem (the Magdalen Choir sing it from the top of their tower at sunrise)—most impressive and beautiful it was. A great crowd of many hundreds gathered on the bridge and up 'the High' and in boats on the Cher—all dead silent listening to the far-away, clear, quite unearthly carolling of little white blobs on the tower! We then went on into the country on our bicycles—got our breakfast (consisting of fried eggs and home-cured bacon more welcome than any manna) at a charming old farm 5 or 6 miles away—and returned laden with cherry-boughs just as the clocks were striking nine.

Both men had good voices and Tony was again having ideas about himself and opera. He arranged for another singing teacher in London to 'hear him'. He agreed to sing for the Tunbridge Wells Operatic Society in *Iolanthe* and went off on vacation with Christopher to Bavaria, with the express purpose of hearing grand opera at its grandest. But as regards the Voice, there was even a bit of discouragement, this time from the Muse herself. Mother wrote,

> . . . about your acting—you are far too unsimple—same about your singing—you try to cram in far too much expression which detracts from your voice tones—that was where Scaife's singing was so pleasant. He just sang the words very distinctly but quite plainly and unemphasized and his voice was the prominent feature.
>
> Your very loving   N.G.

Mother and son were writing to each other now as adult equals. But this kind of criticism could hurt. Was it jealousy? He might address her as 'Madame Gutheroe', 'Mrs. G.' or (naughty corruption of Titania) 'Titsina', but in that lifelong love affair the real affection was serious and unwavering:

My darling Tit,
> . . . your birthday comes in May: I've always quite un-consciously associated you and that month—so that my impressions of you are against a sort of May and Spring and flowery background—and my impressions of May are all coloured by your personality. Then it goes further than that. May-trees remind me not of you exactly but of being with you and dependent on you . . .

He wrote to her again, after being involved in practice with the Bach Choir:

. . . the B Minor Mass . . . To sing it excites me so that I can't sleep for hours after getting home—*it's much the most intense emotional experience I've ever had* [Author's italics] . . . The Vaughan Williams Sea Symphony . . . it's a fine thing . . . the scherzo movement is a big thrill—you'll love it—choir and orchestra shriek and scream as loud and as fast as they can—the effect of whistling screaming winds through ropes—of dashing through the air—and being soaked in spray—quite the greatest effect I've ever heard in the way of reproducing 'atmosphere' *but* it's but the porch where Bach is the temple.

Literally worshipping music he went on to dabble in drama; and first stumbled on his gift for directing (or producing, as it was called till films and TV altered the term). The O.U.D.S. were to do Molière's *Le Bourgeois Gentilhomme*. He was allocated the parts of the Mufti and the Arcadian Shepherd. The first satisfied his appetite for fun and grotesquerie. The second—he wrote home —gave him a fine wig, Arcadian furs and a Dresden-china make-up which to his alarm turned him, he said, into the spitting image of his sister. He was given also the job of producing the ballet within the play.

It was at this point that Kenneth Rae—who ended his distinguished career as secretary of the National Theatre—came in to Guthrie's life and the rehearsal room. The dancer-players were assembled. Guthrie was at the piano and, with hardly time, Rae thought, to see him come in, Guthrie called, 'Do you play the piano?' Being shy of musical responsibility he started to answer, hesitantly, 'Well . . . yes, but I . . .' 'Can you read music?' was rapped back. 'Well, yes, I can, but what . . .' 'Read that. Play that.' He found himself on the piano stool, and Guthrie Tyrannos giving the famous clap and clarion call. 'Everybody!!—Right, into the minuet!' And they were off and away willy-nilly. 'Never a dull moment with W.T.G.,' Rae was to report of the Oxford days.

And there was one hilarious, and significant, expedition by punt with Scaife.

Punting was one of the joys of the Guthrie life which was to recur again in Cambridge and in Stratford-upon-Avon. With such shoulders at such height and hands as deft as his surgeon father's, the punt pole for him was an ideal propulsive instrument. But this particular Guthrie/Scaife vacational expedition was not just

pleasure. It was field-work—or, more properly, canal-work—on a
Folk Art experiment. It entailed punting miles of canal for eight
days and singing nightly at canal-side pubs, to assess the rustic's
reaction to Folk Song. Guthrie, being the organizational genius,
organized the business side, as well as being potentially the chief
propellor. It was arranged with the London *Times* and the journal
of the English Folk Dance Society that articles would be written
and submitted for a fee sufficient to pay for hire of punt, hire of
'dulcitone' (a portable source of music more all-weather and
smaller than a celeste) and to defray some of the expenses on food
and on paraffin for the primus stove.

There was one lurid wet night when the punt got wedged
for'ard in a lock-gate and water rose when punt prow did not.
And dulcitone and primus and all almost went overboard. But the
damp Folk Art crew continued through all weathers. They
would tie up of an evening and proceed to a rural pub. In its snug
they would start by a baiting of the cultural hook with a rousing,
vulgar, Guthrie 'Because' or 'Roses of Picardy'. Then, the
'carrying' voice having advertised their presence, the Scaife
'golden' would try 'Waley, Waley', 'Barbara Allen', or Guthrie
get in again with 'Lord Ruthven's Daughter' or 'The Erl King'.

The fun of this is obvious, the significance is its relation to his
love of getting out of town and taking Art, by entertainment, to
the People. With his links with the Irish folk there would be no
condescension in these evenings with the Warwickshire rustics.
In fact an angry letter went home when, at a Morris Dancing
evening in a village hall, he found Mrs. John Buchan to be to his
mind too patronizing—so that he chose to refer to her as 'Mrs. 39
Steps'.

With these delightfully distracting years on their way to conclusion in what was bound to be a not too honourable class of
academic degree, the feeling for Theatre finally found a real
commitment.

Again I was invited to act . . . in the Oxford University
Dramatic Society's annual Shakespearean production . . . they
rented the New Theatre [*in London's West End*] for a week;
London critics attended and wrote notices with what we never
recognized as indulgent condescension. The play was *Henry IV*,
Part I. My part was Glendower. The producer was James B.
Fagan, whose work we had all seen and admired, whose work

was serious and intelligent, who was an Irishman from Belfast. My fate was sealed.*

Rehearsal again fascinated him. Just as he learned about placing from Bridges Adams, he learnt from Fagan—who was an established playwright as well as producer—how a producer might work to bring all the elements of the theatre arts—especially lighting—into one total stage vitality, of light, movement, costume, décor; and where speech marched with it all. And how 'a script of a play, even of a great play, a masterpiece, is still only a *part* of the raw material of performance'.

He gave his whole heart to his part in it. His friend, Kenneth Rae, playing alongside him, had many of the same fears as Guthrie's mother, that zest would be the ruin of his acting. 'Given to gesture' even in his writings, he did 'saw the air' and all he did was nothing if not exaggerated. But the personality and presence even impressed Fagan. Because, just at the point when he had to face his father with the fact that he would make his exit from Oxford with a very second-rate History degree, Fagan wrote to him and opened up a way ahead—on the Stage.

James B. Fagan was founding a new theatre and company—in Oxford—and he wanted Tyrone Guthrie to play. Dr. Guthrie could not deny that, within the so-called profession of Theatre, Mr. Fagan's aims were laudably high. In an appeal for public support Fagan said:

The breach between literature and the stage which the modern commercial theatre in this country does little to remedy is a matter of concern to all who are interested in dramatic literature. It appears to us only right that Oxford should encourage the efforts which are being made sporadically by individuals to raise the standard of the acted Drama in England—the only great country in the world where neither Government nor Municipality will move a finger to support the most democratic of the arts.

The Oxford Playhouse will open its doors on October 22nd for a season of seven weeks, during which the Oxford Players a company of talented actors and actresses, will present plays by de Musset, Goldoni, Hankin, Ibsen, Shaw, Sheridan and Wilde.

* *A Life In the Theatre*, Tyrone Guthrie. Hamish Hamilton, 1959.

Among the twenty-three eminent signatories to this appeal were J. M. Barrie, Arnold Bennett, Robert Bridges, Edward Elgar, John Galsworthy, Thomas Hardy, John Masefield, A. A. Milne, Gilbert Murray, Arthur Pinero, Nigel Playfair and Bernard Shaw.

Fagan's playhouse was not the *old* Oxford Playhouse, where the visiting companies of the past had come. It was a new Oxford Playhouse, for a resident company, where the entire profits would be devoted to the scheme for the foundation of 'a permanent theatre for classical repertory *during term time* [author's italics] in Oxford'. It was new in concept and in its limited technical equipment, but in fact it was the ramshackle old Red Barn on the Woodstock Road, not far out beyond St. John's. It had not so long since been a big game museum. There had been a previous attempt to open it up for 'varied entertainment', but this had been firmly quashed by the Vice-Chancellor's putting it 'out of bounds'. He could now hardly do so against such an assemblage of eminent signatories.

The first play was to be Shaw's *Heartbreak House*. The opening would be in the Michaelmas term and Guthrie, the actor from the O.U.D.S., was to play the role of Captain Shotover, a plum part. And with all the off-stage security of a promised salary of £5 a week, he studied Shotover and played wonderful tennis that summer in Tunbridge Wells. He reported, word-perfect, in London for the first morning's rehearsal. With all he had he gave the astounded company the full Captain Shotover, larger than life, and much louder. By lunch James B. Fagan found a quiet Irish moment to tell the young man that he had made an error of judgment. Mr. Guthrie could leave now, with no hard feelings, one hoped, on either side. He could on the other hand stay, swallow this hard lesson in casting and start learning a lot more; as assistant to the Stage Manager.

This was as much the crash from a great height for the hopes of Guthrie the Actor as it had been for Guthrie the Singer when Señor Garcia brought that hope down. It was also rather more sudden. He knew and respected Fagan and now he loved the Theatre, so he knuckled down and did what he could do to serve the new company. For consolation prize—as well as economy—he was allowed to play Hector Hushabye. Playing alongside him was a young actress whom he wrote of as 'a tall, dark girl with beautiful grey eyes'. He and she were the youngest members of the company; she was Flora Robson.

When the play opened at Oxford it did so to a distinguished audience which included the author himself. Shaw seemed to be the least impressed of anybody and in a curtain speech, typically, he said so; because he maintained there was no heartbreak here in this *Heartbreak House*. One cannot but believe there must have been some temptation for the young gentleman with the Irish, and the Power in him, to dream that had he been playing Shotover, at least he would have been moving to the great Irishman.

But he was too happy in his work for jealousy and his first professional First Night was for him a great affair. For he was in amongst all the back-stage business of Theatre. He wrote with enthusiasm to his mother:

> Yesterday . . . a terrific day. I was on the go from 9.30, when I first arrived at the Playhouse till 1.15 this morning when our rehearsal ended . . . (Dress Rehearsal 6 p.m. tonight, Sunday.) . . . Wee Luggie and I get on quite well together because he likes tying knots in rope and toying with electric batteries and in fact all the things I'm so hopelessly dull over and bad at—while I like messing about with paint brushes and gum etc. . . . Friday evening was spent by Fagan, myself and Molly Anderson . . . in painting the backcloth blue to represent sky . . . you can imagine what an amusing scene there was at 10 p.m. on Friday in the hall gangs of carpenters erecting the stalls, on stage we three splashing blue paint about, and electricians up innumerable ladders all over the place!

And his report on the opening is very much from the proud A.S.M. and modest player.

> You will be wanting to hear how the 'First Night' went off. Let me tell you at once that if you have seen an extremely laudatory notice in 'The Times' all about 'W. T. Guthrie' it's a mistake and the praise is intended for Richard Goolden (who simply brought the house down . . .) whereas poor pathetic T.G. was too bad even to be mentioned . . .

It all went well, but the one disappointment was

> the big explosion; which was the tamest of affairs . . . But that was Fagan's fault because the maroon at the dress rehearsal having blown the bottom out of a bucket he funked letting it off on the night and ordered a bang on the drum instead—!!

The bucket was an elderly affair whereas we were going to have used a stout tank at the perf. However in view of the feebleness of the effect I persuaded him to try a maroon this morning and we let one off in the tank with great eclat and perfect safety— so tonight we shall have a better explo.

Christopher Scaife was not in the Oxford Players. He had a further academic year to go and had his hands quite full with all the business attendant on being President of the Oxford Union and the serious academic study out of which he achieved an excellent degree. But they still lodged together and Tony brought Flora to tea. Like Christopher and unlike Tony she was not new to the Theatre. She had been trained at what is now the Royal Academy of Dramatic Art, had played in London in *Will Shakespeare* and had been on tour with the Ben Greet Company. But the whole atmosphere of Oxford was utterly new and to her something of a dream. Her impression of Tony Guthrie at the time was of a shy, tall and handsome young man, very much belonging to the upper-crust of society and the university intellectuals. She 'could never talk their language', she said, but the company was stimulating and the friendship with him grew, as they slaved happily together for the greater glory of 'classical theatre', conceived within the economy of Fagan's 'presentational' approach to the art. This seemed to the hard-worked pair to come down, in practical terms, to presenting every play with the minimum of set and furnishings and on a simple outer and inner stage in which all drapes and flats, etc., would be off-white.

The first new theatre in the Guthrie career was, however, such a place of joy to him that he described it uncritically at the time as '. . . delightful—stage quite beautiful and very spacious— auditorium ugly but I think will be very comfy; dressing-rooms excellent—clean as pins!'

In fact, to John Gielgud's brother, Val, it was 'a building devoid of cheer, foyer or bar' with seats 'surely the most uncomfortable in any theatre in the world'. John Gielgud joined the company and had signal success until, as Tony reported home, 'Young Jack Gielgud's got the mumps'—and it fell to him to fumigate Jack's dressing-room so that the whole company might not be stricken down.

Emlyn Williams—an undergraduate at the time—spent his all on tickets to Mr. Fagan's theatre and had this to say:

The players were not always word-perfect; loyal first-nighters began to notice that long speeches tended to be directed thoughtfully at the hidden backs of chairs . . . I was to see a maypole named Tyrone Guthrie, as Vedio in *Monna Vanna* . . . hasten on with a message, trip, fall his full impossible length, rise and deliver the line, 'But, Sire, you are hurt—let me sustain you!' On the other hand I was to see in his first leading part . . . in *Love For Love*, a youth whose name in the programme caused a woman behind me [*to say*], 'Poor boy! how *does* he pronounce it, John Jeel-gud?'*

In the season and a half (October 1923–March 1924) that Guthrie was with the company they presented: *Heartbreak House, The Importance of Being Ernest, Mirandolina* (Lady Gregory's version of Goldoni), *Love For Love, The Return of The Prodigal* (St. John Hankin), *Monna Vanna* (Maeterlinck), *No Trifling With Love* (de Musset), *The Master Builder, The Rivals, The Man of Destiny, The Land of Heart's Desire* (Yeats) and, finally, *Oedipus Rex* (in Gilbert Murray's translation). For Guthrie it was a baptism of total immersion in 'the classical repertoire'.

What he got out of it all was a love and feeling for the whole backstage organization and physical work in a theatre. In playing many small parts it became obvious to him, and more obvious to J. B. Fagan that this undoubtedly talented young man was no actor. Yet, this was not easy to take, for the playing of three parts had meant much to him. And in the playing of the third he actually ran away with the notices. These parts were two Irish, one Greek: that old favourite of Tyrone Power's, Sir Lucius O'Trigger in *The Rivals*; Shawn Bruin in Yeats's haunting *The Land of Heart's Desire*; and Tiresias in *Oedipus Rex* . . . of which the press notice said on March 13, 1924: 'The outstanding performance of the evening was certainly that of Mr. Tyrone Guthrie as Tiresias; he alone of the players raised the drama to real heights of tragedy and passion . . . he *was* Tiresias.'

It was ironic, and a little bitter, that right after that minor triumph in a major role, J. B. Fagan informed him that he would not want his services any more. It is some consolation, looking back, that he also dismissed that young aspiring actress, Flora Robson. They were both out of a job; and his first full commitment to the Stage had actually ended in rejection. Not a singer;

* *George, An Early Autobiography*, Emlyn Williams. Hamish Hamilton, 1961.

not an actor; and certainly not now a history don or a brilliant solicitor. No—it had to be Drama somewhere, somehow. He was an awfully oversize actor for any stage; but the Voice—maybe not as a singer . . . the Spoken Word?

. . . Spoken Word?. . . .

A job was advertised at the BBC: Wireless? . . . the disembodied Voice over the air? He applied through the University Appointment Bureau. The response from Savoy Hill, London (the citadel of the British Broadcasting Company), was to suggest he come 'at once' to see them. Then fears set in. He wrote from Oxford in June 1924:

> Have heard from BBC . . . and it looks as if they might want me . . . I can't *bear* broadcasting and should die of shame if I had to be Uncle Ananaias and bandy facetious jokes with Aunt Toots all over the Empire . . . On the other hand I can see that b'casting, dismal as it is just now, has a future—both artistic and financial. The pay is good and the promotion (they say) rapid. Right!

He put on his 'best blue' and took the train for London, Savoy Hill and an interview:

> I was interviewed by the Controller—i.e. boss—who seemed nice—an ex-admiral with a son at Wellington. I think I made a good impression and at all events have been offered a job . . . My business will be to assist in the arrangement of programmes and engagement of artistes . . . I shan't have to mind the machines and I needn't wish Louise Brash and Fiji Sprott many happy returns more than *extremely* seldom, need not be called Uncle anything . . . I shall be given a preference of Station . . . i.e. there's a good chance of working either in London, Edinboro' as opposed to Cardiff or Hull. I am being chosen on account of my 'artistic propensities combined with organising abilities'!

He accepted the job and was told that in September he should report as junior member of a brand new staff in a brand new 'station' opening in—of all places—Belfast. Ireland, and a few hours' journey away from Annagh-ma-Kerrig! With all summer between and the University Appointments Board fixing his salary (£280 per annum—1924 currency), he decided to have what he thought then was his 'last theatrical fling'.

Xtopher had written a play—'in verse—melodious and melancholy', he said. It was called by not the most lively of titles, *The Triumph of Death*. He got all his 'organising abilities' going to gather together a company of friends. He persuaded Flora Robson to come and Gillian Scaife, the elder sister of Christopher (who was already a distinguished actress), needed no persuasion; she was as devoted to Xtopher as Peggy was to Tony. The actor Guy Bolton, also Robert Speaight and Cecil Bellamy on their way out of Oxford into the profession, joined them. A barn theatre in Oxted, Surrey, was hired. *Mirandolina* was added to the bill (*The Triumph of Death* was not a full-length play). Tony played Death. He made his spectacular entry from below, a black figure rising higher and higher than any normal expectation about the height of Man. Then the figure added to its own startling height by slowly raising white-winged arms, till, joined above the head, they made the spectre top some eight-feet-plus. Very impressive. Very Guthrie. Flora was the woman raised from the grave to be given immortality just so long as her sensualist lover (Xtopher) kept to the renunciation he had made of love of woman. The Great Moment came when, as sensualist lover, he stooped to kiss the woman and found that what was Flora had turned into a green skull-like death mask of dead female. A lady fainted in the audience and had to be carried out. It was somewhat of a triumph for effect, but not entirely a triumph for the whole play. When the takings for the two plays were counted, 'we found,' says Tony, 'that, if each of the company paid ten shillings and Christopher and I each paid a pound, receipts and expenditure would balance'.

He went off to Belfast, in accordance with the instructions of '2LO', to report to '2BE'. Flora, who had now met the Guthrie family, said sad farewells and departed for her Welwyn Garden City home, and the weary business of chasing jobs in a Theatre that, rightly, could not see her as the typical young ingenue and, wrongly, could not discern in her a unique genius. W. T. Guthrie *could* see it and was not to let the talent go to waste in Welwyn Garden City. But the grimly real city to which he made the Irish journey was quite a shock to the English public school boy with the sharp Oxford accent.

CHAPTER FOUR

BELFAST AND 'THE WIRELESS'
(1924-1926)

IT WAS at Oxford that Guthrie took active part in the fashion-able movement towards Folk Art. It was in Belfast that he first savoured the sense and the deep sentiment in a local culture, and in Art related to Community. He was forced to rub shoulders with the people Folk Art was principally intended to serve: '. . . the folk art revival . . . aimed to keep alive simple and ancient expressions [of joy] in danger of disappearing with the change-over from a predominantly agricultural to a predominantly industrial society . . .'

Belfast was his first industrial city; its economy built very much upon shipbuilding, shipping and the mills of the linen trade. And, outside it were the country folk.

The North of Ireland, with its strongly provincial feeling, its wealth of beautiful folk music and legend . . . I had never before lived in a city with this strong provincial character. London is too huge and cosmopolitan; Oxford too small; anyway, in Oxford, town and gown form two separate com-munities. I found a great new interest in the effect of locality—through climate, history, economics, religion—upon people's character.

In this Irish city, which stirred his own roots, he said, 'I became militantly provincial, the sworn foe of all that was fashionable and metropolitan.'*

But the letters kept going home with the same Oxbridge journalism and the revolution in him, from Oxford theatrical to militant provincial, definitely did not begin on the day of his arrival:

* *A Life In The Theatre.*

Midland Station Hotel, Belfast.
Saturday August 18th 1924.

Darling Titsina,

I had a *dire* journey: *wedged* into the corner of a 3rd Class compartment accompanied by 41 hot fat-women with kippers in string bags and 63 peevish old men who insisted on keeping the window shut (from the above figures you will realise from this that there were 105 humans in the compartment). Moreover we were the very last carriage of an enormous train . . . with the result that we swirled about and by the time Fleetwood [*just north of Liverpool*] was reached I—fragile tender flow'ret that I am—felt quite—yes!—quite train-sick . . .

The boat was full before our train came in (an excursion comprising the entire population of Blackpool) and our train-load was succeeded by another excursion composed of the entire adolescent population of Preston.

Fortunately it wasn't rough a bit just a slight roll—but even that was sufficient to cause numerous casualties and the saloons and passages presented veritable Crimean spectacles—elderly ladies being sick into strange gentlemen's tweed caps and people literally piled in heaps on the floor. I was lucky and lay full-length on the floor of a secluded corridor wedged tight between two Prestonites who fortunately 'contained themselves' . . . After depositing luggage here and having a lovely bath and some costly eggs—I tried Mrs. Payne, one of Ethel's recommendees. She was a decent little body in a lavender silk golf jersey with big, big 'pearls' and 'jade' hung about her here and there. But her lodgings didn't do at all. The house is entitled 'Belgravia' and is on the peak of a remote mountain. There were red plush saloons *crammed* with spinsters and I was shown a vault sans any furniture but prison bedstead and Edgar and a sort of tent with pegs in it—3 pegs for one's entire wardrobe. There was no fireplace and if you lent out of the window you could pull the plug of the next door W. For this I was to pay £3:15 . . . I ran violently down the steep place into Belfast.

It was now about 10.15 so I repaired to 'the office' and found painters and plasterers at work.

This was to be a recurrent factor in the life of Guthrie, the natural pioneer; to start the new job as the building was still going up around him. In his first job, in Oxford, it had been old big-game museum being converted into theatre; here it was old linen warehouse being converted into 'studio' and offices. When he arrived there was nothing for him to do and nowhere to do it anyway. However, he met his seniors, busy on plans in their various unfinished corners. And the gossipy communiqué went back home.

> Major W.D.M-s seems quite nice and easy to get on with. He didn't appear to be the least efficient but probably that was only the manner—Time will show. Wee T was quite sweet—clearly intending to be friendly. He seems quite efficient and capable but I suspect him of being idle. The man Brown who is the musical director seems to be a decent lowish class body, none too much gumption but very kind and has asked me out to tea at his home . . . Ingram the head engineer is five years of age and peers with baby wonderment but mechanical acumen from behind the vastest 'horn-rims'—I said 'How do you do?' I said—whereupon he pressed my hand and held it for a long time *hard* and said *'very* well thanks and I hope you are the same'. I laughed outright and had to pretend it was a nervous giggle of confusion at meeting so many strangers!

Impossible, gifted young prig. But very observant. It was pioneering days in broadcasting on the wireless; the engineer was king and the engineers seemed to know what they were doing, so:

> The work seeming well en train and there being nothing particular for me to do—I left quite soon after on the pretext of finding rooms. My job is going to be running the dramatic side: engaging people to give 'talks'—editing talks—and doing my share of the announcing.

The 'dramatic side' of the wireless had been very limited up till then. It was only as recently as June of that year that the London station 2 LO had commissioned Richard Hughes to write the first ever play conceived for effect in sound only: *Danger*, about a group of people trapped down a coal mine. There had already been excerpts from classics and a complete transmission of *Twelfth Night* but wireless drama was a very, very new thing. What if it was *the* thing and the Stage was dead from now on? It hardly seemed likely. Guthrie had the vision to see that it *was* just possible. The *Amateur Wireless* had a circulation of 100,000 in autumn 1924; the *Popular Wireless Weekly*, 125,000; the *Wireless Constructor*, 250,000. The 'Radio Craze' was on. Folk Art *could* reach the Folk in their thousands, in their homes. And here was he inside the national monopoly from which he could reach them —in Ireland at least. It was to be a later discovery and joy, that he would be listened to in the Warwick Lodge drawing-room. He, who had been the star of family theatricals on the family carpet, could now be the star in the corner of the room; and the height and physicality of the performer did not come into it at all. It was all voice. Exciting horizons. But then came the deeply feared part of the whole operation. 'We are going to have a "Children's Hour"—I shall try and be firm on the subject of avuncular archness but don't expect my opinion will count much for some time yet.'

With the 'station' still in preparation he started to look around him. He loved the nearness to the mountains, Strangford sea Lough, the gentle green and gorse-covered hills, the river estuary and all the nearness, westward, to open country and, eastward, to open sea. All this added to the fact that such a short journey could take him, south, to Annagh-ma-Kerrig. This bit of Ireland was, and is, culturally very close to Scotland; he could even see the Scottish coast on a clear day from the Antrim coast. But did he really like the grim industrial seaport? Could he get to like the enslavement to an institution? He wrote to that most free of creatures, Christopher Scaife:

Oh Christopher,
    Isn't it foul to think that Oxted really was the final episode of a period of one's existence. I'm now a 'business man' with 3 *weeks* holiday in the year. Christ! Three weeks to see Italy, Spain, America. It's not long enough to 'do' The Isle of Wight! . . .
    Your Oedipus sings no more—the strings of the lyre are broken—the muse (as yet) shuns the noise, the smoke, the smell of Belfast . . . my quips find no echo in the stern and literal Northness . . . the talents of an Oedipus may be wrapped in the napkin of industrialism but they will rust . . . Honestly this place is awful. There are loads of merchant princes but they are all Presbyterians and *save* all their money—dress in fustian, eat tripe, drive Fords—eschew all that makes for anything other

than a sternly material 'utility' . . . If I stay long in this place it
will turn me into an R.C.!

It ceased to be a comfort to get from Aunt Sue such comments as
'I remember Belfast from 2 days 30 years ago . . . the impression
remains of sordid squalor . . . Meantime I am mailing your white
tennis socks.'

There was that other thing too—the fierce religious bigotry
all wrapped up in the political tension of Ireland's perennial
'Troubles'. The grand white house of Stormont, of the Parlia-
ment of Ulster, had been built just the year before. Suddenly in
this year over 300 people had been killed in an upsurge of the
'Troubles'. He could not just walk the streets at night, as in
Oxford or Tunbridge Wells. In his pocket was a curfew permit.

However, at this time he was rather a political innocent even
for a second-rate scholar of History, and his eye was firmly on the
job. From Fagan's dismissal from the acting profession he was as
internally scarred as any young man with high ambitions. *This*
job was jolly well not going to end in any sort of failure. He was
keen to get going.

The engineers transformed the linen warehouse into an opera-
tive studio and got the new station 'on the air'. The thousands of
crystal set enthusiasts—as well as the wireless avant garde who
now possessed sets with 'valves'—might suddenly hear a new call
coming through the 'atmospherics' and into their ebonite 'ear-
phones': '2 BE calling!' Irish the station might be but it could
be very English in accent and crystal-clear if the call was coming
from the station's junior announcer. He had to tame that 'carrying' voice to let itself be carried by a 'carrier wave', not by the
strength of his large lungs. A new technique would be required
not to blast the ear of the distant listener or—much more probably—ruin the substantial but sensitive box situated like a holy
relic within the shrouded and windowless chamber they called the
'studio'. The age of the Microphone had begun. The Voice
would have to find free vent elsewhere. The young announcer
took singing lessons with Herbert Scott. This splendid Belfast
singer-teacher made the discovery that not only in height was his
pupil extraordinary. Tony wrote home:

My singing lessons yesterday . . . Herbert Scott . . . said in
awestruck tones '*Do you realise* you've got a bigger voice than
Jimmy Newell?' Jimmy Newell is Belfast's King of Song.

Having a louder voice does not mean that I have automatically become Belfast's *Emperor* of Song, for Jimmy Newell is a very fine singer and has reigned undisputed king for, I believe, about 15 years!

Bertie Scott was later to have an important part in more than Guthrie's vocal and musical development. But now the youngest member of the station had to get out and about and arrange Talks for and consultations with every section of the community: heads of universities, civic bodies, schools, Industry, etc. It was a time of an almost shocking enlargement of his contacts with society, coming after a period—through Tunbridge Wells, boarding school and University—when he had almost entirely moved within his own class of rather privileged citizens. The walls of Class were crumbling and he stepped out beyond them. He was fascinated for instance by the great shipyards of Harland and Woolf. In the first days he had seen them as a mere grim source of grime, noise and smoke, *and* of estuary pollution. He met management, he met the shop-stewards, he met 'the men', he met 'the workers', all for the first time. And these were Irish folk; but not quite the Irish folk of the creations of W. B. Yeats on the page or the devoted servants of Annagh-ma-Kerrig, in the cottages and the lands of the bog. These lived in 'workers' rows', with slate roofs. The Irish Mist for them was sea-mist smoke-polluted from no open peat fire but hundreds of little coal grates contributing to the pall of industrial smoke which on a still day could hang over the city. As Micháel MacLiammóir puts it: 'But for the blue mountains at the end of the streets, the quality of light, the sigh of the wind, certain faces and voices, certain hints of melancholy and magic lightly touching you as day passes into night, you might easily believe yourself to be in Bradford or Manchester.'*

Harland and Woolf's shipyards employed literally thousands of both men and women. In their recreation parks, welders, shop-floor managers and clerks all met as equals. Guthrie noted this with surprise when writing to his mother. Would these Irish folk accept Folk Art, or what were their needs? Lover of the procession and the 'big day', he had yet to see for himself the street parades which split the population clean in two. If these were Folk Art then their wild drums were a reversion to something

* *Ireland*. Thames and Hudson, 1966.

perhaps *too* ancient, something as barbaric as tribal warfare. It could be an exciting, perhaps even dangerous, mission to get out and see what the People of the Community needed.

The Official Opening—no official opening could be fun to him unless it were a piece of well-directed ceremonial:

> I caught a cold sitting in a draught among hydrangeas last Friday at the Official Opening. It was a dire function: one of those 'brilliant occasions' when nobs stand on red carpets and pay trite compliments to one another. The d. of Abercorn is a big fuzz-buzz with a well-preserved Duchess. Craig [*representative in Scotland and Ireland of the Controller, Mr. Carpendale*] was there like an old cattle-dealer but a *charming* speaker with a most admirable 'delivery' . . . There was *boundless* enthusiasm about things like The British Empire or The Duchess of Abercorn . . .

One can see his fingers snapping silently and impatiently to 'get on with it'. 'It' in this context was the one sphere in which Guthrie was totally fulfilled and forever in his element, Work: 'I can get along with people all right if there is anything to do, and co-operate with them in, but I am very poor at just "meeting people" . . .'

The work was demanding. But hard work to him was always more a matter of boast than of complaint:

> I have been just *that* busy . . . The 'Double-sided Records' proved an immense success . . . 200 letters of congrats about them—to be read and sorted—besides a mass of other correspondence. Then there has been the Talks Programme for the 1st quarter of next year to get under way; then I have to produce a dramatised version of Dickens's Xmas Carol on Xmas Eve and though it ought to be well en train by now I haven't even cast it. However it's all rather fun and I am definitely enjoying the work.

The off-duty week-ends were made more pleasant by visits from his Oxford friend Hubert Butler, who had also gravitated to the land of his ancestors, and been appointed librarian to the Carnegie Libraries. He was located up on the northern coast at Portstewart. Butler came to see 'the Wire'. They walked the autumn hills together and spent one delightful country-house week-end at Annagh-ma-Kerrig, where there were more walks, boating trips on the lake and evenings by the drawing-room fire, playing intellectual parlour games, like 'writing biographical poems'. He wrote to his sister, Peggy, 'I like him so much, he's very absentminded but has a lot of character and a sense of humour.'

In fact, since Oxford visits to her brother's college, Peggy had been somewhat attracted to the courteous, quiet young man she referred to in her letters now as 'St. Hubert'. It was a relationship which was to grow. And, in another letter from Belfast, Tony wrote, 'Have been introduced by Hubert B. to a new author— E. M. Forster.' The book Butler had recommended was to be quite a turning point in his cutting away from all the Tunbridge Wells influence. It evidenced to a degree the first revolt against Mother: 'He's sent me Forster's *Room With A View* . . . 1st pub. 1908 but I've never heard of it *or* E. M. Forster, have you? . . . You must get it . . . There's a quite marvellous T. Wells "girl" in it—(it mentions St. Peter's Church) who went to Florence. Hubert was, enthusiastic about this Forster's books—I don't know if it's a man or a woman . . .'

Well, as Peggy had now been some months among the young intelligentsia at the London Polytechnic Art School, she might at least have known the sex of the author.

The breakdown of class barriers, in literature as well as in life, was fascinating him, and here was a brave romance across the class barrier. This had relevance to Flora Robson, who thought of herself—as upbringing made him think of her—as of another class. Since leaving Oxford they had kept in touch. Part of his respect for her stemmed from her sincerity and strength of character, which came out of a family background of strong sea-faring stock of Scottish origin, and then of merchant success in the North of England. Her father had been a sea captain. Well, here was he savouring the culture of his Irish seaport. And there was she, as much of a cultural exile in Welwyn Garden City now as he had been in Tunbridge Wells. Then a letter came to say that she had a part, in London, in a play called *Fata Morgana*. It was produced by Reginald Denham, who had produced them both in the Oxford Playhouse days. She had not a big part but the play was a 'success' and was transferring to the Comedy from the Ambassadors. She wrote: 'My time is very full . . . started singing lessons again and I love them. I am very popular at home just now too, and I have hardly anything to worry me except some debts . . .'

A few days later a cheque arrived from Belfast that made her
doubt if she should have said what she had about debts. But given
in a realistic way by someone who could well afford it, she
accepted it. The debts arose because there was no pay for the
weeks of rehearsal. Guthrie was convinced in any case about
Flora's talent. And he was about to offer her work on the wireless;
he also urged his mother and Peggy to go and see *Fata Morgana*,
and young Flora Robson in it.

They went. Mother wrote that she found the play 'disgusting'.
Son wrote back firmly:

> Sorry you found *Fata Morgana* so disgusting . . . not having
> seen it I won't attempt to argue with you. I am sure you are
> wrong about the piece being 'the kind of thing that brings the
> theatre into disrepute'. It is obviously by what has been
> written about it not merely an attempt to exploit the boy's
> seduction simply for the sake of dabbling in the unsavoury;
> but is a serious attempt to comment upon the incident—and to
> show in the action without any trite generalization how shabby
> of the woman (and she is *not* a bad woman at all but intelligent
> and wholesome) it was to tarnish the boy's first experience of
> 'love'. I think surely there's nothing 'disgusting' in being frank
> about that; and I think it is more wholesome than hints and
> whispers. If you don't like Peggy to see 'such a piece' how can
> you allow her to go to a place where she draws *naked bodies*??
> . . . I think people like you are very intolerant and unjust . . .
> Be sure and get *A Room With A View* by E. M. Forster—it's
> simply splendid.

Life was being very hard to Norah Guthrie. She was not well.
Her husband was threatened by an illness she would not talk of
to the children. Her own illness was mysterious in source, and
now harsh revolt was coming from the quarter she was least able
to take it from. Also Christmas, that previous family time, was
coming on and he would be tied to Belfast and possibly the
horrors of a hearty 'Children's Corner'. Tony wrote to his Aunt
Nan in Sevenoaks,

> I fear the poor Warwick Lodgers had a melancholy Yule, and
> I am worried about Mum; she seems so easily bowled over now
> by microbes and gets so depressed and unlike herself . . . Be
> sure the Aunties and Uncles of 2 B E made heroic efforts to be

sprightly and make Yuletide Jollity for their thousand and one
tots.

So, it *had* happened. His contract had obliged him to become
Uncle Will of the 2BE Children's Hour. And it should be noted
that his great success as a director or in rehearsal at the height of
his career had much to do with the authoritative capacity to treat
all players like temperamental children, all longing to be loved
and corrected too. A story is told that is not entirely apocryphal.
In New York's Metropolitan Opera House he brought shocked
silence, and the desired result of stopping the useless hand
gestures of a world-class prima donna, by leaping over the
orchestra pit, grabbing her by the hand and breaking the tense
silence by an avuncular slap to the hand, merely saying to the
great lady as he gave it the unforgettable remark: 'Naughty
handies!'

The first Christmas party at the Belfast station went with a
swing which was to be characteristic of future spectacular, and
non-proscenium, Guthrie productions. Many critics hereafter
were to say that Guthrie could clear a stage of a crowd quicker
and with a sweeter flow than any other living director. Perhaps it
all started at 2BE, with Uncle Will.

At the end it was time to go—so we got out all the packages of
sweets (which we'd put into a big wooden crate)—Tom Corrin
[*Music Inspector, Education*] played a march and led round the
room—all holding hands—with Aunt Evva on a chair in the
middle guarding the box o'tweets. We led round the room
forming a sea-serpent . . . that converged upon the box (where
each child seized his packet) and then out again—without ever
stopping—right out thro' the door and downstairs to the cloak-
rooms so there should be no possible mistake about the
moment of departure—a brilliant inspiration of which I am
proud! No child cried. No child got hurt. No child sulked.
There were no appalling pauses.

There was another and sentimental satisfaction for him in the
job. He reported to his mother something that would surely have
made her forget *Fata Morgana*. On going out to supper in the city
with one of the families of a growing circle of self-chosen friends,
he was asked to go upstairs to see their two children now abed.
And he witnessed at close quarters the childish thrill it gave them
to receive this visitation from 'Uncle Will of the Wireless'. With

the children of the community, at least, he had become an Irish institution.

Under another nom de plume or rather nom de théâtre, his voice was to become for a time also much loved. He wrote to Peggy,

My dearest Myde,

. . . please explain to your mamma that 'Tyrone Power, was *of course* me—how *could* she and your aunt be such utter gomies as to suppose it was anyone else. I didn't want to appear under my own name lest people should say either 'The BBC is so hard up they have to employ their staff to do their plays for them' or '*That* young Guthrie thinks he can jolly well do everything'—both of which statements would have been inconvenient altho' founded on fact.

Fond love to all

Agapanthus Flynn

And letters then came home signed variously 'Featherstone Finn', 'Agrippa Philpot', 'Tannhauser Flinn', 'Tothill Block', or 'Yours in the spirit, Jellicoe Beatty Armistice Jutland Bing'. It became a kind of long-distance family game in which Peggy responded in kind, 'Yr. moderately doting, Kasha Balt' or 'Miss Paris Lamb', etc.

He was happy in his work. Happiest of all was the discovery he himself comments upon, that he found that he loved Rehearsal; found that actors, readers, singers, too, seemed actually to *like* being rehearsed by him. Here he had struck—within the happiness of Work—the work he most wanted to do for the rest of his life: to prepare and rehearse plays.

The wireless was also developing in him a taste for a theatre of non-physical illusion; a theatre of the audience's imagination; and a theatre where the spoken word was potent. He had started writing his own dramatic pieces.

In February 1925, now secure enough in his job to be pushing his own ideas, he had his first real success on the air. Still under the name of 'Tyrone Power' he wrote and produced a winner with his listeners—who after all tended to be mostly his parents' generation—*A Night in a Mid-Victorian Drawing-Room*. He called it a play, but it was really a gathering of caricatured characters performing songs and recitations, within the framework of a very slight dramatic construction. But letters poured in

to 2BE. This was success for him and the station. He also
succeeded, in getting London, 2LO, to take it up.

From Warwick Lodge postcards went out to all relatives and
friends, and within the family circle the reaction was near to
rapturous. To his mother it was better than medicine:

> ... About the Victoriana! ... We had a loud speaker attached
> and all sat round in great comfort and real enjoyment. Dad and
> Sandy [*Tony's uncle from Edinburgh*] giggling most satis-
> factorily. Aunt had been invited to Probins who were all qui
> vive also Adamsons and many others whom Fanny had post-
> carded ... The only criticisms to hand so far were from
> Brethertown—a bunch of roses and congrats for *me* ... Pop
> had been to London on Sat. and the man he goes to for treat-
> ment in course of conversation said he had had a most enjoy-
> able evening listening to a mid-Vic play and was too thrilled to
> hear Pop actually knew the talented young author!!!
>
> Much love precious, your very loving
Mother.

Fata Morgana was wiped from the slate. But now, when his
word would be listened to, he was determined to get Flora
involved in the Wire at the first opportunity. He had tried to
enroll Xtopher, but all offers to play were gently turned down.

> I can give you a rather amusing engagement on Jan 7th ... If
> you let me know at once I'll book you and will give you as
> many engagements following as I decently can—so as to help
> pay expenses! ... then we can have a really good discussion of
> plans for the Future ... Another plan ... would you like a
> month's engagement at £5 a week? ... work would roughly be
> —Act in 1 play per week, give 1 poetry or literary recital (15
> mins) per week, appear 4 times per week in Ch. Hour ...

This was not just getting his friends on to the bandwaggon.
Flora's talent is well known. What is not so well known is that
Christopher Scaife had gone back to join his sister Gillian in the
Theatre and that he had had sufficient success for Basil Dean to
offer him the part in Noël Coward's *The Constant Nymph* before it
was offered to John Gielgud. But he said that at that point he was
'unable to stand any more back-stage dressing-room society'. He
went off Drama, and took on the job of tutoring the fifteen-year-
old son of an American, 'who had made millions in guts' (the
offal trade). He had to 'do' Europe with them.

To 'Tyrone Power' of 2BE this was a sad waste of talent. But when he turned from Xtopher to Flora, the response was very positive. She was ready to come. He was getting her over to play Iphigenia, in the *Iphigenia in Tauris* of Euripides. The choice of play is, to say the least, illuminating.

A brother and sister play. Beloved sister across the sea (Iphigenia) is condemned to serve as priestess to an anti-male goddess (Artemis); the beloved brother, who has murdered his mother to avenge his father, is wrecked upon the shore, where the sister's temple stands; and the sister-priestess, pledged to sacrifice him on the foreign altar, saves him and he saves her. Flora was a magnificent Iphigenia in a production which troubled the Celtic Presbyterians but pleased the Celtic scholars no end, and was a succès d'estime for Belfast BBC.

This allowed Flora to visit Annagh-ma-Kerrig. For the first time she saw Tony not as the brilliant Oxford graduate of the bright set of upper-crust friends, but as the sober young squire-potential of the lands around the lake; and the big house with all its familiar Irish Folk, so friendly to 'Master Tony'.

He obviously loved having her there. He rowed her out on the Irish lake, where the wild swans came. It was spring—Mother's month of May. There were walks in the tall hushed pinewoods and quiet evenings beside the turf fire. It was a magic and memorable time for them both. Flora went back, but to a fruitless search for work in the Theatre, and—because she owed it to her family to bring in some money—she had to take what work she could get. She became welfare officer in a Welwyn Garden City Shredded Wheat factory.

It must have seemed to Guthrie that the Theatre was dead. He went on to his next essay in dramatic poetry, for the new medium. This time not the Greeks but the native Celtic thing, Yeats's *The Land of Heart's Desire*. He had played it in Oxford for J. B. Fagan, but here it would drift with the native wind and reach—he hoped —the Irish at their own fires; touch their roots with true Folk Art.

There is personal significance in this choice too. It touches the inner Guthrie so at home with the mists off the hills by Strangford Lough, the hush of the swaying woods round Annagh-ma-Kerrig, where thistles and hemlock mimicked the tall trees by growing up into their mossy hush to shoulder height. It is a play about a fey child come in out of the woods to lure away, into outer darkness and inner wildness, the young wife who longed for passion in Life. It may seem all Celtic Twilight and folksiness but, in the bone of Ireland, it is not too far away from the knock on the door opened to darkness, the gun blast and wild oblivion. The young woman's soul is lured away to where, out in the woods, there are dancing wraiths; and, on the wing out there, the sort of white bird that took up and away when its great wings beat the surface of the Annagh-ma-Kerrig lake.

FATHER HART:
> Thus do the spirits of evil snatch their prey
> Almost out of the very hand of God;
> And day by day their power is more and more
> And men and women leave old paths, for pride
> Comes knocking with thin knuckles on the heart.*

This was the Wireless and the Spoken Word at their best, at their most committed to Art, the medium and the community. But the response from the community of listeners was nothing like the little flood of fan-mail for *An Evening in a Mid-Victorian Drawing-Room*. The Folk were not affected by ageless drama from a dateless cottage. The drama they were all affected by was something Guthrie at that time seems not to have been able to assess seriously—a form of street theatre somewhere between Folk Dance and a barbaric preparation for Tribal War. Processions always fascinated him. And, this summer of success on the Wire, he was to see his first 'Twelfth of July'—the annual memorial demonstration to the memory of the victory at the Battle of the Boyne in 1690, when the Protestant army of William of Orange overcame those forces determined to see a Catholic sit on the throne of England.

Guthrie did some inoffensive wireless documentary on the 'big day' without fully realizing what he was handling. The drum, with the painted portrait of Queen Victoria, must have seemed to him just another bit of Victoriana. The Lambeg Drum!

As an instrument for the production of rhythmic noise it is unique . . . The combination [*in the procession*] is usually composed of 4 or 6 gigantic drums, huge engines of percussive might . . . The drums are beaten not by drumsticks but by schoolmasters' canes, and no drummer is thought to be worth his salt until two livid semi-circles of his blood stain the skins

* W. B. Yeats *The Land of Heart's Desire.*

at each side of his instrument, drawn from the laceration of his knuckles on the wooden rims as he beats out his message of defiance to His Holiness of the Seven Hills . . .

. . . Few districts in the civilized world have any annual festival to compare with Ulster's Twelfth of July. Sashes and banners of . . . fiery orange hue are everywhere in this all-male rhapsody of fever and fervour, sashes and medals and badges worn by boys of eight and men of eighty: bowler hats, black suits, stiff collars and dark ties are de rigueur; the streets are impassable and uncrossable, sometimes for hours together, and the poor Papists remain—if they are wise—indoors and wait, presumably for the dawn of the Thirteenth to break . . . It is an astonishing sight . . . whether one witnesses it in some little country town or on the historical streets of Derry, or parading on Donegal Square about the City Hall of Belfast . . .*

Recalling his early penchant for the Big Days and thinking forward to how much the concept of *Festival* attached to his own great successes to come, here indeed was a Big Day he could not entirely ignore in his coverage of the cultural needs of the community. But, if he seemed strangely non-committal about it, we must remember too that Religion and Politics were taboo subjects for the British Broadcasting Company.

Beyond his dramatic success as 'Tyrone Power' and the second successful Christmas as 'Uncle Will', he got into critical debate with the Controller. There was a kind of Kiplingesque exchange of letters on points of principle and finance. The community was registering its approval of 'Tyrone Power' and the young man was beginning to assert himself and show signs of restlessness.

There were spring floods at Annagh-ma-Kerrig. He was wanting to stretch his wings and get away from the institutional cage. First he hoped that contacts with the Scottish station would get him across the sea to his father's native country, and he visited Glasgow for an interview. He was itching to do more Drama on the radio. But the surprise outcome of the Glasgow visit was that he was invited to become the Producer of the Scottish National Players, a theatre company. To the despair of some of his more cautious colleagues he seemed to be giving up a great future in a secure occupation to go romping about the Scottish countryside with a group of tartan amateurs. But he sailed out of Belfast and

* *In Praise of Ulster*, Richard Hayward. Mullon & Son, Belfast, 1939.

steered away for the Firth of Clyde and that other great shipbuilding seaport, Glasgow. He was free again. He was going back
to Drama on stage and, for the first time, he would have a
company of his own.

But it was not easy to sail away from Belfast. There was a
gentle lure—this wonderful sense of belonging to a community.
There were touchingly happy memories; comic ones, too. A
letter from a listener:

> Please sir, will you take care of the cold you have. We love to
> hear you speak at the Microbe and would like you to give us a
> wee talk some night yourself. We can hear you cough at the
> machine and hope you will soon get rid of it.
>
> From
>   'the Mother of the family' to
> Mr. Guthrie
>   Announcer,
>   at the Study room,
>   B.B.C., Belfast

and one from an Oxford colleague—evidence of the national
notoriety: 'I see your name as Announcer in the *Broadcasting
News*—If you have announced things every night since September
you must now feel like the Archangel Gabriel . . .'

Belfast dropped astern. Yet why—if it was Drama and the
Stage he wanted, why not stay, when the Irish Literary Theatre
had just asked him to be a producer with them? In fact this distinguished Irish theatre company had just come through ten of
the worst years of its history. It was limping along. In 1927, the
next year, there would be no Ulster theatre season anywhere.
Theatre in Belfast was due for a regeneration. Guthrie had begun
to find his feet in rehearsal and make many contacts with playing
groups via the BBC. If he had stayed there is no doubt that the
history of Ulster Theatre would have been given a new direction.
But, instead, he sailed into the Broomielaw in an August morning
of 1926 and took a second crack at Theatre; in his father's
country.

CHAPTER FIVE

GLASGOW AND THEATRE ON A SHOESTRING

(1926–1928)

SCOTLAND MAY have been his father's land, but Edinburgh was his father's city. And there was a deal of difference between that governmental 'Athens of the North' and the huge, smokey, industrial spread of Glasgow, second largest city of the Empire. Of it his father now wrote to him, 'I have shadowy and unhappy memories.' He recalled that he had been sent, as a lean and keen young schoolboy, to Glasgow's Kelvinside Academy. But, after only a few weeks of subjection to the rigours of Glaswegian education and the pollution of its industrial atmosphere, he had been anxiously hurried back home, with advanced pneumonia and a fifty-fifty chance of survival. It was on the storm-wrecked night of the great Tay Bridge Disaster that the Good Lord had decided Thomas Clement Guthrie would survive. Unknown to Tony, he was again struggling to survive.

Glasgow *was* a tough town. It was also a great provincial football town. The 'big day' for that sport was highly sectarian and fascinated Guthrie: the great dramatic conflict between the two famous teams of Rangers (Protestant) and Celtic (Catholic). Why, in supporters and players, it divided the city this way even Glaswegians never knew; but it did. On any of his first autumn Saturdays he could see the flood of folk (with cloth cap and muffler still the standard answer to fog and cold) moving towards the arenas with the great roar. (As the excitement rose and fell the 'Hampden Park roar' could be heard over the whole South of the City and was a nationally known phenomenon.) These were the Roman amphitheatres of the Industrial Revolution.

The next most popular activity to football was 'going to the Pictures'. The Cinema was the new thing threatening Theatre, as films moved towards talkies. And in Glasgow was the new and 'largest cinema in Europe', Green's Playhouse. When the tall Guthrie stooped to the pay-box grille, before going into one of his first Glasgow cinemas, the voice behind it said—in sympathetic amazement: 'Gawd!—whit height are yeu?' He replied with icy clarity, 'Six feet five, and I think you are very impertinent'. He was in touch with The People; but on his own terms.

The terms of his employment were, to direct or 'produce' for a theatre company formed with these objectives in mind: 'To encourage the initiation and development of a purely Scottish drama by providing a stage and acting company which will be peculiarly adapted for the production of plays, national in character, written by Scottish men and women of letters.'

His own response to this sort of assignment was: 'It was exactly the sort of wheel to which I wanted to put my shoulder. It exactly chimed in with my anti-metropolitan, provincial feelings, and there was enough of the Scot in my ancestry to attach me passionately to the nationalist side of what we liked to call The Movement.'*

Though this would be his first experience of a company 'of his own', it should be made clear that he was not *founding* a company; or a theatre. The Scottish National Players had been founded in 1913 to do more or less for Scotland what the Abbey Theatre had done for Ireland. Their first resident producer (A. P. Wilson) had in fact come (by courtesy of Annie Horniman) *from* the Abbey; the second, in 1925, was Frank Clewlow, from that other famous foundation of Annie Horniman—the Birmingham Repertory Theatre. Now, in 1926, it was W. T. Guthrie of the Oxford Players and the BBC. Of these Scottish players he wrote that they were far more experienced in Theatre and Life than he was at this point in his career. And he made a distinction he was to preserve clearly throughout his career: just because these players were non-commercial—i.e. did not make their living in the Theatre— it did *not* mean that they were amateurs in their attitude and commitment to the work; or in the level of their skill. They were professed to the Art and were dedicated professionals in this sense. Jean Taylor-Smith was a qualified woman dentist; Halbert Tatlock carried a responsible position in a family scientific instrument business of international repute, and tartan-sounding Glen MacKemmie, the Chairman at whose office Guthrie had to report on his first day there, was not unfamiliar with the workings of show business. He had done the equivalent of a CEMA service to troops of the 1914–18 War, through an organization still lettered on his office door 'Harry Lauder Fund'.

* *A Life In The Theatre.*

On their first day MacKemmie gave the young man a hearty welcome, reinforced by a 'high tea' in one of the famous Glasgow tea-rooms. He then led him up steep streets of granite to a grey-stone building in the business quarter and to the tiny little upstairs office assigned to 'the producer'.

> The room is very nice but small . . . with a desk and a telephone. There is also a gas-cooker on the premises . . . I think I shall do all my writing here. It is a blessing to find that one will now have a little time and energy to write . . . I am inclined to like Glasgow very much. Oh the joy of being released from the Wire! So looking forward to rehearsals . . . and to seeing what the players are like—Oh, if only they are talented.

It was not long before he wrote home, 'The Players have great *talent*.' It also was not long before he sensed the other, grim side of the city and developed that love-hate relationship which was much deeper than mere like or dislike:

> . . . endless tram lines gleaming in the wet . . . and losing themselves in the murk and mist between high grey walls—horrid boot shops and pork butchers on the ground floor—and flat upon squalid residential flat piled high. I hate it.
> The climate—if nothing else—makes existence such a struggle that it's no wonder the inhabitants are hard and dour and materialistic . . . It's so repellent that these squalid, precipitate streets are just a filthy crust upon the hills of the Clyde. And yet I'd rather have Glasgow for all its muck than South-borough [*Tunbridge Wells*] or Colinton [*Edinburgh*] . . . It's alive.

Belfast was the first break from the sort of society in which he was brought up. Glasgow was a further step away and it also developed in him a growing attachment to this sort of provincial industrial town of tough people intent upon the work-a-day business of the world. His tall, broad-shouldered figure began to appear less and less in 'best blue', or tweed suit with bow-tie, and more and more in rough woolly sweater with polo neck, and slacks and sandals—the Guthrie garb for the two situations in which he was most in his element: rehearsal hours or Annagh-ma-Kerrig days.

It would be a false impression if it were thought by this that he was plunged into the Workers' or the People's Theatre. In a term coming into his vocabulary at the time, the whole operation he was now involved in would be very, very 'bourgeois'. Tough it was, but not rough. In fact, in a town with a very tough upper-crust, he became closely related to the local 'merchant princes', because they were the patrons of all Arts, including Theatre.

Miss Elliot Mason was one member of the company, who did not have to work for a living, but who worked like ten for the sake of the art and the company. She became his 'right-hand man' and hers was the one household in Glasgow which earned the sort of Guthrie label given to the Bretherton house in Tunbridge Wells, 'Brethertown'. The atmosphere of 'Masonlund' is best indicated by his letter about the first New Year's gathering there:

> Old Ma Mason . . . about 9 rings on each finger of either hand and her entire front bedecked with a complete 'set' of cairngorms—each the size of a large paperweight . . . innumerable married daughters and husbands (this one 'in Paint', that one 'in Timber' and the other 'in Linen')—all clever and interesting . . .

Elliot Mason was a niece of one of the rich Miss Cranstons of the famous tea-rooms and she was the gifted actress of the family. Unmarried and considerably older than Tony Guthrie, she was another aunt figure to add to the gallery of monumental female influences in the Guthrie gallery.

He was blessed with talented players, and a sensible and sympathetic governing board, but the Players were not blessed with a theatre of their own. They mainly had to perform in the old Royalty Theatre, now called the Lyric, attached to the Y.M.C.A.

Even so, he was an extremely happy young man, 'have never for 5 mins. regretted the decision to come here'. And these players were disciplined to doing things 'on a shoestring'. This echoed his own personal disciplines: always to put people before things and never to spend on 'silly things'. But, when he got down to rehearsal, one thing hardly went along with his 'zest'. This was a hangover from a tradition established by 'Pat' Wilson. It was an export from the ethos of Dublin and Lady Gregory. The theory of the Abbey founders was that almost everything depended on the Spoken Word and that exaggerated gesture (a Guthrie failing throughout), like over-attractive décor, simply detracted from the beauty of the speech. (The Abbey lot were reputed to have rehearsed in tubs, thus making Samuel Beckett a cultural throw-back). This was to produce the right effect of 'stillness'. Guthrie accepted the non-distracting décor but 'stillness' was not the most natural state for him. The characteristic innovation young Guthrie brought was typically restless: tented tours—one-night stands all over the Highland landscape, in all weathers and on the go like theatrical gypsies.

But, before any innovation, he got down right away to the work he really loved: rehearsal. It was a tight schedule likely to defeat his hopes of spare time for writing. And writing was important to him now. Just as he had once nursed hopes of Tyrone Guthrie the opera singer he now had considerable hopes of Tyrone Guthrie the playwright. Out of fourteen productions in fourteen months, nine were 'first performance on any stage' (and all but one of Scottish authorship—the exception being *Victorian Nights* (his stage adaptation of *A Night in a Mid-Victorian Drawing-Room*).

By the middle of his first October he had produced *Weir of Hermiston*, an adaptation of the Robert Louis Stevenson novel and already a tried favourite in the company's repertoire; *The Glen Is Mine*, by the established Scottish playwright John Brandane; *Ayont the Hill*, by Cormac Simpson; and before October was out he and the company had achieved a total success with a one-act play by a member of the company, Morland Graham, called *C'est La Guerre*; a slight but touchingly truthful piece about a Scottish miner, a soldier, in France during the Great War. Gordon Bottomley's *Britain's Daughter* kept the flag flying for the Spoken Word and Poetic Drama. But as preparations went on with a play for Christmas called *Bridget in the Heather*, Guthrie began to learn that from one nation's resources it is unwise to expect other than a very limited supply of new plays of top quality. But he was rehearsing many plays, and he was moving now in an aura of success.

He was also enjoying doing on the side some reasonably lucrative jobs for the Scottish BBC—as a performing artiste. He got in touch with Flora to see if she would join him in touring a half-hour radio show (of short play, short stories and folk songs and verse) at three guineas a week, all expenses paid. It would even include a return visit to 2BE. But Flora was unable to get away. However, he did have the satisfaction of being invited over with his Scottish National Players to Belfast BBC.

All in all, this was definitely the life for Tyrone Guthrie and he began to organize time to write. This he did in his little office or in his lodgings, close to a coal fire. Then fog—the Glasgow pea-soup variety, fed by thousands of domestic 'lums' and thickened up by factory and steelwork sulphurous fumes—descended. It used to induce the sort of hush of a fall of snow. The coalmen, standing on the decks of their wagons, would not be able to see further for'ard than their horse's ears, as they moved like wraiths, hoarsely broadcasting the price of a hundredweight into the heavy gloom. Tyrone Guthrie went on writing, by the fire, to complete his own play, *Emmy* or *A Passenger to London*. The experienced John Brandane encouraged the aspiring dramatist. The play was completed and dispatched to Gillian Scaife, now somewhat of a star of the London stage. She showed it to her friend and admirer A. B. Horne, of the Prudential Assurance Company. He had backed the Cambridge and London seasons by which she—and Christopher—were now achieving London success. Horne offered to help—cautiously. He would assist, up to the sum of £50, anybody Guthrie could persuade to produce the play. The script was also sent to a London agent who was more than cautious; and a chill fog of discouragement settled upon the playwright. 'Our reader's report' said:

> The story is that of a young girl who, with some encourage-ment for she has musical talents, breaks away from 'pro-vincialism' and her family, and goes to seek a career in London. Her father, whom she leaves behind, is heartbroken. But, hav-ing made the mistake when he was young of not venturing through timidity, he lets her go. It is very well written but not well enough worked out. I regret that we should not be justified . . .

But now came cheering news. Both Oxford friends, Hubert Butler and Christopher Scaife, were to visit. But when Christopher came there was also unsettling news. He was finally renouncing all ambitions in the Theatre. He had committed himself to going to Egypt on January 16, as Assistant Editor on the English Language *Egyptian Gazette*, in Alexandria. Again—to Tony—a waste of talent. But it was the festive season. While he and Elliot Mason togged themselves up to attend the BBC New Year's Fancy Dress Ball, he sent Christopher and Hubert off to see what he reckoned to be one of the most impressive pieces of real and native Theatre in Glasgow: the annual Christmas Pantomime at the Princess's Theatre, in the Gorbals (the same theatre building which has become the Glasgow Citizen's Theatre). Of course he had seen the visiting giants, like Henry Ainley in *Prince Fazil*, and been bowled over by Sybil Thorndike twice, in the Old Vic Company's *Henry VIII* and Bernard Shaw's new play *St. Joan*. But the Pantomime, to Glasgow, was in a way true and lively Folk Art. At its heart in the Princess's was a giant of pathetic comedy, Tommy Lorne: a true, deeply sad, white-faced comedian universally adored by Glaswegians old and young and by Guthrie too:

> . . . he would hold that rough, excited audience in the hollow of his great boney paw. He was A One, too, for pathos. Many's the tear I've shed at Tommy Lorne, and many's the time I've gasped and ached, and gasped again, in an utter exhaustion of merriment.*

Tribute indeed from one given to gesture and a taste for the macabre. On New Year's night, that taste was being fully indulged by Guthrie himself. This is what he wrote home, and it must have been a very macabre letter to receive at Warwick Lodge, where Dr. Guthrie was having to face solemn medical facts about his own mortality:

> . . . to the BBC Fancy Ball. Elliot wore a white shroud—I wore Death and the Demon face and operating gloves and carried a long black trailer attached to one finger. The appearance was terrific and had a profound sensation. When we arrived at the Dance Hall the page boy shrieked aloud (in *real* fear)—strong men cried aloud and women threw their jewelry in the air. We won the prizes for Best Gent and Best Lady.

But spring came, and with it the decision that his father should retire and that Warwick Lodge should be sold up. Annagh-ma-Kerrig was truly to be home. His father now wrote a letter which was one of a precious few from Father to Son which Tony kept, safely put away. The description is of arriving by boat—the old summer journey—at Dublin, at dawn:

> . . . There was no moon, but the sea was pearly grey in the dawning light on the way to Amiens station and the shore and

* *A Life In The Theatre.*

shallows peopled by a multitude of ghostly seafowl. I enjoyed a really wonderful sunrise after leaving Dublin, all the tidal ways were brimming and still; and mirrored the clouds that glowed with rose, chocolate, grey, blue and even green, crowned—when the sun rose looking immense on the horizon —and of intolerable brightness, the light sharply confined to the sphere like the moon at its best and biggest, one of the most wonderful sunrises I ever saw. Needless to say by the time I got outside breakfast and reached Dundalk it was raining and it is raining still. I am writing this at a turf fire in the morning-room. This place is as seedy, weedy and homey as ever, and the task of rescuing it from becoming *quite* like the palace of the Sleeping Beauty appears hopeless, there's so much drying out to be done. I feel that Nature is too strong and life too short . . .

When he saw his father at Annagh-ma-Kerrig in May, he looked 'seedy' and Tony said to his mother, 'You'll have to "feed him up".' But, delighted that the 'sickaneedy' were finally being left to somebody else's care and the Power house would now fully be the Guthrie house, he went back to furiously healthy activity in one of his innovatory 'tented tours'.

. . . a month's tour under the auspices of the Carnegie Trust: 7 of us—in a caravan and lorry—doing one-night stands at small places in N. of Scotland . . . 3 one-act Scots plays; 3 ballads done in mime; and a group of sentimental Folk-songs sung by a woman standing at a long French window in artificial moonlight in a black velvet 'costume' period 1850! . . . Have designed masks for 'Wullie's Gane Tae Melville Castle' . . .

It may sound all very arch and arty but it certainly impressed the then Labour Prime Minister, Ramsay MacDonald, when he saw their performance at his native Lossiemouth. And there must have been some Guthrie real magic about it, because that fine actress Lennox Milne, then aged sixteen, saw it in Callander, in the village hall. There was a short play—about Prince Charlie on the run—then songs and poetry, with 'a highly pictorial effect', she recalled; not just people standing up and singing or reciting. It was *new* . . . they wore cowls and tunics and the set was a table with candles set on it to light the scene. She was into Theatre for life, one of the first of hundreds of Guthrie 'converts'.

He loved being the sort of circus-come-to-town ringmaster of the whole show; not just backstage or on-stage as at Oxford but handling the whole management and organization of Theatre at its most basic.

Nell [*Buchanan*] is the cook aided by Charlie Brookes who is O.C. tents. The lorry man [*Archie Frew*] does motors and lights (the acetylene is a high success). Ethel [*Lewis*] does wardrobe and of course drives her car. [*She also played the spinet and sang.*] Elliot looks after props and business; Moultrie [*Kelsall*] assists Elliot, and he and I and Maley do the stage . . . We all at least have 3 changes of costume—scenery and props are simplified to a minimum. Nell and I not being in the first act have to sell the programmes and usher the patrons to their seats . . . It's amusing how the Wireless has helped. Everywhere in the country places people have come because they have heard either the Players, Ethel or me on the Wire . . . I began this in camp on the golf course at Cullen but am now in Ethel's car . . . the drives are lovely . . . just gorgeous scenery . . . the tour is being enormous fun and quite *invaluable* theatrical experience. I now feel that nothing will daunt me in the way of halls . . . We rise at 6 and are seldom bedded before 1 . . . getting everything on to one lorry is a fine art. However we manage it by cooperation and are *very* happy.

. . . Weather terrific . . . when unloading . . . a great 15 foot flat was caught up off the lorry blown clean over a house and dashed to pieces on a spiked fence! That was our only casualty —bar a pail of which I blew the bottom out exploding bombs in 'C'est la Guerre'! . . .

Two things from the Scottish experience were to stick with him for life; realistic budgeting and the love of a company become by work a kind of 'family'; a sense as he later said, of precious 'solidarity'. And it was all such fun.

. . . Friday we played Dunoon . . . After the show, back to boarding house . . . cooked eggs and bacon . . . a riotous meal . . . then we made up a 'paddling party'—It was then 12.30. Only 5 would go—Maley, Meg Buchanan, Elliot, Jimmy Allan and I . . . Dunoon I must explain is the Margate of Glasgow . . . We saw a boat in somebody's garden and broke in and carried it off and boated in the bay—such Fun—moonlight and large waves—then we paddled—an excruciating experience—and then went a long mountaineering walk returning at 3.30 to the boarding ho. After that people told ghost stories and recited ballads and sang songs till 5, when we retired.

In one game the company played, each member had to give only *one* quality of his character to the question, 'What do you consider the one thing that most characterizes you?' After the usual thoughtful pause and intake of breath through the big aquiline nose, he said, 'Oh, I don't know . . . A gift for administration?'

Elliot Mason grew very fond of him. He might joke away the obvious by saying aloud there was nothing in the rumours about them and anyway 'these tents are too small for sin'—yet one day he proposed marriage to Elliot. It must have been an endearing and flattering proposition to her. But she was considerably older than he and not really the marrying kind. Seen with the liberty of Olympian hindsight, this was marrying the mother-figure, this was Oedipus Biggs getting into real complexity. At any rate, it came to nothing but an increase of their mutual respect.

Then came the whirlwind. It almost seemed as if, by that fancy-dress mockery at the New Year's Ball, he had been in some nightmare where, in surgeon's gloves, he played the messenger of mortality to his father's Everyman. He wrote to Egypt, on November 19, 1927:

Dear Christopher,
We have suddenly plunged catastrophically into the whirlwind.
My father is very, very ill and the doctors do not think he will recover—it may be weeks, months, possibly three years—a growth in the lung.
My mother is going blind . . . suffering from the same mysterious disease that has been troubling her for some years. It has finally lodged itself in her eyes—she can hardly see now—cannot read, can barely write and cannot go out in daylight even in black goggles without great suffering . . . I was down in Tunbridge Wells last week . . . One can *do* absolutely nothing . . . One struggles to preserve some sense of detachment; to consider the whole situation with an icy aloofness . . .

Christopher Scaife said that, from this time of utter shock, when something struck at the whole foundation of his stability—

Family—he was a changed man; a coldness crept in. He went on working with the Players simply to complete his contract; and the letters to Christopher continued: '. . . lacking subtlety still— I can hammer and drill and browbeat the people into a galvanic performance but am not successful in gently leading them into an intellectual one . . .'

Even into that working-bliss, rehearsal, a sadness was creeping. By December 29 he wrote: 'I can give you little better news . . .'

Then on February 18, Dr. Thomas Clement Guthrie died, of cancer of the lung. The *British Medical Journal* said:

> . . . he never spared himself . . . gave best service with equal hands to rich and poor. Though suffering from a fatal malady he performed many major operations till within a few months from the end . . .
>
> Senior Surgeon of the Tunbridge Wells and County General Hospital; Chairman of the Tunbridge Wells Division of the British Medical Association; Honorary Surgeon to Dr. Barnardo's Home for Crippled Children . . . A man of the highest integrity of character, tall, cheerful, and possessing the best type of Scottish humour . . . tennis player, first-rate angler and a good shot . . .
>
> Nature he loved, and in his approaching retirement he looked forward to life in the fresh air devoted to country pursuits and pastimes . . .

Life produced in this suddenly grown-up son a new line in angry profanity that was to stick. His adjectives became pathetically profane. It was not just the loss of a loved father to a sinister disease. His mother was suffering a strange sort of mortal corruption too. It had come out of the exhausting days of the Great War. The family blamed it upon some infection picked up from the soiled linen of the refugees and wounded 'Tommies' she cared for. Anyway for Tony it was too much to take in any clarity of mind. A sense of career had come to an end.

He hung on to the comfort of Christopher's friendship, continuing to write to him in Egypt.

> She [*Mother*] returned from Paris [*a convent-cum-nursing home*] in a state of complete nervous and physical collapse but is now (after 3 weeks) very much better and stronger and the doctors have great hopes that she will have some measure of

sight . . . Meantime she is to have bi-weekly injections for
another 6 months. So we have taken a small furnished house in
London and I have given the S.N.P. up in order to join them.
15 Albion Street, Hyde Park.

'Them' meant his mother, Peggy—who he said had been a
marvellous support—also Miss 'Bunty' Worby (a former nursing
sister in the Doctor's hospital who now became Mrs. Guthrie's
nursing companion).

And before he left Glasgow he dealt with another sadness. This
had to do with Christopher, who he confessed was the person in
the world he felt closest to, next to Peggy. He had come home
from Egypt on leave, had bought a little touring car, and he and
Tony had gone over to Ireland together. There they spent some
vacational days of pure pastoral peace. But Tony was troubled by
the way his great friend was drifting—the homosexuals' way.
Despite the moral judgments of the times—especially in Scotland
—there was no standing in judgment on his part. He had grown
up in this, too. He now saw that 'it was a sentimental maiden
aunt's dream of mine' that Xtopher might be 'redeemed by a good
woman's love'. He accepted what was and he just wanted to tell
his closest friend that, in the way of life he was taking in Gizeh,
by the Nile—which the world might censure—'you will be more
than usually in need of the constancy of friends and I'd like to
think that you felt *sure* of mine . . .'

It was a statement of very pure love, at a time when life had
drained him of any passion. He went—a very shocked passenger
—to London. Shocked even by the fact that he, for whom Work
was salvation, was unemployed, and in the metropolis. These
were probably the lowest days of his life.

CHAPTER SIX

LONDON AND
THE MICROPHONE PLAY
(1928–1929)

THAT BLEAK Christmas of 1928 he had handed over the direction of the Scottish National Players to Elliot Mason. All his gift for organization and administration was suddenly narrowed to the domestic business which falls to the male head of the family in such circumstances: selling the Tunbridge Wells house; renting and setting up the London house, where his mother would be within easy reach of her specialist; interpreting the will, etc. There was Peggy and there was Miss Worby, with her medical expertise, but with the cruel loss of 'The Doctor' there was a need that he should keep close to them. London to Norah Guthrie was the hum and throb of the capital and blurred images through black glass. To him it was still the hateful metropolis.

He had always liked reading, and reading aloud, but here—through a real necessity—he became one of *the* best readers of the spoken word. Through the wireless, in Belfast, he had developed a technique to broadcast the words, like the biblical seed cast abroad in the hope that some would fall where they would be fruitful. Now, he could see his audience of one, and could trim his reading skill to an observed effect. There was no need for the letters now, but to be his mother's eyes in all matters of print was an activity that satisfied him and also solaced her.

For a time he did little but come and go on domestic business, and quite a bit of that, of necessity, was a coming and going between London and Tunbridge Wells. In 'The Wals' he had opportunity to renew the friendship with the sympathetic Brethertons. Judith was now twenty-five, rather beautiful and very nearly as tall as himself. Peggy was studying Art at the Polytechnic.

Not to be in some job did not suit him. There was no desperate need for him to be making money immediately but he was now the breadwinner of the family. He was not disposed to like London and he was not greatly in sympathy with what he knew of its Theatre then, though perhaps it had more effect on him than he admitted. Sir Barry Jackson's Company at the Court did *Macbeth* in khaki. But that could be taken as just the Great War catching up with Drama; because at the same time *Journey's End* hit London. A young actor named Laurence Olivier had 'created' the character of Stanhope in two performances of a Stage Society try-out. Charles Laughton too had got mixed up with War as subject matter, playing the Irishman, Harry Heegan, returned, paralysed—in Sean O'Casey's *The Silver Tassie*. Maybe he could dismiss as metropolitan triviality Noël Coward's *Bitter Sweet* and Marie Tempest in her 600th performance of *The First Mrs. Frazer*, but it is some indication of his own state that he seemed more interested in films, with the Talkies beginning to draw crowds, and to close several theatrical touring houses.

He set himself against the Theatre and, though Cinema interested him, he turned as a writer to the new medium in which he had some experience: Radio. There his whole sensitivity to the Spoken Word would have effect. He had started to write a play for the wireless. He called it a 'microphone play'. And within a year he was committing himself to this statement in print:

> The microphone play lacks the glamour and physical magnetism of the stage, but lacks also the too, too solid flesh. Because its pictures are solely of the mind, they are less substantial but more real than the cardboard grottoes, the calico rosebuds, the dusty grandeur of the stage; . . . more real because the impression is partly created by the listener himself. From the author's clues the listener collects his materials, and embodies them in a picture of his own creation. It is therefore an expression of his own experience—whether physical or psychological—and therefore more real to him . . .*

He began to doubt if Theatre would survive against the popular 'canned' drama of film and radio, except as an expensive minority pursuit.

The play he wrote was *Squirrel's Cage*. It was submitted to the BBC at Savoy Hill and was immediately accepted. Small wonder. It is technically a brilliant piece of radio-writing, startlingly ahead of its time in its use of the medium; and it has the compassion

* *Squirrel's Cage and Two Other Microphone Plays*, Tyrone Guthrie. Cobden and Sanderson, 1931.

which would make it popular. It was an anti-metropolitan, anti-establishment piece about the conditioning of a young man by his conservative suburban father, so that he no longer has the spirit needed to rebel. He longs to go off to pioneer in Africa, but capitulates to the daily round of city employment, suburban commuting, bowler hat, furled umbrella, etc.—a squirrel's cage existence. It was a success.

Unemployment came to an end. The BBC offered him a staff job, as a sort of script editor, with hopes held out of becoming a producer. He began to be very busy again. His mother was getting over the shock of his father's death; Miss Worby was proving a very devoted and efficient nurse-companion. In the spring he went over to Ireland to adjudicate at a Drama Festival in Sligo and from this he organized what he reckoned was 'a perfect week's holiday'. Judy Bretherton, Peggy and Hubert Butler joined him. The four did a walking tour plus a short sea-trip on a tramp steamer. The sky was brightening. Wounds were healing and he began to appreciate the company of Judy Bretherton.

Back in London he wrote another 'microphone play'. It was a slighter piece than *Squirrel's Cage* and did not enjoy the same success but technically it is fascinating in its use of a sort of 'stream of consciousness' technique:

ANNOUNCER: What follows is supposed to be happening in the mind of Miss Florence Kippings—who is sitting alone in a cheap restaurant in the Strand, in London. The time is about a quarter to twelve, midday. She has ordered a cup of coffee . . . Remember you are overhearing her thoughts. She is alone . . .

It is the story of a shy and lonely spinster who dares to answer an advert in the *Matrimonial News* despite the ridicule of a suppressive mother. She is keeping an appointment with the man, but at the moment when he should turn up she can not face the situation and turns and runs back to her safe suburban loneliness; and her tyrannical mother.

It was not exactly pre-Pinter Pinter but it was new. It expressed the loneliness of urban living. But, though he could do this writing within the steady employment at the BBC, the institutional life irked him and he began to see even the benevolent embrace of Savoy Hill as a squirrel's cage. Then something happened, his reaction to which was completely to deny his despair about Theatre: 'A.B.H. yesterday proposed a thrilling project rc Festival Theatre Cambridge . . . so perfect can't possibly happen.'

A.B.H.' stands for A. B. Horne. It was he who had read *Passenger to London* at Gillian Scaife's request, and had offered to help promote it up to £50. It was he who had come down to Oxted, Surrey, that blissful summer after Oxford, to see Xtopher's play; because his two great interests in life were Theatre and Gillian Scaife. He was a keen amateur actor, very rich and a most considerate and generous patron of an art in which he had hopes of becoming an impresario. So it was he who had in 1925 taken on the Cambridge University Amateur Dramatic Club's theatre and put on plays with both Gillian and Christopher in them. Some of these had transferred to London. Now, under the nom de théâtre of Anmer Hall he was taking a lease on the little eighteenth-century Festival Theatre in Cambridge, with a view to putting on a weekly programme of interesting plays during the three eight-week periods of the university term. It would be a fully professional venture for which he needed a resident producer. The Scaifes suggested Tony Guthrie, so recently back from all that practical experience with the Scots. His own company, professional, and with a theatre! And not in London. Of course he accepted.

His mother's sight had steadied at dim and was now getting no worse. With Miss Worby, Peggy and the help of Aunt Sue, who was to join them later, Mrs. Guthrie was moved over to Ireland and took up residence from then on in Annagh-ma-Kerrig. It must have stirred painful memories. But Norah Guthrie was a very strong character and no sentimentalist. She was soon striking out blindly at a typewriter and in eccentric spelling sending contented letters to Tony and friends. One came to Xtopher that year:

> December UU th 1931
> Dear Christopher,
> My stupid eyes are I suppose a wee bit better . . . I am still not able to go about alone or do anything to make myself less of a nuisance . . . I fear I have dabbed down on many wrong letters today . . .

But only the date was wrongly typed. Things were better for her, and Tony was over in England and on the go again.

In that summer of 1929, with the Cambridge excitement ahead of him, he went to Welwyn Garden City, to adjudicate in its amateur drama festival. One of the companies in the festival was directed by Flora Robson—her Welwyn Garden City Barn-stormers, from the Shredded Wheat factory. She was still out of the Theatre, disillusioned and disappointed by the miserable parts and pittance she had been able to collect, but not dispirited. The Robsons were tough in spirit. Tony was invited home. He met her parents and over tea the talk was brought round to Theatre. Tony broke the news of his involvement in the new Anmer Hall Cambridge venture. Flora naturally wanted to know all about it; but she was not at this point at all assured that the world wanted what she had to give as much as it wanted breakfast cereal. She was happy with her work people and they liked her. Her parents were also concerned about the insecurity of the acting business. It proved to be a critical crossroads for her. Tony was not sure what he was entitled to offer, but he certainly wanted her in his company. Besides, they were in fact more attracted to each other personally than they were prepared to admit. He arranged for her to go to London to Anmer Hall's apartments in Albany for an audition. Anmer Hall engaged her for Cambridge.

CHAPTER SEVEN

CAMBRIDGE—
THE FESTIVAL THEATRE
(1929-1930)

THIS WAS the first time that Guthrie had artistic control of a theatre. It stood a mile away from the centre of Cambridge on the Newmarket Road—an eighteenth-century building which had been subjected to the 'modern' surface décor of its previous manager, Terence Gray. This was mainly a matter of paint applied in triangles of scarlet, black and emerald green. Abstract Art was beginning to show on the surfaces of domestic and industrial design. The stage had no footlights or proscenium barrier between stage and house. Terence Gray had been much given to use of rostrums, platforms, cyclorama and 'modernistic' lighting. One of the facilities of this theatre, to have a lasting effect on Tyrone Guthrie, was a splendidly up-to-date lighting system: also a brilliant resident electrician, Mr. Steen, who taught Guthrie a great deal about how to light actors and sets without the time-wasting process of trial and error. The experience with the Scottish National Players had trained him from sheer practical necessity to reduce setting, costume, and lighting to a workable simplicity, but the nature of many of the plays had forced him to relate this simplicity to box sets and naturalistic effects. The kind of simplicity of style of Gordon Craig and Jacques Copeau was in the air, and here he had a stage ideally suited to a stylistic, non-naturalistic setting, eminently 'theatrical' and greatly aided by lighting effect. Anmer Hall proved to be an almost ideal patron, with all the prudence of the Prudential in management matters but liberal to an unusual degree in the freedom he offered his producer in matters of taste, choice of play, etc. The recruitment of the company went apace. The quotient of professional talent was high. To Gillian Scaife and Flora Robson another notable name was added, Robert Donat—whom Tony had met up in Glasgow, seen on film, and also used on radio. His stage manager was an unusually intellectual and argumentative colleague, Evan

4

John. Tony was excited, happy, and dead keen to get into
rehearsal and get going.

In the Michaelmas term, October 1929, they got off to the flying
start of an immediate and resounding success: Pirandello's *Six
Characters in Search of an Author*. It was success for the company,
for Anmer Hall, for Tony; but, above all, for Flora. And one
should remember that she was the young actress he had believed
in before anyone else; and who, but for him, might never have
risen above that initial discouragement, but gone on to be simply
the beloved social worker. His tribute to her performance, years
later, is one which she prizes to this day:

> . . . Flora as the stepdaughter gave an electrifying performance.
> No one who saw her in that part could doubt that here was the
> makings of a great actress.
>   . . . I visited Cambridge thirty years later, and a group of
> senior Fellows over dinner recalled it with the sentiment which
> we all reserve for the exciting impressions of our youth.
> Unanimously they declared that in thirty years of subsequent
> playgoing they had never seen a performance to equal its
> dazzling originality and force.*

It was a thrilling return to the stage for her. But to realize the
terrific step forward this production was for Guthrie, one has to
realize that for the first time he was dealing with a modern
masterpiece; a play right in the mainstream of what was then a
move in Art and in the Art of Theatre. It was very new to
English audiences. It was a totally different piece to any of the
somewhat parochial national plays he had been doing up in
Glasgow. Finally, it had within it the sort of playful artifice and
non-naturalism which he, as an artist, kept looking for: something frankly 'theatrical' and yet informed by very deeply ordinary
human conflict. As a style of play it absolutely fitted the style of
his bare stage with its flexible lighting means. And it gave Flora
one of the most marvellous entries into action any play gives any
talented young actress. All in all it could hardly have been a more
fortunate choice—for the company, the theatre and the audience
which the Cambridge community could supply. In the first scene
there was a Guthrie coup de théâtre. In the text, the six characters
edge on to the stage while the Manager is starting up rehearsal
with his Players. Guthrie had two stage-hands come on with a

* *A Life In The Theatre.*

large flat, pause centre backstage and—at the appropriate moment when they moved on—a spotlight came in, and there was this group of mournfully dressed, anxious intruders suddenly and unaccountably slap in the middle of the stage. Note the fact that this was *a family play* (like *Hamlet*, like *Iphigenia*, like *Oedipus*, *Rosmersholm*, the *Oresteia*, *The Three Sisters*...and all his great loves).

As he said, Cambridge was a happy time. Autumn, misty mornings, the sun coming through on to the falling saffron leaves of Cambridge's willows, clear skies and, in the busy activity of town and gown, talk getting around about the superb avant-garde production of that avant-garde play out there at the Festival Theatre. Mother was secure and surrounded at Annagh-ma-Kerrig by warm and practical care—English and Irish; Flora had been 'saved', theatrically, adoring Judy Bretherton was a frequent visitor, and was even sometimes one of the amateur extras on stage. There was every reason to be glad to be alive. But no time to indulge in a leisured love of it.

Thirty plays were ahead—one per week (till it proved too much to maintain the quality) then they did two in three weeks. The little company lived a hard-working, almost monastically disciplined existence. Six of them were in a house attached to the theatre, the rest in lodgings nearby: an intensification of theatre 'family'. Every day they were at it from ten till one, rehearsing, and again from two till five (unless they were playing in a matinee). Then there was the performance at night and on Sunday no 'day of rest' at all. On the Sunday morning the setting of the previous week's play was struck—All hands!—and the scenery of the next play set up. With the slickness of action between Mr. Guthrie and Mr. Steen the play was lit in the afternoon; in the evening the dress rehearsal went on till all hours of the morning.

It was here that he acquired the professional disciplines—and the artistic regrets—related to the pros and cons of Weekly Rep. Of the thirty plays, all of which were of quality typical of an Art Theatre's mixed repertoire, if only nine are named here it is because these have special significance to him: *Six Characters in Search of an Author*, *The Machine Wreckers* (Toller), *The Rivals* (Sheridan), *Marriage* (Gogol), *Rosmersholm* (Ibsen), *Measure for Measure* (Shakespeare), *Tobias and the Angel* (Bridie), *Iphigenia in Tauris* (Euripides) and *The Merry Wives of Windsor* (Shakespeare). In the whole repertoire only two plays were Shakespeare's, and Guthrie only attempted to direct the second of the two—*The*

Merry Wives of Windsor. *Measure for Measure* was directed by his Stage Manager, Evan John, and was a 'modern dress' production, done with great taste and no gimmickry.

The significance of *Iphigenia in Tauris* is not only that he thought this to be, of all productions, 'our best effort', but that it had the link with Flora, Ireland, Family, and was the sort of archetypal and non-realistic play upon which his whole appetite for Theatre was finally to focus. Flora again played the saviour-sister-priestess and Robert Donat the brother, Orestes—a potent pair, and at that time bursting with talents clamouring to be used.

It was also a first lesson on the relativity of success. A great success to him, it did poor business, this despite the fact that Cambridge at that time was bursting with talent and had exactly the sort of audience to appreciate it. For example, the young Michael Redgrave was writing undergraduate poetry in competition with William Empson, Ronald Bottrall and two poets-presumptive, Jacob Bronowski and Basil Wright. George Rylands and young Alistair Cooke, were writing pieces for the theatre's magazine. Hesketh Pearson was there. Maynard Keynes would come and go as a Fellow of his college. Robert Eddison was student audience till he found his way on stage and into the profession, via Anmer Hall.

Iphigenia, Six Characters and finally *Rosmersholm*—quite apart from their artistic success—focused Tony's attention on Flora, as a woman, and what she meant to him. He was being drawn to her personally, and she was obviously destined for a considerable career as an actress. For her part, she was back in university city bliss, with the added happiness of personal success. She now had the time and opportunity to know the full character and quality of the man, and she was deeply drawn to Tony. He was thirty years old and a very eligible marriage partner for any young lady of the Arts. But she saw Judy Bretherton come and go from Tunbridge Wells—a witty and delightful tall companion to Tony. Judy spoke the same language, came right out of the same stable as it were, was brought up exactly like his sister and *must* be the family's candidate. In fact the company, and Flora too, assumed that Judy must be Tony's bride to be, and left it at that.

The only significance of *Marriage*—Gogol's one-acter—was that it kept a suppressed subject in play. In *The Rivals* Tony once again, as in Oxford, played that favourite part of his great-grandfather Tyrone Power—Sir Lucius O'Trigger.

In the second season—January 1930—he produced Ernst Toller's *The Machine Wreckers*. He also played—and, according to Flora, impressively—the part of the Engineer. This play developed the then budding Socialist in him and stirred all the sympathies he had found with the industrial Folk of the Harland and Woolf workers in Belfast. It was very much the new drama of the socially-conscious and he was handling it just ahead of all the employment problems related to Britain's Great Depression. Secondly it brought into full consideration the question of how to handle 'the crowd' on stage.

At a later date, in a more caustic state of mind about the matter of on-stage crowds, he was approached by a tiresome lady who said to him, 'Mr. Guthrie—how is it you so wonderfully manage your crowds?' 'Madam,' he said, 'you have to know their bloody names,' and went on with his work. Within that rude reply is the essence of his undoubted success. A crowd is animate—not a thing. A crowd is people, and people are individuals all with personalities, all with names precious to them. In his programme note at the time is the quotation from Lord Byron's speech to the House of Lords in 1812 (on the Nottingham weavers' riots—the machine wreckers):

> ... You call *these men* a mob, desperate, dangerous and ignorant ... Are we aware of our obligation to the mob? It is the mob that labour in our fields, and serve in your houses—that man your navy—and recruit your army—that have enabled you to defy all the world, and can also defy you when neglect and calumny have driven them to despair! You may call the people a mob; but do not forget that a mob too often speaks with the sentiments of the people.

And in Guthrie's own words in the programme he states the problem of the crowd as a 'personality':

> ... to convey the energy and vitality of the masses in contrast to the detached attitude of the Great Ones in the Prologue ... Crowd-Personality of which not only is each member a highly developed mechanical organism, but which in itself becomes one ... [*and he finishes*] I wish to thank the crowd for working hard and intelligently to give their scenes significance and vitality.

A gracious dismissal to those amateurs and extras who had

come in to take part. He gave a less gracious, but as meaningful, dismissal to the local Edinburgh extras who had come in to help him at the height of his career. When the stage management reminded him how long and hard they had worked and that they had to rise early to face their regular day's work in the city: 'Right!' (clap of hands) 'Want you to know, never worked with a more intelligent lot in my life. Now, bugger off!' They loved it.

From Cambridge on, in a Guthrie production, there were no 'extras' no 'walk-ons', they were all players, all essential to the play—no matter how small the part. (And it could go right down to a child led by the hand by the last member of crowd in the last seconds of a scene.) A particular gift was developing. And one of the willing small-part unpaid players now experiencing this respect could be Judith Bretherton. In the outrageously vamped up box-office success of *Lady Audley's Secret* she did a mock 'rustic dance' with a group of ultra-Mary Morris, Isadora Duncan dancers. She was a very beautiful young woman now. His affections fluctuated between Judy and Flora. But still the work was everything. That they were both doing work with him was added fun.

Yet, despite all the Cambridge work-load, he had found the time to write another—and his best—'microphone play', *The Flowers Are Not For You To Pick*. The BBC wanted to do it in the Christmas vacation (1929–30). It was to be produced by John Gielgud's brother, Val—a pioneering young producer of 2 LO. It is a very beautifully, tenderly childlike play of male frustration. The dramatic framework, within which its 'stream-of-consciousness' technique operates, is the flashing before him of a young clergyman's life in the last moments before he drowns. Its imagery comes straight from Annagh-ma-Kerrig: Mother's garden, the flowers, the dark woods beyond, where voices echo from tall trunk to trunk in the mossy hush, and all the landscape of the lake. There is in his play a delicate love scene very close to the heart of its hero, Edward, and very revealing of its author. Edward has a stammer and is short-sighted. The girl is Vanessa:

(. . . *the creak of oars is heard and the light trickle of water broken by the bow of their boat*)

VANESSA: Oh, Edward, what a heavenly wonderful sunset . . .
    Look, look at the colour.
EDWARD: Look at the reflection in the water.

VANESSA: Don't row any more . . . let her just drift.

(*Silence . . . for a second*)

EDWARD: It's as still as g-glass . . . as if the water were asleep.

VANESSA: Look at the trees and the sunset in the water . . . the reflections are as clear as the real trees.

EDWARD: They often are . . . and even clearer sometimes . . . if you know what I m-mean.

VANESSA: Yes. I believe I do.

EDWARD: Do you, Vanessa?

VANESSA: Rooks flying home to bed . . . look down; they're reflected too . . . there's one trailing home behind the others . . . late.

EDWARD: That's m-me.

VANESSA: Oh, Edward, why?

EDWARD: (*not sentimental this . . . humourously*). Oh, it's just something Fanny said , . . And now if ever one looks at the rooks flying home there's nearly always an Edward one labouring along behind the rest.

VANESSA: The Edward rook seems tired tonight . . . it's flying so slowly.

EDWARD: Is it? . . .

(*Pause*)

VANESSA: Look, Edward, the first star . . . funny to think of it racing and spinning through space . . .

EDWARD: Yes. And funny to think of us sitting here in this absurd little boat.

VANESSA: Yes . . . one certainly feels more important indoors . . . but I'd rather be out here.

EDWARD: Would you?

VANESSA: Yes.

EDWARD: Vanessa.

VANESSA: Yes?

EDWARD: I want . . . you're shivering . . . you're cold.

VANESSA: No, I'm not.

EDWARD: But, of course, you must be . . . what a fool I am . . . I never noticed, here's my coat.

VANESSA: But you want it yourself.

EDWARD: No, no, no, I don't . . . here . . . I'll wrap it . . . round you . . . so.

VANESSA: (*gently*) Edward . . . Edward, don't . . . Take your arms away.

EDWARD: Vanessa.
VANESSA: *Please* let me go.
EDWARD: I love you.
VANESSA: But, Edward . . .*

And it gets as awkward as Edward is, and, in Vanessa's case, she says she cannot love him. But then this is a play about the way establishment figures—starting with Mother and her sudden slap when the child picks the flower—say 'Don't' and 'Don't' till the child becomes this shy, original and highly self-critical man. Here was the eternal child under the Guthrie skin.

Flora was to play Vanessa. She did. He was not directing it. He could listen to his work, and to her; so could Judy—and wonder who was in the boat. The play was a bigger success than *Squirrel's Cage*.

Elliot Mason came down from Glasgow, bringing her Scottish National Players to play as guest company at the Festival Theatre. They gave Cambridge *Campbell of Kilmhor* and *C'est la Guerre*—with the author of the latter, Morland Graham, among the players. Friendships were renewed and Guthrie was able to see the contrast between what he had been doing with the Scots and what he was doing now; also to see the contrast between Elliot and the other two, younger, objects of his affections.

Suddenly, in the spring of 1930, marriage came up over the Irish horizon, and startled him more than it should. Yet his first reaction was to exclaim how deucedly odd to think of his dear friend Hubert Butler as 'brother-in-law'. Peggy and Hubert were to be married. On that 'perfect summer holiday', which he had organized the year before, when they walked the west coast from Sligo, it must have been clear to him that Hubert and his sister were coming close together. The other pair to that summer quartet was himself and Judy.

The Butler/Guthrie marriage was a truly Irish affair, cele-brated at Annagh-ma-Kerrig in June. Tony went over, but immediately afterwards had to nip back in time to see Flora and Robert Donat launched in *Rosmersholm*, that doom-ridden Norwegian play about a family house outside a small country town. It was a play of which, a few years later, he was prepared to say in print 'my favourite play'. But the heavy, fateful Ibsen atmosphere and the too, too tragic end for the unhappy pair as

* *Squirrel's Cage and Two Other Microphone Plays*, Cobden and Sanderson, 1931.

they walked off to make their final exit in the mill race—this was too much for buoyant Robert and Flora. They tended to finish up off-stage and out of view in hysterical giggles—not quite proper appreciation of somebody's favourite play. But pent-up players have to let off steam. Pent-up producer began to over-organize Flora. When they played Feuchtwanger's *Warren Hastings*, Flora in a small part was required to sing—to guitar. Tony had told her that during the vacation she must learn to play the guitar. She arrived back to say that she had no money either to buy a guitar or pay for lessons. He sharply sent her to a woman teacher to learn to play the instrument within the week. Of course the teacher said this was quite impossible. Flora reported this. He flew into a rage. A week was long enough for anybody to play 'Surabaya Johnny' on any instrument. He might be Flora's Master in the Art, and she might be meek at heart, but she was not docile. And at last she revolted. They were doing outright melodrama (Townsend's *The Fatal Brand*). When he was giving directions for the final curtain, she refused to do what he wanted her to do, which was to snatch away a bouquet of flowers from another actress. They had a row. Next day they met, and he said something he had a lifelong habit of saying whenever things or nerves got frayed, 'Let's go for a walk.' He walked her up the river, they talked it all out, and, on the towpath, he proposed to her.

It is hardly surprising that the exact dialogue is not remembered. But Flora—apart from a quite natural thrill—*was* surprised. 'We all thought it was to be Judy.' No, it was Flora he loved, he said. Judy was like a sister. The nervous talk went on, on both sides. Of course, it was utterly wonderful in a way, but the talk got round to children. Flora said she would want children. It was then that he said words to the effect that that was not his way. Before one jumps to conclusions, one must remember that he was very ambitious—for himself and for her; and that later in life he *did* want children. Choosing 'a way' was a critical crossroads situation. With his prospects and the prospects he saw for her within the profession, the idea of being lumbered with the mundane chores of bringing up babies was just not proper; not professional. Anyway the exchange brought a little chill to the air. But Flora gave no positive 'No' to his proposal. Tacitly they assumed each to be 'engaged' to the other. And, for the moment, they left it that way, and got on with the work, all the more devotedly.

4*

Peggy, who had been such a close companion of Judy (they were like sisters), Peggy knew that for Judy there just was no other man in the world than Tony. Peggy was devoted to Tony herself; in fact to such an extent that she hated anything that would take him away—and for this reason later hated the Theatre. But, if he married Judy, it would be almost like keeping him in the family.

After *Rosmersholm*, the most significant production for Tony was *Tobias and the Angel*, by a Glasgow doctor turned playwright. James Bridie was Dr. Osborne Mavor's adopted theatre name. Two years back all Guthrie's new plays had been Scottish ones and here was another; but this was a full-length play that he believed to be in the world class. He persuaded Anmer Hall to put it on, there at Cambridge.

Guthrie took to Bridie at their first meeting. This mature medical Scot, with his own father's dry wit and a 'cheeky' kind of intellect, was totally in tune with the Guthrie sense of fun. And so it was that, in his last season at Cambridge, Guthrie was able to present, in a theatre he knew with a company he had mostly trained, the world premiere of an important new play of his choice. And he chose not to direct it himself. Instead he played the part of the Archangel Gabriel—a role in which his stature was an advantage—letting Evan John direct the play.

During rehearsals of the new play, the Archangel Gabriel leaned over to the Scottish doctor, who was in the stalls watching Flora play, and whispered, angelically, 'No one knows it except me till now, but that is going to be a great actress. Watch her. You must write a play for her.'

To Egypt he wrote about *Tobias and the Angel* and in the letter raised the subject of a new development:

Dear Christopher,
. . . the new play was a huge success, at which I was much relieved as I was instrumental in getting it done . . . Oh! The Canadian National people came on Saty and I had hour-long chats with them—Mr. England and Mr. Weir the very grand boss from Canada.

The 'Canadian National' was the Canadian National Railways. His success as radio-writer and radio personality had reached the New World and in Canada they were interested in the new medium. The C.N.R., with no lack of funds to back it, wanted to do a great radio series on 'The Romance of Canada' and to send it out from Montreal. They needed experts on radio drama. They already had a distinguished Canadian writer on the job—Merrill Denison—but they needed an editor-cum-producer. Would Mr. Guthrie be interested?—because they had heard great things about his handling of the new medium.

Mr. Guthrie, however, was now desperately interested all over again in the *old* medium, Theatre, British Theatre. In fact he was being made aware for the first time of a concept as national as Canadian National Railways: British National Theatre. 'Granville Barker is lecturing in Cambridge this afternoon and we do be all in dread lest he comes to the evening performance,' he added to the letter to Egypt. Granville Barker had just published his 134-page comprehensive proposition on 'A National Theatre'.

However, the Canadian money was good; it would be a pioneering expedition to a new country he had wanted to go to (and where James Bridie had a theatrical cousin, Mrs. Dora Mavor Moore, who was prepared to show him around). Finally he was relieved to find that it could be done in the interval between the end of the Cambridge season and an even more exciting theatre venture which Anmer Hall had been cooking up for London.

> I telephoned the Big Guys from way over today to say that if the offer were made I should accept . . . Six months is a very different kettle of fish from a year . . . I've discussed it all fully with A.B.H. . . . he is very seriously considering taking over and converting the St. James's Picture House (London)—but would not likely be opening till autumn—So, you see, if I got back in July that would be perfect, in fact too good to be true . . .

The Canadian offer was positive and substantial and was accepted. There was a great and sentimental farewell party on stage at the Festival Theatre. Even Mother was brought over from Ireland to be there. And, like a true descendant of Tyrone Power, she sat just off-stage on a theatrical hamper, held her son's hand and vaguely saw but clearly heard Anmer Hall make a touching speech of tribute to the Passenger for Montreal. Farewells were made to Flora, Judy and all, and then Mother reported on her typewriter to Xtopher:

> Well, Tony is off . . . Bunty [*Miss Worby*] and I went up to

help him at the end, he and I sorted his things and Bunty packed while he dictated letter after letter to his Secretary. The company all united in giving a very handsome 'revelation' suitcase as a parting token . . . Peggy and Hubert went down to Southampton to see him off. I could not manage that and I know I would be an anxiety and nuisance being pulled over gangways, etc., so I said goodbye to him here [*Aunt Sue's 'Crossways' Tunbridge Wells,*] . . . the pair [*Hubert and Peggy*] go over to spend Xmas with Butlers of all sorts in Kilkenny and will join Bunty and me at Annagh-ma-Kerrig when we go home about the middle of January . . . my little Frenchman gives me a very good report and says I am cured of the disease and may never have to have any more inoculations . . .

The blackest of years, for her, was over; and though her adored and adoring son would be physically out of touch for a time he would write his vivid letters. Peggy would not be there to read them to her, but Bunty was becoming very much a member of the family and was now the reader. In June, as soon as he got back to Cambridge from Peggy and Hubert's wedding, he wrote one letter any mother would have been delighted to receive:

Now I am going to write what will be difficult for the person who reads you this letter because it is so private—but I must say it . . . You are *never never never* to feel that your work in the world is done because it *isn't* . . . Peggy and I and Aunt Sue and others too—many others—are *extraordinarily* dependent on you . . . not for what you do but what you are. P and I are quite strong and dominant personalities but you wouldn't believe how much we lean on you . . . and just because we are Awful Modern Young People who argue and don't wear gloves, you *know* it doesn't mean that we think we can stand on our own legs . . . And partly because suffering has made something wonderful of you and given you a power and influence that I see can only belong to people with hearts that are warm enough to be terribly sensitive to sorrow but who have the fortitude and faith to resist being broken or embittered by their suffering . . . when you feel old and depressed and lonely try and remember . . . and when (as I know I often do) I seem to be hard and unsympathetic and angular and impersonal and a lot of other beastly things—it doesn't mean that underneath I don't just dote on you. And when I feel depressed and despise myself I feel—and I know—that I must be *some* good because I have yours and Daddy's blood in my veins.

The notepaper reaching Xtopher in Cairo had a picture of the ship, with four erect smokestacks trailing four elegant wisps of smoke astern and her straight-down prow slicing through the Atlantic wave.

> On Board
> Cunard R.M.S. Mauretania,
> Wednesday Dec. 10th '30.

My Dearest Christopher,
Behold me esconced in Floating Palace en route for New York en route for Canada . . .

It was a scrimmage to get away from Cambridge . . . packing, passport, medical examination and a dozen other pestilent preliminaries to travel in foreign parts. The last perf; at Cambridge *The Merry Wives of Windsor* [*his production*] was on Satdy night and the boat train left Waterloo at 9 on Tuesday morning . . . I am going to be on a 6 months contract to produce a series of quite dire, dim, dowdy, dubious dramas for radio under the auspices of the Canadian National Railways. It's doosid well paid and I've always wanted to see Canada . . . I shall try to find you *a good job*—it's quite time you left Egypt.

This was to be the first of many Atlantic voyages—and not the last to Canada.

CHAPTER EIGHT

MONTREAL AND
'THE ROMANCE OF CANADA'
(1930–1931)

As EVER, he was impatient to get there; for floating palaces soon became floating prisons—even if they were gold-plated. It was a mid-winter crossing, and he was never too good a sailor. When feeling sick he just lay in first-class luxury and read and read. *The White Peacock* developed in him a new respect for D. H. Lawrence, and in his letters he suggested that Hubert read it aloud to Mother. The home scene he was leaving astern was very satisfactory. Hubert and Peggy had moved into rooms within the old house and were keeping an eye on Mother and Annagh-ma-Kerrig; and rescuing the bog-garden from years of neglect.

Flora was launched towards London and still vaguely 'engaged' to him; Judy Bretherton was continuing her private and educational 'finishing'—with dance, singing, flower arranging, etc.—and was somewhat tied to the Tunbridge Wells scene looking after *her* mother; as for Xtopher, Tony was determined to dislodge and rescue him from the seductions of Egypt. For himself he had the hope and promise of returning to the Anmer Hall theatre plan in London. But the watery end to his great-grandfather *and* to his hero in *The Flowers Are Not For You To Pick* could be ominously in mind,

> . . . watching the restless enormous, grey, powerful mass of the waters—they are *powerless* against the force of the imagination and the steadfast projection of spirit, will, personality—though they could swallow all the tiny puny bodies so easily . . .
>
> It's an odd feeling to be in a shell like this ship tossing with several hundred strangers in a wilderness of ocean . . .

But it was more exciting than 'odd'. He was travelling as a V.I.P. in Radio on one of the world's largest ships, holder of the Blue Riband for the Atlantic Crossing, and he was steaming towards what was still the great New World. However, he had

under-rated the C.N.R. job in the beginning, it was a *national* job
for a great and growing nation, and he was on international travel
with some of the international personalities of the day: 'Tell
Peggie that the little rather dusty French-looking woman we saw
come on board with a bouquet was Madame Galli-Curci—the
other triple-starred red-letter passenger is M. Henri Matisse . . .'

He was bowled over by the Manhattan skyline. Merrill Denison
and Austin Weir were on the cold snowy quay to welcome him—
Denison was startled by the fellow's height, which was measured
from the chin all way down to his boots by a knitted muffler,
trophy of the Oxford years.

Before seeking forbidden drinks in that chill day in Prohibition
America, they walked down Broadway: 'like a Satan's dream of
Heaven' it seemed to the Presbyterian soul of Guthrie. Merrill
Denison was Canada's foremost playwright and he would be the
writer of all the scripts for the 'Romance of Canada'. It was he
who had first put Austin Weir of the C.N.R. on to Guthrie.
Scripts of *Squirrel's Cage* and *The Flowers Are Not For You To
Pick* had been dug out by Denison in New York (where they had
recently been turned down by the N.B.C. broadcasting station).
He had started reading them on a journey up-town on a 5th
Avenue bus. Before he had reached 52nd Street he realized that
here was the master of Radio Drama they were looking for. He
immediately alerted Austin Weir to go for the hatless Irish giant
who was now walking with them down Broadway.

After two days of New York Tony wrote to the banks of the
Nile: '. . . *wonderfully* beautiful . . . But . . . the vulgarity . . . It is
a terrible indictment of Capitalist Democracy . . . the railway
stations . . . far larger than St. Paul's cathedral and have more
religious atmosphere—the dollar is worshipped far more
conscientiously than the cross.'

Then he launched into prophecy, from the basis of his growing
belief in a Christian Socialism: 'One feels that the next big world
struggle will be Russian *v* American conceptions of Politics
and morals . . .'

The two days' introduction to New York had been so liberally
laced with Anglo-Canadian bonhomie and prohibition liquor that
he had to be restrained from undressing in the open-ended
bookstall in Grand Central Station, in the belief that it was the
Pullman for Montreal. But the three of them—at that point
employees of a great railway company—got into their sleeper and

were on their way. It was a journey mostly through the snowy night.

In Montreal he was swept into the grandeur of the monumental seven-storey Windsor Hotel; but he very soon shifted to the Y.M.C.A. This is entirely in the Guthrie character. He would not want to spend his grand salary on 'silly things'; his own comfort he always counted as such. The 'Y' gave him a decent bed to sleep in at night and the C.N.R. gave him a superb office to work in by day.

He had very little time to look at cosmopolitan Montreal, he was too busy setting up what was virtually his own radio station. He was making broadcasting history, in a country whose vast area gave to radio an unusual importance. In 1918 Montreal had set up its first broadcasting station and in the 'twenties Canada developed a feature characteristic of the requirements of such a vast continent—the 'phantom' station. This was a practical arrangement whereby companies not owning the actual hardware of a station could operate for specific hours under licence and be responsible for the programme material only; not for the technical operation of the station's equipment. One of these 'phantoms' was the Canadian National Railways, using the Montreal station CKAC.

Now, in the winter of 1931, the C.N.R. were promoting a scheme for a national broadcast of twenty-five episodes of a dramatized popular history: 'The Romance of Canada'. It needed special station equipment and a special studio. Merrill Denison describes 'the hardware':

There were no studios in the city sufficiently large to accommodate an orchestra, sound effect equipment and casts which would often number fifty persons . . . Guthrie promptly took over an entire floor of the King's Hall Building . . . and proceeded to instal the first multiple broadcasting layout ever used in North America. He ripped out the interior partitions and built the multiple studios, so there'd be action in one, a crowd in another, sound in another, and the like. He built a special sound room which was occupied by a huge tank of water. He put the orchestra in yet another studio. His control panel contained 19 microphone lead-ins and required three engineers, who were kept on cue by Guthrie standing behind them with a long pointer in his hand. The only way to cue people (players, etc.) was by a series of lights, for which Guthrie devised a red-amber-green traffic control system.*

When it came to specific sound effects he was meticulous. He had half a dozen technicians weaving their way through Montreal's Woolworths in search of a toy 'which would convey the impression of the grinding and crushing of ice' (for the first episode 'Hudson'). No luck, till he himself came triumphantly in 'with a small balloon which he inflated with impish delight. Then, he dipped his fingers in resin and produced a sound rarely heard south of the Arctic Circle'. Icebergs groaned and 'calved' in the sound studio.

So far, all was going nervously well; nervously, because he said he found it rather a strain to live up to the reputation of smart young genius from the Old Country with all the new answers.

The next problem was to recruit the necessary number of skilled players; and there was not much in the way of professional theatre—certainly English-speaking theatre—in Canada at that time. So the company became what his companies were so often to become, 'the Guthrie mixture': professional, amateur and small-part players who had never seen stage or studio in their lives before. He saw the Montreal Repertory Company and did some recruiting. He did more recruiting in Ottawa; he even recruited the Windsor Hotel bell-boy (because of his old-country accent) and he went recruiting in Toronto—where there was much amateur activity of the same sort of professional but non-commercial kind he had dealt with so happily in Scotland.

This was the outside, the travelling part of the job. The train journeys were a delight to him. Ever since 'the train' had meant the journey which in boyhood summertime would end up at Newbliss, he loved trains. He wrote delightedly home: 'As an official of the CNR had very grandest observation car at end of train with little platform at the back to "observe" from. I sat and stood there a lot tho' it was pretty chill.'

He could look right back down the line, and watch the countryside slip by, the cultivated vistas down to the great lake to his right and the sparsely populated countryside to his left, going in the imagination away up to the wild lakeland territory between him and the even more frozen North. He had to travel regularly on that long lakeside journey to Toronto and the other

* *Mugwump Canadian*, Dick Macdonald, Content Publishing Ltd., Montreal, 1973.

end of Lake Ontario, where Merrill Denison lived. There he would consult over scripts; consult and agonize. Because it was evident to both men that, in their historic broadcast, dearth of historic incident was going to make it exceedingly difficult to sustain dramatic quality much beyond the twelfth episode. By now he had seen how patronizingly wrong he had been to label the job 'dire, dim and dubious'. It was very important, and very important to him that it should not be a failure.

On all these Canadian rail journeys he was to hear a background sound which was to come back—'a sound effect' to his own life drama: the 'lonely moose' wail of the whistle of the great Canadian railway engines as they steamed their way across the continent. It is one of these romantically haunting sounds from the Age of Steam which the Canadian railways have had the sense and sensitivity to retain and reproduce electronically on their modern engines.

In Toronto he met a lady who would later play an important part in the events leading up to the triumph of his career. For the moment she was of interest to him by the fact that she knew a great deal about who was who in Canadian theatre, and she ran a barn theatre, members of whose playing company might be casting material for 'The Romance of Canada'. She was Mrs. Dora Mavor Moore, who had received a letter from her cousin, James Bridie, warning her to expect 'a tall wraith of a man' called Tyrone Guthrie who was the only radio playwright of any consequence. Guthrie found a warm-hearted, formidable woman, with some of the qualities he later found in Lilian Baylis. She had in fact not only the link with the old country through his play-wright friend, Bridie, but had been—like Flora Robson later—a young member of the Ben Greet Company. Mrs. Mavor Moore had been ascending the ladder of success and, having been promoted from Pimple, to Constance, to Kate, in *She Stoops To Conquer*, she had finally played Viola in *Twelfth Night* on the Old Vic stage. She took him to see her own production of *Twelfth Night* in her barn theatre.

Back in Montreal his principal aide in recruiting cast was Rupert Caplan, an actor with a family business in Montreal and a leading figure in the Montreal Repertory Theatre. The shuttling back and forth to Toronto went on, and script conferences continued when rehearsals began in Montreal. It was a big operation. He was suddenly a 'big guy' himself, at a big desk, in a big office; and he had a big studio. Big publicity drums were beaten:

BRINGS NEW ART TO CANADA

. . . celebrated radio dramatist . . . 'Romance of Canada' . . . to be heard each Thursday evening over the transcontinental network of the Canadian National Railways . . . Tyrone Guthrie has developed a technique which will be quite new to all listeners in Canada.

The first episode, 'Henry Hudson', was ready. The green light was given. The play went out on the air towards the end of January. On January 26, he was able to write home: 'First performance a *huge* success—such a relief! Flow of telegrams from all over the country.'

This was success in the new medium and on a grand scale. It was also in the pattern of Irish-boy-goes-to-New-World-and-strikes-rich. He wrote home: 'By the way I am *very rich*—so if the farm accounts are really low and the dividends not paying will you not borrow some money? I have about £100 in hand at the moment . . . Discuss economics with Eddy [*Daly*]—but please don't allow economy to harm either the place or the employees; because I have the money and I would *like* it spent that way . . .'

Very shortly royalties from Australia—on *Squirrel's Cage* and *The Flowers Are Not For You To Pick*—came in. Then news arrived that his Oxford friend and Kentish neighbour, Kenneth Rae, was in publishing and arranging to publish his three 'microphone plays'. When he got round to writing the introduction to this volume, he was so on the crest of the new thing in the New World that he was prepared to begin thus:

> It is my regretful belief that the Drama of the Stage is going to be forced, by economic pressure, to abandon the unequal struggle with the 'canned' products of the Film Industry and Broadcasting corporations. Already, by slow degrees but sure, 'the legitimate' is being forced off the road and confined to select nooks and corners of the largest metropolitan cities. Soon theatre-going will have become, like polo, attainable only by the rich.*

It is not recorded what Anmer Hall felt, reading this. He was preparing to invest heavily in, and launch, a new London theatre, in harness with the 'celebrated radio dramatist'. For, in February,

---

* *Squirrel's Cage and Two Other Microphone Plays*, Cobden and Sanderson, 1931.

the news had reached Montreal and Guthrie that the theatre plan was going ahead and that he definitely wanted Tony as its producer.

He was in a kind of ferment of considerations at this time. He had written to Xtopher to say that he would like to get right away and work for the summer on a farm on the prairies—would he join him? At the back of this was a kind of Guthrie rescue plan; Xtopher was considered by him to be going to pieces. He wrote now to Kenneth Rae:

> I am working very hard to get him out here . . . excellent job on the radio and very suited to Christopher's particular gifts . . . For myself and with myself I feel a growing dissatisfaction and very nearly contempt . . . I think I am on the high road to 'success', if I continue to bother; and probably I shall continue to bother—more I think from force of habit and force of public opinion—than from inner conviction that success is desirable. As a writer I think I have something near first-rate faculties of expression . . . but nowhere near a first-rate intellect . . . if I am to write anything that will justify my existence it will not be of 'intellectual appeal' it will have to be the fruit of *feeling* of '*living*'—and that's where I seem to be falling so short. I seem to have so little zest with which to accept heartily a mature life—I go ahead with practical things with an artificial briskness and efficiency that means nothing at all—expresses nothing at all but a fairly dominating will; but nearly all my capacities for thought and feeling are turned towards and backwards à la recherche du temps perdu—such a *decadent* pursuit . . .
>
> If you haven't been and it's still running, please go and see Flora Robson in *Desire Under the Elms*, at the Gate, and tell me what it's like.

The ferment was both personal and political. Flora had received disturbing letters from him. Their coldness had frightened her; the 'engagement' no longer needed much 'breaking off'. He wrote to his mother about Flora in a detached way in February: 'I think she is sure to go a long way in spite of not being pretty—she has great gifts and fine qualities apart from her professional life.'

Then in May he got on to the subject of Family, Motherhood and Children:

> . . . a mother's is such a very wholetime and absorbing career

that it's difficult during that period not to lose touch with all the interests and affairs one needs to fall back on later. It's high time 'Science' discovered a more satisfactory method of producing children . . .

I think there are many arguments in favour of communal nurseries. Those women with a vocation for motherhood (many of whom don't have any children under present circumstances) would be the nurses. The possessive aspect of motherhood would disappear and I can't help feeling that it would be better for parents and children . . . The Family as an institution is by no means unassailable . . .

Now he was kicking at the very foundations of his life, and it was all being done with the detachment and coldness of being away out there in Canada, looking back. He was thrashing about politically, too. The Wall Street Crash had hit New York. He was beginning to see the results hitting Canada. 'The depression here is ghastly . . . all are creeping about in hourly dread of the sack.' By the next year there would be fifteen million Americans out of work (and three million unemployed in Britain, too). Then he castigated his mother for worrying about money.

You have *more* than enough to keep Peggy and me from penury even if we both went paralysed tomorrow; and, in any case, I think in our lifetime ownership of capital will be, if not legally abolished, frowned on by intelligent and progressive public opinion to such an extent that we shall prefer to give it up . . . I think there can be no doubt that Communism—doubtless considerably modified from the present Russian Formula— will sweep like a wave over the world. I'm sure that the more we accustom ourselves to the idea of not owning things privately the easier it will be to adjust ourselves to the new conditions. Personally I don't think I should mind a bit!

While still under the cloud of Depression, two events raised his spirits. At Easter he was able to direct and produce a singing cast in a radio performance of John Masefield's oratorio *Good Friday*. He had continued in Montreal with his own singing lessons and now, to conduct this choral work, was to rise above political perplexities and 'feel' where he was sure; not intellectualize where he was uncertain. The other inspiriting thing was that James Bridie had sent him the script of a new play. It was called *The Anatomist*. He was very excited by it. So was Anmer Hall at home. So were his colleagues in Montreal, to whom he read it out aloud.

'The Romance of Canada' had reached seventeen episodes under his direction, then, as he said, 'It fell sick of a disease to which all serial undertakings are liable: gradual exhaustion of the author . . . Poor Merrill was in trouble. He would deliver the current script just in time for the first rehearsal and then, exhausted, with no ideas, no enthusiasm, he would have to sit right down and beat his brains afresh . . .' Merrill Denison was also dealing with 'the only considerable radio playwright' and one who would like to have written much of 'The Romance of Canada' himself. Denison says they had 'struck a balance of antagonistic harmony'. Guthrie had fulfilled his contractual conditions and was beginning to think with pleasure of going home. Austin Weir—as a sort of bonus to supplement his salary—arranged for him to have a vacational trip all over Canada, as a guest traveller on the Canadian National Railways. To someone who loved both travel and trains, this was a wonderful parting present. In three weeks he 'did' Winnipeg, Edmonton, Jasper, Fort Rupert, Vancouver, Victoria and back to Toronto. He then took two days in New York to see the insides of as many theatres as he could. Then he returned to Montreal, sailed down the St. Lawrence to Pointe au Pic and caught his Hamburg–American ship *Megantic*, to sail back across the summery Atlantic, with fine weather all the way, to Galway, Ireland and home. He landed on Irish soil on his birthday, July 2, in glorious weather.

His report to the family was that he loved Canada, the country and the people. He says in his autobiography that he determined there and then to find some good cause to return. Merrill Denison, in fact, recalls how he, Guthrie and Rupert Caplan would adjourn for discussion to a nearby Montreal café, during breaks in the radio rehearsals. Guthrie would talk theatre architecture and enthusiastically draw plans, on the café proprietor's napkins, of his own idea of how Shakespeare should be staged. Had these napkins been preserved, one would now be in no doubt in which theatre's archives they should be displayed.

CHAPTER NINE

MARRIAGE AND THE WESTMINSTER
(1931–1932)

HE WAS back, bursting with health and breathing success from a man's world where he had found himself highly acceptable. And he had prospects to look forward to in the capital city of the Old Country.

He had not been home for a week when he was off to Glasgow to see James Bridie and then to London to see Anmer Hall: and to talk over all the plans for October, when the new theatre was to be ready. It was the old St. James's Picture House in Palace Street, just south of Buckingham Palace and not five minutes away from Wellington Barracks, where he had once offered himself to the Lord of Hosts as an Irish guardsman. Builders and electricians were hard at work turning it into the Westminster Theatre (named so after Anmer Hall's old school). This, of course, could not be the sort of theatre building Guthrie drew on the Montreal café napkins, but the Company was just what he wanted. There would be Gillian Scaife, Flora Robson, Robert Eddison; and Morland Graham and Meg Buchanan, these great troupers of the S.N.P. troupe, because Bridie's *The Anatomist* was to be the first play. Casting was set in motion and Tony went back to Ireland for an August vacation.

These were the happiest of summer days. Xtopher came over to Annagh-ma-Kerrig and Judy Bretherton, too. Evan John, of the Cambridge days, joined them for a time. Days of sweated 'estate work' took place; 'all hands' under Tony's direction. Areas of rhododendron bushes and briars were hacked away to give clear views to the lake. He was determined to make the place look less—as his father had said—like the palace of the Sleeping Beauty. Mother loved it all. After work 'the young people' swam in the lake, and ate ravenously, and there she would be, in the evening, by oil lamplight, sitting at a spinning wheel, a skill which more required touch than sight. Judy Bretherton was regular accompanist at the grand piano. Xtopher and Tony sang Somerville's song settings.

Then Evan John—a very intense man at most times—'took the stage' by the piano and recited 'Don John of Austria' till the veins stood out on his neck; and Mary, Bob Burns the chauffeur's fiancée, going up the big stairs with hot water bottles, would be misled into thinking there was an argument on.

During this month of summer days—so many of them spent out in the open with swimming, boating, and picnic meals across the lake—Tony at last came really close to Judy Bretherton. Xtopher went back to London. There he received a letter from Tony, dated August 6: '. . . Just a line to tell you that Judy and I are going to be married.'

Peggy was delighted and took full part in preparations for the event. Tony continued his letter to Xtopher:

> We feel *very* happy and a little silly—but truly happy. I hope you feel pleased, Chris, and do realise that you will *never* need to feel excluded . . . I value you very, very much; this is a crux in our friendship that will have to be surmounted (can a crux be surmounted?—it sounds rather rude) but which can be and must be. I'm WORN RIGHT OUT with the effort of it all—breaking the news and all that. So is Judy. We have never done anything so brave in our lives either of us. See you in London I hope.

Judy—deeply happy—wrote, with a nervous, affected lightness:

> Dear Christopher,
> You have now heard our pretty news and we are having a piano with another manual made so that we can play *trios* . . .
> Kindest thoughts are sent
> from
> J. D. Bretherton
> (Miss)

Mother wrote:

> My dear Christopher,
> . . . The Marriage of our 'creature' is settled for September 5th and to be here. Everyone, including the bride, desired a very quiet affair and where quieter than Aghabog. So the plan is that Judy leaves here on Friday, does her final show with

Ethel Lewis [*the ballad singer*] Saturday, and then home to gather up wedding garments . . . You know how happy I am to have Judy for Tony's wife, she has all her life been a second daughter to me and is fond of us and our ways so it will not be a bit of a stranger coming in among us.

On the announcement of the engagement a bonfire was lit on the hill nearby. All the family and the servants went up on Stewarts' Hill and danced around the fire with the young pair. A feast; a festival; a 'big day', and the stirring of old folk memories of tribal betrothals. And Mother said to the young pair, as if to solve forever the problem she knew to be worrying her son, '*You* have the babies, *I'll* look after them.'

In the morning sunlight, by the open door of what used to be the coachman's quarters, Becky, Tony's Irish nurse, sat. The young couple saw her. She had her hand out, rocking a pram. In the pram lay one of the young children of the Irish servants. So Master Tony, stopping by with Miss Judy, his betrothed, on his arm, said lightly, 'Now, Becky, not to do that. Stunts the growth of the child. Not to rock.' So she stopped her rocking of the pram, looked up at the full six foot five of him and said, 'Many's the time I've rocked you. Are you stunted?' And she continued rocking the Irish babe. The happy pair walked on, laughing, towards the woods. They were light-hearted days.

The wedding was solemnized in the little stone Aghabog Church on the green hill, a mile of winding lanes beyond the Annagh-ma-Kerrig forest. Judy was now the proud owner of a little yellow 'touring' car and after the big house reception they set off for God knew where with a tent strapped to the back of the car. The first night of their honeymoon they pitched their small tent, which one must hope was not 'too small for sin', on the banks of lovely Lough Erne. The rain came bucketing down.

The honeymoon was over; the new life partnership of Tony and Judy Guthrie was a-move on the boat for London and Work— the work he loved and she would now take part in.

They now became Londoners. They set up home in Lincoln's Inn, Old Buildings. At number 23, up several turns of ancient and scrubbed wooden stairs, they lived in an attic above legal chambers. For the tall young couple it was tiny in terms of accommodation. In terms of urban architecture they could hardly have found anything more like a tent. But then he was at his happiest as a theatrical nomad and Judy was a sort of gypsy littératrice. Life in this distinguished attic had the order and disorder of camping out. And they loved it. Both had been brought up to be intolerant of all ostentation. Soon it would be Earl Grey tea in high-quality cracked crockery and high-quality guests ducking the laundry line to reach the sitting-room section of this bit of Brethertown Bohemia. It was the first home of their own; and Judy's first *and* last. Except perhaps in a tented punt on the Warwickshire Avon she was never to be so much the mistress of her own place as here. It may seem surprising that these young theatrical folk were allowed to rent the chambers above the Master of the Rolls, and within the precincts of the select legal Inn. But the Bretherton family was in Law and at that time the Trustees of the Inn were, in fact, encouraging non-legal members of the city community to take up a proportion of the residential accommodation. It must have been quite a squeeze to get the hired Broadwood upright up the stairs past the small wooden doorways with their legal name-plates and on into the attic. The piano was one essential piece of first-rate equipment in the Guthrie urban 'tent'. If the windows were open, on a calm Sunday afternoon, august and sedate members of the legal profession were liable to hear loud-voiced versions of Moody and Sankey's hymns, or anything from 'Lord Raglan's Daughter' to:

> 'When I was a lad I served a term
> As office boy to an Attorney's firm,
> I cleaned the windows and I swept the floor,
> And I polished up the handle of the big front door.
> I polished up the handle so carefullee
> That now I am the ruler of the Queen's Navee! . . .'

Judy would be the accompanist on the Broadwood. Their kitten (there would always be a cat in their lives) would be on the windowsill staring down and up, level with the foliage of the great London plane tree which rose out of the yard. This yard during the day was a thoroughfare for the legal profession and also for the public passing on foot from the great iron gates at Lincoln's Inn Fields through to the arched gateway which gave out on to the busy traffic of Chancery Lane. On week-day daytimes the whole grounds of the Inn community was as busy with people as an ant's nest. But in the evening the tide of city activity gradually ebbed away; the head porter, in his faded maroon coat, brass buttons and silk top-hat, would issue forth from his lodge, look at his fob watch and, with assured dignity, walk out to see that the gates were closed and secure for the night. The Inn then became a select and enclosed community. Within it only the denizens or their guests moved; the cracked bell would be heard clearly telling the hours. A positively medieval atmosphere would take over.

Away west beyond Fleet Street and the Strand at the far end of the Royal Mall, rehearsals were to start right away. For the first time, Guthrie would be originating a production in London. *The Anatomist*, which had been first produced at the Edinburgh Lyceum in the summer of 1930, was a play he liked, by a playwright he liked. It was set in Edinburgh, which he knew. It was about medical Scots—his father's sphere. The central character was Dr. Robert Knox, an early nineteenth-century lecturer in anatomy in the Edinburgh Medical Schools, who took the same provocative delight in shocking conventional folks with outrageous truths as he himself did. It touched his own love of the macabre too: for it was about Burke and Hare—the graveyard body-snatchers—and the dubious source of supply of the bodies brought to Dr. Knox for his scientific dissection.

He was at home with the two Irish players who played Burke and Hare—Harry Hutchinson and J. A. O'Rourke. He had full and familiar response from the Cambridge players, Gillian Scaife, Robert Eddison, and also from those stalwarts of the Scottish 'tented tours', Meg Buchanan and Morland Graham. And there was Flora—playing the small but telling part of an Edinburgh prostitute destined for the dissection table. Judy was on duty in the dim stalls, keeping her brilliant and handsome husband supplied with cigarettes and refreshment from the picnic bag. The whole set-up was amenable to a degree. But there was one member of the cast and company he was not quite at ease with. Anmer Hall had engaged the great Henry Ainley to play the star part of the voluble Dr. Knox. Of course Tony had agreed that it made sense to have 'a name' to draw audiences. After all the theatre was new and in an unfamiliar locale; the public had to be drawn there. This was the first evidence of that distaste which Tony Guthrie sustained all his life for the 'star' who acted in a starlike way. He had enormous respect for talent but he had an absolute antipathy towards any signs of starry superiority.

The clash came in rehearsal. On his first entry Guthrie wanted Ainley to come on at a spanking pace, and, with the verve indicative of Knox's character, to start holding forth right away with all his witty verbosity. Ainley paused at this bit of misplaced direction from the young man. He gently advised him that this was a mistake. He must take into account that in this play Henry Ainley was making his 'return to the London stage' after an absence. The London audience would therefore applaud as soon as he came on stage. He was right—they did. On the night, Ainley paused, took his due tribute, relished the moment and then went on with the play. But Tony Guthrie did not like it at all. Nor did he enjoy many of the particular tensions leading up to this First Night, so critical for his career. Ainley was courageously fighting off the devil of drink. Tense builders, technicians and company worked all hours to have the building ready in time. That equitable and generous gentleman, Anmer Hall, had personal tensions attendant too. From her nearby town apartment his wife was adamantly refusing to consider divorce so that he could marry Gillian Scaife to whom he was truly devoted; as was she to him. Guthrie wrote to Xtopher (now in his University of Egypt in Cairo)

> . . . it was a sad struggle at the end of all . . . the builders were not out till a month after their appointed time. We hardly got any rehearsal on stage; where there were hods still a-carrying as the pit queues filed in to the first performance; the electrical plant was actually being tinkered at *during* the first act!

But James Bridie had written a superb first act. Even with Henry Ainley's pause for applause the whole evening was a huge theatrical success; Guthrie's first in London. It is interesting that, even before that first act, there was a Guthrie touch of originality. Instead of gramophone or instruments to play 'God Save the Queen', a lady, dressed in the crinoline costume of the play's time, came before the curtain and *sang* the National Anthem and brought the audience to its feet to join in.

The Times said 'a play of absorbing interest' and echoed the other papers in praising Ainley but picking out, for special mention, Miss Robson. Its critic said of the scene where the woman of the town is decoyed to her death by the Irish ruffians who supply Knox with his bodies: 'It is a supremely well-acted scene in which Miss Robson, who brings out with the most delicate skill the tenderness which may be latent in the depths of degradation, carries off all honours . . .'

So—Flora was triumphant again and Tony could write from his happy attic in Lincoln's Inn to the one man he considered had all the gifts for huge success, but no ambition to seek it:

Flora, David (Morland Graham), and the Irishmen are all good and the Tavern scene goes very well . . . Ainley I find pretty teasing in his part. He has been consistently reasonable, patient and polite to work with; but, Christopher, he's not intelligent: he doesn't understand what things mean. He's carried through by wonderful, wonderful, God-given bel aire—and his voice is a fine organ . . .

But it all mounted to success for the new Westminster and everyone concerned: '. . . as far as I can see the play will run for some time to come . . . your little boy-friend will have practically nothing to do (but full pay) till Xmas anyway—delightful.' Then he added—looking to these hours of leisure ahead: 'I'm writing a play—a *very* great one—in collaboration with Judy; about St. Matthew in a setting of modern Glasgow.'

In the Lincoln's Inn attic, screeds of foolscap paper were being covered in two sorts of bold clear handwriting—his and Judy's. But they had ample time to go and look at other plays in performance and—as the successful young London producer with his beautiful wife—to socialize a bit. This was around the time when the Depression had moved George V to request the Labour Prime Minister, Ramsay MacDonald, to form a coalition government to plan for national economic survival. Miss Ellen Wilkinson was a notable Minister in MacDonald's government.

Judy and I went to an awful party last night in Hampstead . . . everyone was either 'labour' or clever. No 7 Parsifal Road was crowded out—and all so pasty in the face—such *dark* blue shirts and such *art*—ties . . . Miss Ellen Wilkinson was there . . . she has a *great* big head with lovely red hair and the face of a beautiful dreamy slum child—only her face and head are proportionate to a splendid Juno of 6 feet 4 inches. I had to talk most of the time to Mrs. Naomi Mitchison; it seemed to me that she was 'expecting' but Judy said the maternity gown was mere affectation and that she stood that way for effect . . . I felt profoundly glad to be just a simple Pleasant Person—just

a hometown body—not one of those clever *Modern* Young
Folks.

In fact, they were as happy as a pair of children. Kenneth Rae,
who was working near the British Museum, would often walk to
Lincoln's Inn. There he would share their favourite lunch—
boiled egg followed by toast and marmalade. One day, they
asked Kenneth if he could recommend them to a nice family
doctor, who could tell them 'rather late in the day', as Tony said,
'the facts of Life'. He did. They went to the doctor who was
utterly disarmed by their frank childlikeness.

After Christmas at Annagh-ma-Kerrig with Peggy and
Hubert, Tony and Judy returned to London for the production of
Six Characters in Search of an Author at the Westminster—which was
now on the London theatrical map. As predictably as anything in
the Theatre, here was another triumph for both Tony and Flora.
But things were not happy with Flora. She did not look well. One
day, in the theatre, she fainted. Tony took her in hand. She was to
come to the Lincoln's Inn attic and tell Judy and him what it was
all about. She came, and poured out her troubles. She might be
feeling famous but she was certainly feeling the strain. In terms of
hard cash she was hardly able to dress even reasonably well; none
of the Company had princely salaries. The curtain came down too
late each night for her to get back to Welwyn Garden City. This
meant she had the expense of London lodgings. These lodgings,
in a club near Victoria Station, were depressing in the extreme.
Neighbours complained if she learnt her parts aloud. And she was
very worried that already she had a £12 debt to Anmer Hall, and
. . . Tony interrupted, as he always did if he could cut short an
emotional scene. Sharp but sympathetic words to this effect were
given to her: *Mustn't* wallow in one's misery—was sure he could
get the sympathetic and generous Anmer Hall to cancel a debt—
£12 was hardly likely to run the Prudential Assurance on the
rocks—as to lodgings, a miserable domestic background was no
use to anybody—up-and-coming actress must be able to learn her
lines loudly and without threat of police. Did she have any other
place she . . . Yes, Flora knew of an unfurnished room next door
to their Cambridge friend, Geoffrey Toone. This was available,
but though she could manage to rent, she could not afford to
furnish it. 'Right!' Tony and Judy persuaded the confused Flora
to accept a loan of £10—enough, he said, to buy a bed, some

blankets and the bare necessities. To a pair who honeymooned by choice in a tent and preferred their snug slum of an attic to any palace, the 'bare necessities' were an attraction rather than a privation. Flora's Scottish blood was stirred to resist. She did not want to be further in debt; and to them. She just could not see herself being able, in anything like the near future, to pay them back. 'In that case we can always take the bed, can't we?' Tony made this typically astringent Guthrie comment, which, also typically, was very near the bone. Flora was thus briskly picked up, dusted and set on her way again.

News of success at the Westminster was getting around. J. B. Priestley—then successful author of the best-selling novel *The Good Companions*—had written his first play, *Dangerous Corner*. It was to be presented in the West End. He came to the Westminster. He liked what he saw; including Miss Robson. Now Mr. Guthrie was to direct his play and he wanted Miss Robson to play in it. The play opened at the Lyric, in the heart of theatreland. It had a good press, a successful run, and gave Priestley the start of a distinguished career in the Theatre. It gave Guthrie his first West End success. It set Flora firmly on her way to the top of the theatrical ladder. Other offers were on her horizon; she kept the bed, paid back the Guthrie loan and soon moved into a flat of her own in Mecklenburgh Square, where she could work and live in comfort. It seemed as if the Guthrie/Robson working partnership had reached its conclusion and that for both life could be a steady mounting of the ladder of success. But now the brilliant young director was busy on his own play; and with his co-author, Judy, as playwright.

The summer days of leisure and writing went on, and Lincoln's Inn meals would often be alfresco when they would cart their picnic basket, thermos, travelling rugs down the narrow wooden stairs and eat on a far corner of the walled Inn lawns. And sometimes as Londoners, who both loved public transport even more than Judy's little yellow car, they would explore and picnic in Kew Gardens or on the river banks out at Richmond (he was later to list 'picnics' as his favourite hobby, in *Who's Who In The Theatre*).

And then, more or less by accident, fate directed him towards somebody who would immediately respect a young man who loved trams, public parks and the working-class residents of a remembered Glasgow and an observed South London—Lilian Baylis. In fact fate first directed her towards him.

The Westminster Company had assembled to rehearse what Guthrie considered a somewhat dubious play on Disraeli. Then the principal actor, Ernest Milton, was rushed off to hospital. Guthrie seized the opportunity to substitute another play. And he chose Shakespeare. With very little adjustment it seemed that the Company assembled for the Disraeli might be just right for *Love's Labours Lost*. One of the adjustments was to send to the Cambridge Festival Theatre for the young Anthony Quayle. He had sought a job at the Westminster the previous year and had been guided by Guthrie to go to Frank Birch in Cambridge for more experience. Quayle reflects how Tony and Judy had seen him on his way to Cambridge by driving him past Wellington Barracks in the open yellow tourer. Both Guthries had the wind in their hair, and one long knitted muffler streamed out, almost as dangerously as the one that strangled Isadora Duncan. No strangulation occurred here. They were both singing at the tops of their voices.

What Quayle found at the Westminster now was instant action and intensive rehearsal. It was fast and furious, conducted with the same undergraduate sort of fun as befitted the yellow tourer, *but* punctuated where necessary with sharp snap of fingers and surgically cutting comment. 'They won't understand it anyway, so pace!—rhythm—pace!' was the directional drive given to a company which included Abraham Sofaer, Robert Eddison, Evan John, Richard Goolden, Isobel Scaife, Vivienne Bennet and Joan White. 'Of Mr. Tyrone Guthrie's production of *Love's Labours Lost* at the Westminster Theatre last night it is almost possible to say that perfection was attained,' the *Daily Sketch* said.

Harcourt Williams, the Old Vic's resident producer, was at that time looking around for a successor. He went to see *Love's Labours Lost*. He looked at the Guthrie record. And he advised his employer, Lilian Baylis, to go along and have a look for herself at the young fellow's work.

One night during the run of the play she appeared in the box at the Westminster, she and her personal secretary, Annette Prevost. Word got to Guthrie about who was 'in front'.

We youngsters at the Westminster were very interested to see this legendary figure . . . in the stage box, which at the Westminster is . . . practically on-stage. We had no idea why she had come, but it was mighty interesting to get a close-up view of this thick-set, elderly person in glasses, who looked like a parish worker, who talked throughout the performance to her pretty young lady-chauffeur; in a tone almost as loud as the actors and in the unmistakeable accent of South London suburbia.*

She had crossed Westminster Bridge in the 'Trojan', a solid-tyred economical little car which could develop a suicidal slew when these narrow tyres caught in the shiny tram rails. And it is worth noting that one of the remarks she made to her 'young lady-chauffeur' was how well the young devil handled a number of people on the stage at one time.

She re-crossed the river and that might have been that. It certainly would have been had young Guthrie done, at that point, the sort of production of Shakespeare which had been all the rage since Barry Jackson did his famous modern-dress affairs with Falstaff calling for a taxi; but it was restrained, visually beautiful and not in modern dress. The lady from the Vic had seemed not displeased. She was, however, extremely cautious about the question of the Succession at the Vic. Whoever came in must be 'one of us'. And her 'us' related to her extended 'family' of the Old Vic company and their faithful South Bank following. Clever the young man obviously was—married was he?—and wasn't he rather young for the job, and did he believe in God?

The 'young man' went on writing with his young wife; on two things now. One would very much recommend him as being a lover of God and the lower classes. The other reads like the electioneering manifesto of a candidate determined to be the director of any National Theatre in his day. The first was *Follow Me*, his play about a St. Matthew from Glasgow's working class. The second was *Theatre Prospect*, a slim volume about to be published (1932) by Wishart and Company.

Then the summons came from Miss Prevost. Would Mr. and Mrs. Guthrie be Miss Baylis's guests for week-end tea? She was in her cottage retreat on the North Downs at Box Hill. Great flutterings in the dovecote of 23 Old Buildings, Lincoln's Inn. When the day came, the rains came too. It was a soaker calculated to dampen most spirits, but not those of the two all-weather theatrical gypsies. The Baylis summer cabin retreat was, according to Annette Prevost, 'built into a hawthorn tree' high up on the side of Box Hill. The two Guthries appeared out of the damp

---

* *A Life In The Theatre.*

landscape, sloshing expectantly through the rain, both to the eye
very tall, to the ear very audible, talking as they came. They
sounded very upper-crust but looked very durable. Baylis was
cautious over the whole affair: to engage or not to engage. As
why should she not be? Since her aunt had handed over the
running of the Old Vic to her—thirty-four years before—she
had, by sheer personal conviction and zest, achieved absolute
wonders, by persuading the right people to appear in what
seemed the wrong place to do the right thing. Now the Vic was
the right place. Such was its prestige that the best players in the
world were willing to appear on its stage and at a pittance of a
salary. One could not afford not to have the right person. She
had two theatres now. Sadler's Wells had opened the previous
year to do for the people of North London what the Vic was
doing for the South.

She needed the equivalent of a young archangel to take some of
the fight off her hands. She was, as Guthrie well knew, a lady very
given to prayer. Therefore, either he was the answer to her prayer
and God-sent, or he was not for her. At the first meeting Guthrie
came to the conclusion that he was not the answer to her prayer.
Yet, they had every reason to like each other. She was the same
sort of theatrical nomad at heart. Had she not begun her theatrical
career in a way akin to that boy-wonder of the Putney Empire,
Christopher Scaife, as one of 'The Musical Baylises, Soprano,
Vocalist, Violinist and acknowledged premier lady Mandolinist
and Banjoist of South Africa'? Her sister Ethel was 'the Celebrated Juvenile Whistler'. She had the same shoe-string sense of
economy as he ('Waste not want not'); the same familiarity with
the Bible; and how could he not be drawn to the 'naughty' spirit
and wisdom of a woman who could say to two of her 'children'
(players) about to marry, 'Good. Come to me in your anguish,
dears, come to me in your joy, but don't come to me in between—
I'm too busy.' Apart from the fact that obviously this was one
person whose life he would not be allowed to organize, he had
every reason to admire her; except the tattiness of some of her
stage décor.

Again he was summoned—across Waterloo Bridge this time.
He described his visit to her Old Vic:

As I wait the sapphire plush cover of a side table is violently
agitated and two dogs rush snarling out—Scamp and Sue.

They were quite nasty little dogs, spoiled and bad-tempered . . . Miss Baylis, someone once said, came to dogs late in life. She loved them not wisely but too well. Beneath that table Scamp and Sue had a home from home—basket, water, bones and so on. The top of the table was covered with portfolios, sketches for sets and dresses. But the room was dominated by The Desk; a large affair in oak with a roll top. It was densely covered with papers; on the top were knicknacks. Presents from Margate, Lucerne, the Trossachs, a bowl of Benares brass full of rusty paper clips and shrivelled rubber bands; a bunch of flowers, a tray of dirty tea things and three telephones. Tacked to the roll top was a postcard reproduction of Dürer's 'Praying Hands'.*

If he was after all the answer to her prayers he was not to know for months. He went on correcting the manuscript of *Theatre Prospect*.

This book is now a collector's item in Drama Libraries. It is for the specialist to read, but the list of contents gives some idea of the coverage, and certain passages show where Guthrie stood—artistically—as he waited to hear news from over the river. It is very significant what he puts as Number 1.

   I.   ANALYSIS OF RELATION BETWEEN STAGE AND AUDIENCE.

  II.   RELATION BETWEEN STAGE AND AUDIENCE IN 'NON-POPULAR PLAYS'.

 III.   ORGANISATION IN FRONT OF THE CURTAIN.

 IV.   IS ORGANISATION NECESSARY?

  V.   IS ORGANISATION PRACTICAL?

 VI.   SEASON TICKET SCHEME.

VII.   ORGANISATION BEHIND THE CURTAIN.

VIII.   PROGRAMME: NEW PLAYS VERSUS CLASSICAL REVIVALS.

 IX.   RESPONSIBILITY FOR SELECTING PLAYS.

  X.   PRINCIPLE OF SELECTING PLAYS.

 XI.   FUTURE OF NATURALISM.

XII.   METHODS OF PRODUCTION.

XIII.   A DRAMATIC SCHOOL.

XIV.   EXPERIMENTS IN MUSIC AND DANCING.

 XV.   PROSPECT.

* *A Life In The Theatre.*

In Chapter II he says:

No amount of money can persuade an audience sincerely to enjoy what is not to its taste. And I maintain that without that spontaneous sincere appreciation, without the proper relation between stage and audience, no production can come fully to life. This seems to be the 'catch' in several well-formulated proposals for a National Theatre. They make provision for good productions, but they are content to assume that because there are good reasons why a National Theatre ought to exist, therefore, granted a sufficient subsidy for their productions, a National Theatre would exist. Surely it is more honest to admit . . . that if an intelligent theatre is to survive, it can only be by carefully planned organisation, not only behind the curtain but in front as well. *

This is the man with 'a gift for administration', who has behind him the experience of 'tented tours' taken out to the People; of a Festival theatre run for the intelligentsia of university town, and of the Westminster urban repertoire with no positive policy behind it. And, all the time from this day, his thinking about Theatre was not so much in terms of bricks and mortar but in terms of people and players—the relation between players and audience, the relation betweeen company and community.

In Chapter XI, he says:

I believe the cinema will snip off the withered flower of naturalism that has been blooming in the English theatre since the days of Robertson and the Bancrofts . . . Modern acting has reduced emphasis and exaggeration to the lowest degree compatible with audibility and visibility in the theatre. But 'on' the cinema it is still possible to exploit the naturalistic method still further . . . Fortunately for London it has been possible to see the Tchekov plays interpreted by M. Komisarjevsky with wonderful sensibility . . . Here, if anywhere, lies the future of naturalism in the theatre: in a poetic purpose that is not content merely to imitate the outward appearance of commonplace things and reason about them, but attempts the glorification of the commonplace by arranging it to form a logical, musical, and pictorial pattern of abstract significance . . . The producer

* *Theatre Prospect, Adelphi Quartos No. 3.* Wishart and Co., 1932.

has to 'see' the pattern and 'hear' the symphony in order to direct the actor's interpretation.*

It was not just Komisarjevsky who had influenced him. He was already aware of the work of Jacques Copeau and of the Compagnie des Quinze, evolved as a company in 1931 when Copeau handed over his company of players to his nephew, assistant and disciple, Michel Saint-Denis. The last illustration in the book is a picture of a production by Saint-Denis. It is of André Obey's *Le Viol de Lucrèce*. In appearance, it is the sort of theatre most akin to his own Cambridge *Iphigenia* and *Six Characters in Search of an Author*. The caption to the picture reads: 'No stars, no scenery, precious little "box-office appeal", but an influence that is already fertile.'

Chapter XV indicates his view of his world:

. . . economic pressure, represented by the cinema, and a natural reaction against the convention of an immediately previous generation, both indicate that experiment will take the form of a revolt against naturalism . . . Popular philosophy is on the verge of a revolution. The political turmoils at the beginning of the nineteenth century were the popular expression of the rational philosophies that had been, slowly but steadily, gaining ground since the Reformation . . . From now on the trend of philosophy was more and more extreme toward rationalism . . . Science made barren fig-trees bear fruit, made dumb men speak and lame men walk . . . But Science now admits itself baffled in the pursuit of a First Cause . . . As yet there is only a faint rumbling of doubt; as yet it is only advanced thinkers who find the first chapter of Genesis more convincing than the Darwinian account of the origin of species. But it may well be that the reaction from rationalism will be drastic, invading every department of our civilization with incalculable results, turning all our existing institutions topsy turvy; ending forever the theatre as we know it, or giving to it a renaissance, with another Shakespeare, another Golden Age.†

With this book gone to print he was writing the final revisions to his own play; yet with an enslavement to Naturalism that almost made it a precursor to 'kitchen sink drama', but with an author's note in the flyleaf of the typescript which said: 'This

* Ibid.
† Ibid.

play depends upon the hypothesis that the Incarnation did not take place in the Middle East two thousand years ago; but is taking place in Scotland now.'

It was shown to Anmer Hall. And, for a time, excitement made Judy and him forget the Old Vic. Their play was to be done at the Westminster. It needed a mainly Scottish cast. He recruited Elliot Mason and Morland Graham and took on James Woodburn for the main part. Other recruits to the Westminster included John Moody, Dorothy Holmes-Gore (wife of Evan John), Betty Hardy and Joan White. The play opened on tour, in Glasgow, in a huge theatre designed for vaudeville. It opened at a time when the Depression had hit Britain and taken the heart out of industrial Glasgow. It was a grim winter. Judy and he lodged with Elliot's sister who at that time was actually leaving food outside the back door for hungry scavengers. The audience stayed away. Depression was in the theatre like a chill fog.

It is, in fact, not a very good play. In human sympathy it is lovely, in dialogue it is parochial and colloquial, and its whole vitality is utterly dependent on the off-stage action of an unseen Christ, and that, in its turn, is dependent on the original biblical drama. After a desperate and courageous tour it opened and closed at the Westminster to respectful notices.

He wrote to Egypt and Xtopher, like a man who has lost his first child, and whose wife is too sick to speak.

Well—it's been a very interesting experience; and I am very glad to have been through it, but, at the moment I feel tired and somewhat battered . . . Edinburgh and Glasgow were devastating . . . enormous theatres . . . about 20 people in a wilderness of seats. The play was neither liked nor understood—cast, in my opinion, are admirable . . . The London First Night went really well . . .

And truly the notices were only damning by the restrained respect they gave a sincere play. James Agate found it uninteresting. Ivor Brown (who had been a student at Cambridge and a great supporter of the Festival work there) gave it an honestly respectful notice. The *Evening News* however did find it 'an intensely moving play . . . a fine piece of work'. But:

It was a smack in the eye when I got to the theatre yesterday [*the day after the First Night*] to learn that ABH intends to take the play off next Satdy . . . I was completely winded . . .

However, there it is . . . He's lost a great deal of money, and is acting perfectly within his rights.

This was a bleak end to the London winter. It was the first big personal crisis the two shared together. They were both highly schooled in hiding undignified emotions; but Guthrie had—like most great men—an intense emotional force at the heart of him and he was often given to private tears. He now had someone to share the private anguishes. It must have bound them much closer than success.

He concluded to Xtopher: 'I shall send you a script when I get it tidied up. Till the bitter taste of failure recedes a little further into the background we haven't the heart to tussle with it.'

The play was never published; nor did he talk about it, or mention it in his autobiography. Anmer Hall, the financial loser, had the magnanimity and understanding to offer him the production of a new play James Bridie was finishing. But Bridie was to go on finishing this play for quite a time. And, for Tony, there was the necessary recuperation of an Annagh-ma-Kerrig Christmas. He got rid of feelings of frustration on the limbs of trees with a saw and axe. He and Judy wrapped up and walked out. They helped with the party and the Christmas tree. But when his mother mentioned children—in relation to him and Judy—he lost his temper with a violence that shocked her.

An historical letter came to Lincoln's Inn in January. The notepaper was more impressive than the typing—which was nearly as bad as blind Norah Guthrie's. But, it was an exciting letter to read aloud to Judy, feeding the cat, or finishing breakfast toast and marmalade:

THE OLD VIC

Royal Victoria Hall,
Waterloo Road, S.E.1.

Founded by The Late Miss Emma Cons in 1880
Extended to Sadler's Wells in 1931.

THE	THE
PEOPLE'S	HOME OF SHAKESPEARE
THEATRE	AND OPERA

Licensee and Manager
LILIAN BAYLIS, C.H., M.A.Oxon (Hon.)
(to whom all communications should be addressed)

26/1/33

Dear Mr. Guthrie,

At yesterday's meeting of the Governors I was authorised to offer you the position of producer to our Shakespeare company for the season 1933/34, at the salary of £700.0.0. (seven hundred) a year. I very much hope that you feel you can accept this offer, because I am sure we would work happily together.

There are several points which I might as well make clear now:—

1. The term 'a year' really means from June 1933–June 1934, but the first quarter, i.e. to September 29th next, would have to start this Spring, and cover the preliminaries of getting to know the present company, and selecting plays and artists for the season which would start in September. It would not include any actual production work. Your first salary (a quarter's) payable on September 29th would cover this preliminary work.

To Baylis's famous prayer, 'Dear God, send me good actors—cheap', it looks as if she has added, 'and a good producer to be paid later'. Item 3 leaves no doubts about the terms of her good tyranny:

3. As an annual servant the producer's whole time belongs to the Vic, and no outside work can be undertaken without our permission—even in the summer months when the theatre is closed.
4. The producer must not act here unless written permission is given by the Governors (except in an emergency when I give it gratefully myself!).
5. All costs must be submitted to me not later than the day of the dress rehearsal of the preceding production. Understudies should be shown on these . . .

Various other regulations were almost severely made clear.

I expect that there are many things you would like to talk over with me, and if you decide to accept the engagement perhaps you would ring up, and Miss Williams [*her business, as opposed to her personal, secretary*] could tell you when and where I am free.

I am fighting a horrible cold at the moment but I hope to be

better by the week-end, as next week is a very full one—
Saturday might be possible?

I hope you will come to us and be happy in the work.

Yours sincerely,
Lilian Baylis.

P.S. [*in her own hand*]

Since signing my Dr. tells me I must go away for the
week-end. Tues: or Wed; about 12.30 seem possible,
perhaps you'd ring up Miss Williams on Mon.

At the age of thirty-two he might be a failed playwright,
but here was a job of national importance. Of course, he accepted
the offer. And while still free to do other work, he produced at
the little Arts Theatre in January a double bill of *Lady Audley's
Secret* and *Count Albany*. In the former, Flora was delighted to be
back with him (as Lady Audley to Robert Eddison's Audley);
Elliot Mason was in the other play. Then, in March, he did a
production of Dorothy Massingham's *The Lake*, also at the Arts.
It was very successful and transferred to the Westminster. Spirits
recovered at Lincoln's Inn and over at Annagh-ma-Kerrig Norah
Guthrie added to her drawerful of his letters, a cutting from the
London *Times*: 'Tyrone Guthrie is now recognised as one of the
best of the younger producers, and his work at the Old Vic next
season will be watched with extreme interest.'

As he left the Westminster that theatre and company were
drifting uncertainly, having developed no real policy. Around
Christmas he had written to Egypt:

The Westminster Theatre: well—as far as I can see, by the end
of the year we shall have done only one decent play—*The
Anatomist* . . . A.B.H. will have lost a *ghastly* amount of money
and we shall be no forrader with an efficient theatrical instrument. I can't get him to look at the thing in a big way—i.e. the
way I want it to go. If he had an intelligible alternative (e.g.
making money) I would feel easier; but he has *no* policy . . .
We have become just an ordinary 'commercial' theatre, only our
manager is as un-businesslike as our position geographically is
obscure and our programme informed by no policy whatsoever. *The Anatomist* never made any money . . .

Judy sends love . . . You two must really make *efforts* to get
to know one another . . .

Your loving Auntie Flo.

No despair, just exasperation and good humour; and this written to the one friend in his life to whom he always returned at moments of crisis, to measure the passage of time and change. To Anmer Hall, via Xtopher and the Scaife family, he owed an enormous debt—and said so. They had provided these two stepping-stones, Cambridge and the Westminster. They took him right out of the boggy beginnings and even got him across the first big river towards nationally important theatre; if not yet National Theatre.

CHAPTER TEN

OVER THE WATERLOO BRIDGE
TO THE OLD VIC
(1933–1934)

SPRING 1933. An addictive walker, his route to the Old Vic would best be: out on to Chancery Lane, down riverwards across Fleet Street, to duck through an ancient archway, stride on through the yards of another legal Inn, the Temple, out on to the Embankment of the Thames. With the river on his left, he would strike upstream till he could get up on to Waterloo Bridge, with the tug boats and barges passing under him. If he glanced downstream it would probably be to Blackfriars Bridge, over which he knew scenery shuttled back and forth between the new Sadler's Wells and the Old Vic. At all hours Miss Prevost's small car, stuffed with costumes and properties, would rattle across. One special sight, however, could only be seen before dawn. This was a coster's barrow with several large flats being hurriedly trundled over the bridge. 'Sorry, Ma'am,' the barrow-man had said to Miss Baylis when requested to push off and push on up to the Wells right in the middle of the afternoon, 'Carn't barrer houtsize hobjects over the bridge arter eight a.m.' As Guthrie pushed on over the bridge towards 'THE HOME OF SHAKES-PEARE' he would only be mildly aware that across the Channel and away beyond where the Thames flowed into the sea, the jackboot was on the march in Germany. He was not a very political creature.

By crossing Waterloo Bridge, Guthrie was moving away from 'the commercial theatre', but it should be made quite clear that he was not moving to a 'subsidised' theatre. England had no such thing. But he was moving to a theatre which had the envy of many a commercial management in the matter of full houses. Over the years the Old Vic had built for itself a very loyal audience; much of it a very local one of, as Lilian Baylis would say, 'our people'. These were not quite so totally the working-class resi-dents of the South Bank as Lilian Baylis liked to imagine. But they were not monied people and the West End was to them

almost foreign territory. 'Our people' could not pay the price of
a seat which would make the financial operation of the Vic anything except a perennial worry, but Lilian Baylis never wanted
the 'lah-di-dah' people who *could* pay to cross the bridge; and
perhaps squeeze out her people.

This was, as the notepaper said, 'The People's Theatre'. The
charter of the Old Vic made it so. The charter also made it inevitable that this would be, for Tony Guthrie, a baptism of
Shakespeare. So far he had produced no more of the Bard than
The Merry Wives of Windsor at Cambridge and *Love's Labours Lost*
at the Westminster.

> The Theatre shall be used primarily for the performance of
> high-class drama, especially of the plays of Shakespeare, and of
> high-class opera, or the holding therein of public lectures and
> musical or other entertainments and exhibitions suited for the
> recreation and instruction of the poorer classes . . . Admission
> to the performances, lectures, entertainments and exhibitions
> shall not be gratuitous, but shall be at such prices as will make
> them available to artisans and labourers.

This was not, however, the language of the 1930s. Time and
custom had modified the exercise of the charter to dispense with
the lectures and exhibitions. But the principle of serving the
indigent locals and keeping all expenses down so that the seat
prices could be kept down too, this was a principle to be departed
from at one's peril, so long as Baylis ruled. Besides he entirely
sympathized with the aims. As a sort of Christian Socialist, he was
proud to be over the bridge from pagan West End Theatreland.

As he entered that famous stage door in the Waterloo Road,
the question of plays and players had already been much on his
mind. For the first season at least—and he must have supposed he
would survive more—the question of Company would have to be
a compromise between those already there and those he was
allowed to bring in. One of 'his people' was there ahead of him:
David Morland Graham. He wanted Flora to join. He would
have liked Robert Donat, but Donat was being picked out for
stardom in films, and needed more than the Vic would pay to keep
a young family fed and happy. He was then led to a choice which
was to please many a lot and Lilian Baylis not much at all. Was
this not a concession by the new young man to a system to which
he was supposed to be antipathetic—the star system? Charles

Laughton and his wife, Elsa Lanchester, were friendly with Flora. Laughton was already an international film star and had just begun to enjoy the phenomenal popular success of his Henry in *The Private Life of Henry VIII* (a film in which the unknown Donat took his first step to stardom in the romantic part of young Thomas Culpepper). At a meal shared by the Guthries and the Laughtons, in Flora's flat, the subject was raised: would Charles consider coming to play at the Old Vic? The salary was certainly no worry to him; he was becoming rich. But he very much wanted to put himself to school again in the matter of speech. And he wanted to learn the techniques of Shakespearean acting. Why not in 'the Home of Shakespeare'? Great and splendid players had been schooled there ahead of him: Matheson Lang, Sybil Thorndike, Ernest Milton, and John Gielgud. Elsa would of course come into the company too. They talked it over afterwards with Flora. Her recommendation, of Tony Guthrie as stage director, could hardly have been higher.

The plays of the season were to be *Twelfth Night*, *The Cherry Orchard*, and *Henry VIII*. *Measure for Measure*, *The Tempest*, *The Importance of Being Earnest*, *Love for Love* and *Macbeth* would follow. Laughton let Guthrie know he would come in, but one thing worried him that had also perturbed Guthrie: the costumes and scenery at the Vic were not of a very worthy quality—either in substance or artistry; in fact they often appeared to be—and probably were—a hash-up from the wardrobe of Miss Baylis's first love, the Opera. It would be a condition of Laughton's joining that the company would improve its costumes and scenery. Also, he would willingly help towards this improvement and raise cash for it.

How to break it to Baylis? Guthrie reckoned that Laughton was a real 'catch' for the Vic. But, 'a *film* star?—who had never played Shakespeare before?' Is he a 'nice man'? She had seen him in films, where he was not altogether 'nice'. 'Does he go to church, dear?' and then the eventual bone of contention: 'He'll want a lot of money.' 'So will I.' Her new young producer made one of those clear-cut Guthrie statements of non-compromise. If he was going to serve the Old Vic in the way he considered it needed to be served, then the artistic standard had to be raised—especially in the matter of costume and lighting. More money than usual would therefore be necessary. He was not lashing out on non-necessities. All the plays could be staged on one bare setting, adaptable to each production. But money had to be spent on costume and lighting. However, Mr. Laughton was prepared to go out and find her the necessary funds for the costuming. Very well—she agreed to Mr. Laughton joining them, on that condition. And to her chagrin, the Pilgrim Trust, which had previously turned a deaf ear to all her pleas for more funds for 'the work', responded to Charles Laughton's appeal and made a substantial donation to the Old Vic, but only for use in productions of the plays in which he would appear. His salary would be £20 per week. £15 was high for the Vic, '£20 a week for an actor who had never played Shakespeare!' It hurt her. But she agreed. Guthrie got on with rehearsals of *Twelfth Night*. The company, for this first production, had neither the Laughtons, nor Flora, who were still otherwise engaged. But they had Dennis Arundell, Roger Livesey, Ursula Jeans, Athene Seyler, Leon Quartermaine, young Marius Goring and Peter Copley, Richard Goolden of Oxford days, and a young man who had been a faithful undergraduate member of the audience at Cambridge, James Mason.

Rehearsals would sometimes be in the big, bare, and often cold, rehearsal room at the top of the old building with its narrow backstage passages and stairs. It was all brown-painted stone and shiny brick, not unlike prison corridors, or public urinals. Sometimes they would rehearse in the theatre. Then Miss Baylis, whenever possible, would sit in the stage box. This was at one end of the proscenium arch and level with the stage. She would have her office work brought there. Her secretary-cum-chauffeuse, Annette Prevost, would be sent shuttling back and forth through the pass door, keeping Baylis in her forward battle HQ in constant touch with the action in the business office of Miss Evelyn Williams and the treasury of Mr. Worsley. During rehearsal no one but 'Prevost' was authorized to make these cross-stage journeys.

It must have comforted Lilian Baylis to observe how her young man got down to work immediately and was so unsparing of his energy, and economical in the use of other people's time. Very energetic he would be, pacing the stalls, suddenly appearing up in the circle, clapping hands and surprising everyone on stage with the strength and clarity of his clear commands; then sinking into the dimness of the half-lit auditorium, only to reappear in an impossibly short time, snapping fingers in the circle and calling from there; after which he would miraculously stride down the stalls aisle and finally break the barrier between house and stage by leaping the gap of the orchestra pit. On-stage, and in a hugely caricatured way, he would prove to his players—and to her—that in acting he knew what he was talking about. Very comforting his firmness—very enjoyable his fun; lots of laughter in the company. It was encouraging too that, as she thumbed her accounts in the box, she could see over her spectacles that in all weathers the young wife would cross the Waterloo Bridge to have thermos and sandwiches ready for her husband at the right moment. Took an interest too. The Guthries were perhaps, after all, 'our sort'. Sometimes she would beckon Judy to 'come up and join me, dear'. An almost royal privilege. From that time, Judy, Tony and faithful 'Prevost' were to be life-long friends and workmates.

He was accepted. He was settled in. *Twelfth Night*, always a safely popular play, was a solid success. 'Our people' liked it. A cautious beginning. What he did not like at all was the permanent set, designed by the architect, Wells Coates. He had wished it on himself and he admitted that 'in *Twelfth Night* it completely dominated the evening and suggested not Illyria but a fancy dress ball on a pink battleship.'

The architecture of the old theatre came nowhere near to ful- filling the sort of physical conditions for the staging of Shakes- peare which he had drawn out on those napkins in the Montreal café. This was a proscenium arch theatre which could never establish the relationship between audience and players which he longed for. But he had to accept what was there. On he went with rehearsals for *The Cherry Orchard*: a new English version by his brother-in-law Hubert Butler. Charles Laughton played Lopakin, Flora Varya, and Elsa Lanchester Charlotta Ivanovna. Athene Seyler played Madame Ranevsky. This *Cherry Orchard* is con- sidered by Sir Alec Guinness to be one of the three best produc- tions Guthrie ever did. Chekhov was not then standard fare for a popular audience, but, according to the producer, the new trans- lation made the characters more recognizably normal and their humanity came fully across to the Old Vic audience. There was added satisfaction to the Guthrie family that Hubert had done such a good job on this essentially family play. The production was relieved of any excess solemnity and was successfully played for the comedy it is declared to be. The play ran for twice the number of weeks then customary at the Old Vic. But, however good the production, one can be certain that many people crossed the bridge who would not normally have come. They came not to see the work of the brilliant young director but to be in the presence of the lovable star of *Ruggles of Red Gap* and now *The Private Life of Henry VIII* (during *The Cherry Orchard* this had its London premiere).

Surely Lilian Baylis could now relax a little in her anxieties about the wisdom of the whole plan, and the discretion of her producer. If nothing else, this was brilliantly timed showmanship. The company went on to prepare for 'the real *Henry VIII*', as far as she was concerned. In this, for matters of economy, both she and Guthrie had agreed to accept the generous gesture of Laughton: that he would arrange for the Vic to have the use of the costumes made for the film.

The permanent setting was a bit inhibiting here too. However it all went well and Guthrie was able to write home to Annagh-ma-Kerrig about one notable piece of audience reaction:

> Oh!—a nice thing. I slipped into the back of the gallery at yesterday's matinee and in Flora's death scene [*as Katherine of Aragon*] just to see if it was properly audible. Up there I found a great policeman who had looked in to see that all was well—hadn't been able to tear himself away and was standing weeping—great pear drops—at the poor dear, dying Queen. Rather a tribute!... the dresses are very suitable to her—red velvet with enormous ermine sleeves. Her big exit from the trial scene was applauded—and cheered—to the echo—completely held the play up—very disconcerting for poor Charles who had to play the rest of the scene with a slight feeling of anti-climax.

Mother's friend, Mrs. Katie Gielgud, had been there. But her report to Norah Guthrie deplored a certain lack of sonority in speech, something nobody could ever accuse her John of. Tony took up the cudgels:

> Katie's criticism of *Henry VIII* ... It's the very 'sonority' of traditional Shakespeare that I cannot abide—that, to me, robs it of its humanity and all real meaning ... Shakespeare blank verse enables the speaker to slip imperceptibly from prose-speaking to verse-speaking and therefore a *naturalistic* method of verse-speaking is indicated. The 'traditional' declamatory, rhetorical method is I think of French origin derived from Racine who, unlike Shakespeare, was not a naturalistic writer

at all . . . Anyway every performance is packed out—not that that is any criterion of merit. Indeed I fear the only reason is the personal glamour of Charles Laughton—such is film fame!

Measure for Measure (Laughton, Angelo; Robson, Isabella) finished the year, but not the season. And, with little time for any Christmas celebration, rehearsals for *The Tempest* began.

The routine would be rehearsals, beginning 10.30 and with perhaps a lunch break in the Royal Victoria pub by the stage door. They would then go on till 4.30 or 5.00. The evening curtain went up at 8 p.m. At night, after performance, Flora, Roger Livesey, Ursula Jeans and perhaps Marius Goring would often resort to the Laughtons' rooms in Jermyn Street, to chat, drink beer and eat snacks until 1 or 2 in the morning. Then, for everyone on call, it was up again at 9.30 a.m.

A firm and practical purpose of Laughton's in going to the Vic and making what the papers called 'a spectacular sacrifice' was to improve his voice. Baylis took this as a kind of 'making use of us', and she began to refer to the sensitive and conscientious Laughton as 'that rich film star'. His Prospero, in the early new year, was a challenge in poetic speech that did not reach the lyrical heights required, the play was awkwardly directed and altogether was, as Guthrie freely admitted, 'the worst production of *The Tempest* ever achieved', and his the fault.

The Importance of Being Earnest, a 'galumphing' piece of production followed, then *Love For Love*. Guthrie loved this 'naughty' piece and most of the audience enjoyed it too but there had been some shocked reaction from the governors; over which Baylis came to his aid and endeared herself to him by proving to be not at all the strait-laced lady he had feared.

Macbeth, as is well known, has not the happiest of theatrical records. It was the last play of the Laughton season, and there had been difficulties with the voice. Flora was having troubles too with her performance as Lady Macbeth. Tony had directed her to base her character on a contention in A. C. Bradley's lectures, that Lady Macbeth was a woman without imagination. James Bridie, who was in pursuit of her for his next new play, was in the audience at the first night. He wrote with the rage of artist to artist confronted with artistic heresy:

It's no use lying about it. I thought your Lady Macbeth was wrong, wrong, wrong; lifeless, inept, even stupid. And it isn't all Tony's fault, though the Lord will damn him eternally for his abominable treatment of that immortal black poem. This is probably a left-handed compliment to you as an artist, a woman and friend; but I nearly died of rage, shame and grief . . . You, like the rest of the English theatre people, have gone all psychological as previously Mrs. Kendal made them natural . . . You are to stop being psychological—you know nothing about it and it's a very technical job . . . You are an artist of the theatre and a clumsy amateur of psychology. So is Tony . . .*

Charles Laughton was hit hard before he was many minutes out of Dunsinane. He was in his dressing-room still with costume and make-up on. Guthrie describes the scene:

> . . . Miss Baylis, aware of the need to administer cheerful but honest consolation to My Boys and Girls . . . Charles . . . in his room, painfully aware that his own performance had fallen short of the promise of the dress rehearsal. If ever a human creature is vulnerable it is a leading man at the end of a long exhausting performance which he knows has been a disappointment. Miss Baylis breezes in. She is in the full academic robes to which as an Honorary M.A. of Oxford she is entitled and which she very sensibly puts on for first nights. Beaming benignly through her glasses upon the dejected actor, she gives what I know is a laugh of embarrassment. Anyone who has been to a dressing-room after a difficult first night will know that embarrassment. Charles later declared it was a hyena's yell of triumph. She then catches him a smart crack across the shoulder blades. 'Never mind, dear,' she says, 'I'm sure you did your best. And I am sure that one day you may be a quite good Macbeth.' And she breezes out.†

Laughton never forgave her.

By this time stormy days had begun for Guthrie too. Although a rise in artistic standards had taken place and the pulling-power of his choice of star was putting the Old Vic 'on the map' more than ever before, Miss Baylis was getting complaints from her people about things too clever, too modern—yes—and too many in the audience from over there, the West-End lot. The protests grew, till one tough old regular—Miss Pilgrim—took it upon

* *Flora Robson*, Janet Dunbar. Harrap, 1960.
† *A Life In The Theatre*.

herself to be 'our' people's representative. She started collecting signatures for a petition: to send young Mr. Guthrie back over the river where he belonged. She operated at the stage door with a ruthless disregard for mere honesty. As the company came out one night a weary actor, for whom Guthrie was the God of Drama, recognizing the faithful 'regular', signed her paper happily, in the belief that he was adding to her collection of autographs. Horror struck him when a brother actor informed him that he had just signed a petition to get rid of Tony Guthrie.

Miss Baylis—who was not lacking in forthright honesty—showed the petition, and its strength of signatories, to Guthrie. While standing by him as her appointee she felt he ought to know that such criticism was being widely expressed and that she did not regard it as entirely unfounded.

She then presented to Charles Laughton another piece of paper altogether. And the storm which had been building up broke. It was a bill for more than a thousand pounds: the excess of expenditure the season had had to support beyond the monies Laughton had actually raised. Not unnaturally, he gave full vent to his anger. He more or less consigned her and her bill to the devil. He accused her of dressing anew the whole chorus of her Sadler's Wells Opera from the profits he had brought to the Vic because of his popularity. Her dander was up too. Did this rich film star not understand that even with full houses her theatre could make hardly any profit at all—and largely because she was not prepared to soak her dear people with prices for seats which they could not afford to pay? It seemed to him she was all too prepared to soak 'that rich film star'. They parted. She wrote a letter that Prevost persuaded her not to send. The gist of it was that she had been put to unpredictable expense in renting extra workshop and storage space, etc., in order to cope with the new costumes and scenery that he and Mr. Guthrie demanded for their season and for which he had promised he would get the money. Laughton kept his back turned on Miss Baylis, as he went angrily on to fulfil his final appearance; and to fill the house.

The final curtain of the last night was always a great 'family occasion' at the Vic, when that intolerable barrier for Guthrie—the division between house and stage—was broken, Miss Baylis would speak to her people, and little presents would pass up from the regulars to 'their' actors and actresses. There was no present for Charles Laughton. Flora was as distressed as Charles and Elsa were hurt. She had thought that Tony should have come out more positively on Charles's side. In his book he says: 'I thought a bad situation could be made ten times worse by clumsy diplomacy, so made no attempt either to mediate or to take sides.'*

Years later, when his own book, covering the subject, came out, and he was in the foyer of that other home of Shakespeare, in Stratford-upon-Avon, Charles Laughton turned his back on Guthrie and walked away.

Some weeks after *Macbeth* closed and the season finished, Lilian Baylis, had to her surprise, received from Guthrie a donation to 'the work', of £100.

The Old Vic.

June 25th 1934.

Dear Tyrone Guthrie,

I feel very bad at allowing you to give the work £100 donation. You did some unforgettable good work for us and we paid you little enough for it. We shall certainly look forward to having you with us sometimes.

I don't think I agreed to having an additional electrician at your expense, if an extra man were necessary for the work, *we* should pay him, not you.

It would be good if Laughton realised how he went back on his promises, he must have each production new from beginning to end and he would get us the money for this. Nothing was said about good or bad business, it was a different offer which we accepted and he had failed to carry out.

Your generosity has made me feel really bad over Charles's dishonourable conduct.

I hope you have a lovely summer and great success and much happiness in your future work.

Yours very sincerely,

Lilian Baylis.

He was clearly discharging what he considered his obligation in a matter of finance. Yet, one cannot but feel that this action is a little in the category of 'an apple for the teacher'. What seems an unavoidable implication is that he wanted to go back to the Vic.

While still considering the all too human possibility of clay in the feet of the idol, it is best to deal with another question mark

* *A Life In The Theatre.*

raised at the time by Xtopher. Tony wrote in reply to some obviously disturbing letter from Cairo:

I am rather angry at all that facetious part of your letter about my 'success' and the fact that you no longer know me . . . I don't think I either want or respect 'success', except as a means to doing more interesting and unfettered work. This may not be quite true . . . it's impossible to know if one is wholly sincere . . . In practice, I suppose one does rather strive for the *comfort* (spiritual rather than material) that accompanies even the amount of flattery and respect *I* get! There! That *is* the truth now . . . By now you will have guessed that I am a little vexed you didn't take more trouble with me—and with Judy. The evening here wasn't a success.

That summer Xtopher had made an 'appointment' and met him 'by accident' in the street. Was ambition going to lose him friends? Doubts about the ladder of success—which was such a symbol when he got back to writing another play—those doubts could have begun now. However, the Vic, its company and audience, had meant much to him.

At 23 Old Buildings Judy had a letter from the father of Peter Copley. It brought back the atmosphere of that last night at the Vic and must have made Guthrie sure that Baylis's hope to have him back sometimes would be fulfilled.

Dear Mrs. Guthrie,

Do you remember, after the first night of *Twelfth Night*, when we were all rejoicing in its success and congratulating your husband, your saying that there were still eight months of the season to go, and who knows what would happen before the end? Well the end is come and surely you must be glad of what has happened. The audience said very clearly last night what it thought. I doubt whether it quite realised how much of what it was applauding was the result of the 'production', and your husband does not help them to such knowledge by his abominable habit of hiding on first nights. These productions have gone steadily a triumphal way, but last night crowned the sequence . . . What is so unfailing in your husband's work is the unity. The tale tells itself with perfect clarity from start to finish . . . the use he made of the permanent set was imaginative in the extreme—the blazing castle,

the radiant sunlight of the scene in England, the black hole
into whose darkness characters walked to their deeds and destiny . . . the sense of a house with rooms in which people lived
. . . And the grand finale with its retreating ranks of dark
soldiers and the trail of spears against glittering space, was like
a picture by Tintoretto . . . You must be very proud and your
husband should be very happy.

Who needs critics with an audience like this; summer and most
of one's career ahead; and many offers coming in, one from
Charles Laughton's agent, who had just arranged a very good
film contract for Flora and now was offering to 'place him in
films'?

CHAPTER ELEVEN

WEST END AND BROADWAY
(1934-1935)

THOUGH HE had not quite seemed to be acceptable to her people, Lilian Baylis and the life at the Old Vic had established claims upon him and his hopes of Theatre. It was not entirely diplomacy that made him write in the Old Vic and Sadler's Wells magazine, April 1934: 'I shall treasure always the memory of a company of finely talented, generous and sincere artists; a manager whom I have long admired and now adore; and an audience which must surely be the finest in the world.'

In Lincoln's Inn it was spring. There was one immediate job to do on this side of the river after which it would be Annagh-ma-Kerrig and taking stock. With him there was always this drive to get on to 'the next thing'. The job in question was a production of Norman Ginsbury's play *Viceroy Sarah*, at the little Arts Theatre. With Edith Evans playing the Duchess of Marlborough, and an attractive and effective play, this was again success of a sort. But despite its location in theatreland, the Arts was not assessed as West End. And it was a professional necessity for any young producer as ambitious as he to be able at this point in his career to point to some solid West End 'success' before the next rung on the ladder could be reached.

Stock-taking was the order of the day when they got to Annagh-ma-Kerrig and there he had immediately to consider a new factor in the private sector. He would soon be an uncle. Peggy was pregnant. In the Guthrie family atmosphere, where debate was always very open, and often very loud, it was natural that children should now be under discussion. It was therefore a source of worry to his mother that when the question of babies came up, Tony would change the subject. There was a need to get on with 'the work' and now a need for success. He walked out, did sweated manual work on the estate and took stock.

The Laughtons had gone off into the world of Cinema. Flora too had great film hopes, and a contract with Alexander Korda.

For a time he, too, was tempted. In fact it was on the cards that Korda would welcome him into the Industry. But when the call came it came from the Profession—and the commercial side of it. It was from Hugh 'Binkie' Beaumont, then up-and-coming and on his way to establishing the powerful Tennent management. Would Mr. Guthrie direct, in the autumn, and in the West End, a play by the actress Joyce Carey called *Sweet Aloes*? Mr. Guthrie read it. Yes, he would.

Sweet Aloes at Wyndham's Theatre was Guthrie's first taste of unqualified commercial theatre success. It had a golden glow and when, next spring, the new lot of daffodils came up, which they had planted between the house and the lake, Judy and Tony christened them 'sweet aloes'. In the Guthrie household, daffodils from that day were never referred to otherwise.

Then followed, within the year, four productions in the West End and two on Broadway.

The next production was a strange affair, to which Guthrie makes no reference at all in his autobiography. Yet it had Flora Robson, Robert Donat, James Bridie, and success too, to make it notable. The play was *Mary Read*. It takes us back to the dark of the stalls on that day in the Festival Theatre, Cambridge, when he had lent over to the new playwright, James Bridie, and had whispered into his ear, while they both watched Flora perform on-stage, 'Nobody knows it yet except me, but she is going to be a great actress one day. You should write a play specially for her.' After all sorts of starts and stops, this was it: a play about a formidable eighteenth-century character who, for most of her life, 'passed as a man', first as soldier, then sailor, then as the most notorious pirate practising in the West Indies. It had a large cast, lots of scenes, a good story, and ample opportunity for Guthrie to exhibit director's virtuosity. For Flora it offered a fascinating character in a thumping great romantic part: with a highly original hay-loft love scene between her, as soldier (yet all-woman), and an artist (Donat), an escapee from the military. It was noticeable to Flora that, every time it came to rehearsal of this scene, Tony would simply say, 'Work it out between you', while he got on with other things.

One interesting crisis in the tour—which opened in fog in Manchester—was that it brought into Guthrie's life again Bertie Scott of Belfast. It was he who had trained the great Guthrie voice in the 2BE days. The crisis came when Flora developed that nightmare affliction feared by actors, 'a nodule on the vocal chords'. It means loss of voice and to the sufferer seems the end of his or her career. Tony Guthrie called Belfast. Bertie Scott was there as fast as could be. Flora was out of the tour, forbidden to speak and gradually coached and coaxed till she was in full Robson voice again when she opened in the play in London; and applause followed applause till they could hardly get the curtain down. Mostly the applause was for her. It was a personal triumph.

As a play, Bridie wrote it off as 'fun' but flawed. As a production Alexander Korda found it (his first venture into theatre management) a rather costly loss, and this despite a fair run. Donat got deserved acclaim in an unrewarding role. Guthrie was once again noted as a genius in on-stage organization of busy scenes and in technical complexities.

Before she tackled the star part of Queen Elizabeth I in the film *Fire Over England* Korda offered Flora a holiday of her choice. She chose Egypt. And again she met Christopher Scaife, who showed her round Cairo. Tony wrote to him: '. . . I'm glad you like Flora. She liked you very much. I find her difficult to get on with just now but I am sincerely and deeply fond of her.'

Again it seemed to be the end of a great progress together. She was launched towards film fame and he was in the West End and successful. He did another production at the Comedy, *Mrs. Nobby Clark* by Murray MacDonald and Gilbert Lennox, in which Elliot Mason played, together with Esmé Church and Marie Ney. He then wrote Xtopher another letter which demonstrates his sense of success: 'I believe I've got to a stage now when I could be away for a while and still get offered work afterwards . . . This may be a self-important delusion; but I'm prepared to take the risk. Any offers? . . . Have you any suggestion to make?'

But at this point 'Binkie' Beaumont again came up with an offer, which was to introduce him to the New York Broadway theatre scene for the first time. Jane Cowl, a successful American stage star, had written a play called *Hervey House* and its setting English. It needed to be vetted and directed by an English producer of some taste and tact. Tact, because there would have to be revisions made. Would he go over and discuss it all with Miss Cowl? He went off on his own, across the Atlantic in the early spring. It is a long story well told in his autobiography. To put it shortly—he faced the scintillating lady, trailed her and her husband around while she toured with another play; and as tactfully as he could, faced her with ruthless cuts to the script, and many re-writes; all this to prepare the play for a grand scale of presentation. At this she screamed. It was madness. Her play was an 'intimate' play. But with the firm support of his management back home, he stubbornly maintained that that was how it would have to be, or it just would not suit London or His Majesty's Theatre, Haymarket. Jane Cowl gave in. Binkie assembled a cast with Gertrude Lawrence, Fay Compton, Margaret Rutherford. They took it round all the still extant 'number one' British tour theatres. Then it came in . . . to a resounding flop at His Majesty's. Actress-playwright Cowl was right, Guthrie was wrong and, as always, ready to confess his fault. 'Made a mistake. Sorry. Now what is next?'

Next was the possibility that he would sign a three-year contract to make three films a year. Success in theatreland was losing its glamour. There was a correspondence going on between Donat and him on the need to found another sort of theatre of their own —a theatre with a policy, somewhere outside London. This was not however what Donat wanted: a theatre with a policy, yes, but not outside London. He still felt the need for personal success in the metropolis. Then Binkie Beaumont came up again, showed his continued belief in Guthrie, and this time he got him, and Judy, over to New York to do his first Broadway production. *Call It a Day* was a new Dodie Smith play. It was a production in which the Guthrie pace, applied to a lightweight play, created a faster scramble on-stage than rush-hour on the New York subway. But it worked. Goodish notices and all the skill of Gladys Cooper got it into the category of a success. The Theatre Guild and Beaumont were satisfied and Guthrie was asked to stay on to reproduce the London success of *Sweet Aloes*. It was not a successful transplant, and died an early death. However it allowed Judy and him to be tourists in New York with time to do the sights and ride on the Staten Island Ferry with the same child-like joy as they had once ridden the Kew Gardens tram.

Back in Lincoln's Inn from New York, and with success beginning to pall, he seized an art-theatre opportunity to go over to the Westminster where 'policy' was making its appearance with the London Group Theatre; a policy in favour of all arts—especially poetry. It was at this time, in what had been Anmer

Hall's theatre, that young Benjamin Britten began his apprentice-ship to practical theatre. He wrote the music for the production Tony Guthrie was doing; Henry Moore made a mask; John Piper as designer would soon follow on. Under the artistic direc-tion of Rupert Doone—who had done choreography for Guthrie at Cambridge—poets, painters, musicians, artists were being drawn to work in Theatre. Guthrie produced W. H. Auden's *Dance of Death* in a double bill with Doone's production of T. S. Eliot's *Sweeney Agonistes*.

When Guthrie took on his next commitment to success and commercial Theatre, there was an interesting incident showing his impatience with the West-End-and-Star system. The star was Marie Tempest. The play was Robert Morley's *Short Story*, at the Queen's. Sybil Thorndike, who was in the cast, tells the story. Miss Tempest at rehearsal was

> being very naughty . . . She would try to make you her slave and if you gave way she despised you and treated you like dirt. One day when she'd been awful Tony suddenly snapped his fingers and we all stopped. He came striding down the audi-torium . . . while we all waited. Then, in a loud voice, he said, 'Miss Tempest! Why are you being such a bitch?' There was an awful silence and we all thought, 'Poor young man! Such a promising producer and that's the end of it.' They looked at each other for a long time and then suddenly that gorgeous smile of hers spread across her face and she said very sweetly, 'Very well, Mr. Guthrie, shall we go on with the rehearsal?'*

Right after that slap-down he built her up, by asking her to show the then inexperienced Rex Harrison how to handle a bit of telephone business. She did it brilliantly as he knew she would. Authority and understanding are two things that make the great director.

There was someone else in that company who had the courage and stature to stand up to Miss Tempest. This time it is Guthrie who is telling the story, in *A Life In The Theatre*.

George Chamberlain, assistant stage manager, was 'on the book':

> Prompting Marie Tempest, [*he*] was the absolute model for the craft. He would anticipate a dry-up with the intuition of a

* *Lewis and Sybil*, John Casson. Collins, 1972.

Tiresias and offer the prompt with the tact of a great hostess.
But once he spoke too soon. Madame whirled round on him
with blazing eyes:

'Did you speak?'

'Yes. I gave you the line.'

'Are you acting the part or am I?'

'You are trying to, and you always dry up on that line.'

For the assistant stage manager thus to address Dame Marie
Tempest was like a corporal giving a back-answer to a field-
marshal . . .

There was a long and terrible moment; but neither common
sense was lacking in Marie Tempest, nor humour.

'*Quite* right,' she said, and smiled the smile which no one
was ever able to resist.

I knew then that George Chamberlain was a man with whom
I'd like to be associated.

And the opportunity to work with him was just coming up.
The tutelage to the West End was ending. A summons came from
over the river. Lilian Baylis invited him back, back to where stars
were not allowed to hold sway, success was non-commercial, and
there was a theatre with a policy. On returning to the Old Vic,
one of the early appointments he made, as resident producer, was
George Chamberlain as stage manager.

CHAPTER TWELVE

BACK TO 'THE PEOPLE'S THEATRE'
(1936-1939)

'WITH THE energy of a new broom I was able to sweep Miss
Baylis and the governors into action.'* Clap of hands, snap of
fingers and into action right away was becoming the characteristic Guthrie approach to any piece of work. The action here
referred to was his sudden resort to surgery on those Siamese
twins, the Old Vic and Sadler's Wells. They were bound together
by two things: the Charter, which required that they *both* play
Shakespeare and Opera; and Blackfriars Bridge, which was their
physical lifeline. He did not blow up the bridge but by determined
administrative surgery he managed to sever the constitutional
bonds which made the theatrical traffic across it necessary. From
now on at least people would not turn up at either house to see
the opera or the play which, by the time they got there, was
playing on the other side of the river. Up in the Wells, in Islington,
from now on it would be Opera (with Ballet). Down at the Vic,
in Bermondsey, it would be Drama (with, he hoped, *all* theatre
arts).

As he crossed Waterloo Bridge this spring, he was reporting
to Baylis for a command whose term of duty he hoped would not
be just one single season. She must have nursed this hope. The
health and strength of 'the Manager' were beginning to fail her.
There would have to be serious thoughts of her successor. At the
end of the previous season she had been firmly ordered by her
doctor to take a total rest. For this she retreated to a cottage in a
cove on the Welsh coast. She defied doctor's orders and broke
that holiday in a way that made her more aware than ever Guthrie
was of the troubles looming ahead on the international horizon.
She accepted a flying invitation to Paris, to the Théâtre Populaire
—the Parisian People's Theatre—to see a performance of Romain
Rolland's *Le 14 Juillet*. She reported the event in the Vic-Wells
magazine Sept.–Oct. 1936:

* *A Life In The Theatre.*

... the leading characters were taken by well-known players from the Théâtre Français and the crowds played by the people. At the fall of the curtain the excitement rose to great heights; the players waved red streamers and green branches. A minute's silence was asked for and the huge audience stood, remembering their comrades who had fallen that week in Spain; I too stood and prayed for all those who had died fighting. Then the Marseillaise was sung, and the great multitude stood with raised arms and clenched fists to sing their own anthem— The Red Flag—twice through, everyone at the highest pitch of excitement. When the curtain finally fell the orchestra rose too and sang the anthem as the three thousand earnest, excited people left. It was most moving and I was thrilled from my toes to my hair.

Guthrie's first job was to be choice of plays in relation to the company. And the statement on this in the same magazine reads now as somewhat of a shock. It was not what one would expect from a man who had put starry success behind him.

This season we are hitching our waggon to two stars. From October until the end of 1936 Miss Edith Evans will return to the Vic and plays will be chosen that offer parts for her; for the later part of the season we shall have Mr. Laurence Olivier who will be seen as Iago and, later, as Hamlet.

He quickly tries to correct a wrong impression and then throws in another 'star'—from New York.

This does not mean that other players of reputation and exciting personality will not be seen during the season. In *The Country Wife*, for instance, Miss Evans will be joined by Miss Ruth Gordon. In New York Ruth Gordon is regarded as one of the very few important actresses that have arisen in this generation ...

There then come the rational but rather lame excuses:

At the same time I hope and believe that it may still be possible to preserve something of the corporate feeling—the 'happy family' spirit of a big company, by retaining a small nucleus of permanent members of the company, and by making guest artists feel, during their time of working with us, that they are not outsiders but members of the gang.

Was he trying to convince Baylis that his gift for management equalled his skill in direction? Certainly the Vic still needed the means to get better costumes, sets, etc. But the arrangement about *The Country Wife* might be at the expense of the whole idea of permanent company.

The American theatre manager, Gilbert Miller, had seen Ruth Gordon play Mrs. Pinchwife in Westport, Connecticut. She was marvellous. He wanted to put on the play—for the West End or Broadway. Oliver Messel was to design the décor; and sumptuously. It was Messel who persuaded Miller to let the Old Vic do it first, then he could transfer Miss Gordon and the scenery to New York. Thereby the Vic would get a splendid guest actress, splendid sets free and a bit of international repute thrown in. There was showmanship in it, and the gift for organization too. But, wouldn't this, to Lilian Baylis, just be the Laughton arrangement all over again? Except that this would be more like barter than sale; no money would be involved. Guthrie himself uses the word 'tempted' in his acceptance of the ploy. And he adds, 'Neither Miss Baylis nor I wrestled very long or very hard with Satan!' It was fun, but there was a bit of conscience at work too.

One should in fairness make it quite clear that he was not disrupting or moving in to destroy an established company with a clear policy. It was a theatre with a charter, a reputation, a very faithful audience and a very awkward building. In the matter of company maybe one had to plough in order to sow. He had an eye to a larger future for the Vic and the attraction of top-rank talent.

The London theatre scene at that time was a field very rich in talent. There were four men whose gifts enormously impressed him, and whose careers began to be very influential on his own: Michel Saint-Denis, John Gielgud, Laurence Olivier and Alec Guinness. In 1934 Gielgud had encouraged Michel Saint-Denis to come over from France and reproduce in London his beautiful production of André Obey's *Noah*, with an English cast. Gielgud played Noah. As a producer in London, Saint-Denis's somewhat 'fractured English'—as Alec Guinness called it—made direction difficult. The whole thing lost some of the original peasant simplicity it had had with his own Compagnie. Yet Gielgud and others —including Guthrie—became very convinced that here was a great teacher and theoretician of Theatre who could make a profound contribution to the British Stage. The hope was then raised that some day a Saint-Denis school should be opened where a company of English players could be schooled in the style of the Compagnie des Quinze.

The hope was realized within that same year when the company in Paris broke up. Diaghilev's old studio, in Beak Street, Soho, was rented and Saint-Denis began teaching in London. Soon young actors like George Devine, Marius Goring and Alec Guinness were going along to pay their pound-a-week fee and be subjected to the Saint-Denis magic. For he was, they all agreed, a great and good teacher. Guthrie's help for the project was in accordance with a tenet laid down in his *Theatre Prospect*: that a theatre school was not effective unless it had an attachment to a live and public theatre. The Old Vic did have a school of its own. But it was not Guthrie's idea of a school and perhaps he was looking to larger and future—national—needs. When in this year, 1936, Saint-Denis moved up to Islington and opened up his London Theatre Studio, Guthrie offered the school the facility of the Old Vic Theatre building at such times as it was 'black' or the company playing away. He also lent his name and periodic attention as one of the school governors. What is not generally known is that he lent Saint-Denis a considerable sum of money when his French colleague had a very practical need of it. Guthrie was mean as hell to himself, or to anybody who he thought would spend money unnecessarily on 'silly things'—like a taxi when a bus would do; or on new clothes, when the ones you had were not actually dropping off you—but where he spotted real need or real distress he would give generously.

The influence of Guthrie and Saint-Denis on the British Theatre of our time has been enormous. And there could hardly have been two men more different from each other. If Guthrie was a beanpole, Saint-Denis was a sack of good oats. Guthrie was fast and impatient. Saint-Denis was slow and painstaking. For a play to mean something to Michel it had to be felt in his bowels; feeling was all. Tony had to think and visualize his way in cerebral flashes. Michel spoke between thick lips, with a peasant smile—and deliberately—after deliberate puffs on a pipe. Tony snorted, then rattled statements off like telegraphese while a cigarette stuck to his tight lips. They were my giant and dual godfathers in the Art of Theatre and it was almost impossible to interpret the one to the other. Love of the Theatre was the only real bond between the two. Each in angry professional pride called the other 'bloody amateur!' They were so differently, so professional.

Guthrie's 'naughty' intolerance of the Saint-Denis Gallic exactitude can be seen in the following example. Elderly English actor, about to join cast of a Saint-Denis company, asks, 'What's the Frenchie fellow like, eh?' 'Maa-rvellous producer!' Guthrie raps back. Then he smiles wickedly. 'But *does* require one to live at least two months in a chicken-run before doing *The Ghost Train*!'

John Gielgud, we know, had family links of friendship with the Guthrie family and as 'young Jack Gielgud' joined Fagan's Oxford company just after Guthrie. Now he was managing and directing his own remarkably high-quality companies, and in the classics, and in the West End. Much of the talent he drew to him was influenced or trained by Saint-Denis.

Alec Guinness, shy man that he always has been, had talked his way into Theatre by invading John Gielgud's dressing-room. Gielgud had encouraged him, he had worked hard on himself and then he had gone to classes with Saint-Denis. Now he was playing small parts in the Gielgud companies.

Laurence Olivier had come up his own hard way, through the good schooling of the Birmingham Rep. and several parts in the commercial theatre, until he had alternated the parts of Romeo and Mercutio with Gielgud in his recent West End production. Now he was playing with his good friend Ralph Richardson in *Bees on the Boat Deck* by Priestley before going into production on the film *Fire Over England* with Flora Robson.

It was summer 1936. Laurence Olivier was working on this film and, at a week-end party, Guthrie tracked him down. The party was at the house of the mother of Jill Esmond, who was Olivier's wife. It was on a sunny lawn that Guthrie put the proposition to him: 'How would you like to play Hamlet at the Vic —produced as it was written, that is, in its entirety?' Olivier was a little surprised, a lot flattered. The reputation of Guthrie was of highbrow brilliance. The reputation of the Old Vic then—even before the main Guthrie era—was such that any budding star would welcome the opportunity to play on its stage. After the precaution of consulting Harcourt Williams he gave Guthrie a firm 'yes'. But he could not be free till after Christmas, because of filming. 'Not to worry'—Guthrie would adjust. The full season was planned.

6

To suit Edith Evans, Olivier and Ruth Gordon, the Vic's season of plays for 1936 worked out to: *Love's Labours Lost, The Country Wife, The Witch of Edmonton* (which Saint-Denis would direct), *Hamlet, As You Like It, Twelfth Night,* and *Henry V*.

Guthrie completed his company with Alec Guinness, Michael Redgrave, Alec Clunes, Isobel Scaife, Evan John, Rachel Kempson, Ernest Milton and a player recruited in a way that Guthrie would often follow—going right outside the profession and sticking to his respect for Amateur Theatre—Freddie Bennett. He had seen Bennett, a bank clerk, play, at an amateur drama festival, the Porter in *Macbeth*. He was impressed, tried to see Bennett afterwards, but he had gone home. Guthrie persisted, put the question to him—why had he not considered taking up acting professionally? The question came from the right quarter, and there was bank employee Bennett in the profession for life.

Casting done, the season's programme settled, and his office established at the Old Vic, he and Judy took off for Ireland. They were on a rather special mission, to attend the christening of Peggy's baby daughter, Julia. The expedition turned out to be one of the thrills of their lives; and a thrill they could have done without.

Time was short before rehearsals began. He was a very busy man. He acted somewhat like a tycoon and chartered a private plane. He loved to fly. Back in the Belfast days he had indulged the appetite in several week-end flips. They were flown off from London's Croydon Airport in the equivalent of today's executive jet. They flew straight to a meadow by the bridge at Bennetsbridge, Kilkenny, where Hubert's family home, Maidenhall, sat in its grounds above the river. They bumped down to a successful landing. The child was christened Julia Mary Synolda Butler, and he successfully carried out all duties as godparent, and enjoyed Peggy's big day.

After celebrations and affectionate farewells to Hubert, Peggy and all relatives present, Tony and Judy made for the river meadow again, the waiting pilot and the plane. Villagers gathered. Villagers stared. Villagers saw that these two members of the gentry were not the ideal size to cram in to a little light 'airyoplane'. But they got in; propeller whirled, engine whined, and they roared and bumped along and away towards the far fence, and the distant horizon beyond it of the Leinster Mountains. Hankies waved. Then a great 'be-jaisus' gasp came from the assembled Irish folk. The wheels had caught the fence. The new-fangled flying-machine took a very old-fashioned purler and crashed out of view on the far side. There was not much around in the way of emergency services, but willing Irish hands and thumping Irish hearts went rushing over the meadow to see the extent of the catastrophe. But there was, thank God and His Mother, no burst of flames, and the 'big fellah' and his lady climbed out unhurt. The worst damage sustained was the image of the theatrical tycoon. It was sad anti-climax when he had to alter plans and resort to slow train and slower boat for the return journey.

Baylis was back—even more aware of mortality and saddened by the death of one of the founder fathers of the Old Vic, Sir Philip Ben Greet, the actor-producer. It was Greet who established the Vic habit of doing *Hamlet* every year, if possible to coincide with the time of Shakespeare's birthday. This year it would be a bit late, as Guthrie waited for his popular young star, Laurence Olivier.

Rehearsals began for *Love's Labours Lost*—three or four intensive weeks of sweated rehearsal up in the big, dusty top room of the Old Vic. They started promptly at 10 a.m.—and God help any latecomer. There was no Reading—'You all know the play, of course'—and straight into Act One, Scene One. Hard work, much fun. 'Yes, dearie, *Love's Labour is* a romp. But you are not on court at a Streatham tennis party. You are in the court of Navarre. (Clap.) Now do it again!' There was an element of the military in the number of times he would 'drill' them through a scene.

Ernest Milton, that beautifully affected actor with the superlative voice and Bensonian style, was on-stage in rehearsal:

'Tawn-nay!'

'Yaas?' (From Tony Guthrie in stalls, between sips of thermos flask tea dispensed by Judy Guthrie.)

'Want to career right round the well as I deliver this speech.' (There was a well in the set.)

'Don't know what you mean by "career". Show us, Ernest.'

Ernest Milton makes a beautiful but distractingly exhibitionist parade around the well, while delivering the lines.

Guthrie: 'Yaas! I see. Cut the career! On!' Clap.

Alec Guinness, quietly working like mad, got a shock on the first days on-stage. The cast were all using those little maroon-coloured and well-worn editions of the Temple Shakespeare.

Stub in hand, head down to his book, he was suddenly startled by
the loud hand-clap.

Guthrie: 'What are you doing?'

Guinness: 'I'm marking my moves in my . . .'

Guthrie: 'Then don't do it. Never do that. You have enough
talent in you that if I give you a bad move you'll forget it. If it's
right you'll just naturally not forget. So—*Don't* do it. On!'

Love's Labours Lost was an easy beginning, a good 'romp' that
Guthrie knew all too well. It was a fair success and the part of
Boyet gave Guinness a good beginning at the Vic. It also gave
Guthrie a special piece of satisfaction—in the shape of a letter of
appreciation, from no other than that great authority on Shakespeare, Dover Wilson: 'How very greatly I enjoyed the performance . . . I had (I am glad to say) never seen it before but I
am bold to think that no producer has ever understood it since
the 17th century until you gave it us . . . What a lovely thing the
play is!'

Ruth Gordon arrived, and they found that they got on together
famously. *The Country Wife* in rehearsal was a joy; but not for
Alec Guinness. Once again we see Tony Guthrie standing away
from a skirmish and going ruthlessly on to win the battle.
Guinness was playing a small part (which meant in a Guthrie
production that it should be as important as any star part). It
involved a scene with Ruth Gordon as Mrs. Pinchwife. She
stopped in full flight, 'Tow-nee!' she resorted to broad American
accent in exasperation. 'I cayn't act with this man. C'n we have
another acter?' This really was ruthless, but standard, Broadway
behaviour. Guinness confesses that he was neither good nor happy
in the part. And Broadway professionalism says that if an actor
isn't good he's gotta go. Guthrie dismissed Guinness, recast the
part, and let the shocked actor go, without saying a word more
about it. Hurt and disappointed in himself, as well as in Guthrie,
Guinness went to Miss Baylis's office to collect the compensation
money due to him, if he was to be out of work for some weeks—
£12. He was given £3! You didn't argue with Baylis, but he
expected Guthrie to talk to him of the incident. He never did. It
was Edith Evans who came round to the young actor's dressing-
room. 'You are not to worry . . . Everybody has to lose a part some
day. Better now. And I think you are going to be a star, dear boy.'

This was indeed comfort. Why was there no comfort from
Guthrie? Because, in the Guthrie-Wellingtonian principles of

conduct, hard knocks are good for the young man. One takes the blow, doesn't blub and gets on with the work. I can recollect a day when I, myself, suffered personal tragedy. I was in a deep state of self-pity and I poured out my young heart to Tony. Judy came in. It was at Lincoln's Inn. His report to her of my agony was 'James has been blubbering again'. It cauterized the wound all right. And, in that particular case, I know this was exactly his purpose. Rise above!

The Country Wife was a great success. Edith Evans and Ruth Gordon were both terrific, and Michael Redgrave justified all the Guthrie hopes in him. Oliver Messel's décor was delightful. Eyebrows of governors were raised at the eighteenth-century immorality but the play played to laughter and full houses, the pounds and pence flowed in at the box-office. Happy director (successful showman) saw a happy Miss Gordon—and the scenery —off to New York.

So far so good. Now to *As You Like It*. Edith Evans wanted to play Rosalind. 'Can't agree with that.' 'Why?' they asked Guthrie. And they got the reason with brutal clarity: 'Edith is too old.' But Edith insisted. Guthrie was informed. So he handed over the production to Esmé Church ('wasn't going to be a party to fiasco'). Edith Evans, as Rosalind, was superbly convincing, very moving and utterly lyrical. The curtain came down to loud bravoes. Guthrie hurried round and before all the company he said—as he was always ready to say—'Was *quite* wrong, dear. Marvellous! Well done. Wish I had done it myself, Esmé.'

The Witch of Edmonton, mostly by Dekker, might seem a strange choice for the guest producer, Michel Saint-Denis. Yet Swinburne says of Dekker: '. . . the hand of Dekker; his intimate and familiar sense of wretchedness, his great and gentle spirit of compassion for the poor and suffering with whom his own lot in life was so often cast, in prison and out . . . the poignant simplicity . . .' All this was sympathetic stuff and the right territory for the compassionate man of the people, Saint-Denis. Rehearsals would start with a deliberate and slow exposition of the play and there would be none of the off-the-cuff Guthrie instant-creation. The production was interesting, but not a great success. It was, however, another triumph for Edith Evans. She went from one end of the age-scale, as Rosalind, to the other to play the old Witch—Mother Sawyer. It would take time for the great gifts of Michel Saint-Denis to adjust to the necessities of the Vic. Besides, this politically-conscious man was deeply distracted at the time by what was happening nearer his own country across the English Channel.

Christmas was on the way. The growing international tragedy was obscured by a more domestic and royal drama. Scenes: Buckingham Palace and Palace of Westminster. Cast: Mrs. Wallis Simpson, Edward VIII, Stanley Baldwin. Subject: The Abdication of a Monarch. A more universal family drama however engaged all Guthrie's attention: the tragedy of Hamlet Prince of Denmark. He was deep in the study of the play. He was deep in the study of Freud too. He started via the writings of Ernest Jones, the biographer of Freud. One could say that, as Olivier made his entry into the Old Vic, Freud made his entry too and Tony Guthrie was responsible. He had read, and had been deeply impressed by, a published paper of Ernest Jones's. It dealt with two plays, the *Hamlet* of Shakespeare and the *Oedipus* of Sophocles; both dramas of royal succession, sins of the father, and son's desperate attachment to beloved mother. 'Oedipus Biggs'; he who had played Tiresias; a son who had been haunted by a puzzling dead father—Guthrie being all these things, why should he not be fascinated and deeply affected by what he read? Oedipus comes later into those private anguishes which rightly inform the art of any sensitive artist; and he *was* sensitive. Even Lilian Baylis was now prepared to say that though he had a mind like a crystal he had 'the heart of a child'. *Hamlet* was really the first stage classic he produced in depth, simply because in princeliness and sexuality there was much of Hamlet in him.

This paper of Dr. Jones maintained that Hamlet's famous hesitancy in killing Claudius at prayer had nothing to do with a playwright's cheat to prolong the play to a popular length. It was because the prince was so much in love with his mother the Queen that he secretly longed for all the sexual liberties taken with her by his usurping uncle; that therefore he had good grounds to doubt the purity of his motives in bloody retribution. There is a phrase of Ernest Jones which must have struck below the belt as Guthrie read it in the Lincoln's Inn attic: 'The whole picture is not, as Goethe depicted it, one of a gentle soul crushed beneath a colossal task, but one of a strong man tortured by some mysterious inhibition.'*

In Gielgud's Hamlet he had seen the 'gentle soul' and heard the

---

* *Oedipus and Hamlet*, Essays in Applied Psycho-analysis, Dr. Ernest Jones, The International Psycho-Analytical Press, London and Vienna, 1923.

princely sadness of that wonderful voice, so splendid in authority and sonority. But here, in Ernest Jones, was the tag by which he and his Hamlet—Olivier—could both identify. It might need all that twenty-nine-year-old actor's art to convince an already responsive female public that he suffered from any 'inhibitions' at all; but that he should love his mother, short of incest, that would add joy and increase the bookings from British Motherhood. Rehearsal was an exciting prospect to face.

It is not recorded what Baylis felt about this visitation of Freud through the Vic stage door. She probably felt *Hamlet* could stand it. *She* certainly could. Previously, when young actresses committed to *Measure for Measure* could not summon up the necessary sexuality, she had said, 'Now, dears, all we can do is go on our knees now and pray for lust.' She was a lot less prim than her producer.

The Guthrie-Olivier-Jones *Hamlet* opened on January 5, 1937; and was not an unqualified success. Perhaps Guthrie's company was too much of an ad hoc group, abounding in talent but not with any hope of achieving the ensemble playing necessary: Dorothy Dix (Gertrude), Francis L. Sullivan (Claudius), Robert Newton (Horatio), Cherry Cottrell (Ophelia). Perhaps Olivier, with his great respect for the intellect and intelligence of his director, went too far with him in stage strength and virility, but it was by no means a bad press: 'HAMLET'S FOUR-HOUR TRIUMPH—The best thing of the current theatre season . . .' said the *Daily Telegraph*, and at least one critic proved that Guthrie had put over the Ernest Jones point: 'He is dilatory in revenge, not because he is a gentle soul overwhelmed by his gigantic task. *He is a strong, dexterous man of the world caught by an inhibition.* He hangs back because of some repugnance neither he nor we understand.'*

Dropping into his dressing-room, Guthrie had wished Olivier good luck; then he had added, as Olivier completed his make-up, 'Yaas—every inch a Hamlet . . . Think they will fault you for lack of lyrical quality.' This was probably a way of making a director's last bit of direction tell on someone that he knew could take the spur. And it was true. The critics did. They also tended to fall into the old trap of thinking Hamlet, the part, was the whole play. So did the Welsh oracle himself, Dr. Ernest Jones:

* Ibid.

81, Harley Street,
London.

8th January 1937.

Dear Mr. Guthrie,

. . . I was present at the first three acts last evening, having unfortunately to leave after that time . . .

One very serious fault was the old custom of playing Polonius as a clown, though I have never before seen the terrible gaffe of having Laertes and Ophelia giggling at each other . . . Now for the Prince of Denmark. You will not of course expect me, who have known Hamlet himself, to be content with any human substitute.

Mr. Olivier . . . played well and understandingly the scenes with the Queen. But . . . temperamentally he is not cast for Hamlet. He is, personally what we call 'manic' and so finds it hard to play a melancholic part . . . Then I hastily concur on the severe strictures which have been passed on his gabbling the words, to the ruin of the beautiful and sonorous poetry and philosophy they are meant to convey . . . Hamlet is thinking aloud, not chatting to bystanders . . .

P.S. You will of course not convey my opinion to Mr. Olivier while he is still playing the part.

But the great psychologist was not only a little wrong about the Olivier Hamlet, he was quite wrong about Polonius.

Polonius is admittedly an old bore, and . . . it is common practice to let the young man and his sister show an inclination to catch each other's eye and giggle, and fail to take the old gentleman seriously. Mr. Guthrie follows this practice up to a point . . . But, when he comes to the really fine concluding lines:

> 'This above all, to thine own self be true,
> And it follows, as the night the day,
> Thou canst not then be false to any man—'

he makes Laertes turn suddenly serious and touch his father's hand with a sudden gesture of affection . . . it told us something new and revealing.*

The play ran well. Baylis could note that while de Valois with her Ballet was building up reserves at the Wells, Guthrie with his Drama was plenishing the Vic treasury.

* W. A. Darlington in *The Daily Telegraph*.

Everything was building—except a company. Baylis could not be unpleased. Guthrie was allowed to get out of harness to direct *Love And How To Cure It* at the Globe, the first Thornton Wilder play he ever did. When he was preparing his *Twelfth Night* in which Olivier would play Sir Toby Belch, Guinness, Sir Andrew Aguecheek and Jessica Tandy, Viola, an interesting incident occurred. Esmé Church's production of *As You Like It*, with the Edith Evans Rosalind, had transferred to the West End. It was doing pretty good business at the New but, for some managerial reason, Bronson Albery was taking it off to bring in another play. Edith Evans and the whole company thought this was more than a pity, would Tony please speak to Mr. Albery. 'Ya-as,' he said, got on a bus, went part of the way, got off, came back and said, 'Sorry—not my business.' Again it appeared to be the question of minor tactics which could be damaging to the grand strategy. The grand strategy now was the building up of forces preparatory to assault on the larger objective of National Theatre. Bronson Albery was to be an influential figure in that and was already a governor of the Old Vic; where the real guvn'r, Lilian Baylis, said, 'National Theatre! I don't care a dash about the National Theatre. When I think of all the work that has been done by our three companies . . . I know we are the National Theatre.'

Twelfth Night was no failure, but *Henry V* was to be the big show for that national 'big day'—the Coronation of George VI in May. With its burst of national pride over Agincourt, it was thought suitable fare to be running at the Old Vic then. Tony Guthrie had a weakness for banners. Now, with a national theatre and the cry of 'God for Harry, England and St. George!', it was going to be banners, banners, all the way.

But, for all the flag-waving, both Guthrie and Olivier were next door to pacifists by nature. They really did not greatly subscribe to what they considered to be the Bard's military jingoism. In fact, they had more or less agreed that they would play the play tongue-in-cheek. There would be winks and nudges and definitely no heroic militarism. Olivier actually began by disliking to a considerable degree Henry's great St. Crispin Day speech. Yet, day by day, as they both got more and more involved with the play, Shakespeare and Art began to win, and eventually the nation's pride trumpeted out from that famous Olivier 'baritone with brilliance at the top'. On the night of April 6, 1937, it was

6*

England's impassioned Harry who blazed forth from a forest of banners on the Vic stage. Charles Laughton, breathing hard, and hot from his own triumph as Rembrandt in that glowing film, trundled round from his seat in the stalls and almost embraced Olivier in his dressing-room. 'You *are* England!' he cried. In the stage-box Lilian Baylis cried 'You are outrageous!' at Guthrie. And outrageous it was that *he*—of all people—should have sent the whole cast and company home (a hundred at least) from their last dress rehearsal by taxi! But now that they had the gallery cheering them, Guthrie was given the accolade of instant pardon, from the stage-box.

A piece of remarkable news came from Christopher Scaife. At the Westminster he was going to play Hamlet to Gillian's Gertrude. This was Hamlet time with a vengeance. The Vic company had just been invited to travel to Denmark and to reproduce the Guthrie production of that play on the battlements of Kronborg Castle at Elsinore. (The following summer he would again be tackling *Hamlet*—this time with Guinness.)

The Elsinore visit proved to be of first importance to him on two counts. First, that it drew Lilian Baylis and him to a full and deep understanding of each other. Second, that it suddenly convinced him of the necessity to break away from the tyranny of the proscenium arch stage. At Kronborg Castle, which sits by the sea, rehearsals with the company went ahead, in the castle courtyard, on the ramparts, and in part rain, part shine, and through the Danish night so as not to impede the daily tourist traffic. Sometimes Guthrie in a long, wet flapping mac, damp against flapping flannels, would be bawling out Danish cadets who were trying to be Fortinbras's army, or in sun and wind getting brilliant Olivier to forget that he was madly in love with the actress playing the part opposite and that all he had to do was convince Denmark that Vivien Leigh was simply mad Ophelia; and convince Guthrie too that this was wise casting. Because, right after their return to England, Vivien Leigh and Laurence Olivier were to make the difficult announcement to their respective spouses that they wished to be free to marry again. This disturbed Tony Guthrie who never liked to see families in upheaval. But all was set for the first night. Celebrities and Danish royalty were on the way—to this open air performance. The rain came down, it kept coming down. Lilian Baylis stood in the doorway of the hotel, glanced up at the sky, stabbed an accusing finger at the Author of the bellropes of rain and said, 'This has got to stop!' Should the performance be cancelled? Could it be? Guthrie kept his nerve and, like a general in the field, he made his decision. In their grand hotel the ballroom had sufficient space to seat the audience and to play the play. Shakespeare's company playing in some baronial hall had probably faced worse. Everyone—including international journalists covering the event—became organized under Guthrie direction. Gilded chairs were laid about in a half circle, players were briefed in new exits and new entrances. A crisis occurred in 'our exits and our entrances'. One of the hotel's custodians firmly—and for what seemed a mysterious reason— refused to make one closed door available for any exit or any entrance. The reason proved to be that a bird was nesting above it; eggs or nestlings might have been cruelly cast out. '*Quite* understand,' Guthrie, the countryman of Annagh-ma-Kerrig, would have said.

He watched the play begin, and Lilian Baylis watched too; with scepticism. The play played with quite remarkable effect, entirely liberated from any 'stage'. It started Guthrie revising his whole idea of the sort of playhouse there should be for the plays of Shakespeare. The way he had handled this emergency also fully revised Lilian Baylis's opinion of him. Difficult though Guthrie might have been, he was not the iconoclast she, good Anglo-Catholic, had feared. As she said of him he was 'one of the elect'.

Faithful Prevost noticed the happiness and return of spirit in Baylis, who had lately been so low in health (heart complicated by diabetes). But Evelyn Williams, Annette Prevost and all those close to her were keeping a watchful eye.

Lilian Baylis had said to her beloved confessor, Father Andrew, 'I know that if I go on as I'm going my work will kill me, but I don't see why it should be otherwise.'* Then something of a sign was given to them at the start of the season. On opening night it was the custom of Baylis to give to members of the company and staff sprigs of white heather. This year the sprigs she handed out were symbolic of *Hamlet* and farewell; they were of rosemary.

Xtopher was at the Westminster, rehearsing his *Hamlet*, under the direction of Michael MacOwan. By all accounts the Scaife Hamlet was intelligent, academic, anti-romantic and played with lights more or less full up throughout the performance; a

* *Lilian Baylis*, Richard Findlater. Allen Lane, 1975.

concession to the daylight of the wooden'O' of the play's place of origin. Guthrie came, saw, said little, but he did determine to do *Hamlet* again in the Vic's next season. For the rest of the summer Judy and he were off to the South of France—St. Tropez. This was not for a rich man's holiday. He had at last—in a minor way —been 'placed' in films: as an actor! He went on location in the Mediterranean sun to play a part with Charles Laughton and Elsa Lanchester, in *Vessel of Wrath*. The part he was to play was the Presbyterian equivalent of a whisky priest rotting on a tropical isle. The image he made in the footage allowed was remarkably memorable. In the sun he was cooking plans which were to be announced as 'New Plans For The Vic—The Repertory System'. In fact it was more repertoire than repertory. At Cambridge he'd seen enough of the non-artistic tyranny of 'weekly-rep'. The new plans simply got the company off the hook of having to stick to a specified three-week run, which had tied it to keeping failures on and forced it to take successes off. He was introducing to The People's Theatre a degree of commercial flexibility.

First productions of the season were to be *Richard II* and *Macbeth*. An interesting complication arose, which emphasized the competition and the co-operation between Guthrie at the Old Vic and Gielgud in the West End. It was the culmination then of the Gielgud productions of the classics which had begun at Bronson Albery's New Theatre. To these productions Gielgud drew the sort of company of talented players proper to a national theatre. They were drawn to the famous Queen's Theatre seasons because not only was Gielgud a great actor/director, he was able to pay them an adequate salary, which the Vic was not. The surprising achievement at the Queen's was that he was making the classics succeed—*in the West End*.

In this season, by coincidence, he too planned to produce *Macbeth* and *Richard II*. Guthrie, Olivier and he got together. It was agreed to split the difference; Gielgud, at the Queen's, would play his *Richard II*, Olivier, at the Old Vic, his *Macbeth*. Guthrie invited Saint-Denis (whose greatest London success was probably the superb *The Three Sisters* with the Gielgud company) to produce the Old Vic *Macbeth*. He in turn was invited to direct the Gielgud company in *The School for Scandal*, at the Queen's.

By the time those two productions got into rehearsal it was a grim November, nationally and internationally. Lord Halifax was preaching Appeasement to a growingly aggressive Adolf Hitler. The whole tragedy of the Spanish Civil War was coming through. Many of the more radical players and friends of players at the Westminster's Group Theatre, the Old Vic, and the Gielgud company too, had been volunteers in the International Brigade. They had seen and been appalled by the atrocity of a war where bombers dominated the sky.

At the Vic, November was rendered more grey by the fact that 'The Lady' was beginning to show serious 'heart' symptoms. But rehearsals for *Macbeth* began, with Michel Saint-Denis and company. Guthrie at the Queen's rehearsed *School for Scandal*, and came and went across the bridge, keeping an eye on the office, 'The Lady' and the company.

Laurence Olivier maintains that he probably learnt more from Saint-Denis than from any other producer. The Frenchman simply was an inspired teacher. He was also an inspired director, but his speed of production was geared more to the sort of thorough and laborious work related to the Moscow Arts Theatre and Les Copeaux, than to the semi-commercial pressures of the Old Vic.

Baylis, in her stage-box, saw the sudden contrast to the push and thrust of the finger-snapping Tony Guthrie. And she worried how long the pipe-smoking, thoughtful Frenchman would take over the matter of his masks, lighting, music, when he spent such care and time with the players. Guthrie's production at the Queen's was to open on Thursday the 25th; Saint-Denis's *Macbeth* on Tuesday the 23rd. On the night of the final dress rehearsal at the Vic—Monday the 22nd—Guthrie looked in after his own day's work was done. Baylis was there, with Annette Prevost and George Chamberlain. The Guthrie eagle eye was watching; looks and remarks were passing between the regular staff; Saint-Denis worked on. It was very late and Baylis would not leave her box. At 3 a.m. they were still far from half-way through the play. It became obvious to all the regular company there that they could not possibly be ready to open on the night of that same day. An anxious conference took place. Around dawn, Guthrie took the responsibility of deciding that the opening would have to be postponed, till Friday the 26th. The company went home. It had never happened before. Baylis was driven home, to Stockwell Park Road, by Prevost, tired out and distressed. How could she tell her people there would be no first night on the advertised date? She could not rest and when full morning came she insisted that she must get back to the theatre; she had to arrange to pay the company, and only she could sign the treasury cheques. Prevost prevailed on her to stay while she went to the theatre to get the cheques. Ethel Dunning, Lilian Baylis's sister, who was staying with them, was left at home with her. At the theatre Prevost found George Chamberlain, Miss Williams and others very concerned to know what to tell the press. They were on the telephone. Prevost took the call. To give the real reason might be greatly to hurt Saint-Denis. She said he had been in a taxi accident, which was true if not quite up-to-date, but that the final reason for the postponement was that Laurence Olivier had a severe cold. This was true and she quickly got an obliging Olivier to be ready to vouch for its severity. But the main concern of Olivier and the others there was, how was Lilian? Prevost assured them she was all right and drove back with the pay cheques. Baylis signed them, seemed better and got her to drive her down to the Box Hill summer cabin, so that she could tidy up for the winter.

That evening when they got back to Stockwell Park Road her sister began fussing and fretting over Lilian. Ethel had suffered marital troubles and was in a somewhat neurotic state. She had complained about the quality of the wine in the house. So, they encouraged her to go out and buy whatever wine she wanted. She went, taking Sue, the dog, with her; while Prevost put the car away. Within a surprisingly short time the door flew open, Ethel ran in, crying hysterically and clutching something, which she threw into the lap of the shocked Baylis. It was Sue. She was dead—run over crossing the street. The effect on Baylis was shattering. Signs began to show on her face which alarmed Prevost. It was a mild 'stroke'. She got the inconsolable Ethel calmed down, got the pathetic little corpse out of Baylis's lap, and got her to bed, having called the doctor. By the time the doctor arrived the heart attack was over, but she was not to be moved or excited in any way. However with her dear little bitch dead and no hope of getting to the theatre now, even for the opening on Friday, she was unable to rest, unable to sleep. Next day she said to Prevost, 'I would say a prayer if I wasn't so bad-tempered.' She called Father Andrew to say that she could not come to confession as she had arranged. He said he would come over. 'No. I should hate you to see me as I am. I'm not fit to be seen.' So he said, 'God bless you, my dear.' And she replied, 'I was just waiting for you to say that.'*

That night Guthrie went into the long night of his own dress rehearsal, trying to keep the zest in the comedy. Next day, when *Macbeth* was in its final rehearsal, Annette Prevost came into the theatre. She spoke with George Chamberlain. He asked Michel Saint-Denis to interrupt his rehearsal. They all knew. George Chamberlain announced to the assembled company Miss Baylis was dead. In the shocked silence he added that she had expressly stated before she died that nothing should stand in the way of the play opening, as planned, the following night, Friday.

Guthrie heard the news as he was going into the run up to his first night. It was a great shock to him and Judy; also to Gielgud, Guinness, Redgrave, and all about to play comedy. It was not the easiest of first nights, nor the best of Guthrie productions. After it one can only guess how long he wept up in their Lincoln's Inn flat—for Guthrie was a great private weeper.

Poor Michel Saint-Denis was desperately disturbed, for he felt —not knowing about the shock of Lilian Baylis's beloved dog's death—that the postponement of the first night had been the cause of the stroke which killed her. *Macbeth* opened the following night. And before the curtain went up Lord Lytton, chairman of the governors, came before the curtain and paid a dignified and moving tribute to their great lady. Tony Guthrie rose to his huge height as he saw all around him, in stalls, circle and gallery, rise to their feet, in silent tribute to 'our Miss Baylis'. Eyes went to where, in the stage-box, Miss Williams stood beside an empty chair. Up at the Wells, too, Ninette de Valois spoke before the curtain of her ballet *Job*, and that audience stood in silence too. Next morning, on the same page of *The Times* were three columns, one on the death of Lilian Baylis, one on *Macbeth*, one on *The School for Scandal*. The last two were the least impressive. Yet *Macbeth* drew good houses and later transferred to the New Theatre.

Sybil Thorndike wrote immediately to Guthrie:

I feel I must write to you because I know how you will be feeling Lilian's death. I saw it in the paper coming here from Liverpool to-day and I feel heartbroken. I loved her so and in very difficult years . . . because of the struggle and the war-life

* *Lilian Baylis*, Richard Findlater. Allen Lane, 1975.

then. My thoughts went straight to you in gratitude, that you have been the one helper who has fulfilled somehow her high hope of the Vic . . . She was great and really simple and really good—I know you will feel it. God bless her, she was happy this last year, wasn't she, you understood her so wonderfully . . .

Which he did. In the Guthrie story—one of the great female figures.

Up at the Wells Ninette de Valois kept the Ballet (her own 'Islington Dancers') on course, and Guthrie kept things going at the Vic, greatly assisted by George Chamberlain, who now set up house with his beloved and bereft Prevost. At the end of the season, the *News Chronicle* reported:

> Tyrone Guthrie . . . his lean length swathed in a high-necked sweater and a loose overcoat, sat on a stool and talked yesterday of the fact that the Old Vic and Sadler's Wells had made a working profit for the first time, during the 1936–1937 season.
>
> With regard to The Wells, that's even more amazing (he said). Producing Opera and Ballet, with chorus and orchestra, and still to show a profit—why, it's phenomenal. And if you want yet another answer to the success—you can say 'Shakespeare'. The old man's having a real come-back.

Guthrie was now, de facto, 'the Manager'. If the nation had a future, his future could be in National Theatre. The remaining production in that politically grim year was all fun and fantasy. In the wake of Christmas hundreds of children trooped to the Vic to see the Guthrie *Midsummer Night's Dream*, played to the full Mendelssohn score and with sets by Oliver Messel in Early Victorian style. Robert Helpmann, the emerging star of Ballet, was brought down from the Wells to play Oberon to Vivien Leigh's Titania; the Wells corps de ballet, directed by Ninette de Valois, had added to it a flying ballet of young fairies, a hazardous but thrilling aerial invasion of the Vic stage. Ralph Richardson came back to the company to play Bottom the Weaver. It all added up to a real Christmas festival event. It was made into a royal event when two of the children hurrying to see it were the little Princesses, Elizabeth and Margaret, with their mother the Queen.

After Christmas it was straight into rehearsals for *Othello*, with

On tour with the Scottish National Players

Flora Robson in the Guthrie production of *Iphigenia in Tauris*, the Cambridge Festival Theatre, 1929

Tony with his mother, soon after her
blindness, at the front door of
Annagh-ma-Kerrig (c.1929)

'Prayer session' by the
honeymoon tent;
Tony and Judy

Picnic pairs:
Hubert, Peggy,
Judy, Tony

With Charles Laughton, during Guthrie's first season with the Old Vic
(1933-34)

With Vivien Leigh and Laurence Olivier at rehearsal of the Olivier *Hamlet* in
the courtyard of Kronberg Castle, Elsinore, 1937

The Guthries with the Old Vic group during wartime evacuation at Burnley;
including (6th from left) Annette Prevost; (8th from left) George Chamberlain;
(in front of him, to right) Esmé Church, Evelyn Williams (with bouquet);
Sybil and Lewis Casson

The Three Estates, the Assembly Hall, Edinburgh. *Photo Paul Shillabeer*

Ralph Richardson playing the Moor and Laurence Olivier, Iago. By this they were to renew—and almost to wreck—their happy theatrical partnership. The trouble had to do with Guthrie's return to Psychology—and to Dr. Ernest Jones. This time Guthrie and Olivier went along together to visit the great man in his Regent's Park residence. It was like consulting the oracle. Ernest Jones had a noble, white-haired, head and the manner of a Welsh seer. But where was he leading the pair? Olivier describes his alarm at the direction the consultations were taking: 'The clue to the play (the Doctor maintained) was not Iago's hatred of Othello, but his deep *affection* for him. His jealousy was not because he envied Othello's position, not because he was in love with Desdemona, but because he himself possessed a subconscious affection for the Moor, the homosexual foundation of which he did not understand.'

As they left the house of the priest of Freud, Olivier said to ruminating Guthrie: 'What do you think of it?—the theory?'

Guthrie: 'Think it's inescapable—on an unconscious plane of course.'

Olivier: 'Of course. I don't think we dare tell Ralphy—do you?'*

They did not. Rehearsals went on; with a growing uneasiness in Richardson. The uneasiness came to a climax when Olivier, faithfully following the Guthrie/Jones line, gave the shocked Ralph a kiss. When it was explained to him, he just stared at his Iago, and said, 'Poor fellow.' Richardson then went on to play in a way doubly resistant to Freud and those psychological fellows. This could hardly be a good foundation for Shakespeare in depth. It was not.

In the weeks following the opening of *Othello* there was a reply from Lady Gooch (acting chairman of the governors) to a letter Guthrie had written her. It had to do with internal politics and the future of the Vic, and the now perennial debate about National Theatre. Guthrie had said that he did not want the governors to feel that they were under any obligation to him, 'should the situation arise in which the Old Vic and the National Shakespeare Memorial Theatre might work together or coalesce in the future'. This was an angle Guthrie diplomacy was often to take. He'd seem —in a very Irish way—to render himself dispensable at a time when he was nearly indispensable. The effect was predictable.

* *The Oliviers*, Felix Barker. Hamish Hamilton, 1953.

Lady Gooch assured him that the situation referred to had not come to pass. Besides 'the governors are *entirely* satisfied with the work you have done and are doing at the Old Vic and cannot speak too highly of it'. She also said how thrilled she had been with the *Dream*, and how she had known his father, and would Judy and he come to lunch on Sunday?

It was in an atmosphere of success and with a feeling that he was trusted that he planned the next season. He went to the Queen's Theatre, scouting for talent which could be coaxed over to the Vic. The play at the Queen's was *The Merchant of Venice*, with Gielgud's Shylock and Alec Guinness's Lorenzo. He went round to give praise where praise was due—which was high and general. He had a word with Guinness: 'Like to talk to you. Will be in my office at the Vic tomorrow afternoon.' Guinness went, wondering. Guthrie went straight to the point: 'Thought you were very good. Would like you to come back to us. Now, what is there?...' Then, decisively: 'Think you should give us your Hamlet. What about that?'

It took some time for young Guinness to get his breath. This, so soon, in the shadow of the great Gielgud Hamlets and right in the footsteps of Olivier? Guthrie continued: 'Modern dress—but don't think it should be aggressively modern—no cigarettes.'

Guinness agreed. He had just become engaged to an actress playing one of Portia's ladies in Venetian Belmont, Merula Salaman. Tony and Judy invited them both to come to Annagh-ma-Kerrig right after the marriage. This turned their honeymoon into an incredible 'busman's holiday'. Production discussions during walks to woods and lake were followed by rehearsals which, to a strange degree, brought Theatre back right into the Guthrie home. Upstairs in Annagh-ma-Kerrig at the back of the house is a huge and neglected room with pitched roof and ceiling of dark timbered beams. It had for many years been referred to by the family as 'the concert room'. In fact the report survives from Dr. Moorehead's time of the occasion when Martha, now Lady Power, first introduced her husband, General Sir William, there: the annual Harvest Home celebrations, September 1870. After the introductions and a song, 'Mr. Dane then performed some very amusing tricks. At a subsequent part of the entertainment Mr. Dane and Mr. Maguire gave the celebrated "Dagger Scene" in Macbeth, in a way that "brought down the house" in prolonged applause'.

It was amid these echoes from the past that Guthrie and Guinness rehearsed Shakespeare; and the Guinness Hamlet began to take shape. They both enjoyed themselves enormously. There was an unusual spark of response between these two men of alert intellect.

The production plan for Hamlet was, cautiously, to lead in to London by playing it first up in Buxton. There the Vic company had been invited for the second time to the Buxton Theatre Festival. The full bill was *Hamlet* and *Trelawny of The Wells*, both directed by Guthrie, and *The Rivals* directed by Esmé Church. In Buxton—a spa, like Tunbridge Wells—in its Opera House, the Vic season opened and was a summer success. Back in London *Trelawny* opened the season at the Vic. Then, on October 11, *Hamlet* opened. It was not a star-studded company, but one that played with unusual intelligence and subtlety. Visually it was like a film in black and white. Guthrie ranks it along with his *Enemy of the People* (which he did some months later) as the best of his productions at that time. In retrospect, Guthrie said of Guinness then, 'His youth, combined with rare intelligence, humour, pathos, realized a great deal of the part. He had not yet quite the authority to support, as Hamlet must, a whole evening, or to give the tragedy its full stature. The performance demanded that the public reach out and take what was offered. To this demand the public is rarely equal.'

John Gielgud—who had opened the door that got Guinness into Theatre—wrote to Guthrie:

I saw *Hamlet* yesterday . . . and was stirred and provoked. I was deeply touched by Alec's performance, which I thought grew in distinction and quality all the time as it went on . . . I thought that the Recorder's scene was fussed by the busyness of the production, and you haven't got any further than anyone else in solving the problem of the ghost. I also hated the new punctuation, but perhaps that is only my Terry blood crying out . . . I was terrifically moved by the closet scene, almost the best I have ever seen . . .

Its opening had the misfortune to clash with a Priestley first night in the West End and the first-line critics did not attend. At the end of the week Guthrie, grabbing a rest with the Donat family out in Buckinghamshire, wrote to his mother in some despair:

Hamlet isn't doing well . . . Alec is much *much* better in the part than Larry, but Larry with his beautiful head and athletic sexy movements and bursts of fireworks are what the public wants.

It represents my very utmost effort. It's easily the best work I've done so far and may well be the best I shall do—in this job, as in all semi-creative work experience tends to kill invention and it is a blow to have it fall very flat.

He then went on to show the Guthrie concern and understanding for the actor:

It's been far more difficult for Alec to weather. The actor's position to success or failure is so terribly personal. The work of art is inseparable from himself. It's *him* 'they' like or fail to like. And it's a very personal ordeal to have to tussle thro' that enormous physical effort to empty houses. Still he's got great spirit and sense of proportion and the houses tho' empty are immensely enthusiastic and nearly all the people whose opinion we value have been sincerely and wholeheartedly praising him.

The poor Old Vic . . . The Westminster Bank rings up—but literally *every morning*—to say what about the overdraft.

It was the time of the Munich crisis. Without much heart for rehearsal, Guthrie produced a comedy by Robert Morley called *Goodness How Sad* and it was successful. But rumours were being spread of some Hitler-Mussolini combined plan to attack Britain. Civil Defence was instituted, and the London barrage balloons were going up. Flora, under contract to Hollywood, had sailed from this uneasy scene, to join Olivier and Vivien Leigh in the filming of *Wuthering Heights*. It was too anxious a time for Tony and Judy to go to Annagh-ma-Kerrig for Christmas; and it was bitterly cold. All about old Lincoln's Inn the ancient plumbing was producing a plague of burst pipes. 'We kept the gas fires going all night,' Tony wrote to Ireland as he went on to plan the formation of a company which had been invited to go on a tour of Europe and Asia Minor. It was hardly the right time but, under the firm paternal leadership of Lewis Casson, supported by Esmé Church and thirty-three players, including the Guinnesses and Anthony Quayle, this Vic company was preparing to take *Man and Superman, Henry V, Hamlet, Trelawney of The Wells, The Rivals,*

Libel, I Have Been Here Before, Viceroy Sarah and twelve tons of
scenery to Portugal, Italy, Egypt, Greece and Malta.

Before departure and on the last night of the company's performances at the Vic there came a rumble of protest from the
people of the People's Theatre. Tony wrote home ruefully:

> There's been quite a lot of opposition about the Coy's going
> to Italy ('shaking the bloodstained hand of Mussolini' etc., etc.:)
> letters to newspapers and people parading outside the theatre
> with banners, leaflets distributed to the audience etc. Scotland
> Yard warning of demo in theatre. Letter to Worseley (Vic
> treasurer) 'if no assurance was given of the Italian visit being
> abandoned', the writer would jump from the gallery . . . can
> you imagine??
>
> Lewis came fwd 'made a speech'. Art has no Frontiers etc:
> that the visit represented an offering from the *people*—not the
> government—the *people* who had given the world Shakespeare
> to the people who had given the world Dante and L. da Vinci
> (loud prolonged cheers) . . . all very nice but a teeny bit dis-
> appointing to those of us who were all ears for the thud of a
> body landing in row L.76 . . . It's so *cold*.

On January 20 the company left Waterloo Station, cheered off
by hundreds of enthusiasts. Guthrie went back across the road to
work on and produce a romping and lovely *She Stoops To Conquer*
followed by *An Enemy of the People*. Three days after the opening
of this very satisfactory production, and with the war clouds
gathering overhead, he received a letter from the chairman of
the governors, Lord Lytton. It began:

> Dear Mr. Guthrie,
>   At a special meeting of the Governors held yesterday, it was
> unanimously resolved to ask you to accept the post of Director
> of the two Theatres at a salary of £1,000.0.0. a year, plus a
> car allowance to be agreed. The appointment would be from
> March 25th next, and for a preliminary period of one year . . .

He had officially inherited the Baylis mantle. Her Opera, the
Ballet and the Old Vic—what he called 'the troika'—would now
be guided, and driven, by him. Ten days later Hitler's storm
troops rolled in to Czechoslovakia.

Guthrie went on to do *The Taming of the Shrew* and to plan to bring in true Repertory while preparing for a Third Buxton Festival. There was a brief visit to Annagh-ma-Kerrig that summer and then in to London came a real whiff of the peat fire and old Irish days. Here was the famous son of the house making sure he got away from his desk at the Vic to meet little old Mickie Corrigan at Waterloo Station. Mickie had been the coachman who once drove the jaunting car from Newbliss Station to Annagh-ma-Kerrig. He then became the chauffeur who polished the family motor car till its 'coat' shone like a well-groomed horse. Mickie was retiring. He was on his way to 'see London' *en route* for Tunbridge Wells. Tony walked with him over the bridge to Lincoln's Inn. They lunched and then Judy drove them to Westminster Pier. And if this does not seem important to us—it is important that Guthrie thought it was. From Westminster Tony rode the river-boat with him to Greenwich, all the way pointing out to the ageing little Irishman the historic sights. From the *Cutty Sark* and the Maritime Museum he took Mickie Corrigan back on the top of a bus. He then put him on the train for his destination, having taken as much trouble and time about this representative of their Irish Folk as he would if it had been the American Ambassador. This was typical Guthrie.

It was a considerable relief to welcome back the European Tour Company after their three months away. The European scene was beginning to look ugly. It was even believable now that the trenches and shelters in London would be put to use. As director of both theatres, Guthrie had moved his office up to Sadler's Wells and given the running of the Old Vic over to Murray MacDonald. Plans were completed for the summer and the company moved to Buxton.

On August 23—the day of the signing of the Hitler-Stalin Non-Aggression Pact—the Vic season opened at the Buxton Opera House. On September 1 Hitler's Storm Troops and Panzer Divisions invaded Poland. On the 3rd Neville Chamberlain's ultimatum to Hitler expired, and war was declared with Germany. The first air-raid sirens wailed over London; but no bombers came. On September 11 the Old Vic company opened in Buxton with Goldsmith's *The Good-Natured Man*, and had the distinction of giving England its first wartime first night.

In London the blackout of all lights and windows began. The evacuation of children to the countryside crowded the London rail termini with labelled juniors. Guinness was soon to join the

Navy; Quayle the Artillery. The Cassons' son, John, was off to the Air Force. Ralph Richardson went into the Fleet Air Arm. The drain of young and vital talent had begun from Theatre to 'theatres of war'.

In America, news of the declaration of war came to a shocked Flora in Hollywood. Laurence Olivier got the news on a sky-blue day on a peaceful luxury yacht lying in the blue waters off Los Angeles by Catalina Island. Olivier asked David Niven what they should do to get home; general mobilization was on. Niven had no problem. All he had to do was wait for orders (being a Reserve officer of the Regular Army)—meantime he was going to keep fit for anything. He dived off the boat and sensibly went for a swim.

What was Guthrie to do about the Vic and the company? They were still up in Buxton, with Robert Donat, Constance Cummings, Marie Ney and Max Adrian as leading players. His answer for the moment was: play—keep on playing.

He had written to his mother earlier, to say that if there *was* war he proposed to 'transfer the organization into the most suitable available hands and then volunteer wherever help is needed— *unless* the most helpful thing seems just to be going on with one's work . . .' Buxton became a strange scene. This out-of-the-way uncongested town amid the moorlands of Derbyshire was beginning to be exceptionally full of life; full of people who would have made up the ideal audience for London's West End. As air-raid sirens sounded in London and the larger cities of the South, into rural safety flooded a tide of the well-heeled and the fortunate, those who had no urgent national job to do were over-age and could afford to arrange their own, relatively comfortable, wartime evacuation.

Buxton 'box-office' was splendid. But Guthrie had his own private dilemma; quite apart from the public one of what to do with what he called 'the organization'. This was so different from Wellington in 1914. In his vague politics he was now an international socialist; anti-militarist in mind, yet military to his bones, in discipline, a proud Briton of Irish-Scottish extraction who by conviction could never quite be a pacifist. Yet to join the Army now? And what was the role of a national theatre in a nation at war? There were questions to be asked and answered before he could clearly see his way.

In London bombs did not immediately fall; but theatres closed.

CHAPTER THIRTEEN

WAR AGAIN

(*1939–1946*)

GUTHRIE'S USE of the term 'the troika' came from sleepless nights reading *Anna Karenina*. The three pedigree 'steeds' of the Drama, the Opera and the Ballet companies, which he had been hoping to drive towards one national objective, were now liable to be all over the place in a nation at war.

In his autobiography, he gives this period scant attention, in fact almost treats it as a hateful interruption to his life's work. Of course, for most of us who survived, it was so. And for him it was a period which had little to do with the direction of plays; but—with a vengeance—it had to do with his capacity for administration and executive command; a time of continuous emergencies which used, to a point of exhaustion, his gifts for getting by on a shoestring and rising to crises.

War had been declared. The British Expeditionary Force had crossed the Channel to reinforce the defences of France. But no bombs had fallen and the first thing that happened was, seemingly, nothing. His letters voiced positive annoyance; as if the grand spectacular of The Nation's Entry Into The War was being bloody badly directed. But if nothing seemed to be happening at the highest level, at least at the family level it gave him time for what *could* be a last meeting with Peggy. He wrote home to his mother from his Sadler's Wells office:

> . . . writing this before catching the train to Buxton, which I hope to reach at 10 tonight . . . Saw Hubert and Peggy yesterday. P. and I lunched alone together today . . . a *very nice talk*—happiest most intimate meeting for ages—we were able to feel such *deep* confidence and affection and communion.
>
> Air-raid sirens went at 6.45 y'day morning. I was awake, wakened Judy and we toddled down to our shelter (across yard in chapel) we'd left out warm clothes, g'masks, thermos, rugs etc: all to hand. It was very dull and everyone calm . . . at 9.5 the All Clear . . . I don't think one is likely to be in

London *very* much. Theatres in town are not likely to open . . .
I intend to go on trying to place the Vic-Wells organization
at the service of any authority which can make good use of us
. . . Hubert and P will be arriving with you *very* soon.

So, Mother and family were well placed to survive. Central
London theatres were still not encouraged to open. When the
Old Vic Company moved back down to London it went to the
suburban Streatham Hill Theatre, and played there during
October while Guthrie, George Chamberlain, Annette Prevost
and Miss Williams—now his secretary—established their Sadler's
Wells office as a sort of wartime HQ for the Troika.

During the first months of 1940 Number One of the Troika,
the Vic Drama Company, pulled its weight steadily. In the con-
tinual lull it was even able to get back into the Old Vic. John
Gielgud and Lewis Casson drew faithful audiences to good business. Gielgud played his Lear, followed by his Prospero. But
Guthrie worried specially about Number Two—the Opera. With
a war on, who would go to see Opera? The answer to that
surprised everybody. By September Tony was writing to his
mother and Peggy to say that *Faust* had been so well attended that
'the company had only lost four and sevenpence on the production!' By the end of October—even with bombs now falling—
he wrote again that *Madame Butterfly* had broken all box-office
records at the Wells. The third 'steed' of the Troika, the Ballet
Company, with Ninette de Valois in command, was doing
remarkably well too. And it was the Ballet that gave the Vic-
Wells organization its first brush with the grim realities of
'blitzkrieg'. The Ballet Company had their own Dunkirk.

In the spring of 1940 the company was in Holland. By arrangement with the British Council they had gone to tour the garrison
towns of the British Expeditionary Force. Suddenly the London
headlines announced the 'Nazi Invasion of the Netherlands'.
George and Annette Chamberlain, who now lived not ten
minutes from Sadler's Wells, hurried up from their Wharton
Street house to the Wells HQ. The Guthries came up from
Lincoln's Inn to join Miss Williams and them. Phones started
buzzing to the British Council and the Dutch Embassy. Guthrie
takes up the story:

Thursday night we knew they were dancing at Arnhem.
4 *a.m. Friday* Arnhem invaded.

9 a.m. Friday B. Council in touch with B. Legation at The Hague, all Sadler's Wells ballet together and safe in The Hague.

Friday–Saturday Press reports of bombings, parachutes, etc.

Saturday night Legation phones they hope to get them away by boat.

Sunday morning Legation phones that they are *on* a boat waiting to sail. Meantime pressmen ring up to say Reuter telegraphs that they are on a boat near Amsterdam. Legation phones they are on a boat the mouth of the North Sea Canal (connects Amsterdam with sea).

Monday teatime We hear they are at Harwich.

Monday 9 p.m. Train due L'pool St. Station 11.

At 11 p.m. Liverpool St. Station—Williams, Judy, Bridges Adams (rep. British Council) 20 pressmen and a multitude of tremendously excited Mums, Dads, Aunties and Sympathisers.

At 1 a.m. The train still hadn't left Harwich—hundreds of refugees to be landed and passed thro' customs.

At 2.15 a.m. Mustered at the barrier—station now completely silent, empty and eerily dark. Policemen (arrive) 4 great buses and 6 ambulances . . . for refugees . . . white-coated attendants like ghosts in the gloom of the blacked-out station.

At 2.40 a.m. The train slowly crept in—no lights showing and not a sound—it just sort of rose out of the darkness. And then there slowly got out the most exhausted, dirty, bleary, tatter-demalion crew . . .

We had taxis waiting . . . tremendous scenes of reunion . . . modified by utter exhaustion of travellers . . . Scenery and dresses a total loss, but heavily insured.

By the end of May, not only Liverpool Street Station but all London southern termini were taking streams of refugees. The evacuation from France of the British Expeditionary Force was in progress. Fokkers and Stukas were strafing the fleeing crowds on the roads leading to the overcrowded Channel ports, and the Dunkirk beaches. The loss of life made chilling news. The Ballet Company had to abandon only their scenery; the BEF had to abandon all their vehicles, guns and other equipment. Thousands of troops were trapped and became the first inhabitants of German prisoners-of-war camps. Michael Langham, who later features in the Guthrie story, was one of those.

News of the loss of the young theatrical talent began: 'Missing presumed dead' was the son of Sybil Thorndike, John Casson. He had been shot down into the sea while operating with the Fleet Air Arm as Squadron Leader. His father, Lewis Casson, was at the Vic, playing in *The Tempest*.

At Annagh-ma-Kerrig's safe fireside Peggy read from Tony's letter to his mother:

> In *The Tempest* Lewis plays Gonzago, one of the lords in the shipwrecked party. The King, Ferdinand, keeps lamenting, as you remember, 'my son is lost, my son is drowned'—the night the news came, Lewis weathered all that and got through his performance perfectly all right, till it came to the moment at the end when Ferdinand and Miranda are discovered playing chess in the grotto, and the Father and Son are reunited. Then he just broke down and wept on stage.

In this case life was to be like the play. John Casson did survive to be reunited with his father. But there were to be many bitter announcements that were all too true, and too final.

By June all of France was in the hands of Germany. Mussolini joined with Hitler. The Battle of Britain began with 'dog fights' in the air over Southern England. Back in London from a quick visit to Tunbridge Wells, Tony got off a letter to Annagh-ma-Kerrig: 'Aunt Sue seemed in good form. She's had that wee room properly arranged as a shelter . . . They have been told at T. Wells that it's not impossible that they may be ordered to "evacuate" at 12 hours notice . . . Aunt Sue taking it with complete calm.'

Then—as in the previous war—the Wellington and Oxford historian made his assessment of the situation: His letter went on:

> I feel now that Hitler and Hitlerism has ceased to be significant . . . Hitler is more the *result* of something than the cause. He is the result of the personification of Germany after Versailles. Well—the post-Versailles phase is over—and Hitler is consequently out-of-date and will be increasingly unable to hold the *imagination* of Germany . . . I believe his personality has provided the emotional, almost religious, focussing point, of which the lack has beaten France and looks like beating Britain . . .

We've left a case of clothes at T. Wells. And if both Lincoln's Inn *and* T. Wells are bombed or burnt, we shall either be dead or sufficiently discommoded to regard having no clothes as the merest trife . . .

The London Blitz now began in earnest. Plans were made to get the Vic Company to the fourth annual Buxton Theatre Festival. At Sadler's Wells, 'while Mephistopheles dragged Faust to Hell on the stage, on the theatre's roof Guthrie and others watched the real inferno of the first big raid on London'. *

This was in fact to be the last performance at the Wells for almost five years. Under the resolute leadership of Lawrence Collingwood and Joan Cross, the Opera Company went out on provincial tours and delighted thousands who had never seen opera before. It was a tightly knit team with two pianos and Constant Lambert very active on one of them.

Guthrie held the Sadler's Wells office as a London HQ. There he, the two Chamberlains, George and Annette and Evelyn Williams held the fort. The theatre itself became a refuge and a nightly air-raid shelter for a flood of bombed-out 'refugees' from within the blitzed locality. The theatre suffered only minor damage but the Guthries saw little of Lincoln's Inn for a time while they and the Chamberlains camped out, on duty, back-stage at the Wells. The vanished orchestra's bandroom was turned into a canteen, wardrobe rooms into dormitories, and night after night Guthrie somehow managed to supply them with blankets and a hot meal; then he would take his roof-top watch, chatting with duty stage-staff and keeping an alert for any hellish hardware dropping out of the night sky. His letters to his mother at Annagh-ma-Kerrig, and to others at this time, evoke vivid pictures of that part of London as the blitz built up. He was out and about among it, too. News came that John Moody (a regular player with the Vic Company) had been bombed and cut to pieces by flying glass, while acting as a local ambulance man. When he came-to in hospital, the first person he could vaguely discern, sitting at his bedside, was Tony Guthrie. But his fathering of his extended 'family' was far from being localized to Islington.

News came through that up in Hull there had been a direct hit on the stage door end of the theatre where the Opera Company was playing. The costume skips were a write-off, because they

* *The Story of Sadler's Wells*, Dennis Arundell. Hamish Hamilton, 1965.

were buried under tons of masonry. Guthrie got the company truck and driver, dug out spare hampers from the Wells, and, he and the driver taking turns, drove all through the night, so that the Opera could move on and be fit to play its next date. The day after he was over in Buxton with the visiting Vic Company there, then back to the Wells. Train journeys were now taking an unpredictable time as lines were being bombed. One can therefore see why life had little to do with actual production and how all his energy and resourcefulness went into trying to keep the Troika on the road. In letters home he called himself The Wandering Jew, and felt as fatefully cursed and weary.

The bombs fell faster. It was decided not to bring the Vic Company back from its Midlands tour. An interesting offer had come from the imaginative management at the Victoria Theatre, Burnley, Lancashire. It meant that the company could make that 'Old Victoria' their wartime home. The beloved attic at 23 Old Buildings, Lincoln's Inn, was locked up and wished luck. Suitcases were stuffed heavy enough to dislocate other than Guthrie shoulder joints. And there was of course 'Lizzie' in the cat basket. It was a sad scene. They had to leave the piano standing in the desolate flat, whose sitting-room and kitchen windows were now both blacked-out and broken. The 'hall' (these standard terms flatter this small architectural 'tent') had its ceiling down, and the entire flat was powdered all over by plaster dust, also a very, very fine silvery ash—product of the terrible fires that had raged round Holborn. The gas, now disconnected, had for some time been reduced to a peep, and hot water had been impossible. One winter night of London's fiery ordeal, Tony reported that his 'artificials', left in a glass in the bathroom, had been found in the morning, when they returned from the air-raid shelter, immured in a solid block of ice. At least in Burnley there would be no need to live a camper's night life. For Judy it was doubly sad to go from the one real home of her own where they had started their partnership so blissfully. For Tony, returning from Burnley to keep contact and pick up essentials, London was now a battered and a haunted city:

Did I tell you it took me from 10 in the morning till 9 at night to get from Manchester to Euston. There was a raid on when I got in and London was like a city of the dead most beautiful tho' uncanny—great vistas of deserted thoroughfares under a

wonderful Hunter's Moon. I walked from Euston down the
main road past St. Pancras, past King's Cross, and met *one man*
walking in the same direction and a taxi which refused to take
me, till I got to Grays Inn Road which I walked down and met
one other taxi which did take me and I saw nothing or nobody
else till I got to Sadler's Wells—nine o'clock in London of a
Thursday evening—it's hard to believe, isn't it?

It was on this same night—when the illumination of London
was limited to the cold light from that hunter's moon—that I met
Tony Guthrie for the second time in my life; and my life
became a demonstration of how Guthrie encouraged young
talent into the Theatre. He had arranged this meeting. The first
time I had arranged it, or rather I had gate-crashed his Sadler's
Wells citadel to make an impassioned request. As he wrote to his
mother at the time, I was simply to him a long-haired, intensely
serious young artist from Scotland who had written two fascinating and quite unperformable plays, in green ink. Alec Guinness
and he showed interest. On the basis of this interest the young
Scot had come to put a proposition to him. 'Ya-as?' What was it?
'I am writing from outside the Theatre and a playwright should
be inside the Theatre.' 'Ya-as—agree,' he said. Then I nervously
shot my presumptuous proposition at him. 'I want you to ask me
to write a play—but about which you have no obligation to do
anything at all; beyond the asking. And it must be for a particular
purpose with particular requirements, because I want to work to
realistic limits.' There came the bright light in the eagle eye, the
penetrating look straight at one, but there was no hesitation, just
the opening of the neatly moustachioed mouth, the adenoidal
intake of breath and—and then I nearly lost all concentration on
his reply, because he stood up. It was the first time I had seen the
full imposing six foot five of him. 'Want you to write a play to go
with *Macbeth*.' He paced the limited floor, obviously enjoying the
game. 'Has to go on tour of Welsh mining villages—must have
a meaty part for Sybil Thorndike—Lewis Casson too—perhaps
Larry Olivier. Ya-as—three acts—and—And that's it.' I went to
it. And the bombs started getting bigger and falling faster.
    The play was written—some under the stairs during raids—
and finished up in Glasgow. There I had got my wife and child
away to safety in my parents' home, before trying to exercise some
control over instructions to join the forces fighting Hitler.

By the time I heard from him I was back in London, an unwilling conscript into the Scots Guards. Then his letter reached me in a barrack-room in old Chelsea Barracks. It totally ruined my concentration on spit-and-polish:

> 177 Manchester Road,
> Burnley.
> Jan. 5. 41.

My dear James,

I have read your play. Last night and this morning have literally been the only times since it came that I have had the time and the physical energy needful to concentrate. I have read —devoured—your play once. It has excited and encouraged me more than anything that's happened for months—for years, I think . . . Now for practical matters: I will do absolutely everything I can to get this play before the public. When could we meet? . . . Thursday . . . in London, but *very* busy; could we meet at night?

And that night of the Blitz we met. We talked plans and I walked back with him, towards where he had another even later appointment at the Globe Theatre. And, as we walked through moonlit Piccadilly Circus, the air-raid sirens suddenly ground into startling action, wailed up to the sky, roared down into the streets and echoed eerily away over the moonlit rooftops of what had been theatreland—the West End.

Neither of us increased our pace, past the sand-bagged site of the statue of Eros, though our nerves were bound to take note of the dull, fluctuating drone of Goering's bombers away up there between us and the moon. He was simply not impressed and I was desperately trying to impress him. Also, I was officially supposed to be of the brave, having just been allowed out on to the streets of London after two haircuts in quick succession and two weeks of drilled Hell in Chelsea barracks. My boots hardly fitted as yet, but the hope was that recruit Guardsman Forsyth, having earned half a stripe, would not be an *entire* disgrace to the Brigade. Well he was. Guns cracked into action and sent lethal metal screaming up towards the droning Nazi planes. Bombs would be about to fall. In such circumstances a guardsman was supposed to *feel* seven feet tall. Guthrie almost *was*. The skip of my cap was supposed to take the skin off my nose and make regimentally certain that I looked down on all other mortals.

There was my giant 'civvy' companion, his coat collar turned up (he seemed to wear the same old heavy topcoat for thirty years), his bullet-shaped head, more short back 'n front than mine, and not only utterly bare to the bombers above but seeming to be a full foot nearer them than mine.

No bombs fell, but a hundred yards off the Guthrie objective—the stage door of the Globe—two unexpended anti-aircraft shells hit the street slap by us, and exploded. A citizen of London, not either of us, fell and lay moaning and bleeding into the gutter on the far side of the street.

The Guardsman clattered into action, doubled across, turned over the casualty (to the greater flow of blood and the greater agony of the poor man). Trembling Guardsman then ripped First Field Dressing from groin pocket of battledress; fumbled about frantically in the moonlit muddiness to staunch the unstaunchable; and in the end only succeeded in adding to the anguish of the poor dying man. The wound was ten times the size of the regulation dressing. The well-organized civilian ambulance volunteers moved in and, with Cockney compassion and impressive efficiency, removed the dying man; victim of our own anti-aircraft shells and of our own miserably ineffective Guardsman of our monarch's Household Brigade.

The point about all this, and the point that struck me forcibly, was that through all this untidy, bloody incident the tall Tyrone Guthrie *said* nothing, *did* nothing. He just stood aside, looked down from a cold height and let those who should—including those who should but could not—do what they were trained to do. As I left him to what I thought was *his* theatreland, and as my big shiny boots walked me back to Chelsea Barracks over bomb-rubble and shattered glass, it puzzled me. It puzzled me till I knew his speechless anger at the waste of war and knew what I now know, that deep in his inherited bones was the sort of response traditional to a great general: not to get involved in the hopeless skirmish when one's obligation is to win the battle; not to bemoan the battle lost if the campaign resulted in Victory.

For we lost the battle of the play. It was, as you may remember, to go with *Macbeth* on a tour of Welsh mining villages. 'You have hit Casson and Thorndike off to a T, Tee, Tea(?)'—his letter said. But Casson thought differently. He thought the young man had talent but obviously did not understand Welsh miners at all. Sybil and he were off to Wales, brilliantly playing an abridged

Macbeth to the entire satisfaction of the Welsh miners. By a nice stroke of dramatic irony, I was posted to a Welsh battalion stationed in Ireland, not many miles away across the border from Annagh-ma-Kerrig, and trained there a platoon of Welsh miners for Normandy. Fate had Guthrie and me tied up theatrically from then on.

Back in Burnley on January 28, 1941, the Old Vic Company in the Old Victoria had opened broke. *Twelfth Night* was a non-star production and the salaries of Guthrie and others were reduced voluntarily to help things out. Within eighteen months the Company was solvent. Within three years it was showing a healthy balance at the bank. This was not a little to do with the sudden popularity of Opera and Ballet, and the drabness of war making people simply long for Music and Dance. It had also to do with solid encouragement from CEMA—the Council for the Encouragement of Music and the Arts.

The Carnegie Trust was backing the Opera Company. But it was a remarkable Welshman, Dr. Tom Jones, Administrator of the Anglo-American Pilgrim Trust, who persuaded the British Government to put up pound for pound to start CEMA. Another remarkable Welshman, Lewis Casson, was very vocal in the cause of state-subsidized Theatre. CEMA was undoubtedly a major creative outcome of the war. To quote Tony Guthrie: 'For the first time since the Tudors, the British Treasury has made manifest a belief that Art in general, and the art of theatre in particular, is not merely a graceful amenity but a necessity to a great nation which considers itself, and wishes to be considered, civilized.' This was a positive product of War—as was the forcing of the People's Theatre out among the people.

From Burnley the Companies went out to places as large, as small, and as varied as: Kendal, Ulverston, Glasgow, Leeds, Buxton, Harrogate, Bury, Bradford, Derby, Stafford, Walsall. 'You name it, we were there,' the players could say. So was Guthrie. To keep in touch with 'his troops' he was on the go, travelling by train a tremendous amount of the time. The office work was demanding too:

Tuesday 60 letters (most of them long and involving decisions and plans). I signed and she [*Evelyn Williams*] checked 10 contracts; I signed 24 cheques; and we had teasing trunk calls from Wales (twice), London, Durham and Scotland. Left the

7

house 7.30 a.m. Thursday and got here 1 p.m. after endless delays caused by the raid the previous night on one of the big Midland towns whose name I dare not name.

Burnley—being where the coalfields were—was not, like London, short of fuel. It is therefore small wonder that in the cold of that winter, on the occasions when he had some hours of domestic peace, Tony behaved like a tired business man and, as reported by Judy, did nothing but sit for hours beside the coal fire, in their big, draughty Burnley terrace house, playing with the kitten. He was now forty and feeling more like sixty. It seemed unlikely that he and Judy would have children. He wanted children now.

While he played with that kitten, Judy Guthrie would be seated, preferably on the floor, writing another play on the back of typed sheets discarded by the theatre office. All sorts of war-time economies became ingrained in them then. Tony, in other idle hours, many of them on cold, stranded trains, was writing too: an opera libretto.

He wrote to Midshipman Alec Guinness to say that he thought the post-war form of Drama would be far more like Opera than 'straight' plays: more music, more visual statement, more choreography. The Troika were all to pull together in one direction, one theatre art. For the moment he was in love with Opera. He was not uninfluenced by Ballet. Just before they had to leave the Wells, Ninette de Valois had been able to do *The Sleeping Princess* in its entirety. The story of *his* opera was 'The Sleeping Princess'. And it was set in a great and neglected old house, overwhelmed—as his father once feared Annagh-ma-Kerrig would be—by briar and thorn. Judy's play was about a bed-ridden, tyrannical mother-figure, who ruled in another big house. This domestic scene of the writers at work was in the grim greystone Burnley house which Tony described as having 'absolutely no charm . . . sensible middle class villa . . . excellent repair, nice dull rooms . . . reasonable fittings. It will do.'

And it was cheap; and so convenient that its backdoor, dust-bins, and extra outside lavatory were right there in full view of the stage door of the 'old Victoria'. But it was not depressing to him, who loved the productive realities of cities like Belfast, Glasgow and Liverpool. A short walk would take him to the Wuthering Heights-sort of wilds of the Derbyshire Moors, past

ever so many barracks of great mills—very solid and pros-
perous-looking and madly busy now . . . forests of chimneys, all
smoking . . . Everything files up and down steep hills with
unexpected rushing torrents dashing downwards into the
[*river*] Brun, which appears every now and then in the centre
of the town between tunnels where it dives here under Woolworths, there under the G.P.O. . . . It's compact [*the town*]
and very soon one climbs up and out on to wonderful wild
craggy moors . . .

Laurence Olivier, before he could get free of film contracts,
had cabled back, from the reconstructed *Wuthering Heights* of
Hollywood, £100 to the embattled Vic-Wells headquarters to be
spent at Tony's discretion. Now he flew into Bristol on his way
home—via the premiere in Portugal of *Rebecca*. He and his wife,
Vivien Leigh, travelled up to Burnley to see the Guthries. Vivien
wanted to join the Company; Larry was going into the Fleet Air
Arm. He had kept up his flying in America to prepare himself for
this eventuality. The visit was extremely warm and friendly on
both sides but it was inescapably the visit of two world-famous
film stars, married romantically in California. The whole aura of
success surrounded them, they were the two great 'screen lovers'.
To Vivien's offer, to shed the glamour and join the Vic, Tony was
at first cool. She could not shed the film-star image. The audience
would be there for the wrong reasons. Finally he was totally
discouraging. 'Not a good enough actress'—'Not on stage'. Who
but a Guthrie would have had either the guts, or the cruelty, to
say this straight out? It was hurtful but they knew him well
enough not to take final offence. Olivier very soon joined Ralph
Richardson at Lee-on-Solent, a station of the Fleet Air Arm, thus
cementing a partnership which had begun to build before the war.

Two things occurred now which would have required him to
apply the exhortation to himself of 'Rise above it' (after the title
of a current revue starring Hermione Gingold). The Old Vic was
'badly hit' by a bomb and—like Lilian Baylis's little dog 'Sue'—
his cat Lizzie was fatally run over in the street. All things comforting were subject to destruction now. But at least his great
love—his mother—was out of harm's way. His letters to her
went on:

   . . . Oh, whatever is going on, whatever fate has up its
   capricious sinister sleeve, *so much love—such certainty* that

circumstances cannot, need not dominate us nor alter our feelings. They may part us physically, but only so.

T.

It was now apparent that Britain was not going to be invaded. Britons had not been bombed into submission and Hitler turned away to invade Russia. More London theatres re-opened. Each 'steed' of the Troika was pulling the 'organization' on towards a truly national reputation. The Old Vic had been damaged but, through the co-operation of Bronson Albery, the Vic-Wells companies were able to go and show their mettle at the New. Therefore for a time the companies were in and out of London as well as on tour in the provinces. Their repertoire was *King John*, *The Merchant of Venice*, *The Merry Wives*, *Othello* (in which an important addition to the company was Frederick Valk, a distinguished refugee from Europe), and *The Cherry Orchard* (again in the Hubert Butler translation).

Pearl Harbor hit the Americans disastrously and brought them into the war. With the Grand Alliance of Britain, the U.S.A. and the U.S.S.R. the tide was on the turn, the Burnley days were limited and preparations began for the return to Lincoln's Inn. Vivien Leigh had the bigness of heart to present the bereft Guthries with 'a wee black kitty' as replacement to the beloved Lizzie. A new phase began for them, and all the other survivors, including the Vic-Wells. Sadler's Wells was again the Guthrie office.

Judy's play *Queen Bee* had some measure of success in Bristol and Liverpool. Back in London, she took up local 'war work' in a small munitions factory. Not only was she back into the beloved Lincoln's Inn flat (repaired and renewed), but daily she put a colourful bandana about her head, had a 'ciggy', stubbed it out on the way and went to work in her little local factory, where she simply loved the common camaraderie of the other 'girls' (all ages).

It was the German cities which were now being bombed by waves of Allied bombers. All sorts of debates began within the organization and with CEMA about what the Vic-Wells should become, and where. The Old Vic Theatre would need considerable repair. And the Old Vic Company, was it really in a state to be the national company? Because a National Theatre was now bound to be a post-war project. State subsidy was an accepted fact. And there seemed little doubt that the man with all the qualifications to direct a British National Theatre was Tyrone Guthrie.

In the summer of 1943, he took the Playhouse Theatre, in London, for the Old Vic Company, and put on a season of three plays, one for each nation of the Grand Alliance: for the U.S.A., John Drinkwater's *Abraham Lincoln*; for the U.S.S.R., Simonov's *The Russians* (about Stalingrad); and, for Britain, a new play by a young playwright with a Russian name, Peter Ustinov, called *Blow Your Own Trumpet*.

It was a noble enough conception but Tony Guthrie was spent. He wrote to Annagh-ma-Kerrig:

> Yes—I am sick, yet not ill—just too tired to sleep . . . every ounce of energy has gone into *The Russians* . . . Large cast; difficult sets; innumerable props . . . endless effects—aeroplanes, rifle fire, artillery, machine guns, mines . . . fire . . . snow; wet clothes . . . and everything hard to get, from a hairpin to a star, including stage blood (when use of ketchup would be undermining the war effort).

The proceeds from the Russian play were to 'endow an Old Vic bed in the hospital now rising from the ruins of Stalingrad'. He had

> the close assistance of the Russian embassy, two dreary young men who have come and sat like images at rehearsals . . . Concern only for exact size of collar badges, etc. . . . full of suspicion of putting on the play as a sincere gesture of allied goodwill . . . Their idea was that the Russian soldiers should look and behave like the Horse Guards on parade . . . I lost all patience and put them out of the theatre. After that they were much less bother . . . respected me for the first time—a horrid trait. I can't bear it when people only behave when bullied.

At the Gala Opening in June a house packed with diplomatic notables received the play with storms of cheering: '. . . relieved, because I've been the one who, rather against advice, insisted on our doing the play.'

But altogether the season was a disastrous flop; this at a time when he needed all his energy to look to the complex future. Tony Guthrie was physically and nervously at the point of utter exhaustion. He developed shingles. His was an acute case of war-weariness.

He heard from Flora Robson who, having finished her work in America, was now trapped on the far side of the sub-marine infested Atlantic. She wanted help to get home. Sea berths were few and difficult to get. He had to use his influence to get her back on the basis that she was wanted for a CEMA tour. She came on a banana boat in a convoy in which at least one ship was sunk. Her 'CEMA job' turned out to be the playing of Thérèse in a stage adaptation of Emile Zola's *Thérèse Raquin*—that classic but sinister story of marital murder. It was to open in Liverpool (where Guthrie had established the Liverpool Old Vic Company as a regional Old Vic). At dress rehearsal she complained to Tony that she was demonstrably worse served in the matter of dress than a certain young lady in the cast. He came down on her like a load of bricks. She was shocked. But she could hardly know the strain he was under then and that the image she created would be the Hollywood star, who did not know that 'there was a war on'. It was the same response that Vivien Leigh had evoked.

In London the rumble of war was in fact now limited to the sporadic 'flying-bombs'—V.1s, V.2s—while all troop preparation was for the invasion of France. Wearily he wrote home:

> 'I'm awfully off London . . And—if one's to be realistic—it's pretty clear that one will have to choose between living in London or giving up the Vic.

But he crossed the river with the Vic chairman, Lord Lytton, to survey the damage to the old theatre as it stood derelict amid the blitzed Bermondsey of Baylis's old community. It would need more than repair to take it on to the sort of theatre in which he wanted to see Shakespeare and the other classics staged. He wrote —all too prophetically—that any National Theatre would be a long time in the building.

When it was obvious he would have to continue at the New, he went back to his old favourite, *Hamlet*, and put on a strangely half-hearted production. It disappointed those who now hoped for the great new start at the New. But it was too early. The young he wanted were not home. D-Day was June 6. This was February 1944. He looked for his vitality to the Ballet, so Robert Helpmann played Hamlet while he encouraged another young talent by co-directing the play with Michael Benthall. And he kept on writing letters—as he did throughout the war—to those who dreamed the new dreams of Theatre and were still on active service. It was not the best production of his favourite play, but it was quite a theatrical occasion. And the house could have been sold out ten times over despite a sudden recurrence of air-raids.

The *Alert* went most dramatically at the moment in the play scene when the King calls for lights; and the King's big soliloquy was drowned in a tornado of gunfire . . . The *All Clear* went off during the gravedigger's scene! . . . Another alert during last night's performance . . . a bore . . . because three of the absolutely vital electricians are A.R.P. (Air Raid Precautions) men—so, when 'the purple' is signalled they are phoned for and have to fly post-haste from their perches to Finsbury, Wandsworth and Holborn . . . So far, I have spent a large part of each performance up on the OP perch frantically trying to follow a plot in someone else's handwriting, eked out by a knowledge of how the scene ought to look.

Discussions about the Vic and the future and the National Theatre went on, in the Vic office up in Sadler's Wells between him and his war-veteran team of George and Annette Chamberlain, Evelyn Williams, and Joan Cross. At governors' meetings he found most of them now to be too old and too war-weary to face the huge issues looming. Joan Cross and he, sharing a huge enthusiasm for Opera, were associated in the formulation of a sort of British Opera Manifesto, for presentation to the Board. Lewis Casson, now Drama Director of CEMA, was pushing his ideas. Maynard Keynes, Covent Garden governor and reformer of the nation's economic policy, and husband of Lopokova the ballerina, was complicating things on the Ballet front. And a competition for CEMA's drama funds was arising from Binkie Beaumont's plans. Everybody was making post-war plans. Guthrie wrote in a sort of despair to Annagh-ma-Kerrig:

Unfortunately this kind of long-term and yet practical planning is just what I'm ROTTENLY poor at. I know nobody better, except yourself, at getting a chain of buckets going if the house takes fire; but I don't feel either you or I have any capacity for the far-sighted plan other than on vague visionary terms. I can't organise except on the spur of the moment; I can rap out orders and get people to carry them out happily and even enthusiastically; but without the immediate objective and the

presence of an audience, I find it the greatest task to plan a
campaign.

If only I could delegate this. But at present there just do not
seem to be the suitable people for the job. It needs youth, plus
a real sense of social responsibility, plus business capacity. I'm
seeing a young man on Tuesday who may be useful; he's lame
and therefore not in the forces.

The 'young man' referred to was John Burrell, a small,
courageous and ambitious man, who walked with a stick and had
the steely strength of character of many who triumph over
physical handicap. He had been schooled in the London Theatre
Studio of Michel Saint-Denis and had been for a time in charge of
Drama at that famous social settlement, Toynbee Hall. Burrell
was taken on and he set up office in St. Martin's Court, above the
stage door of the New. He was to be the first of a triumvirate of
directors Guthrie brought in. The other two were Ralph Richardson and Laurence Olivier. Richardson first agreed to join
Burrell, and then both went out to the film studios where Olivier
was now doing the last few weeks of work on his *Henry V*. They
brought the Vic's offer. Olivier agreed to join them. The headquarters of the Triumvirate was the office backstage at the New.
The headquarters of the veterans, Chamberlain and Guthrie,
remained at the Wells, and Guthrie was still overall director of the
whole Vic-Wells organization. It was foreseen that Richardson
would play and take part in planning and that Olivier would do
the same and direct plays too. Burrell would also direct, but be the
main office and administration man. However, it was Guthrie
who directed, in the summer of 1944, the first of those great
productions at the New which were to set the high standard by
which the Old Vic could claim to be the best of the nation's
Theatre. This was *Peer Gynt*, adapted by Norman Ginsbury,
with Peer played by an inspired Richardson; his mother by Sybil
Thorndike; the small part of the Button Moulder, brilliantly, and
in the true spirit of a repertory company, by Laurence Olivier.
A notable and lovely addition brought in from the Birmingham
Repertory Company was young Margaret Leighton, as the Green
Woman.

From then and right through the Burrell productions of *Arms
and the Man*, *Richard III*, *Uncle Vanya*, with Olivier and Richardson
at the very height of their powers, queues at the New Theatre

began to be phenomenally long, and there was an atmosphere of total success.

The lights of London were coming on again. Everything seemed to be on a rising graph. The Triumvirate were proving to be good generals under Guthrie's overall command:

I think the enormous public interest is something more than just the attraction of the two star names. The big scale of the scheme, the large company, large live orchestra, Peer Gynt, Old Vic . . . the whole set-up has captured the people's imagination . . . coming at the tail end of five years of war [*we have now*] a certain momentum that carries things along with far less need to push and shove . . . on a scale that makes all our plans NEWS and obviates . . . a lot of struggling to publicise.

This was classical theatre for the nation in the West End equal to Gielgud's pre-war triumphs there. And, after the resounding personal success of Olivier's first night as Richard Crookback, there came a splendid and generous gesture from John Gielgud. The sword of Edmund Kean, worn by Irving on the first night he made his appearance as Richard III, on January 29, 1877, was presented on stage to Olivier. On its shiny blade the newly-engraved inscription read: 'This sword given him by his mother Kate Terry Gielgud, 1938, is given to Laurence Olivier by his friend John Gielgud in appreciation of his performance of Richard III at the New Theatre, 1944.'

Everything on stage and out front was a shining bright success. Why therefore this depressed letter which Guthrie wrote to me on the night when the whole country was jubilant about Victory in Europe?

I spent VE night alone in Wolverhampton, where depressed elders watched the unfocussed energies of excited 16-year-old hoydens (of both sexes) express themselves in loud animal cries, putting on of paper hats and rosettes, and rather shame-faced attempts at dancing to accordeons in the street. The weather was golden and lovely, but the occasion terribly needed, I felt, a focussing point—the kind of thing that in the capital was provided by St. Paul's Cathedral, to which people could bow down, and did, as to an idol that had survived ordeal; or Mr. Churchill in Whitehall; or Buckingham Palace, with its painted symbolical Mummy and Daddy figures, bowing, bowing, smiling and waving jewelled hands from the balcony.

At the time it did not seem strange. I was flat as a pancake with war-weariness too in shattered Hamburg. But I realize now he was a lonely sort of man and that out there this provincial great man, on provincial tour again, was bitterly realizing what was happening behind all the on-stage success in London. The Troika was pulling itself apart. The two 'horses' of Opera and Ballet began to tear away in different directions. Also the Triumvirate were now beginning to show signs that they found the hand that had held the whole organization together somewhat tiresome. Not a month later he, George Chamberlain, Annette and Miss Williams, too—the old guard of Sadler's Wells and the Burnley battle scars—tabled their resignations.

The crunch had come one day when the two from the Wells, Guthrie and Chamberlain, were in consultation with the Triumvirate in Burrell's office. The whole manner of their talk prompted George Chamberlain to say, 'It almost looks as if you didn't want us around.' It only needed a 'Well . . .' and an interchange of looks for Guthrie to say, 'Raight!' and he was off. Of course he was hurt. But to say of Tony Guthrie that he was a man who would never outstay his welcome is a great understatement. The others, in solidarity, followed suit when he had tendered his resignation. Fortunately for the organization, all sides persuaded George Chamberlain to swallow his anger and stay on. But for Guthrie the fate was Churchillian: essential for the war, expendable for the peace.

There were bitter pills to swallow, too, about the Opera and the Ballet. There had always been a sort of Wells family battle between him and Ninette de Valois. Perhaps it was the Irish in both of them, because she was born Edris Stannus of the Wicklow Hills. He could never be convinced that Ballet should be anything more than part and parcel of the one art which was Opera. De Valois on the other hand fought all the time for Ballet as a separate Art. She was in fact the Ballet's St. Joan fighting to liberate her dancers from 'Operatic Dancing'. And she had her 'voices', one of which was the great Diaghilev, saying in Paris that from the growing field of talent among British dancers the next great advance in the international art of Ballet would come. And the Royal Ballet of Covent Garden was duly created.

More serious still to Guthrie—with his growing love of Opera, and his campaigning along with Joan Cross for a native opera in English and for all the people, not just the upper classes—was the break up of the Wells Opera Company. In the last years of the war, when the company had been making money, Joan Cross introduced one or two new productions. One was a new Guthrie *Traviata*. Later in his career he was to say of it:

> It was my first, and last, experience of an operatic production when there was enough time for the dramatic presentation. In this case all the principal singers were not only thoroughly familiar with the work, they also had long experience as a team . . . the result was an effort on which I look back with some pride.*

Now—and without what he considered due consultation with Joan Cross—arrangements were undertaken whereby the cream of the singers were to move to Covent Garden and the whole Wells ensemble be broken up. It was on this issue that Joan Cross also resigned. At least before she went, she had the satisfaction of seeing on to the stage the first of the new English operas that both Tony Guthrie and she had dreamed of, *Peter Grimes*.

This new opera by Britten had its first performance on the night that Sadler's Wells re-opened after the war. It was a strange night for Tony Guthrie, and for George Chamberlain too. Guthrie knew he was on the way out, and both of them felt rather like ghosts at the wedding. The fate of Opera at the Wells had not yet been decided, but Guthrie had committed himself to saying that the whole future of the Company hung on the standard of performance reached in this new work. This was anxiety enough, but George Chamberlain and he, who had weathered all the bombs at the Wells, had another very physical and specific anxiety. In a typical letter Guthrie—but with a final note of ruefulness—he reported home:

> . . . our anxiety . . . that 'vibrations' would bring the great chandelier crashing down upon their Excellencies' heads in the stalls. It was taken down when the raids began, and only hoisted up a few days ago . . . these sorts of occasions are so much easier to deal with when one has definite duties and occupations. As it was I had NOTHING to do except grin like a Cheshire cat, which I did to the point of lockjaw, with stomach *churning*, while inwardly I bled for the crash of the chandelier, played every instrument in the orchestra, sang every

* *A Life In The Theatre.*

top note with Madam, shrieked every chorus—checked every ticket, balanced every cup of coffee, tested every fire appliance, pulled the curtain up *and* down, wiped every lavatory seat, shifted every piece of scenery and every single prop and put on and took off every costume and wig . . . all in feverish imagination with that gay serene spontaneous grin FIXED. A terrible, terrible evening. Far worse than the raids . . .

The opera was received with loud acclaim, whose vibrations the chandelier survived.

So we locked up the safe and tottered in a state of physical and psychic collapse to one of those ill-judged post-first-night parties . . . at the Savoy . . .

And by the time he and George got there the food had run out and the party was dispersing, so—

. . . resorted to 23 OB [*Old Buildings, Lincoln's Inn*] with Judy and Prevost and enjoyed a dried-egg omelette and chocolate made of dried milk!

On his resignation from the Vic, there were no bitter recriminations and when the Triumvirate asked him to do another production that year at the New, as a guest director, he agreed. It was that other play which, next to *Hamlet* he was most fascinated by, the *Oedipus Rex* of Sophocles. Sybil Thorndike was to be his Jocasta and Olivier his Oedipus. But that would not be until October.

It was Peace. It was summer; he was—in a somewhat sad sense —free. Judy too was free—'demobilised' from her daily war work. London was drab and damaged; for six years nothing had had a coat of paint; people's clothes had suffered war-weariness too. He noted that the total addition to his wardrobe over these years had been one vest and underpants and two shirts. As if taking off an armour he and Judy went out to Windsor, hired a punt and bathed in the river, slept in the sun and picnicked under overhanging willows reminiscent of Oxford and Cambridge days. Free?—but what to do? Well, there was *Oedipus*, his choice of play for the old firm, in October.

Meanwhile, the Theatre Guild had asked him to go to New York, to do a production of his own choice. And there was an offer which the devil in him tempted him to accept—to join with

Binkie Beaumont in his project of the Company of Four. The Four were H. M. Tennent, Glyndebourne, the Cambridge Arts Theatre, and Tyrone Guthrie. (He yielded to the temptation and his participation lasted a year.) There was, more immediately, his own play. He was working on one which he called for a time *The Picture of Success*—a very personal sort of a tragedy. So, there was plenty to consider while both Tony and Judy—bound so much closer by the ordeals of the war—recovered physically from the depredations of those years. No responsibility. Bliss to punt out from under the gentle brush of limp willows and under a sky from which no threat came. Happiness enough to bus home and let the lights blaze out and into the upper branches of the great plane tree in the Lincoln's Inn yard. Piano . . . life pianissimo . . .

He got back into *Oedipus*, and production preparations were begun. Then suddenly, and indirectly, word came to him that the plan of the Triumvirate was that *Oedipus* would be only one part of a double bill. The other half of the evening would be Sheridan's *The Critic*—in which Olivier would also play as Mr. Puff. *Oedipus*, true enough, is a short play. But Oedipus and Puff! Guthrie's reaction was, 'over my dead body!' He went to see the three— Olivier, Richardson and Burrell. He was no longer the senior authority—and it was their considered decision. It was also Olivier's wish, and they were sure it would be a great success. 'Then not with me—I won't do it,' Guthrie said. And he didn't. Judy and he accepted the offer to go to New York and he chose to do her version of *He Who Gets Slapped*. They looked up ways and means to go without spending money on 'silly things' such as 'floating palaces'.

Ten days before joining a small cargo-passenger ship sailing from Avonmouth, they went with Tanya Moiseiwitsch to be at the first night of Olivier's *Oedipus Rex* (and *The Critic*) now directed by Michel Saint-Denis. It was a huge popular success. But two things need explanation here: the presence of Tanya Moiseiwitsch with them, and the re-appearance of Saint-Denis on the Old Vic scene.

From the time of the fall of France, Michel Saint-Denis had worked for the French Section of the BBC, broadcasting under the pseudonym of 'Jacques Duchêne'. His inspired broadcasts to his occupied country not only kept hope alive in many of his countrymen but passed essential information on to the French Resistance. He was now free and if Olivier could not have

Guthrie he was happy to have Saint-Denis, with whom—despite the sadness attending it then—he had loved working on *Macbeth*.

Tanya Moiseiwitsch was there for two reasons: she had designed *The Critic* and she was indebted to Tony Guthrie for her wartime introduction to the Vic. It was one of the great theatrical partnerships between director and designer, which would last his lifetime, and it had begun in this way. In 1944, she had been working as assistant designer at the Oxford Playhouse. Her father was the famous pianist—and favourite of the Guthrie family—Benno Moiseiwitsch. Tony Guthrie had met her mother when she had come over to Belfast to play on the Wireless, when he was at 2BE. She was the Australian violinist, Daisy Kennedy—a striking character he immediately took to. Tanya had crossed his path, in London once before, when he was first at the Old Vic in 1934. She was an apprentice on the paint frame, learning how to paint scenery, so she was not unknown to him. But suddenly in 1944 a tragic factor came into her young life: one that would greatly affect Guthrie.

She had come over from work at the Dublin Abbey Theatre to Oxford to fill the place of a resident designer who had been called up into the Army. At Oxford she met somebody else who had been called up: Felix Krish, assistant stage manager. He had come back to visit the company—in Air Force uniform. For them it was a classic case of love at first sight. They married without delay. Within months her mother was having to find some way to tell Tanya that Felix had been killed in action. Very shortly after this, Guthrie asked her to consider getting out of Oxford and coming to join the Liverpool Old Vic Company. Nothing was ever said about Felix and the tragedy. But, knowing him, there would be somewhere deep down in the man, a flaming anger at the human affront of such waste of youth, and such hurt to what he saw as a shy, sensitive and very gifted girl. Tanya stayed on at Liverpool and designed four or five productions in the one year, one of which was with him, *The Alchemist*.

When the Vic Company started their grand plan with the Triumvirate at the New, Guthrie persuaded Tanya to join, and she designed Burrell's successful *Uncle Vanya*. Then followed *The Critic*.

Of the other play in the double-bill, *Oedipus Rex*, he wrote:

Laurence Olivier played the part with deserved and immense

acclaim. But when he re-entered for this final scene festooned with plastic streams of crimson lake . . . to suggest rivers of blood pouring from ruined sockets, we both [*Tanya and he*] felt that the attempt was mistaken not only in practice but in theory. It was exposing what had been deliberately concealed by the author from the audience; it was doing again what had been better done in the words of the Messenger. By forcing the audience's attention, but not its conviction, upon material details of the blinding, it was detracting attention from the spiritual meaning.

He was from this moment determined somehow to do his production of the play.

Judy and he prepared for the Atlantic voyage. 'After 3 days of hanging about' in a Bristol still badly battered by the war, they sailed out of a very gusty Avon's mouth, in a cargo ship with no cargo, because of a dockers' strike, and into the open sea, and the wintry Atlantic beyond Ireland.

It must have been the sailing-ship forebears of Judy that made her love any form of life at sea. Tony struggled with writing what he called his 'ladder play', gave up, was sick and decided against the title *Our Father*. The storms took the S.S. *Malancha* and them not to New York, as planned, but to Baltimore, Maryland. Three and a half hours on the train carried them to New York.

In New York at that time, anyone out of beleaguered Britain was treated as though he had just emerged starving from Dickens' Dotheboys Hall. From Ruth Gordon and all their New York friends, they had hospitality lavished on them. It was difficult to adjust to the affluence—and the waste—after all the waste-not-want-not years, of ration books, clothes coupons, and food queues. Judy Guthrie, in a letter home, like someone entombed who had just seen the sun, gave a whoop of incredulity, 'There are bananas!' The whole expedition might have been one luxurious convalescence. The Guild laid everything on for them.

The production was of a play in which Judy's adaptation had proved to be successful before; and it was Russian and, in those days of victory, Russia was still the great and heroic ally.

They opened in Washington, D.C., on March 5 and came into the Booth Theatre on March 19, and it turned out to be a disappointing and rather dull affair. The Liverpool cast had been able to convey—in this 'rather ninetyish Russian play about the circus'—both poignant melancholy, and humour. In New York, Guthrie said the final effect was of 'Chopin scored for military band'. It was too difficult to get ebullient Americans to see that humour was not a laugh a line, and could mix with melancholy. But something else about the visit heartened them.

Before the play opened they had made a quick trip to Canada, to old associates of Tony, in Montreal and Toronto. At Kingston-on-Lake, Ontario, they celebrated Christmas with Robertson Davies and his family. As a player Davies had already shared Shakespeare with him in that non-ideal theatre, the Old Vic. He had also written the new prologue to *The Good-Natured Man* when the Vic opened in Buxton on that first first night of the war. As a Canadian, he had then had to report home. Guthrie now expressed his own high hopes of getting back to Canada. He pumped Davies about the current state of theatre in Canada. And he talked a great deal, on this visit to Kingston, about a tent theatre and how Shakespeare should be staged. He insisted that a tent could be a rather beautiful travelling theatre. He talked about having an inner tent in a beautiful colour, which would give a festive air to the whole pavilion for Theatre. The entire visit reinforced his interest in Canada as an obviously potential sphere for future operations.

CHAPTER FOURTEEN

HERE THERE AND EVERYWHERE
(1946–1948)

THE GUTHRIES got home in April and soon after they had the real pleasure of going to see Alec Guinness's post-war return to the London stage. He was playing Mitya in his own adaptation of *The Brothers Karamazov*. It was being presented at the Lyric Theatre, Hammersmith, where the Company of Four were usefully devoting profit from their 'non-profit-making' West End productions to the encouragement of young talent. The play was directed by the twenty-one-year-old Peter Brook.

Guinness was about to re-join the Old Vic, at the New, to play the Fool to Olivier's King Lear. Guthrie himself agreed to do another guest production for the Triumvirate, *Cyrano de Bergerac*.

The Vic was in an interesting and dangerously extended condition, and he was well-informed on this. George Chamberlain was still there and, the year before, the Joint Council of the National Theatre and the Old Vic had come into being. On to its board, as secretary, Guthrie had been able to introduce his old Oxford colleague, Kenneth Rae, (just out of the wartime Ministry of Information). The London County Council now (1946) offered to this planning body a site for the National Theatre, on the South Bank.

The Triumvirate battled on with what had been a twelve-year plan. The first phase of this had been to bring in another three directors, Michel Saint-Denis, George Devine (who had been Saint-Denis's assistant at his London Theatre Studio), and Glen Byam Shaw. To distinguish them from the three of the Triumvirate these three were affectionately referred to as 'the three boys'— the experimental boys. All were devoted to the ideas of the Compagnie des Quinze and had worked together in the Gielgud companies before the war. The repaired Old Vic Theatre was to be the centre for an exciting experiment incorporating three things: the Young Vic, The Old Vic School, and the Old Vic as an experimental theatre. Saint-Denis was already at work on the stage alterations at the Old Vic. The senior company was to remain with the Triumvirate on the West End side of the river while The Old Vic Centre was to be on the south side.

The Old Vic board was uneasy about the expensive plans of the Triumvirate. Guthrie was requested to attend a governors' meeting. After it, he reported home that there was about to be 'no end of a flutter in that dovecote'. This was said with an understandable but wicked pleasure, just short of malice. But he made it clear to the board that anything he had to say had no personal animus in it. What he said was that he thought the Triumvirate ought to be made aware that their 'actor-management' was 'not infinitely expansive'. The warning took into account the facts that Olivier was preparing to be temporarily excused from Old Vic duties in order to make a major film of *Hamlet,* and Richardson was having to be absent from the company for other work in the U.S.A. And Guthrie knew how much the organization needed to keep at its heart an inspiring presence. He saw this as Olivier's responsibility. On the other hand, if you are committed to the life of 'a star', there is a practical need to make much more income than Old Vic salaries. The absence of the two stars meant that John Burrell was over-extended. It is evidence of Guthrie's uncertainty about his way ahead now that he let it be known that he was prepared to undertake the launching and running of a second Old Vic Company. With Michael Benthall, he had also made a proposition about building a new Globe, or Shakespearean theatre, on the South Bank site of the Old Globe.

It was with this confused background that Guthrie launched into what must have been one of the most romantically delightful of all his productions, *Cyrano de Bergerac.*

It was also at this time that—on the recommendation of Guthrie and the expressed interest of Olivier—I was welcomed back from the wars and into the Old Vic Company. At half a week's pay, I was to be number one in a post-war scheme to encourage promising playwrights who had been denied practical theatre experience by their war service. Taking up this 'apprenticeship' to the art, I therefore saw the whole Vic set-up from the inside. I was however too much of a theatrical innocent to register what was going on in internal and external politics at the time.

In rehearsal for *Cyrano* I was, however, to witness a clash of the giants, and the electric atmosphere probably had more to do with internal politics than I was aware. It was a mixture of technical rehearsal and dress rehearsal. The actors were meeting their lights for the first time. We were in the middle of the famous balcony scene—with Richardson as Cyrano, Margaret Leighton as Roxane and Michael Warre as Christian. Junior members of the company were slumped around the dim auditorium, watching. Guthrie was —as always—on the move in the aisles, eagle eyes alert as he backed away, cut across the back of the stalls, disappeared to re-appear with startling swiftness in the dress circle. Suddenly the handclap came, then the cry, 'For godsake, Ralph, play the scene! —play the play!' All action stopped on-stage. In the stalls we sat up, shocked and expectant. Here was to be the big row. 'Star Walks Out!' In tense silence, Ralph Richardson came from up-stage, slowly, right to the downstage edge. Peering, gimlet-eyed, from both sides of the great de Bergerac nose straight to the spot where Guthrie stood, he said clearly and coldly, 'I was brought up to find my lights. And I'm finding them; and for the first time in your production. So . . . don't call me a bloody fool—old cock.' In my innocence of theatrical professionalism, I was keyed up to hear Guthrie crack back at him. Instead he said 'Raight!' (clap of hands) 'On we go!' Richardson returned calmly to where he had been, and the rehearsal went on.

On October 3, 1946, *Cyrano* opened. It had been designed by Tanya Moiseiwitsch. In costume and setting it had a marvellous mellow integrity of tones; the whole thing deeply romantic. It moved with amazing fluency from scene to scene and Richardson had the wind of genius in him. Margaret Leighton was a dream of a Roxane, Alec Guinness such a stylish De Guiche. But the revelation of that production was the sweep of the Guthrie direction; and its effectiveness in the crowd scenes. In the first scene of the play, in the courtyard of the Hôtel de Bourgogne, the way in which one character (Cyrano) was made to emerge as the product of his whole society till he was finally the focal point of the whole play—this was superb. And then how the whole social tide of humanity surrounding him could smoothly ebb away—to leave him alone and suddenly so approachable by the whole audience— this was the Guthrie touch.

Within six months there followed two productions of immense satisfaction to him. He was asked by the Habimah Theatre to come to Palestine to direct a play of his choice. He thought it best that it should be something other than Shakespeare. Here was the opportunity he had hoped for—to do *Oedipus Rex*, a play of mythological universality. He was also invited to Covent Garden to do *Peter Grimes*, and with the original Sadler's Wells trio of talents, Benjamin Britten, Joan Cross and Peter Pears.

The Palestine expedition (for it was not yet Israel) is something everybody should read about in Guthrie's autobiography, *A Life in the Theatre*. The account cannot be bettered. Briefly, though, here were Judy and he in Tel-Aviv, guarded by armed Jewish irregulars, and living amid terrorist activity directed against the British Army. In the middle of it all he pulled off a production which thrilled Tel-Aviv and after which he and Judy had to be hurried out of the country; more or less at dawn after the first night. To get the play on they had risked remaining when the Embassy had advised all Britons to leave. In the year before, 300 civilians—British, Arab and Jew—had been murdered or injured by terrorists and, weeks before, a British Major and three British N.C.O.s had been seized and flogged in reprisal for the birching of a young Jewish terrorist. Yet they met with nothing except loving kindness. And a letter got back to Lincoln's Inn to say that his *Oedipus* had reached its tenth performance, that it had already played to 10,000 people, and that his name was 'the most popular in the Yishuv!' Later the production was to go, successfully, to Broadway. One can see what a success his patriarchal figure and kingship of command would be in that nation and that national company. The fact that the play had to be in their language, not his, only increased his attachment to *Oedipus* as universal, international, and the sort of drama that he had predicted to Guinness would be the drama of the future; for it had all the arts—music, too.

Peter Grimes: opened on a bitterly cold night, with a London fog sneaking into Covent Garden with the furs and tiaras. It even crept in backstage and some wraiths of the real stuff kept confluence with the artificial stage fog which swirled around the sea-timbers of Tanya Moiseiwitsch's set. This fisherman's structure ranged the whole width of the Covent Garden stage and had a grandeur in total harmony with the power and surge of the sea in Britten's big orchestral moments. Guthrie was, self-confessedly, a sucker for big moments. It was certainly a big occasion, and a successful one; and he was asked back to direct one of his other favourite operas, *La Traviata*.

1947 was a happy year, if restless. At the start of it he had even made his first visit to Australia, at the invitation of the Australian Government. In a sort of 'whistle-stop' tour, of six weeks, he tried to fulfil their request to report on the readiness of that nation to embark on some form of national theatre. His answer was negative at that time.

Christmas was spent at Annagh-ma-Kerrig, and made all the merrier by a quite unique and characteristic present he managed to engineer for his half-blind mother. She had loved to play cards. (He was addicted to Solitaire too.) The Christmas present was the biggest pack of cards you ever saw. While in America he had found that, in the town where his mother's mother had come from, Cincinnati, there was a company which made huge playing cards, 7 x 4½ inches, 'jumbo size'. They were for advertising purposes. But through the good offices and persistence of a Dr. Gus Eckstein—whom his mother would bless for many a day —two or three sets of these great cards found their way back to Annagh-ma-Kerrig. To see the Guthrie giant trio and Bunty play 'family' bridge with these cards was, as Alec Guinness said, to feel like Alice in Wonderland. To become involved in playing was not only to be embarrassed by such a huge fistful but to find that the rules of play were bent every way to let Tony direct everybody's hand, as if we were all players in his production.

News of the Old Vic was that the Centre was in operation, that the Young Vic Company had been out on tour, and lost a considerable amount of money in the good cause of taking first-rate theatre to young audiences, that the Old Vic School had moved from temporary premises in the Royal Ballet School to better quarters in Dulwich and was proving to be a positive and profitable success. Honours were in the air for the Old Vic directorate. Michel Saint-Denis, who had been given a C.B.E. for his war-time service in the BBC, had apparently turned down the honour of being director of the Comédie Française in order to develop the Old Vic Centre. In the New Year's Honours of 1947, a knighthood had been given to Ralph Richardson, and within months this was followed by an honour which made Laurence Olivier the youngest ever theatrical knight. There was some bitterness in the Guthrie camp about national honour related to national effort— aggravated by the amount the two stars appeared to be committed to in film and commercial theatre. There was bound to be some bitterness in Guthrie, but he genuinely liked and admired these two great men and no bitterness was shown.

While Olivier was worrying his governing board by having to postpone a planned tour of Australia with an Old Vic Company (because of delays in his *Hamlet* film), Guthrie, without much care in the world, was off with Judy to Finland to do another production of *Oedipus*, at the Swedish Theatre, in Helsinki. Again Sophocles and the play stood up to his expectations; and, as much of Guthrie's development in the art was devoted to productions of this particular play, it should be noted that neither the Habimah nor the Helsinki production was masked.

When he got back that spring, a news item was of immense interest to him. The Chancellor of the Exchequer, in April, had made a statement to the House of Commons that the Treasury was now prepared to allot one million pounds towards the building of a national theatre. There was, by summer, another, and shocking, piece of theatre news reached him: the Triumvirate were sacked. Sir Laurence Olivier had received his notice while he was leading the Old Vic Company, in Sydney, Australia. Sir Ralph Richardson had received his while he was in the U.S.A. John Burrell had gasped as he got his, cold at his desk in St. Martin's Court. The Old Vic Centre was in turmoil. The national press were sharpening pencils to report a national scandal. Guthrie was otherwise involved; trying to convince the Glasgow Citizens Theatre Company—on tour in Belfast—that they would perform an unperformable old Scottish play at the Edinburgh Festival.

CHAPTER FIFTEEN

FESTIVAL
(1948-1952)

IN THE previous year, 1947, the first Edinburgh International Festival of Music and Art had been successful enough for the second to be planned. And there were certain people in Scottish Theatre who were not happy that in the first festival the term 'international' had not extended to a drama contribution from their own nation. It was agreed by the Festival Committee that there should be some classic of the Scottish drama in the 1948 festival. James Bridie was authorized to approach Guthrie to see if he would produce such a play. Guthrie was interested—would always be—in a concept where Drama served a 'big day' or a community in festival, especially in his famous great-grandfather's city. There was, however, a very limited choice of play, among the Scottish classics. Out of a field of three he picked a play by Sir David Lindsay called *Ane Satire in the Thrie Estaites*. It was a sixteenth-century sort of morality, hugely long and in thick vernacular Scots.

The choice of play having being made, Robert Kemp, the Scottish playwright, was commissioned to bring it down from nearly seven hours' playing time to nearer two. The question was now to find a theatre. Guthrie came up to Edinburgh. The theatres were very few, and were either already booked or quite unsuitable for what he had in mind. What he had in mind was very vague. He knew that he wanted not so much the production of a play as the staging of a drama event, in the spirit and in the manner related to celebration in a city in festival. It is not inappropriate to remind ourselves that Edinburgh is called 'The Athens of the North' and that Guthrie was fascinated by the Greek city festivals. Just as Athens has its Acropolis high up at its centre, so Edinburgh has that temple of the military, the Castle, on its rocky mount. Both these sites are in fact quite unique: on one is the temple of Pallas Athena, on the other, the Chapel of St. Margaret, the oldest ecclesiastical building in Scotland.

Though not quite at the same height on the mount, there is another ecclesiastical building, the Assembly Hall of the Kirk of Scotland; where his great-grandfather was once enthroned, as Moderator General. The whole of one wet day, Guthrie, Bridie, Kemp and William Graham of the Festival office toured the city and tramped through a variety of '. . . halls ancient and modern, halls secular and halls holy, halls upstairs and halls in cellars, dance halls, skating rinks, lecture halls and beer halls'. It was in the vaguest of hopes, at the weariest of moments, that Robert Kemp said that, of course, there was the Assembly Hall.

It is a place specially designed to accommodate the great general assemblies of the Church of Scotland. They can there be seated in congregation, with the Moderator General on his throne. It is therefore, in its seating, all addressed downwards towards the throne and the area surrounding it, where the senior pastors of the flock and officials would sit. In this sense it is an amphitheatre. But, despite its seating accommodation plus lots of changing and committee rooms, it was nobody's idea of a 'theatre' at that time. The other wet weary searchers could have been excused if they had thought that James Bridie's provision of rum had inflated the Guthrie vision into flights of fantasy. He declared *this was it*. It was not simply the right end to this day's hunt through Edinburgh, but of years of tentative searching for the sort of shape for a playhouse for Shakespeare or classics like *Oedipus*. It must have seemed that fate was on his side from the start, because the Church of Scotland officials, who might well have raised their hands in horror at the very idea, calmly gave the go-ahead—just so long as he wouldn't be driving nails into the Moderator's Throne. (He nearly drove the caretakers to distraction, with his love of candles. Candle-wax was all over the good oak and stage 'blood' all over the floor.)

With his penchant for provocative shock, it was a god-given opportunity to turn the sacred stamping ground of respectable Scottish dogmatism into a theatre; and with a play whose verbal currency he knew would bring blushes to the cheeks of the lady burgesses. Here he was in his element as *enfant terrible*. Great-grandfather Guthrie's statue stood proudly down there below the Castle and the Assembly Hall. And there was a painting actually in the Assembly Hall of the Rev. Dr. Thomas preaching to a congregation, but with no roof between him and the vaults of heaven. Guthrie was determined to draw on all the local resources he could from a town in festival. The Castle would yield him soldiers, there would be boys' choirs related to the many city spires; citizens for small parts would be needed too. The community event was in his bones. To Guthrie Tyrannos, on his mount looking down, the only plague of this city could be its hard crust of conventionality. Would the people come up the Mound to see what was an unknown play in what was not a theatre?

There were others more doubtful than he, and more familiar with the scene—the company. James Bridie had hoped that the company could essentially be the Glasgow Citizen's Theatre Company. At the beginning of August they were on tour, and in Belfast. Guthrie came up from Annagh-ma-Kerrig to meet them and, in a Belfast rehearsal hall, he faced his principal players with the fact that the play *would* be staged in the Assembly Hall. They had their doubts about Sir David Lindsay's suitability as a playwright for modern ears, and for an international audience, many of whom would have difficulty in even understanding the King's English. 'Not to worry', the play was more to be seen and felt than 'understood'. Their doubts about the 'theatre' he dealt with by pacing out in the Belfast hall the stage he alone foresaw. Here was how he would box over the sacrosanct Moderator's throne; how steps from it would lead down to shallow staging covering the area forward of it right over to where the raked seating rose; how from the staging there would be a step or two down to the aisles. In fact, it would be what we now call a 'thrust' stage. But at that point he was thrusting out into unknown territory in the history of theatre architecture. And what was driving him on was the desire to strike a better relationship between players and audience than could ever be possible with any proscenium stage. Costumes would be important; and banners—lots of banners—not scenery.

They decided he was mad—but creatively so. But better his madness than most directors' sanity. Also a Guthrie fiasco would be preceded by Guthrie rehearsals, and these, the old S.N.P. players knew, were a joy. The Citizen's Theatre Company included some he had worked with in Glasgow, such as Molly Urquhart, Moultrie Kelsall, Fulton Mackay, Jean Taylor Smith, also Lennox Milne; one of the 'tented tours' converts to Theatre. One notable player to join them now was Douglas Campbell, a Glaswegian by birth, who had played for Guthrie at the Old

Vic. Rehearsal started as abruptly as ever: a very brief note on
the play and notes of utter brevity on the characters:

'Jean!'—(playing Chastitie) 'The Head of the Salvation
Army.'

'Lennox!'—(playing Veritie) 'Head of the Post Office.' Clap—
snap—and away! Three sessions a day for three weeks, morning,
afternoon and evening.

Every day at 1 o'clock they could almost feel rather than hear
that punctuation of the Edinburgh scene—the One o'clock Gun—
as it thundered over the city below from a high gun battery up at
the Castle, about half of the Royal Mile away. Guthrie made
contact with the military and reached a close understanding with
the garrison officer in charge of that thunderingly good open-air
show, the Edinburgh Floodlit Tattoo. In fact Guthrie's theatrical
know-how was sought, and he suggested some improvements in
the scaffolded seating which is erected round the Castle fore-
court and makes of it a whole playing area for this annual
'spectacular'. Several keen soldiers marched daily down to
rehearsals in the Assembly Hall. There they found themselves
under the sweeping command of a theatrical giant.

Music by the Scottish composer, Cedric Thorpe-Davie, was
worked in to become an integral part of the theatrical statement.
Mollie MacEwan did the stage design. Robert Kemp stood
by for script alterations (some of them more Guthrie than
Lindsay, or Kemp). They all worked furiously until the whole
alchemical brew was brought to the boil and the ingredients
of all the arts became substantially his sort of Theatre. But,
at the box office there was dull despair; an old, unknown play;
no stars; the *Church* Assembly Hall!

At the dress rehearsal the civic heads came to see, were
impressed, but the heads shook—dreadful booking—sorry—but
they must cut down the proposed length of the run. They did.
The first night came. Those there were thrilled to the point of
amazement. But too many of them were there on complimentary
tickets given away in final despair.

The next morning there was a thumping great queue at the box
office. It is one feature of such a Festival that there are lots of
talkative people around. By word-of-mouth the news spread that
something extraordinarily good was on up at the Assembly Hall.
People poured up the Mound.

Out of this came two crucial convictions for Guthrie: he now knew the sort of *stage* he wanted, and that the theatre he wanted should be in a recognizable community. It had all happened by accident, providence, fate—what you will. He had not had his eye on Edinburgh. He had had his eye on Canada. He had had his eye on Liverpool, even Stratford-upon-Avon, and of course National Theatre and London. But, in London, the Old Vic organization was now in danger of total collapse.

It had taken the Triumvirate's breath away suddenly to receive thanks and notice that their services would no longer be required after September 1949. It had been unfortunately hurtful that the chairman, Lord Esher, should have had to do this by letter, especially so for Olivier, who received his in Australia when he was acting with such spirit for the touring Vic Company that he had badly damaged a knee in a spectacular on-stage leap. The Australian company limped back up the Thames into Tilbury on a drear November day and Olivier consulted with a depressed Burrell who had battled on with productions of *Doctor Faustus* and *The Way of the World*. He had persuaded Hugh Hunt, director of the Bristol Old Vic, to direct a *Cherry Orchard*, and Alec Guinness had been taken on to direct *Twelfth Night*. Olivier now gave the new year at the New a lift with his *School for Scandal*, directing and playing opposite Vivien Leigh (now Lady Olivier); and John Burrell revived his *Richard III*. The 'three boys' went ahead with the Old Vic Centre—but it did not need the keen eye of Guthrie to see that the whole National Theatre scene was miserably confused.

After Edinburgh, things had continued happily for him. The New English Opera Group asked him to direct for them a new musical version of John Gay's *The Beggar's Opera* with music composed by Benjamin Britten. He made it an opportunity to work again with Tanya Moiseiwitsch, and the whole company took off for beloved Cambridge, where he found himself again rehearsing in the old Festival Theatre on the Newmarket Road. Peter Pears was to play Macheath; Flora Neilsen, Mrs. Peachum; Nancy Evans, Polly Peachum, and Otakar Kraus, Locket. They lived and worked as the old company had done; in community. He was pushing Acting within Opera. He had Peter Pears leaping on to a table at the same time as he had to hit a high note. He treated the chorus in a way that opera choruses were not very used to: 'Stop!! Stop! Ladies—to remember, please—you are whores in a whorehouse, not typists at tea. On!' It opened at the

Arts Theatre in Cambridge and moved on to Amsterdam, Utrecht, Rotterdam and Knocke, in Belgium.

A freelance now, he tried to plan his time to give as much of it as he could to Annagh-ma-Kerrig and his mother. Never other than mentally alert she was yet getting to be an old lady. Pressure had slackened and he was trying to promote his own play. He was also preparing to produce *Carmen* at Sadler's Wells. He did what work he could at home. For hours he would sit, in old chain-knit sweater, slippers on feet, smoking and listening to the Gram, on which he would play the opera through and through again. There would be a notepad on his knee (U.S. legal yellow if possible). He would be scribbling settings, in diagram, writing notes and, momentarily, even the Guthrie voice would come into play.

He had not long got back from a second visit to Helsinki, where he shook the Finns out of their dignity with a cheeky production of *The Taming of the Shrew*, and now, in the summer of 1949, there was one of the happiest professional expeditions he and Judy were ever engaged in—directing *Henry VIII* for Anthony Quayle at Stratford-upon-Avon.

Quayle had succeeded Sir Barry Jackson as artistic director of the Shakespeare Memorial Theatre (as it was then called). It was a heavenly summer. The question of lodgings for the Guthries came up. Suggestions were sent. The reply came. 'Don't want lodgings. Ask Dot [*Dorothy Hyson, Quayle's wife*] to hire for us *a covered punt*!' And a punt it was, with hooped canvas cover to keep off rain, wind and sun. The limited wardrobe they had (and they dressed forever as if there was a war on) was hung in a cupboard in the front of the house manager's office in the theatre. After the day's work they would walk out of that red brick memorial to the Bard, cross the front parking lot, descend a few steps, frighten off a few ducks, unhitch the painter and punt away, travelling smoothly up-river to their evening anchorage. In the punt would be the bare necessities of life; and both would be rich, very rich in what they had: peace, freedom and work that was fun to do. Looking back beyond their rippled wake, rocking ducks and suspicious swans, he would be facing the Shakespeare Memorial Theatre—a building with the appearance of a power station less the chimneys—and he might be thinking of what he advised Tony Quayle should be done with it. They had been talking about the sort of theatre proper for Shakespeare, a lovely shell that need be no more than a tent and that certainly should in no way be a too, too solid monument. 'You should build a "tin theatre"* on the river bank by the Dirty Duck' (a favourite actors' pub at Stratford). 'But, Tony—we can't have two theatres here. What would I do with the Memorial Theatre?' said Quayle. 'Push the monstrosity in the river,' was the reply.

The designer for *Henry VIII* was Tanya—she was beginning to be *his* designer. They had a rare understanding. He would scribble rough sets and costumes on backs of envelopes, sides of scripts, etc., and she would go to work from then on, completely trusted by him. All debates would be very open, remarkably unstrained. They both agonized over the Stratford stage, wrestling with steps and solid scenic elements, and here began years of discussion between them on the design of theatres. She had not yet seen the Assembly Hall staging. Theatres—'tin', tented and of all sorts— were in his mind then. As he punted away from the Memorial he could see the green bank-sides of the Avon and perhaps even recall that Garrick had done something he would like to do—for a Big Day, a Festival. In 1769 Garrick had tyrannized the authorities into building *his* tented, pavilion theatre: the Garrick Jubilee Rotunda. From the river one would have looked beyond a line of cannon to what appeared to be a big top rising from the meadow. Topping the canvas rotunda was a 'lantern' worthy to crown a cathedral, surrounded by flying pennants and with one huge central pennant floating in the wind. To the glory of Shakespeare, for Garrick's big day the cannon puffed and thundered, music was heard, flags fluttered in all colours; and James Boswell, dressed up as a Corsican chief, got royally drunk in the Masquerade. Guthrie would have loved it.

Punting or paddling, Tony and Judy would pass the big house Avoncliffe on the way and wave to Tanya and others of the company staying there, before they moved smoothly on to 'harbour' under willows about two miles out, towards Warwick. To their punt certain invitations would bring guests to take tea or 'dinner' of an evening. 'Evening dress' would be shorts or bathing trunks, loose shirt and sweater. The kitchen resources would be primus stove and an eccentric and small collection of provender from Judy's shopping in Stratford. Even Tanya, who knew by now the Bohemian range of crockery, cutlery—and

* He used this term for temporary theatre—the reference being to tin chapel as opposed to stone cathedral.

menu—at Lincoln's Inn, was a little shocked to see that the water
for tea was scooped straight up from the river. 'Not to worry.'
It all came out in the boiling, according to Judy. Inexperienced
actors would turn up to 'dinner' in best suits and find that gin
cocktails could be drunk out of anything from a china cup to the
tea-stained top of the rehearsal thermos flask. Soup straight out of
the tin would somehow be transformed into something quite
special by their gracious hostess. These sorts of gypsy occasions
saw Judy at her best. And somehow during it all she would be
able to emanate a quite remarkable dignity. However, from a
series of such events, the punt would begin to develop in a
genteel way an accumulative squalor, though this did not seem to
trouble them one little bit.

If the event at the theatre was not quite as much Festival as the
Edinburgh one, at least it was, as a play, a feast of colour. There
were banners enough and a fourteen-strong, on-stage contingent
of the Royal Warwickshire Regiment. Anthony Quayle was a
more than convincing Henry. Diana Wynyard was a delight to her
producer and her audience as Queen Katherine. The last night
was received with roars of applause that would not die down
with the final curtain. But Guthrie certainly made this beautiful
actress work for her success. She was in the middle of that great
inquisitorial scene, fighting for her life and dignity as Katherine,
the several clerical recorders of the court's proceedings bent over
manuscripts. But with their quill pens—under direct encouragement from the director—they were noisily scratching away to her
total distraction. She thought this was surely a mistake. 'No,'
Tony said. 'Wanted it—still want it.' 'And am I really to play over
that frightful noise?' 'Yaas,' was the reply. He might be wrong.
He was seldom uncertain. And he knew when, and exactly when,
he wanted the noise to stop, and intense and total focus to fall on
Katherine. In fact this was one of his great gifts: how to keep the
focus of attention on the point that mattered most in the process
of the story and the progress of the play. That point could sometimes be quite other than the star performer in full verbal flight.
Stars did not like this. People said he hated stars. It was not true.
He loved playing, and the play. And, of course, he hated self-
importance or pomposity. Diana Wynyard suffered from neither,
so she put up with the scratching quills and came gloriously
through into highlighted focus when she was meant most to be.

In 1950 Guthrie directed *Hamlet* again, in Dublin; produced

Falstaff and *The Barber of Seville* at the Wells; directed James Bridie's new play *The Queen's Comedy*, in Edinburgh at the Festival and in Glasgow. But the most crucial event for him was his production of his own play *Top of the Ladder*. For this, Laurence Olivier and he once more came together—Sir Laurence as management, he as playwright-director. On the conclusion of his directorship at the Old Vic, Olivier set up his own production company. He had taken a lease, together with Vivien Leigh, of the, now sadly departed, St. James's Theatre. And, as one of his plays, he chose to present *Top of the Ladder*, by his old colleague. Both men could now feel what Tony Guthrie once said to his Irish friend, John Gibson, about the ladder of success: 'On the way up everyone is excited to see the ascent, but once you're at the top there are hundreds of pairs of hands just waiting to drag you down.' Guthrie and Olivier had both been at the top of that ladder where the prize was presumed to be the direction of the National Theatre. At the St. James's, in October 1950, Guthrie produced his own play. It says something for Olivier and friendship (even allowing for his sense of showmanship) that he went against considerable opposition in his production office about doing it at all.

It was a considerable theatrical occasion. The play had a composite setting of scenic elements to be played with, rather than sets to be changed. These were designed by Roger Ramsdell, a scenic artist who over the years did much stalwart service backstage at the Old Vic. There were office elements, house elements and two features common to both—a ladder leading up and off into the flies, and a great patchwork quilt making a backcloth to all the action. At this quilt sat, and worked steadily throughout the play, Mookie; in Art a sort of universal Nannie figure, and in life Becky Daly, his own Irish nannie. The house of the play, Stone Lodge, though related to London, was a symbol of a residence not far away from that villa of suburban success, Warwick Lodge. Mookie was played by Esmé Church, with whom he had done so much work at the Vic.

The 'hero' of the play is in the executive class and is boss of a city firm. The theme of the play is more or less how a mother can smother and a father overshadow a son, so that he kills himself in the ascent of the ladder of success. The father in the play has been an overworked family doctor, the mother an over-fond parent who keeps his accounts and dotes on the son. Mikie—a

kind of valet—is not far away from Mickie Corrigan. As for Kath,
the secretary, Guthrie was a secretary's hero and in his life there
were several successes to the marvellous Miss Williams of the Vic.
Below the surface of the play moves a depth of symbolism. In
the introduction to the published version he says that at the top of
his ladder there were these four equivalents to Hamlet's ghostly
Father: Sir James Frazer, Sigmund Freud, James Joyce and Our
Father Which Is In Heaven. The action of the play—as with *The
Flowers Are Not For You To Pick*—takes place within the last
dying minutes of the hero. Much of the action, as with his radio
plays, is 'in the mind'. It can be argued that 'in the mind' is more
at home on Radio than Stage. It can also be argued that his own
dictum, that 'the last person to know what he has written is the
playwright', was something he had forgotten and that he was too
close to the play to produce it well.

There is one stage direction he put in the play which stands out
as unusual: 'The following is the key scene of the play and must
be given all possible stress.'

Bertie's son, Thomas, has just broken away and sailed out of
their life. He has left his mother, Katie, hysterical and his father,
Bertie, subject to her accusations that it is all his fault for 'forever
dominating, overshadowing him . . .' 'No one would think he
was your son. He might be a stranger. An absolute stranger . . .'

> Bertie moves into the 'office' part of the set . . . Kath, the
> secretary is there. And the crisis of the argument between
> them is:
> KATH: Bertie——
> BERTIE: Yes? . . .
> KATH: Your attitude to the firm, to Wingate, Tyrrell and Pitt.
>   All this time I've imagined—imagined you felt about it like
>   I did. But I see now that I was wrong. To you it meant—you
>   hoped it would be a means of extending yourself through
>   your son—my son shall succeed me in the Firm—it was to be
>   a means of dominating him, as compensation for—
> BERTIE: For what? Compensation for what?
> KATH: For the domination of *your* Father.
> BERTIE: (reacting sharply) Kath, there are some things that—
> KATH: No. I'm right. Do you know what has been the chief
>   incentive of your career? The desire—the need to excel your
>   Father.

BERTIE: How dare you. My Father has nothing whatever to
   do with—I loved and admired my Father more than anyone
   in the whole— You've absolutely no right to—
KATH: My dear, do be *reasonable*!
BERTIE: Reasonable! How *can* I be reasonable? How can *anyone*
   be reasonable? You make the most loathesome, detestable,
   disgusting, accusations about—*
There follows an irrational outburst from Bertie; after which
Kath walks out—out of his life.

and if it *is* the most important scene to the playwright 'and must
be given all possible stress', then the important thing is the
assertion—in the degree of violent denial of the 'hero' Bertie—
that sons pursue their ambitions only in order to outstrip their
fathers.

It is a very conventionally moral play of almost embarrassing
immaturity: childlike, verging on the childish, clever often to a
foolish degree. That was the man. But you cannot make the sort
of big and intimately personal declaration in public which this play
is without making yourself very vulnerable. It was not quite the
Follow Me hurt again. But it hurt him that the response was again
mainly respectful and mostly lukewarm. Despite the popularity of
John Mills and a fine performance by him as Bertie, it was obvious
that the play would not run. This was a somewhat disillusioning
conclusion to his biggest effort as theatre playwright. It was with
distaste for the whole business of West End theatre that he
turned away and went back to other theatrical plans—but not
Theatre plans.

For several months before this he had been involved in discussions with the Liverpool Festival Society. They hoped to
celebrate the 1951 Festival of Britain in their own way; and it was
his way—a way that takes one right back to public rituals seen
from the Tunbridge Wells nursery window: a sort of Street
Theatre. He was going to be directorial master of ceremonies in
10,000-strong street pageants. There might be river-boat spec-
taculars and all sorts of extravaganzas; all with the sense of a
Big Day. With plans for Liverpool confirmed with their organizer,
Alfred Francis, he was off, across to Belfast where Ulster's contribution to the Festival of Britain was to be a greatly augmented
version of the annual Belfast Festival of the Arts. There he was to

* *The Top Of The Ladder*, *Plays of the Year*, Paul Elek, 1950.
8

recruit a new Northern Ireland Festival Company. It was to play three new plays by Ulstermen: *The Passing Day* by George Sheils, *Danger Men At Work* by John D. Stewart and *The Sham Prince*, an adaptation by Jack Loudan of a nineteenth-century play by Charles Shadwell. These were due for the Belfast Festival in May but were to be taken across to London in March, to be presented at the Lyric Theatre, Hammersmith. On March 20 *The Passing Day* opened in London and was an immediate success. It had a strong cast and an excellent set, by Tanya Moiseiwitsch again. The very success had a bitter-sweet consequence for Drama in Belfast. It brought over to London such talented players as Joseph Tomelty, J. G. Devlin, Allan McClelland and Patrick Magee—all of whom left Belfast, where there was insufficient theatre work, got on to the ladder of success, and became part of the London Theatre and Film scene. The other two plays had not the same success, but altogether the season was a notable Irish event.

It attracted to it two visiting Irishmen very important to Guthrie's career: Bertie Scott and John Coulter. They saw their successful Ulster compatriots at the theatre, and on the night of Friday, April 6, they dined with Tony and Judy Guthrie in their Lincoln's Inn flat. Both men brought news of interesting developments in the theatrical scene in Canada. Bertie Scott, who had been Tony's voice teacher in Belfast, had been out in Canada very recently, on consultations to do with the Royal Canadian Conservatory of Music. While there, Coulter and he had got together. John Coulter was a distinguished Irish-Canadian playwright and man of letters, who had been editor of the *New Adelphi* magazine in London and was writing radio scripts for the BBC when Guthrie was known to him only as a bright young man at the Belfast station. In 1936 he married a Canadian girl and settled in Canada. As the author of a play on one of Canada's folk heroes, *Riel*, and of the libretto of a popular opera, *Deirdre of the Sorrows*, he became one of the pillars of the Toronto Arts and Letters Club. In 1945, he had alerted Guthrie to a matter being much debated there and in which he knew him to be really interested: the new post-war wave of enthusiasm in Canada for some form of National Theatre. Guthrie wrote back to Coulter at that time to say that, if the Canadian National Theatre idea went ahead, then he would come over to Canada at cost of transportation and maintenance only'. It is also interesting to note that he had said in 1945, that he would bring over Ralph Richardson to open with *Peer Gynt* as the first Canadian National production under his direction.

Now, in 1951, at supper in Lincoln's Inn, Coulter and Scott gave Tony Guthrie up-to-date information on the Canadian theatrical scene. It was all very promising but the debate was still going on and nothing was yet decided. Nine days after this happy and talkative Irish evening, Judy and Tony Guthrie had the shock of hearing that Bertie Scott had suffered a fatal heart attack and had in fact died in the arms of his old friend, John Coulter.

Another Canadian reunion happened very shortly after this. Robertson Davies and his wife and children visited London. They had a night at the opera with Tony and Judy, and again the talk got around to theatrical developments in Toronto, Ottawa and Montreal. Canada was therefore very much in his mind when, in May, he went off to Liverpool to prepare it for its celebration of the Festival of Britain. One should remember that the concept of festival was popularized by a post-war longing to get right away from the drab years of the war. In London the whole of the South Bank site—where the foundation stone of a National Theatre lay—was turned into a super-fairground where people danced to music in the open. Guthrie was in the middle of planning his processions of thousands when, on May 30, two sudden and simultaneous arrivals in Liverpool claimed his attention: Stephen Arlen, the company manager at the Old Vic, and an urgent letter from his old friend John Moody (now Director of Drama at the Arts Council). Both carried an anxious appeal: would Guthrie come back to London and try to save the Old Vic from imminent collapse? To Arlen—emissary for Hugh Hunt (who had succeeded the Triumvirate as Artistic Director at the Vic)—he made the typical Guthrie suggestion in moments of stress: 'Let's go for a walk.' And they took the ferry across the Mersey to Birkenhead and walked the docks and talked it out. Out of this conversation, and from Moody's letter, he gathered that the three responsible for the Old Vic Centre—Saint-Denis, Byam Shaw and Devine—had tendered their resignations; that the Artistic Director, Hugh Hunt, was in conflict with the Administrative Director, Llewellyn Rees; that the Chairman, Lord Esher, had offended most parties concerned with an acute attack of autocracy, before falling seriously ill; that the quality of the productions had

fallen off and finance was more than worrying. In these circumstances, Lady Violet Bonham-Carter and half the other governors
at least, plus George Chamberlain at the Vic, and John Moody
and Charles Landstone at the Arts Council, all agreed that a
strong hand at the wheel was the only thing to save the ship from
total wreck. Guthrie was the man for the job.

After much thought, but without delay or indecision, he said,
'Yes—it's time I came back.' And Arlen returned with a letter in
his pocket giving Guthrie's willingness to return if he had wide
powers to act and the governors could persuade the Liverpool
Festival Society to release him from his contract to them.

He could not have wanted to leave all the fun and public
panoply of his street processions. But there was a certain bitter
satisfaction in the fact that the Vic had found out that it could
not do without him. Lady Violet Bonham Carter wrote on
behalf of the governors to Alfred Francis and his Festival
Committee in Liverpool. Reluctantly—and with bitterness from
some—Guthrie was released, to pack and go, right away, to
London.

He returned to a hugely complex situation complicated by a great
collection of remarkable characters.* The Old Vic Company had
continued at the New while Saint-Denis continued to run the
Young Vic Company from the School, preparatory to moving the
Centre into the reconstructed Old Vic Theatre. But the senior playing company could not forever continue at the New; a proposal
was therefore put forward to find some other theatre on which
the Vic could take out a five years' lease (looking beyond this
probably to the day when a National Theatre would be built on
the South Bank site). As the Festival of Britain was being planned,
grants were allotted and it was thought at the Old Vic Company
that their grant could be used to help finance the leasing of such a
theatre; which on their current critical financial state they could
not otherwise afford. But the Treasury ruled out this use of the
funds granted. It then became obvious that the one economical
place for the Company to go to was back across the river to the
rebuilt Old Vic. However, a condition of Saint-Denis's taking on
the directorship of the Centre was understood by him to be the
assurance that the Old Vic Theatre would be his—for the Centre.
It was around this situation that the fur flew and 'the three boys'
angrily tendered resignations (not without the hope that the

* See Charles Landstone's *Off-Stage*. Elek Books, 1953.

predictable and outraged outcry this raised throughout the profession would lead them to be re-instated).

As Tony Guthrie crossed Waterloo Bridge and the Festival pennants flew from the South Bank site, all the committees concerned, and the Queen, were, ironically enough, preparing to re-lay the foundation stone of the National Theatre on its second site there, between the bridge and the new Festival Hall.

It was no easy job for Guthrie. And it has often been assumed that he moved in and ruthlessly closed down Michel Saint-Denis's School. But, the Old Vic School was demonstrably the most successful part of the three parts of the organization, the students at the School were in revolt in support of their beloved theatrical guru, Saint-Denis, and Guthrie was always on the side of the young. One of the first things he did was to see Saint-Denis and his two colleagues, George Devine and Glen Byam Shaw. He requested the three to honour their obligation to their students and to keep the School going for a further year. He then went to the Governors. Llewellyn Rees, the Administrative Director, had already been requested, by the board, to resign. It was decided that Guthrie should be Artistic Director. And he accepted, but only on condition that he had wide powers in the matter of policy and reorganization. Hugh Hunt was to stay, as Administrative Director. The whole grand plan of the Old Vic Theatre Centre was broken up, with the scrapping of the Young Vic Company. The old theatre was given to the Drama Company. The School was still in the Dulwich premises. Guthrie encouraged various attempts to attach the School to another professional school and keep it in existence. But the heart had gone out of the angry students and the offended Saint-Denis. All the 'three boys' thought they had been treated like boys, with scant respect shown by Lord Esher and the governing body. The School lasted another year; long enough to see its students out into the hard world of Theatre.

In this sad, surgical dismemberment of the organization and in his efforts to get the main Company back to a financially viable state, Guthrie had little time to do more than register that another letter had arrived from Canada, from John Coulter. It advised him seriously to 'investigate what is going on in Stratford, Ontario'. In that railway town some inspired and theatrically ignorant man had got going on some crazy scheme for a Shakespeare Theatre.

There was no time for much investigation while he supervised the recruitment of the next season's Old Vic Company and made a flying visit to New York to discuss a production of *Carmen* for the Metropolitan Opera House in the early new year. Meantime he took on the production of *Tamburlaine* for the Old Vic. In this he was adventurous enough to cast in the name part one of the English stage's most potent and difficult personalities, Donald Wolfit. In the event, two sorts of inspired tyrant co-operated, to stage one of the most exciting productions of that barbaric play anyone was ever likely to see (with superb sets designed by Leslie Hurry). On stage there were tents everywhere and the Tamburlaine encampment was a magnificent sight. Later in the year Guthrie produced (but only because John Gielgud was suddenly unable to) a not so fortunate *Midsummer Night's Dream*. With the Vic at least out of disaster he took off in the early New Year for the New York Met. As he flew he noted that in the New Year's Honours List a C.B.E. had been given to Flora Robson. He was, literally, a prophet without honour in his own country. All the more reason that he was anxious to hear just what was going on in Canada. He had at this point no wish to be tied more than necessary to the Old Vic—or Old England.

Carmen at the Met (for Rudolf Bing) let him put into effect on a grander scale the innovations he had brought into his earlier production at the Wells: notably, changing the location of the murder scene from outside the bull-ring to a sleazy inn. A self-confessed 'sucker for great moments' he had Carmen, when stabbed by Jose, clutch at the long red curtain of the window alcove and drag it down with her as she sank, dying, to the floor. He said he could not have wished for a better Carmen than Risë Stevens.

He returned to London to complete his obligations to the Vic with a searing production of that bitter play on man's ingratitude to man, *Timon of Athens*. But he also did something that contradicts my statement that he was without honour in Britain. One honour he was proud of came to him in 1948, when he was made a Fellow of the Royal Society of Arts. He now did something which was to be a regular feature of the Guthrie life: he gave a lecture to the Society. For a natural performer with great presence, wit, and that 'carrying' voice, lectures were almost his consolation for being a frustrated actor. They were also enormously useful to him at a later stage as a source of income.

The lecture was on the producer's art ('producer' equals director). He talked of the producer as 'a conductor'. In the whole orchestration of a production Guthrie often acted and looked like an orchestral conductor (Toscanini was one of his heroes). He said that the performance of a play was analogous with the performance of a piece of music. And he often used musical terms in directing players—'More brio, Chris! . . . in crescendo, crowd, please! . . . Pianissimo! Patricia.' On the question of playwrights he made a striking and apparently arrogant comment, that much of the process of playwriting was subconscious and that the first thing a producer had to do was to decide what the play was about, and the last person to consult should be the author. 'If the play had the potentialities of being an important work of art . . . the author would not have the faintest idea what he had written. I would lay any money that Shakespeare had only the vaguest idea of what he was about when he wrote *Hamlet*. It was produced from the subconscious.'* He went on to talk about the producer working from the audience's point of view.

It was in March of that year, 1952, that I saw him again, after several years of little contact. It was in the auditorium of the New Theatre at Oxford. The Vic Company was on tour—I think it was *A Midsummer Night's Dream* because a considerable number of that cast were also in the cast of my play *The Other Heart*. This they were rehearsing during the day. It was not Guthrie, my godfather in the art, who had brought the new play into the repertory. It was Irene Worth. She had taken it to Hunt and Guthrie when she joined the Company, saying that she wanted them to do it if she could play Catherine; which she did, beautifully. The Oxford incident is personal evidence of something several people have commented on: that Guthrie was not much given to praising and that generally praise came very obliquely. It also strangely links with his own play; in that both of us, without benefit of any mutual influence, had ended our plays with a ladder going off and up. Mine did not lead to any shadow of God The Father, or even to Freud. It led up to the noose of a substantial gallows on which François Villon was about to mount; in order to slip out of this world, as an act of final self-judgment. I was in the dark stalls. Michael Langham was directing Alan Badel, and Paul Rogers in

* *Cantor Lecture on The Modern Theatre*, Journal of the Royal Society of Arts, 2nd May, 1952. Vol. c.

this last scene. Badel, as Villon, had completed his reconciliation scene with his surrogate father, old William Villon. He turned towards the lower rungs of the ladder, began to mount . . . and a hand came from behind me, rested on my arm and pressed it. I turned to see Tony Guthrie nodding. It was the height of praise, coming from him. He was off, without a word, to see about another production for the Edinburgh Festival.

But John Coulter was in London. He was urgently trying to find out where Guthrie was. A wire from Toronto had overtaken him in London. It was dated May 5, 1952. And it read:

SEEKING TYRONE GUTHRIE'S HELP WITH AN UN-
LIKELY THEATRE PROJECT IN STRATFORD, ONTARIO.
WOULD YOU HELP.

DORA MAVOR MOORE

CHAPTER SIXTEEN

CANADA, TRIUMPH AND A TENT
(1952–1953)

JOHN COULTER went to Lincoln's Inn, found there only Judy Guthrie and Myrtle, their most memorable theatrical cat. Tony was in Edinburgh, preparing plans for the production of *The Highland Fair* for the Festival. Right on the heels of her cable Dora Mavor Moore had followed with a letter to Coulter enclosing one for Guthrie. This last he got to Guthrie on May 10, as the latter was on his way back to London. It was from the Old Vic Guthrie made his reply. And it is worthwhile noting his state when he wrote it. In detaching himself from the organization, he had proposed a long-term Administrator (to replace Hugh Hunt who had been obliged to become interim Administrative Director while Guthrie 'tidied up'). His proposed Administrator was Alfred Francis—the Merseyside businessman and organizer of the Liverpool Festival celebrations. Michael Benthall was brought in as Artistic Director. At this time he had considered the board of governors so rude to these two men that he had walked out of a board meeting, 'not to be seen again'. The nomad was obviously itching to move on. His reply to Mrs. Mavor Moore (whose letter was 'unofficial') was as follows:

> Yes; I am very interested in your 'unofficial' proposal. But, naturally, before I can commit myself, I want to know a bit more.
>
> Frankly I am not very attracted to the usual idea of 'pastoral' Shakespeare—viz; a rather impromptu stage in questionably suitable 'natural surroundings'. On the other hand I am intensely interested to produce Shakespeare on a stage which might reproduce the actor/audience relation for which he wrote—viz: the audience closely packed *round* the actors.
>
> I assume that at Stratford, Ont, the stage and auditorium are still to be made. And, if I could influence their design, I would be very happy to do so. Do, at an early opportunity, suggest to

8*

those responsible that it would be wise to avoid the usual course
of entrusting the essentially functional design of a theatre—even
an operation theatre—to the local Borough Surveyor, or a
landscape gardener, or—worst of all—to a committee!

I shall wait to hear further, assuring you that I am most
interested in the project, if it offers possibilities for a fresh
advance in Shakesperian production.

I have no *definite* commitments after this coming August; but
a good many 'possibilities'; so I'd like to hear soon.

Obviously he was raring to go. And, cunning gentleman that he
was, he had so talked himself into the job that they might feel it an
offence to put him off now. And, cunning too, he had flattered
them with the hope that they—way out there in Ontario—might
make 'a fresh advance in Shakespearean production'. And it is
worth stressing now that, from the start, it was to be a theatre for
Shakespeare.

He hoped to hear *soon*. But the summer came. Alfred Francis
took over at the Vic. He went 'home' to Annagh-ma-Kerrig, with
summer weeks and the Edinburgh Festival ahead. And he waited.
And he wondered. And, on July 8, a call came through to Newbliss 3. He lifted the heavy, old, black ebonite phone that sat in the
hall: 'Yaas?' And—according to him—from Toronto:

'This is Tom Patterson,' said a still, small voice out of the everywhere. 'Will you come to Canada and give advice? We want to
start a Shakespeare festival in Stratford Ontario. We will pay
your expenses and a small fee.'
  'When do you want me?'
  'At once. To-morrow, if you can.'
  Naturally, I said yes. I had some time at my disposal. It would
be fun to have another look at Canada after all these years. I did
not take the advice part or the Shakespeare festival very
seriously . . .*

Didn't take it seriously? He was so prepared and so keen to go that
before he had even sent that letter off to Dora Mavor Moore he
had preceded it, immediately, with a wire: 'INTERESTED AIR
LETTER FOLLOWS.' This was the one that must not get away.
This is what he had been after years before, when he had said to
his friends out there, 'If ever . . . I'll come for transportation and
subsistence.'

* *A Life In The Theatre.*

Tom Patterson, the 'small voice out of the everywhere' was a physically small man with a big idea. He was born in Stratford, Ontario, completed his education in the University of Toronto and was now a publicity man in the employment of McLeans the publishers. And being a publicity man in a big city of a big nation he was trained to have big ideas. He was, according to a close friend, 'well up on Civic Administration; and the best authority around on Municipal Sewerage but he knew Hell-all about Theatre'. Yet he wanted to provide his birthplace with a theatre.

There was a practical reason behind this fanciful desire. Stratford had, as the heart of its economy, the great railway workshops. He had seen what cruel things had happened to his home town when its economic heart came under threat during the 1930s Depression. And now, in the 1950s, the new railway engines were to be diesel engines. The Age of Steam with its roaring giants was over; and the great Stratford workshops were under threat of closing down. If they did, the heart would go out of Stratford. What to do? Then he got his big idea.

His town was not only called Stratford, a river—well, almost a river—ran through it, called the Avon. The wards of the town were called Falstaff and Romeo and there was a street called Hamlet. If Stratford-upon-Avon in England could be a bonanza town for the tourist trade, why could not Stratford-on-Avon, Ontario, be also? It did not seem to occur to him that the other Stratford was the birthplace of someone with even more universal ideas than he—and that that was quite a draw for the public. His idea became an obsession and he began to be a very positive nuisance, promoting it in the face of all sorts of 'wise' opposition. It was about this time that John Coulter directed Guthrie's attention to what was going on around Stratford.

Patterson's persistence got him a committee and at its head a citizen who had a big heart, a stubborn resoluteness and a strong streak of religious rectitude—Dr. Harry Showalter. A man neither to be pushed into foolish dreams nor panicked out of proper ones, Showalter ran a highly successful business dealing in non-alcoholic beverages. One of these was called Kist. (The great publicity gimmick for this product was a shop-front banner which all its Stratford purveyors displayed, 'COME IN AND GET KIST') Tony Guthrie blessed this beverage with the name of 'Château Showalter', and had every reason eventually to bless the man.

It is of interest in the Guthrie history that before ever he came on the scene, Olivier (unbeknown to him) was almost brought in. The Committee authorized Tom Patterson to spend $125 to get himself down to New York, where Sir Laurence Olivier was performing. By sheer native push he was to get through to the great man and convince him that it would be great for him to lend his name, and perhaps his presence too, to this New World Stratford Shakespeare Festival. But even Tom Patterson's push was not enough to get through the defences thrown up around the world star. He came back from New York defeated.

Then came an unpredictably helpful result of all the talk and rumour. Some Shakespeare enthusiast from Edinboro, Pennsylvania, came to Stratford and to Tom Patterson, when Tony Guthrie was still in Edinburgh, Scotland. He was in hope of a job in what the papers said was a new Shakespeare Festival Theatre. There was not much hope of a festival at the time, let alone a theatre. There was not even a job in it then for Patterson. So he took the man along to meet his friend Mavor Moore, son of Dora. As Mavor was in the middle of setting up the TV in Toronto, there might be some job with him for an enthusiastic arts man. Whether the man got a job or a return ticket to Edinboro, Penn., does not concern us; what does is that Tom Patterson got together with the Mavor Moore family. Tom did not really know which way to turn. 'Have you talked to my mother about the idea?' Mavor Moore said. Tom had not. So Mavor directed him to her office. And this is where Guthrie in 1952 reaped from seeds sown in 1931—when via James Bridie's introduction he had met that vital lady of the Toronto theatrical scene—Mrs. Dora Mavor Moore.

It became obvious to her that Patterson knew very little about what she knew so much about—Theatre. What he needed for his project was not so much a 'star' like Olivier, but a 'name' director. The name she had in mind was Tyrone Guthrie, the brilliant young man who had produced 'The Romance of Canada' and who she knew had done wonders now with her cousin in the old country. It was after this visit from Tom Patterson that she sent off the cable to John Coulter, and the letters to him and Guthrie.

When she got Guthrie's more than favourable reply, she summoned Tom Patterson to her office again. 'I have the man you want, and I know that he is interested—Tyrone Guthrie.' She had the right to expect an excited reaction. What Tom Patterson said to her was a non-committal 'Fine'. Because what he said to himself was, 'Who the hell's Tyrone Guthrie?' And it was not till he had had time to nip into a public library and look Guthrie up that he enthusiastically responded. She suggested that he should put a call through right away to Guthrie at his home in Ireland. That was when the ancient, upright telephone rang in the high hall at Annagh-ma-Kerrig. And after answering it Tony did literally fly out the next day.

Now that Tyrone Guthrie was coming, one thing about that telephone call worried Patterson. He had nervously told him what he could, about town, the site, etc. Then the question of a fee was mentioned and Patterson had more cause for nervousness, because nobody had given him any authority to offer anything. He found himself mentioning a figure of say $500. What he did not know was that, just before he mentioned the figure, some leprechaun on the Irish line cut them off. When they got connected again everything else was briefly agreed and Tom Patterson rang off under the impression that the great man was coming for $500. He wasn't to know that he would have come for $5.

So, 'Doctor Guthrie' was due to arrive (in 1950 he had been made an honorary Doctor of Law at St. Andrew's University, Scotland, and, in Canada, he enjoyed this form of address which so ran in the Guthrie family). Tom Patterson was sent to the airport in a small Volkswagen, with instructions to look for a 'tall wraith of a man' with an almost military haircut and eyes as piercingly observant as Leo Tolstoy's. (The Mavors had been friends of the Tolstoys.) Off the plane came a whole posse of tall men answering this description. It was a deputation of Canadian Mounties in civilian clothes. But one tall figure, bare-headed and in 'best blue', did not move off with this police posse. Little Tom Patterson, feeling like David in the approach to Goliath, got near enough to identify the Anglo-Irish giant.

The talk about the project started so immediately and went off at such a spanking pace, that by the time Dr. Guthrie was trying to compress himself into the small Volkswagen, Tom Patterson was surprised by—and comforted by—the banality of, 'Jesus Christ!—my luggage!' 'Never mind. I'll fix it,' said Patterson. And the little bespectacled Canadian impressed Guthrie by the alacrity with which he did so. This was a more youthful and zestful member than usual, in Guthrie's experience of committee members. He would have been impressed too by the economy with

which Patterson fixed his Toronto accommodation for the night.
He had gone to Dora Mavor Moore in despair: 'I haven't got the
cash to put him up in a respectable hotel.' (If he had known Tony
Guthrie beyond the pages of *Who's Who* he would have known
that Guthrie was happiest at a Y.M.C.A. or a two-star hotel with
the one-star bill.)

Dora was not keen to get stuck with more than the $25 of that
telephone bill. But she was not going to see the visit spoilt on its
very first night. 'He can come to us—for tonight anyway.' 'To us'
was to one of the oldest wooden-built houses in Toronto; built in
1814. When Guthrie first entered it, he said, 'It reminds me of my
mother's home.' Indeed there were ways in which the matronly
authority of Mrs. Mavor Moore would remind him of his own
mother; the same intelligence, warmth, and impatience.

Next day Tom Patterson drove Dora Mavor Moore and
Guthrie the 125 miles or so out to Stratford. And all the way his
ranging eye would be telling him—because he was a fateful man—
that this was 'his way' to travel. In fact there was something
dreamlike in a journey which began as they left the Toronto
suburbs with a sign which said 'Islington', and that they should
roll on through open corn country of the county of 'Perth' to
reach 'Stratford', north of 'London', passing through a hamlet
called 'Shakespeare'. In Stratford, the bridge which spanned the
Avon carried a 'Waterloo' road; and around the verges of the
Avon waters there were great willows which would have been at
home on the banks of the Cam or the Isis. It was rather like a
dream. On the way, he got to know Tom Patterson, and Patterson
got a whiff of Guthrie common sense and Guthrie command. In
the embarrassing position of having taken a wrong turning and
having lost his way in his own native territory, Patterson stopped
at a gas station to ask the way, 'No,' said Dr. Guthrie, firmly.
'Takes two to find the way when lost. *I'll* ask the questions, *you*
listen to the answers.'

Without delay he met the Committee. And using to the full the
aura of exotic authority brought all the way from old England,
and speaking to keen but theatrically innocent folk who looked
eminently responsible and responsive, he had the courage to tell
them that they had better call the whole thing off now if they were
not prepared to find a lot of money and, for the first year, lose most
of it. Also, he was not for a moment prepared to commit himself
to their proposed Festival if—Tom Patterson had the Guthrie eyes

fixed on him—if they were just thinking of it as a good promotional gimmick which would bring busloads of tourists from
Detroit and make the shopkeepers' cash registers ring to a merry
tune. *However* (and one can hear the Guthrie nasal intake of breath
and the pause for effect) *if* they were prepared to do something of
such significance, in the Art of Theatre, and the presentation of
Shakespeare, that the above would merely follow as a by-product
of other aims more spiritual—both for the benefit of Stratford
and the Canadian nation as a whole—*then* he would do what he
could to realize Mr. Patterson's dream; and to see it through with
them.

It was a thrilling moment. Yes, they would. Then Yes, he
would. The project was 'on'.

It was a heavenly July evening and all were forgathered to end
the day in the elegant house of engineer Mr. Alf Bell and his
dynamic architect wife, Dama. This was on the other side of the
Avon from where he had been shown a sort of public park bandstand. This bandstand had been the first choice of Tom Patterson,
as the place where the plays might be played. But after the Guthrie
address this could only be referred to apologetically. No, a
special site must be chosen; theatres from the 'tin' to the tented
must be talked of; but for the moment he must recross the Stratford, Ont., Waterloo bridge and get some sleep. They crossed it.
And not for the first time on that historic day Tom Patterson had
a red face. At the Windsor Hotel, where he had booked Dr.
Guthrie in, there was not a sign of a soul. True, it was late, but an
empty reception desk and no night porter? 'Not to worry,' said
the Doctor and strode up to the derelict desk. There he thumped
not the reception bell but the cash register. And he persisted in
thumping it till a bleary-eyed night porter, with a limp, came into
the hall, saw the giant, and with understandable alarm said, 'What
y' doin?' Purpose firmly but quietly explained, the Doctor from
England was shown up to his room and the nervously exhausted
Tom Patterson drove back over the Avon to his parents' house.
There was no sign of exhaustion in the Doctor. He came back
downstairs, struck up an acquaintance with the lame night porter,
and talked till 3 a.m., no doubt quietly provoking his companion
by his questions into the answers that gave him a rundown on
the town and what was going on. In the quiet Stratford night the
sound of the 'lonely moose' hooter on the great trains could
remind him of the great railway town it had been; and also of his

own Canadian National Railways days. Things had definitely taken a fateful turn.

In the remaining days of this first visit he had time to see the town; and liked what he saw. It was large enough to have the necessary core of imaginative and intelligent people to get things going. It was small enough to feel itself to be one community. Theatrically it *could* be his chosen community; for his sort of Theatre—they were the sort of people who would respond to his benevolent tyranny. His Canadian friend, Robertson Davies, later wrote of him:

> His greatest gift was not specifically theatrical; it was that power to discern what was best of each one of a group of widely differing people and to use them in a common cause, which is characteristic of great leaders in politics and the church . . . Let no one suppose that I underestimated his powers as an artist . . . But it was this power as a leader that pulled us through, gave us a faith in our own abilities.

The immediate things that had to be decided within these limited days were choice of site and type of theatre. For a moment, in the Canadian air, in the morning sun, his love of festival and the extravaganza almost tempted him back to the pageantry of an open-air affair. Standing on the slope of the park at tree-top level to the willows, with swans and the Avon waters of the lake some hundred yards away, he had talked of barges, island stagings and . . . 'No! Quite nonsensical,' he checked himself. He was not going to settle for the open air, noisy birds, even train whistles, and uncontrollable children off. This was not what he had come here for. It had to be a new theatre constructed to the old recipe of playhouse for which Shakespeare wrote the plays. But the high cost of bricks, mortar and labour daunted him; and it petrified Patterson. He knew, in a way Guthrie did not know then, that the whole town was by no means behind him. By the time the milk-man (who was to become one of the world's best front-of-house men) had done his own unofficial public opinion poll—during his milk-rounds—it was pretty obvious there would be as much opposition as support. Also, the next-door town of London considered that it could show a much better history of theatrical activity, and if Guthrie was coming to pioneer theatre, why not in London? (The name, at that point, would have been no recommendation to Guthrie.)

With various forms of structure under discussion, they drove Guthrie the three-hour journey back down to Toronto. Further talks went on with Dora and her son, Mavor Moore. She offered to be helpful in suggesting who was who in the recruiting of Canadian company. And Rupert Caplan of the Montreal days also offered the same help. Both offers were accepted. But, although Guthrie wanted the whole concern eventually to be entirely native to Canada, he knew that the North American public was not going to flow to that little township out there, just because it happened to have some parallels to Stratford, England, or some crazy new Canadian Shakespeare Show. Of course he knew that Canadians were used to jumping in large cars with packed picnic hampers, and to travelling huge distances in order to see something spectacular. But it was essential, he thought, to go back to the sort of idea which sent Patterson after Larry Olivier. There had to be, in the package offered the public, at least one 'name', one worldwide star. He, or they, should come and play as the nucleus of a Canadian playing company. But before one approached any star, one would have to know wherein he was going to play.

Guthrie the nomad, Guthrie of the tent, spoke of tents. Mavor Moore remembered that, outside Toronto, there was the Summer Theatre of the Melody Fair. They played musicals in a big-top tent. They were playing one now. Again they bundled into the little Patterson car. They paid their way into the Fair's big top. They sat right through the performance of the musical. Guthrie sat totally silent, entirely observant. The show was over. They drifted back to the parking lot, then Dr. Guthrie turned back, looked at the tent from all possible angles again. They waited for him to come to the car. As he got his long legs in, he broke the silence: 'The tent's the thing.' All the Guthrie loves were coming together in the one place: tents, theatre, trains, pioneering and an adequate community with much Scottish—and Irish—blood in its veins.

With this decision made about the tent, Patterson and he went back up to Stratford. There they prepared to face a full committee meeting in formal session in the Town Hall. In the Windsor Hotel, Tom Patterson began to go from awe to laughing admiration of the man. For he now could see how unstuffy he was and how his own people, of pioneer stock, would warm to the Doctor's 'wicked' humanity. 'Christ!' he heard come from the bathroom—where he thought the splashing meant his guest was washing his

face—'I've washed the clean one!' Travelling lighter than light
was a Guthrie art, and he had recently blessed the technological
age for the invention of the nylon shirt. He now travelled all over
the world with only two: one on, one off. He was now left in the
summer heat with the soiled one (and he was a great shedder of
perspiration). To buy a new one would outrage the Guthrie sense
of economy. So, Rise above it!—on went the soiled one. On their
reconnaissance runs round Ontario they would stop at a petrol
station for 'gas' and—with the discipline of a punt-dweller—the
great Doctor would resort to the toilet, wash through the dirty
shirt and then, as they drove away, drape it out to dry in the
baking hot back of the car.

Off they went to the Town Hall and when the Doctor stood up
to speak—to the shock of some and the delight of most—he threw
off his jacket, apologized for soiled shirt and cracked right into
action. Speaking with urgency and wit from notes written on the
back of a cigarette packet, these were the requirements he laid
down:

1. Theatre to be on the site he had indicated, on the park slope
   overlooking the Avon's lake.
2. Theatre to be specially designed and its fabric—at least at first
   —to be not bricks and mortar but canvas: a pavilion to the Art
   of Theatre.
3. The stage within the tented shell to be specially designed and
   the designer to be Miss Tanya Moiseiwitsch; who should work
   in conjunction with a Canadian architect.
4. Somebody here—'Not me—not my business to be your agent'
   —should go to Britain on 'a shopping tour' to get us an
   international star. Suggestion—Alec Guinness (brilliant actor
   now a 'name' and a world star through the film screen).

Having established the principles of his tyranny, he swept off
to visit Rob and Brenda Davies, in Toronto, saw his godchild of
the Davies brood, and flew off home. And so ended the first visit.
There was planned to be a second visit to audition and recruit
company and to see architect about tent. Also a third on which
Judy should accompany him.

Before he left, Harry Showalter had seen to it that Dr. Guthrie
was rewarded with a respectable fee. Showalter had raised the
necessary cash by the simple expedient of not asking but telling
specific fellow citizens that they would give such and such an

amount; and, now they had seen and heard Guthrie, they did. This alone shows the infectious enthusiasm Guthrie left at work in Stratford while he got back to his Edinburgh Festival commitments, and with fascinating news for James Bridie.

In Canada he left the Voice of Guthrie; to be heard throughout the land. The following is from a CBC recording he had made during the visit and which was loosed on the nation now:

. . . What likelihood is there that there will be a more flourishing theatre in Canada? None—*unless* Canadians begin to feel that a serious theatre is not merely an amenity—but a *necessity*. Don't mistake me: naturally nobody thinks that the theatre is a necessity in the same category as bread. It is perfectly possible to live without any theatrical art as it is perfectly possible to live without being able to read . . . but . . . it now looks as though Canada might well be the richest and, in a material sense the most powerful community in the world, indeed, that the world has ever seen. This community will eventually be judged by posterity. In the eyes of posterity mere richness will only be a cause of envy and even possibly contempt. It will avail little that owing to superb nutrition, achieved with small regard to the condition of the rest of the world, the busts of the females, the biceps of the males, were of stupendous size; that such and such a proportion of the population possessed a helicopter or even a washing machine. These tangible standards of civilization, that seem so important and real because they are measureable, do not mean much after the washing machines, the helicopters, the busts and the biceps have crumbled to dust. Posterity will judge us on our achievements in the spiritual sphere.*

'Our achievements'—he surely had thrown in his lot with the Canadian nation. If only the Pattersons, Showalters, Bells, Mavor Moores, Gaffneys, Griffiths and all would face the challenge. They were facing it; and what they were most facing was the probable cost. They were talking in terms of $15,000. Dora Mavor Moore and Tom Patterson went to see James Cowan, the PRO of the powerful J. Arthur Rank film concern in Canada. He was born in Shakespeare. They went to him about finance but also about Alec Guinness. They badly needed both, and Guinness was under

* *Our Special Speaker* series, CBC Trans-Canada Radio Service, 1952.

contract to Rank's in London. They were taken by Cowan to see
the Canadian President of Rank of Canada, Leonard Brockington.
From him they got firm advice on both matters. About finance?—
they would need nearer $75,000, not $15,000. And as a carrot to
get the donkey moving he was prepared, on behalf of the Rank
Organization, to guarantee the last $15,000 of that sum. About
Guinness?—'Get to London and go after him. I'll speak to the
London office.'

In August Tom Patterson and his wife set off for Scotland,
taking his mother along to see where the Patterson ancestral roots
were; and first to see Guthrie, who was in Edinburgh. There
Patterson also saw the Assembly Hall in action. The Old Vic
Company was there, with Alan Badel playing Romeo to Claire
Bloom's Juliet. Guthrie talked again of theatrical tents and sent
the two female Pattersons off up to Pitlochry, to a theatre which
began as a tent—and went on to be a building containing the tent
fabric. Tom Patterson he dispatched to London to seek out Alec
Guinness, who was now playing in Sam Spewack's *Under the
Sycamore Tree*. If it came to talking of plays, 'offer him *Hamlet*,'
Guthrie said. But if it came to talking of fees? Tom Patterson
wanted anxiously to know, for it was very vague what authority
he had from home except to seek Guinness's 'interest'. 'Fee? Your
business, Tom. Not proper,' said Guthrie again, 'for me to act as
your agent.' Patterson took a deep breath, and made for London.
Tony had written Judy, who was at Lincoln's Inn, to make
arrangements for Alec Guinness to meet Mr. Tom Patterson. In
fact they first met in Guinness's dressing-room, between matinee
and evening performance. It was an awkward conversation, a
defensively shy star meeting a defensively uncertain and over-
awed novice manager. Tom tried to explain the scheme: that the
festival would have two Shakespeare plays, six weeks of rehearsal
plus four weeks' playing. And fee? Well, what about $3,500? He
was delighted that this stab at it brought a calm, 'Yes—all right,
but I must know more about it, of course.' The meeting had to be
brief. They met again for lunch the next day. Tom said that, about
plays, Dr. Guthrie had said to suggest *Hamlet*. This suggestion
was not taken at all well—a coldness crept in. Tom Patterson was
not to know that in the previous year Alec Guinness had taken on
to play and produce, at the New, what turned out to be a somewhat disastrous production of *Hamlet*. Could it be that Guthrie
was going to show him? A remark was made that a certain

gentleman was very good at encouraging actors and quite good too at slapping them down when they became stars. But a long letter from Guthrie arrived to say why he had not himself made the approach—not to put any obligation on him, as friend. He stressed the international importance of the scheme and the importance to it and to Canada of having a star. Guinness decided to go. After all he loved to work with Guthrie. Rank in London were co-operative and agreed to release him for the required time. But *Hamlet* was discarded and in further discussions with Guthrie it was decided that the 'more melodramatic *Richard III*' would better suit the sort of open stage he had in mind.

Now Tanya—who knew next to nothing of the plans—was invited to dinner at the Lincoln's Inn flat; and accepted the invitation, thinking it was to be just with Tony and Judy. However she had not consulted her diary. She arrived breathless at the top of the worn wooden stair, knocked, and, hardly before she was inside, apologized that she 'had made a terrible mistake'. Please, could she switch on the radio. Old Mo was on—at the Albert Hall. (Her father, Benno Moiseiwitsch, was at that moment playing her favourite Rachmaninov piano concerto at the Proms.) Tony immediately switched on, the Albert Hall applause for the entry of the soloist came through, and, gratefully, Tanya subsided in a chair. She noticed another stranger, a little man, in the flat, but all listened in rapt silence and heard the whole concerto right through. Then Tony switched off and said, 'I want you to meet Mr. Tom Patterson, who—Well, Tom will explain.' And over dinner Tom Patterson did. Tony put it to her, 'We want you to come.' This was a somewhat sudden arrival at what she could see was quite a crossroads in her career. But, to the Guthries' delight (and to Tom Patterson's, too), she decided on the spot that she would go. Before Tom Patterson went back, Irene Worth had agreed to be the second imported star for the Stratford, Ontario, opening season: an actress greatly respected by Guthrie and all the more right for this adventure that she was born on the American side of the Atlantic.

By challenging and persuading—in a manner that made each of them feel they were facing an important moment of choice in their lives—Guthrie got 'Stratters, Ont' (as the Guthries and Tanya called it now) a superb stage director, Cecil Clarke; a splendid maker of costume, Ray Diffen; and a whole production team known to him as professionally first-rate. Cecil Clarke was a key man. He had come into the Old Vic after the war, in which he had been a very young and very successful staff officer. It must have endeared him to Guthrie-of-the-street-processions that Clarke organized the Victory Parade in Berlin. He was still stage director with the Vic Company when in that summer he and Guthrie travelled up to Edinburgh, by train. Guthrie leaned forward to his fellow passenger and started the Stratford story. Before they reached the end of the journey, Cecil Clarke too was 'on'. It was he who first would have to go to Canada in charge of the advance party.

With all plans on the move both at his and at the Canadian end, Guthrie could look towards next summer as very probably one of the most important for him. With the remains of this summer comparatively free he went over on his own to Annagh ma-Kerrig to see how things fared with his mother. She had not been well. He reported back to Judy at Lincoln's Inn that he had taken his mother up through her garden in a wheelchair in lovely weather. Thinking of Canada and the possibility of being a considerable time out of the country, it was a matter of some concern to him that she should have the care and attention she needed now. But there was her faithful companion-nurse, Miss Worby ('Bunty'), and there were the Irish Folk: with Mary Burns and her gentle husband Bob (Nickie Corrigan's successor) as servants in the house. She was well surrounded by affectionate helpers. And Peggy was near, always ready. By October, when he checked up again, heavy autumn gales had stripped the trees of most of their colour, but he was able to report his mother stronger. He also announced with wicked confidence, 'I am completely re-writing Mr. Pirandello's 3rd Act—cutting reams of rather dull shallow metaphysics that we've already had in Act I.' He was preparing an entirely new version of *Six Characters in Search of an Author*.

He had added to this letter, 'No word from Canada re whole project!' But then he heard. Letters began to flow. He was to make his second visit in December to plan for a June opening. By now he was committed to another and earlier event in 1953. In June the new Queen, Elizabeth II, was to be crowned. As their coronation production the Old Vic planned to do that play about the celebration of the birth of Elizabeth I, *Henry VIII*. Who better to direct it than the man for banners and the big day? So, he and Tanya worked on two projects: the design of the Stratford,

Ontario tent, and the staging, and also the designs of costume and settings for *Henry VIII*.

As Tony and Tanya got to the point where she could construct a scale model of the proposed stage, Tom Patterson, in Stratford, was pushing ahead at top speed. He was now the first full-time employee of the newly established 'Stratford Shakespearean Festival of Canada Foundation'. Money was the major concern. The budget was predicated at the more realistic figure of $150,000. To little Stratford this was phenomenal—and to some of its citizens a wicked sum to squander on a theatre. The local *Beacon Herald* was vastly sceptical too. But first responses to fund-raising were not at all bad and the Committee had the encouraging support, all the way, of the Governor-General of Canada, Vincent Massey.

Dr. Guthrie was to make his second visit in the first week in December, and only for a week. Its prime object would be recruitment of the playing company. From England the British quotient was to be strengthened by two strong 'supporting players'—Douglas Campbell (now at the Vic) and Michael Bates. Tanya completed her scale model of the proposed stage and got it to the Lincoln's Inn apartment two days before Tony flew off for Montreal with it in a hat box.

He 'did' Montreal, 'did' Ottawa, and Toronto, at a speed well beyond the capacity of most American tourists; nothing to do with seeing the sights. He was seeing players; hundreds of them. He 'auditioned' or rather interviewed 317 players in five of his seven days. He took advice from those he trusted—like Rupert Caplan in Montreal, Amelia Hall in Ottawa and Dora Mavor Moore in Toronto. Of the hundreds he says:

> I narrowed this down to about sixty probables, about whom I had notes as to size, shape, colouring and my own very personal reaction to our meeting . . . The rejects were those who had no experience or who failed to convince me that they were seriously prepared to do a job of work. I turned no one down for being plain or shy or because of the way he was dressed.*

He was wise enough in the business not to value auditions highly anyway. Either you know the players from whom you are casting or you take a chance. Some of the best are at their very worst on the sort of slave market block an audition stage can very well be.

* *A Life In The Theatre.*

Some of those most impressive at auditions turn out to be exhibitionist fade-outs when it comes to rehearsals and work. He would not take on anybody who was not prepared to *work*.

In Stratford he found that the site on the park slope facing the lake had been donated by the authorities and confirmed as suitable by the Toronto architect taken on to design the tent, Robert Fairfield. At all stages along the way, of interviews and conferences, the hat box, with its model of the stage, went along. The architect was impressed. A firm was found over in Chicago willing to make a tent big enough to cover stage, auditorium, dressing-rooms. At this point it cannot be over-emphasized that this project was beginning right from scratch. 'Scratch' was a hole in the ground, a belief in the value of Theatre, and sheer faith; in a community of people who mostly did not know the meaning of such a word as 'auditorium' and were blessedly ignorant of the enormity of the task they were taking on. Down in Toronto many know-alls said it could not be done. Up in little Stratford they did not know it could not be done. So they did it.

But even in Stratford the town became divided within itself. Gossip got around about Alec Guinness coming. Who? Somebody was having somebody on. Alec Guinness? He'd never come here! That dreamer, Tom Patterson, was moving back into his home town and talking big about thousands coming to his theatre who would bring the tourist trade. All right, but where were they to go? There weren't the hotels for them. Next thing, they'll be asking us to open up our own homes to strangers, for bed and breakfast! (Which they did, some getting a fat fee and some asking for the first year nothing at all.) But despite the various murmurings, Harry Showalter and his team of enthusiasts grew and work went on, much encouraged by the spirit of Oliver Gaffney, the building contractor, who agreed to start with little sight of the money needed. But, within their responsible councils there were so many 'buts'. Cecil Clarke was the one who first met them all, in their frightening practicality. With his arrival, there was introduced a note of impressive professionalism to which the local enthusiasts would have to measure up. At Guthrie's request he reviewed the players so far chosen, so that there should be a second opinion, then he went into contractual problems, saw Fairfield about the tent, and so on.

He soon returned to conferences in London with Guthrie, Moiseiwitsch and Guinness, at the Old Vic and at Lincoln's Inn.

It was now confirmed that the companion play to *Richard III* would be *All's Well That Ends Well*. This was chosen as a play which would be as new to Guthrie as it would be to a Canadian audience. It also would be a contrast to the grimmer *Richard III*. Tony and Tanya got down to the designs for both plays, and when Cecil Clarke left again in March he took Tanya's designs along. Also along with him went his wife, Jacqueline Cundall, principal property designer at The Vic. Through the goodness of Dora Mavor Moore the Clarkes were able to set up a costume and property workshop in her barn theatre workshops in Toronto. In the city, materials were more to hand than out at Stratford. It should be remembered that 'scenery' would have no part in the Stratford stage, but costume and properties would be of prime importance. Cecil Clarke literally tramped the streets, searching stores, and looking at any concern that might supply boots, armour, drapings, etc. It emphasizes the contrast to London, with its theatrical traditions, that the place where he at last found the skill and the stuff to create the footwear for the productions was 'The Snugfit Spat and Slipper Factory'. A slipper in the window led him in. Inside he discovered a skilled craftsman, a modest man, and his son, whose sense of craft was positively Elizabethan and who had a deep nostalgia for the culture from which he had come, in the heart of Europe. He rose to the challenge of Clarke's demands and the Snugfit Spat and Slipper Factory began to make footwear to walk a Shakespearean stage.

By the time that spring had started to stir in Ontario, time and money available were suddenly seen to be quite inadequate. Clarke and his workshop workers had now moved up into Stratford. All Tanya Moiseiwitsch's designs had arrived, and had thrilled those concerned. Costumes and props were well on their way. Promotion had gone forward. Bookings suggested there was going to be a healthy box office income; this would begin to come in by June. But it was a question of the outgoings *now*. And even when money from bookings came in, it would be untouchable, for the chilling reason that, if things went wrong, if they did not open, the money would have to be returned to the customer. The tent alone was going to cost as much as their first guess at a budget figure— around $15,000. And that was a sum that would have to be paid on the nail, before delivery. In April the worried board thought it might be wise to postpone. It was not at all a happy time—either for the dedicated group of voluntary local workers or for Cecil

Clarke and his workshop crew. But, despite chilling forebodings, the resolute men on the Stratford board decided they could not turn back, and on April 15, 1953, Dr. Harry Showalter took up a spade to cut out of the cold parkside the first sod. His words to those assembled reflect the courage needed then:

> This country in which we live is relatively a very new country. Well within the past two hundred years our forebears were advancing into it with tools such as the one I hold in my hand, to make a new home ... The period of which I speak knew the blows of the axe and the thrust of the spade as picturesque symbols of the attack being made on the first objectives of our national march forward. Now I should like to mark the end of that era and the beginning of another, by this thrust of the spade ...

If it went on to get a bit euphoric, who could blame him? It needed the spirit of a poetic thrust to face the practical consequences of cutting that bit out of the Stratford turf and letting the excavators and bulldozers get busy while snow was still in the air, spring storms on the way, and 'Festival' a word not easy to apply. This had started—the physical theatre; an amphitheatre gouged out of sloping park.

Hardly a month later, in May, the telephone rang in Lincoln's Inn. Showalter spoke with Guthrie. Things were now really worrying. Serious debate had forced the Committee to consider delaying the opening by a year. In Stratford this had much to do with a nightmare Cecil Clarke was going through. The tent people over in Chicago had downed tools. Telephones buzzed. Tempers rose. No, they were not going to complete and deliver the tent without payment down, now in Chicago. The money was not there in Stratford.

The board treasurer, Alf Bell, and Cecil Clarke decided to fly to Chicago. Alf Bell is a courteous, quiet but not un-tough precision engineer. Cecil Clarke has steel at the centre, but he had only managed to get a one-day visa to be allowed to cross into America. He flew out of Toronto at the crack of dawn and joined forces with Alf Bell, who had come straight to Chicago by train from the Stratford station. They had a wash and breakfast in a hotel and drove on into the equivalent of New York's Harlem, to keep a ten o'clock appointment with the manager of the tent firm. There was their tent, spread out in a vast upper room. Its expanse

of canvas was a bright brickish pink and all around its spread, on
the wooden floor, were many, many little stools; for the women
workers who should be stitching the seams. But there was nobody
there in this silent loft, except the manager; and he was not silent.
Unless $15,000 were in his hands by Monday morning there
would be no work done. 'And if we don't work Monday you
don't get your tent in time. Do you?' It was Friday. Further
discussion did no good. When Cecil Clarke got on to his return
plane there was little left of the day. At time for take-off an
announcement came, 'All off!—engine trouble.' He did not move.
In no time at all his one-day visa would be exhausted and he would
have no right to be on American soil. He could not risk being held
in Chicago. He sat tight and prayed while outside men in white
overalls with powerful torches swarmed over the plane's wing.
By the time it took off he was an illegal immigrant, but he got
back. On Saturday Mrs. Mavor Moore saw him in Toronto. He
looked ill. She took him to lunch and he told her the situation.
Not only were the tent people holding out for $15,000, but
costume material was being withheld too because of $350 due. It
was $15,350 altogether. Dora Mavor Moore said that by Monday
she could get the $350 out of her own bank. But $15,000! Cecil
wearily said he was due to be in Ottawa on Sunday, to give some
promotional pep-talk. She got on to the phone and called an
influential woman friend who was close to the Governor-General.
Stratford must have $15,000 by Monday morning or the Festival
was sunk. Mr. Clarke was coming to Ottawa and he would
explain. The lady concerned belonged to the same university
sorority as did Dora Mavor Moore. It is some justification of that
elitist institution, the sorority house, that on the Monday $15,000
arrived from an anonymous donor. The lady stitchers of Chicago
could again be on their little stools sewing away at the seams of
the voluminous tent. Yet the larger financial crisis was not over.
All sorts of other bills were outstanding. So Dr. Showalter now
cabled London.

Tony Guthrie and Tanya Moiseiwitsch were on the eve of dress
rehearsals for their Coronation Year *Henry VIII*, and hard at work
in the Old Vic. Alec Guinness was packing ready to sail for
Canada, so that he could get in a visit to New York and a short
holiday before the Stratford rehearsals began. A cable came to the
Old Vic from Dr. Showalter: for Guthrie to stand by for an
important phone call on the Saturday. Guthrie and Tanya feared

the worst. Guinness was due to board the *Mauretania* on the Monday, and to sail for New York on the Tuesday. Guthrie takes up the tale from his end:

> My wife and I rallied Tanya and Alec for lunch at our house. It was a tense feast. Then the telephone rang. I lifted the receiver. The others clustered close. All of us were, to coin a phrase, white to the lips. It was my sister, calling to ask if she had left her spectacles on the mantelpiece. When the bell rang again we all felt better. Harry Showalter gave a brief résumé of the financial situation. It was serious but not yet utterly desperate. The committee was divided as to the best course to pursue. How did I feel about postponing the whole thing for a year?
>
> I should like to be able to report that across the ether my voice rang strong and clear—a rallying call that saved the day, a note of steady confidence, the horn of Roland. In fact I asked a few footling questions, hummed and stuttered, said I must consult my colleagues and would call back in half an hour.
>
> I then (half an hour later) reported that we felt postponement would be utterly fatal. Better to abandon the whole plan than either to postpone or to proceed with faint hearts and a reduced budget.*

The London group then backed this up with a cable to Stratford:

> CONFIRMING CONVERSATION MUST HAVE FIRM DECISION WHETHER FESTIVAL PROCEEDING STOP GUINNESS HAVING BOOKED TO SAIL TUESDAY MORNING WOULD WELCOME EARLIEST DECISION HUMANLY POSSIBLE STOP REGRET NECESSITY COMPEL IMMEDIATE DECISION STOP IN VIEW MY INTENSE PREOCCUPATION OLD VIC PLEASE CABLE OR TELEPHONE GUINNESS LONDON RIVERSIDE 5542
>
> GUTHRIE

Rehearsing at the Vic the next day, Guthrie was in the middle of the death scene of Katharine of Aragon when a cable was passed to him:

> DECIDED TO PROCEED STOP ASSURE YOU FULL STEAM AHEAD

* *A Life In The Theatre.*

And following on its heels came a local wire from Guinness:

AM AWAY STOP GOOD WISHES FOR HENRY THE
EIGHTH STOP RECEIVED FOLLOWING TELEGRAM FROM
SHOWALTER STOP SITUATION IMPROVING THOUGH
STILL HAZARDOUS BUT DETERMINED TO GO THROUGH
PLEASE SAIL AS PLANNED STOP

LOVE ALEC

Reinforcing the resoluteness at the London end, what had
happened at Stratford was that a courageous branch manager of
one of the Stratford banks, without any authorization from above,
risked the exercise of personal discretion and in civic pride had
guaranteed $5,000. Also, the Perth Mutual Insurance Company
had come through with $25,000. Confidence was restored, work
was 'full-steam ahead' now in all departments.

With *Henry VIII* off to a good start on the Wednesday, the
Guthries set out with Tanya for the docks at Tilbury to board the
Beaverford, a slow boat, for Montreal. Travelling with them was
the model of the stage, making its second journey, also several
swords and properties not available in Toronto. They sailed down
the Thames by daylight. It was early summer 1953. On deck Tony
read aloud, to his two ladies, passages from *All's Well That Ends
Well*. But this was not the end . . . It was a completely fresh
beginning.

The reception committee at the station looked down the line
towards Toronto. The 'lonely moose' call of the great engine
could be heard; the warning bells clanged and the train came
in and drew to a halt. Guthrie stepped down, smiling, off the
train, looking like de Gaulle come to claim Quebec. His fellow
voyagers, Mrs. Guthrie and Miss Moiseiwitsch, were introduced.
Welcomes over, he found that on the site the concrete auditorium
was all but complete, the stage too. But the tent was not yet there,
and rehearsals were due to start right away—on June 1. Rehearsals
were therefore begun in a long wooden shed with a corrugated
iron roof out on the fairground; and on a mock-up of the stage
set up by the most faithful of contractors, Oliver Gaffney, who—
when all had despaired—had gone on working.

The acoustics in the shed were dreadful. The heat was intense.
And it was loud with the noisy chatter of resident sparrows.
Guthrie said that days passed and the words of the plays were

known, but nobody had heard any lines but his own. 'Lips are seen to move, gigantic but unintelligible noises resound in the building, punctuated by the thumps of baby sparrows hurtling to their doom. These noises make a Wagnerian accompaniment to the *miming* of two Shakespearean plays. It is an interesting new art form; avant garde but searing to the nerves.'

More days passed and still the tent did not come. But a tent man—Skip Manley—did, to look the ground over and prepare it. This wiry mid-westerner was a remarkable sort of man. He would look at the parched ground, check on the behaviour of the ants, and then say, 'The rain'll hold off another hour.' (Otherwise the ants would not have foraged so far out.) Guthrie had a great admiration for him:

> He travels the world putting up, looking after and taking down enormous tents. He had come from Iowa, where he had been in charge of a gospel tent. Nightly, several hundred people had plunged fully clad into a baptismal tank. After a season of Shakespeare with us, he was booked to look after a circus tent in Venezuela.*

When the tent came, Skip Manley was to be resident in a compartment of it and, with his small crew, always to be on call. The crew's job was to be like that of a sailing ship's crew: constantly adjusting cord and canvas to wind and weather. But the tent was not there. And before it came, there arrived 'the worst rainfall and flooding for thirty years in Stratford, Ontario'. The noise on the tin shed roof made Guthrie think of what such torrents might do to a standing tent. But the storms cleared, the hot sun soon dried the site and the tent came. As preparations went on to put its canvas between the open auditorium and the sky, Cecil Clarke found himself sitting with one of the foremen builders, a rugged chap, up on the rim of the concrete auditorium. Daylight was going and a June moon was coming up as both weary men stared down towards the wooden structure of the stage. Beyond was Avon's lake. And the big simple Canadian said to the small intelligent Englishman: 'I don't care what they say— that's a thing of beauty there.'

Two weeks before an audience was due to take their seats and watch a play, Skip Manley had 'her' ready to go up. Like a ship-master with a ship, he always referred to the tent as 'her'. And on

* *A Life In The Theatre.*

Sunday, June 28, 'she went up'. It really was spectacular, and it took all and more of that very hot day. Guthrie, reduced to sandals, shorts and flapping shirt tail, watched, fascinated—with intervals only to picnic and bathe with Judy and some of the company in a sort of lake pool they called 'the quarry' or 'the sandpit'.

Half Stratford turned out to see 'her' go up . . . Four eighty-foot poles of Douglas pine were moored in position by guys of steel wire. Skip directed this operation like Toscanini conducting a symphony. Each pole was drawn up and held in position by four [wire] guys. Two of these were [hauled up] by hand—two teams of fifteen men; the other two were attached to tractors. Skip would sign first to this group to pull so far, then to that; then, with the sweep of a jewelled hand, he would bring the first tractor into play, holding the remainder of his forces at the ready as though they were trombones waiting to make an entry. The whole tricky, delicate operation took a day and a half. Thereafter the great expanse of canvas was hoisted comparatively quickly and easily. In another day or two we were able to rehearse in the tent.*

That spread of canvas was *'the largest theatrical tent in the Western hemisphere*, second only to the Ringling Brothers' circus big top'. It was later to extend to two extra outside poles, and then to be 'the largest area of unsupported canvas in North America'. This was full-scale Guthrie at work.

Rehearsals now went on apace and the company began fully to realize what it was to be under the direction of such a man. This was Guthrie at the height of his powers. His apparently free and off-the-cuff direction was based upon a great deal of private preparation. As Douglas Campbell, who was now very experienced in work with Guthrie, says, 'You never quite knew what was going to happen next . . . but you constantly felt that you were in a creative process.' Apart from Alec Guinness and Irene Worth, these players were slightly unprepared for this sort of Instant Creation. But they had been engaged to *work* and work they did, not only immensely stimulated by Guthrie, but encouraged to reach out to give of their best because they were playing in the company of two of England's top talents in the art, Alec Guinness and Irene Worth. Though there was little leisure,

* *A Life In The Theatre.*

there was lots of fun. With his authority Guthrie could always afford to have fun without any loss of discipline. And it was an exciting life, to be in this smallish, friendly town, hoping by the nationally important nature of the scheme to draw audiences from all over the nation. In certain ways it was like being members of a circus family. The big top was up, the ringmaster was preparing the show. And there was quite a bit of thumping of the drum. Cecil Clarke was instructed to secure a big bell (similar to the one which was a regular piece of equipment in Shakespeare's own theatre). A gun or guns and a platoon of the local militia were also ordered by Guthrie. He was going to see to it that the whole town of Stratford knew—percussively—when the play had started.

The Sunday before the first night, the Dedication of the Theatre took place. After morning church, no less than five ministers of separate denominations all had their say in blessing the tent. But one ominous thing was that fears were confirmed about troubles they had in rehearsal with the tent's acoustics. These were not made less by the words of a lady as she turned to go . . . 'Don't worry, dear, neither could I, but they'll have microphones, of course, for the plays.'

In rehearsal the acoustics had not been good. But it had been bliss compared to the tin shed and it had been thought that, when the seats were in and the theatre full, it would be quite different. What they had been most concerned about was the noise that came in through the thinness of the tent walls. Guthrie used cajolery and benevolent tyranny over the townspeople to cut out the noise of their boys playing baseball. He even persuaded the railway to stop that whistle call of their engines till they were well beyond the town. But now they faced real trouble inside, for the auditorium *had* been filled with people at the Dedication.

They got back to work on final rehearsal. There was no doubt about it. The acoustics were bad and there were just two days to go to first night. Guthrie sat down in some dejection on an upper tier of the concrete auditorium—not in a seat, but on coils of Skip Manley's rope. Campbell joined him in despair. 'Do you notice something?' Guthrie said to him as the rehearsal went on. 'Am I wrong, or is it better from here? Go to the other side, Douglas, and listen there.' And Campbell did and came back and listened again. 'It does seem to be better here.' 'Because we are sitting on coils of rope?' 'Could be.' They were not quite certain, but suddenly Guthrie took the plunge. It was a time for definite decisions. 'Cancel the rehearsal! Get coconut matting and cover the whole thing in it.' Gaffney and his men somehow found a supply, and everyone pitched in and lent a hand. When they got all the seating in on top of that, the improvement was near to miraculous.

The first night came. The cars rolled up all day. The evening came, the crowds poured in. The Governor-General, Vincent Massey, honoured the occasion. The young volunteer ushers, in black slacks and white shirts, moved slickly about their business. They had been thoroughly drilled by the milkman-turned-house-manager (Norman Freeman) and briefed by Guthrie with the words, 'Yours is the show before the show; the eyes of everyone will be on you.' They moved like naval cadets putting the ship to sea; got people aboard and seated with courtesy. Trumpets blew. The red geraniums were in place round the tent. A yellow pennant —present from Stratford-upon-Avon, England—floated from the top of the tent. A gun fired. The play was on. Guinness took the stage, as Richard III

'Now is the Winter of our discontent made glorious Summer . . .'

They loved it. They came, not like a sophisticated London audience to make comparisons, they came to see something to them quite new; and, with the feeling of festival, and pilgrimage, they were prepared to enjoy what they were offered. What they were bowled over by was the colour and the quality of the costumes, the props, banners; the sheer professionalism and the movement of it all coupled with the eloquence of the language. There was a quality about it that nobody but the informed minority had expected way out there in Ontario. This theatre was probably going to play to 1,500 people a night. Guinness's personal triumph was followed on the very next night by Irene Worth's triumph as Helena in *All's Well That Ends Well* (a character Guthrie came to believe was Shakespeare's finest female creation). *All's Well* was in modern dress. But this too was taken as no upsetting innovation; everything was so much of an innovation.

It had worked. The bookings were good. All the doubting Thomases were defeated and the Festival was obviously now something the Stratford community could be proud of. Also, Guthrie had proved his theory that Shakespeare would be in vital communication with audience on this sort of stage and in that

9

sort of auditorium. There were snags of course. For instance rain *could* stop play if it drummed down on that canvas roof, but this was an on-going concern and the tent was not to be forever. Was this what his whole career had led up to? And would Guthrie, the nomad, stay? Would the tent really give way to bricks and mortar?

Guthrie, typically, was soon on his way. But the next year was planned. He would stay till the Canadians totally took over and no longer depended on talent from the old country.

Before we leave Stratford, something should be said of the Guthrie ménage, because domestically they were terribly happy there. To Judy it was the next best thing to the Lincoln's Inn Bohemia. They had their own pleasant house and could run it their way. Their way did not always coincide with local conventions of the Law. There was sometimes a state of more than gypsy undress that, even in a country used to dress informality, seemed a little surprising. Dr. Guthrie might greet board members dressed in bathing trunks and his only other covering a torn dressing-gown that had once done duty on-stage in Cyprus, for Othello's second honeymoon. There were rainy days when all that stood between the Doctor and total shame was underwear and a see-through plastic mac. Mrs. Guthrie was sometimes to be seen by conservative congregationalists sunbathing almost as though she were one of Nature's original and sinless children. One day both of them broke the law. They were inclined to drink whiskey or gin in measures more proper to giant lumberjacks off-duty—and to show no after-effects. They were liberally entertaining friends and members of the company on the rough equivalent of an English front lawn, an unfenced area of parched grass around their Princess Street house. And the Law stepped in. But all it did was step courteously across the thirsty grass and quietly inform Dr. Guthrie that he probably didn't know, but you couldn't drink in public like this. 'Can't entertain my own friends in my own garden? Oh, dear!'

Inside—as with all Guthrie temporary tenancies—accommodation was inclined to grow cumulatively untidy. When the Guthries went and the Guinnesses stayed on (and were to follow into the same accommodation) certain members of the theatre community, who were all now quite in love with the two great Guthries, quickly and without comment moved in to mop up, repair and somewhat reduce the aristocratic squalor.

Daily, from that disreputably happy house on the far side of the Avon's lake from where the tented theatre stood, Guthrie would go to work across the bridge at Waterloo Street. He used one of the town's biggest available bicycles. Guinness would perambulate on a bicycle too, trilby on head and decently clad, moving smoothly and sedately along the tree-lined streets, like a character right out of one of his Ealing Studios comedies. Guthrie would race along, shirt tails flying in the morning air. One day he overtook that conscientious company actor, Mervyn Blake, breathlessly footing it, and at a time when without benefit of bicycle he would be bound to be late for rehearsal. Came the loud clear hail: 'See the advantage, Mervyn, of the Wheel?' Guthrie sailed past and pedalled on and for Blake there would be hell to pay, if he kept others waiting at rehearsal.

When the Guthries left, the season went on. And every evening some minutes before the play began, families at peace on the summery front porches of houses in the streets nearest to the theatre could be seen raising their hands to their ears; to take them down again only after the gun had gone, and the play was on. The tent was lovely to look at in its salmon pink and blue-grey. But there were nights when rain stopped the play till the drumming on the canvas roof died down. Also, it had wounds to show; great wounds stitched up, by the end of the season. For there had been storms when the heavens opened, the waters came down and great reservoirs of rainwater gathered on the canvas roof and bulged dangerously downwards. They threatened to uproot the guy-ropes and bring the whole thing down. Skip Manley came to the rescue with a knife on a pole and with skilful surgery lanced 'her' great tumours so that 'she' sent cascades into the auditorium, which then steamed like a laundry as the sun came through. Later he got up aloft and scrambled all over the canvas with his needle and twine.

At the end of the Festival, when the tent came down to be stored till next summer and the stage was put into a sort of winter cocoon, the product of Tom Patterson's vague dream, linked to the precise Guthrie vision, had begun to affect the Stratford economy with a new sort of tourism. And that, after all, was the Patterson purpose, whatever had been the Guthrie one. It was highly satisfactory that both purposes should now be so serving each other.

CHAPTER SEVENTEEN

FROM SHAKESPEARE TO SOPHOCLES
(1953–1956)

HE WAS back in Stratford, Ontario, before the year was out to confirm plans for 1954. The tent had been stored away and the boxed-in stage cocooned against frost in a snowy auditorium, made a strange sort of monument to the summer. Cecil Clarke and he got down to discussion of the next season. The first had run on for six weeks. They planned next time to run for nine. The demand was good and there was the need to recoup from the inevitable expense of an initial year. As was desirable, most of the 1953 company would return. The star attractions this year were to be James Mason, now an international film star. Frances Hyland was to play Isabella in *Measure for Measure*, James Mason Angelo. At Tony's suggestion Cecil Clarke would branch out into production and direct the play. He himself wanted to do *The Taming of the Shrew*, but not in an Italian setting, in a Mid-Western one, with Petruchio almost a bronco-busting cowboy. There was talk of a possible third item in the repertoire, something perhaps non-Shakespearean; an experimental production, Guthrie thought, which might be done not in costume at all, and with the concentration on quality of acting. It was suggested that in their sort of amphitheatre and on that stage one of the Greek plays might be at home. *Oedipus*? As soon as it came up, Guthrie pounced on the idea. James Mason, in his opinion, could play a splendid Oedipus.

With further details of the new season settled, he got back home, where there was some worry about the situation with his mother. For the moment, however, he found her all right, and he did what seemed a strange thing. He decided to produce an early play of Emlyn Williams called *Pen Don*. And not only that, he decided he did not want to do it with professional players. He wanted to produce it in Wales, and with amateurs. He did it with the Swansea Amateur Dramatic Society.

The choice of play is not so strange when one realizes that he had now begun to be very interested in mythology. Study for *Oedipus* went on and when he got to Wales he wrote to tell Judy to be sure to send on to him the Yeats' version. Pen Don, in Welsh legend, is the sacred mountain of the goddess, Don— Mother of the World.

It must have seemed extremely strange to Ruth Gordon and her husband Garson Kanin that, when everything had been arranged by Binkie Beaumont for Tony Guthrie to do a slap-up production with her of Thornton Wilder's *The Matchmaker*—and when he had such plans for his Stratford Festival, too—that he should go off to Wales to produce amateurs. Tantalizing enough for the Kanins to follow the Guthries to 'Oystimyth'. At least that is what Tony called Oyster Bay, near Swansea. And, despite a cold hotel and an April chill off the sea, they would not have missed the event for anything.

The play, it turned out, was being presented in the Swansea Natural History Museum. They got there to find Judy on her knees, her mouth full of pins, and plying a needle to repair the hem of one of the costumes. She was surrounded by glass cases of natural history specimens. Guthrie produced the play without scenery on an oblong rostrum in a large gallery, where the roof leaked, but Ruth Gordon maintained it was a miracle of staging and had utterly magical moments. The scene of the action was the mountain top and the moment was the eve of May Day. (Mother's month, the Mother mountain.) The moment Ruth Gordon could never forget was when the small boy, son of the bard Rhodri, said, 'No. I will not go,' and refused to leave the mountain. In nature and the nature of theatre he was seeking now, the event of *Pen Don*, with its legendary simplicity, was right on the line of Guthrie development.

There was not much time between this unsung triumph and the May day when the Guthries boarded the *Empress of Canada* to sail once more for Montreal. He would see Ruth Gordon in August in Edinburgh for rehearsals of *The Matchmaker*. On May 14 they caught the familiar train, out of Montreal, had breakfast in Toronto station and chugged their way on in a slow train to Stratford. This time the welcome awaiting them was almost presidential. The Mayor, all the Committee, Cecil Clarke (now Artistic Director), Tanya, John Hayes (the new stage director), Tom Brown (an Australian who had assisted Clarke at the Old Vic), and all the old friends were there. It was May 15.

his mother's birthday for him. That day Cecil Clarke could tell him that by the end of the month they expected there would not be a single seat left for the whole season. Bookings were booming, 'she' had wintered well and Skip Manley was fetching the new great poles from somewhere West, which would make her 'the largest unsupported area of canvas in the whole of North America'.

When he strode the streets, complete strangers hailed him with a 'Welcome back!' from their front porches. It was their royal welcome to a king-size man. But he failed to see the kerb while watching some kids play games on bicycles, and he crashed to the dust. A bone in the ankle was chipped, the foot swelled up. With mythology much in mind, it must have seemed as if Oedipus (the word means 'swollen foot') had wished the Furies on to him. For weeks he prepared for *Oedipus* and *The Shrew* from a cane chair. But in the regulation Guthrie soft shoes he was ready for rehearsal. Meantime, James Mason, who was to play Oedipus, had walked Stratford like an unassuming monarch. Mason was followed by hushed whispers and gathering crowds around any shop into which he went. 'It's *him*—James Mason.' One day a shocked lady member of his theatre staff exclaimed to Guthrie, 'Tony! You've got the handsomest actor in the world, and I hear you're going to put him in a mask!' *Oedipus* had started as an experimental idea, and this time (his third as director) it was going to be a masked production. Mason had no objection. Artistically, it was exciting and would force him into a new scale, in voice and movement (two things films inhibited). In fact the whole experiment gained momentum and was to be the first step towards a more symbolic, less realistic style of theatre which Guthrie continued to pursue till his dying day.

Tanya was deeply involved. They were striking a level of artifice suitable to their stage, which was not suited to an illusory presentation. Cecil Clarke laboured anxiously with his first major production of a play (not an easy play for any director), *Measure for Measure*. It proved unwise to have pushed him into it, and in the end it became a co-production with Guthrie. Fun went on with the Mid-Western *Shrew*. A cowboy Petruchio entered on a hobby horse and Vincentio was driven to Padua in a pantomime cut-out of a vintage car chauffeured by Hortensio. It had, however, an important effect. Some Canadians considered its Americanized presentation to be a sort of 'talking down' to them.

And it reinforced existing fears of a faction in Stratford who thought that 'Doctor' Guthrie lacked discretion and might well be too provocative, too 'naughty', to be encouraged to stay as perennial director of their festival.

As to *Oedipus*, that was somewhat to divide the town too. But, from being the extra item to be done in rehearsal dress, it became number one in the season. For Tanya there were memories of the first days of working together at Liverpool. Then (on *The Alchemist*) he had said to her, 'No. Let's not complete the costumes now. Let's take them so far and rehearse on till we are sure of what we need. Wouldn't it be wonderful if we could say to the carpenters, "Don't build the whole set. Just do the door now." ' Now at Stratford, they tried out masks, for rehearsal only —costumes, too. They started working towards total completion in all the arts and crafts involved, so that all ingredients in the alchemy should come to the boil at the one time: the actor's, the designer's, the director's contribution. And within the Stratford tyranny this was almost possible. This was the way he wanted to work: making, breaking, re-making—nothing too set till the right moment, creation of the moment, leading up to the crux of completion 'on the day', and only on the day. Was this not what Sophocles wrote for—the Festival event, not 'the run of a play'?

Unfortunately this was Stratters, Ont., not Athens, and it was a short play without other dramatic additions. He was damned if he would add another play (as they had done at the Vic with *The Critic*). But, it had to be faced, *Oedipus Rex* was not long enough to give picnickers who had motored hundreds of miles the feeling that they had had their money's worth. So he split the play into two parts and had an interval when the Messenger comes running in and announces, 'Good news!' The convention he chose to span that interval was in a sense 'the freeze'. He then froze the action on stage, had a blackout and took up after the interval again with the action frozen at the same point. It rather broke the rhythm and build of the play, but this was a notable production. It had a profound effect on a serious audience and he was asked to repeat it the following year.

The season ended with plans to bring in another director who might succeed him. For he now made it clear that he had been founder-father only to their Festival; it was now theirs and he was not going to stay.

Back home again, he launched Thornton Wilder's *The Match-*

maker in Edinburgh, successfully got it into London's Haymarket Theatre. He then joined Peggy, anxious to see that things were in order at Annagh-ma-Kerrig, where his mother's failing health was now a critical worry. The new year 1955, would be complex and mostly pledged once again to the far side of the Atlantic.

Because the 'next thing' beyond Stratford which he was moving towards was the idea of founding in the U.S.A. a theatre of true repertory, and on a scale of national importance; something America had always failed in before. And there was Canadian dissatisfaction with Guthrie: that, out of what had initially been a post-war movement towards a form of national theatre, he had channelled that wave of enthusiasms—and the resources of talent and money raised—into a regional success with a seasonal theatre just serving a summer festival. Nobody could deny that he had thereby set exemplary standards for the whole nation in the quality of direction, design and playing, but even so . . . And Guthrie shared in this 'but' too. All-the-year-round repertory, and in a theatre not specially designed for Shakespeare, this was the way his thinking was going when in the fall of 1955 he made contact with the Phoenix Theatre, 2nd Avenue, in downtown New York.

In fact the contact was made by Michael Langham, the director Guthrie had brought in that summer to do *Julius Caesar* at Stratford, and who was to succeed him there. The men Langham met at the Phoenix were known to Guthrie and admired by him because of what they had been doing in a form of repertory—T. Edward Hambleton and Norris Houghton. When the young Englishman walked into their office, it was at a time when Albert Marre had unfortunately had to tell them that he could not, as promised, direct their next play, *Six Characters in Search of an Author*. It must be remembered that Guthrie had been 're-writing Mr. Pirandello' and 'cutting reams' out of that play to make his own version. Norris Houghton takes up the story:

As he [*Langham*] was about to leave he remarked, 'Oh, yes, I almost forgot—I bring you greetings from Tony Guthrie. He's over in Brooklyn, you know, staying at Oliver Smith's house. He said to tell you if you need any help he has a bit of spare time while he waits to start rehearsals for *The Matchmaker* for David Merrick.' Thus casually did Tyrone Guthrie enter the life of the Phoenix and that of its two leaders. He was probably the greatest influence on our thinking and our labours in our early Phoenix years, and remained one of T.'s and my greatest friends until his death . . . Needless to say, we accepted with alacrity the offer of one of the most distinguished stage directors in the world.*

Now Guthrie was under contract to Merrick not to undertake other work. However, taking as much wicked liberty as he had with Pirandello's text, he stopped watching the big ships go by, came down off the Brooklyn Heights, strode across Brooklyn Bridge, and took on the production at the Phoenix on 2nd Avenue. The Pirandello Estate was somewhat taken aback at Mr. Guthrie's 'jokes' but he argued Hambleton and Houghton into using a version finally described as: 'Prepared from Dr. Guthrie's adaptation and a new translation by Mr. [*Michael*] Wager and Frank Tavritz.'

Wager had already done a version with Albert Marre—in Boston. He was a handsome young American Jew, whose distinguished father was then the head of the Weizmann Institute in Israel. On meeting, Wager found that Guthrie and he shared a love of Opera and the Habimah. They got along well together and thrashed out one version, in which the main Guthrie liberty was to write in dialogue for the scene in the play in which 'the players' of Pirandello improvise. A liberty with the ending, referred to in a programme note, was a breath-taking Guthrie coup de théâtre. When the character of the daughter (the part Flora Robson first played for him) makes her final exit, Guthrie had her start at the bare brick wall, back of the stage, and run, gathering speed all the way, straight at the alarmed audience, and then suddenly plummet and disappear into the orchestra pit. It was as if she had vanished into the thin air of Pirandellesque imagination. Actually, she was alive and well, and on several thicknesses of mattress. He was not the first to play tricks with the end of the play; Max Reinhardt used to face the out-going audience with the character of The Boy crouched, weeping in the foyer.

But the whole thing nearly did not happen. When rehearsals were due to start, Tony and Judy were in Philadelphia with *The Matchmaker* and the cat was out of the bag. A cable came to Hambleton:

* *Phoenix Rising, 1953–72* (Memorial Booklet, 1972), the Phoenix Theatre Company, New York.

I HAVE NOT AT ANY TIME GIVEN GUTHRIE PER-
MISSION TO ENGAGE HIS SERVICES FOR YOUR PROJECT
OR ANY OTHER.

MERRICK

Guthrie wrote home: 'Having a First-Class slam-bang
SCHEMOZZLE with Merrick, who threatens to sue. I am Rising
Above in the very biggest way.' Finally it was agreed to release
him to the Phoenix, 'for a minimum of 4 consecutive hours
between 10 a.m. and midnight on November 28, 29, 30,
December 1, 2, 3.'

Poor Norris Houghton was obliged to take rehearsals with a
perplexed cast for Monday to Friday of the first week. He asked
Guthrie, 'How do you want it "blocked"?' 'You just do what you
want, Norris. It will be fine.' At 1 p.m. on Sunday, Tony and
Judy Guthrie arrived from Philadelphia, armed with rehearsal
basket, thermos, etc. Then started what Norris Houghton called
'the most extraordinary day, I think, I ever spent in a theatre'.
Guthrie got off his jacket, put on carpet slippers, threw his tie to
Judy and rolled up his sleeves. 'Raight!—Run it as you've done
it.' Up till now the company had viewed the play as deep, intellectual and properly heavy stuff. Houghton had, also very
properly, given it as little interpretation as he could. Guthrie says
in his autobiography, 'I regarded the play as a light-hearted and
essentially theatrical *tour de force*, a juggling trick with metaphysics in place of billiard balls.'

They hardly knew what had hit them, for at the end of the run-
through the hand-clap echoed through the empty house and he
stood up. 'Now . . .' And he changed everything, and everything
he did was positive, assured, and it was work, work, drill, work—
with him pacing, sweating, smoking, joking, cajoling. 'Stop!
Mandy! No!' (to Michael Wager who was playing the Son) 'I
don't want any juvenile prince coming in. I want myopia, itchy
scalp, running nose, knock knees! Again!' Wager says, 'It was
like the First Day of Creation.' He broke them down and rebuilt
their characters all in that day. And Instant Creation was in the
air. On entering, away up-stage against the back wall, Wager had
edged in (in order to listen and to see). He was now standing
behind a ladder which rested against the back wall. Guthrie saw
the image, wanted it, kept it in. It was an image with certainly a
lot of meaning for him; the Son, as behind prison bars, behind

the rungs of a ladder which reached up to . . . God knows who? Frank Hauser, the British director, says he has never seen greater concentration in any director during rehearsals than Guthrie gave to the job. And, like his hero Toscanini, who in rehearsal could break a baton in temperamental intensity, Guthrie, in his intensity, almost broke a limb. It was at a rehearsal in the Stratford tent of *The Merchant of Venice*. It was late into a heavenly evening in June. Down on the stage the young actress playing Jessica was lying back enjoying her work—in love's languishment, on 'a grassy bank'. It was all rather beautiful and pianissimo when suddenly the handclap came crack! Guthrie rose from the auditorium, marched down towards the stage and, reaching the actress, he gave her a near karate blow on the bare leg and spoke in fury: 'You're feeling it, you silly little bitch! Your business is to make *them* feel it! [*pointing to the auditorium where the 2,000 would sit on the night.*] Do it again!'

Shocking but not surprising. To Guthrie such selfish playing, such enjoyment by the player at the expense of the audience was worse than treason. Now—in New York—he had his knife in 'the Method' for seeming to do that very same thing: making the thing 'real' and 'true' for the player but not actively communicating at all with the audience. The producer of a play, he had said in his Royal Society lecture, had to look to the interest of the audience. When one of the actresses in the Phoenix cast said, 'But, Dr. Guthrie, I don't *feel* this. It doesn't seem real to me,' he said, 'My dear, if it's reality you want, go out and watch street accidents. This play is a work of art and all we need from you now is nasal resonance. Speak up! Play on!' And on they did go that Sunday till the Equity representative in the company came in some anxiety to Norris Houghton. 'Mr. Houghton, sorry, but they've been rehearsing solid for six hours!' 'Have they?' Houghton rose and spoke to Guthrie—Equity regulations, etc. 'Raight! Break for lunch.' 'Oh no!' The phenomenon happened. The cast insisted, 'Please—if we break now we'll lose all concentration. Can't we go on?' So, sandwiches were sent for, and they all went on working. They finished up with at least nine hours of solid work. Then Guthrie Tyrannos took off again for Philadelphia or Boston and left poor Norris Houghton to 'follow that!' for the rest of the week.

'A triumph for the Phoenix Theatre,' said Brooks Atkinson in the *New York Times*, and happy Houghton and Hambleton were able to announce to their Phoenix faithfuls: '. . . enormous success has forced us to extend its run for three weeks more.'

Norris Houghton gratefully records that out of that initial association came other successes: two years later *Maria Stuart* and *The Makropoulos Secret*, also under Guthrie's direction. Before and after these productions, and sometimes during their preparation, Guthrie bombarded Hambleton and Houghton with harangues on the error of their ways, on potentials they were missing, on high hopes he had for them. They must create a permanent company, he reiterated. Articles from his pen, which the *Sunday Times* was always ready to print, gave them oblique support. Houghton goes on:

> He was unstinting of time on behalf of the cause of our kind of theatre. He allowed himself to be trundled off by T. and me to fund-raising teas and meetings in Park Avenue salons where dowagers delightedly listened and occasionally succumbed to his witty and impassioned cajolery with a check. If he could have been persuaded to stay with us . . .*

But he had handed over the Stratford Festival to Michael Langham, and he was beginning to look like a commanding general on reconnaissance at the start of a whole campaign: the campaign for all-American all-the-year-round repertory theatre.

He kept his link with the New York scene by giving winter employment in 1956 to Stratford players and bringing down from Toronto a spectacular production that until this day divides opinion on whether it was a form of flop or the greatest thing he ever did. Roger Stevens (who had given solid support to the Phoenix aims). He had fair claims to be at that time New York's top impresario. He went along with the Guthrie idea to bring the Stratford, Ontario, company into New York with *Tamburlaine*. Guthrie's old colleague, Anthony Quayle, played Tamburlaine, and Leslie Hurry once more did the designs. Again there were tents galore, but there were also too many technical tricks; too much resort to stage mechanics. It was awkward and expensive. It did not run.

By April he was back to *Oedipus* again, but this time as a film and with a new partner in production. He had struck up a friendship with Leonid Kipnis, cousin to the great singer Alexander Kipnis.

* *Phoenix Rising, 1953–72* (Memorial Booklet) 1972, the Phoenix Theatre Company, New York.

And Leonid—known to his family and friends as Lola—formed with Guthrie the Leonid Kipnis Film Productions Company Ltd. They would make a film of the Guthrie production of *Oedipus Rex*; make it in Stratford and in the theatre. It was proposed that this would be the first of several film versions of classical productions of the Festival repertoire. Douglas Campbell who played Oedipus in the second year would repeat the role in the film. Guthrie was like a boy with a new toy. He directed the production and was able to be understudy to an experienced film director and cameraman, whom Lola Kipnis had brought in. The film is in fact an enormously impressive record of the play and the stage production. Having got the company back into the playing of the play, the plan was to take the stage production to the Edinburgh Festival along with *Henry V*, which Langham had produced at Stratford, with Christopher Plummer as Henry.

By the time they all met in Montreal to fly straight to Scotland, Tyrone Guthrie was a different man. The most important loss in his whole life had suddenly taken place. His mother was dead.

In June he had been in America. His last letters to her told of how he was working happily on Martha's Vineyard, preparing for a production of *Candide*, with Lilian Hellman and Leonard Bernstein; how he had had to fly off to Hollywood with Lola Kipnis, to edit the *Oedipus* film; how, while there, one of the film moguls had offered him the direction of the film of *The Matchmaker* (the play which became *Hello, Dolly!*); and how he was determined to turn it down. In reply to these gossipy letters she was still banging blindly away at her typewriter, and hitting a fair number of the right letters too. When he got back to her after that, it was full summer at Annagh-ma-Kerrig. And, though she was not too good on her feet by now, she started for some reason to begin to do a great deal of tidying up. She started with the flowers and the pots in the greenhouse. It became disturbingly obvious to him that this was what the folk about the district called 'the gathering up'—a premonitory preparation for death. Her activity spread to the house and she said to him, 'I'm throwing out the useless things, and, when I'm through, you throw me out too.' Very shortly afterwards she suffered a stroke. A week later—on July 5—she died. Peggy and he were quite shattered.

A hearse drawn by black horses with black plumes took her coffin from the old house. And as its black wheels ground away

over the gravel towards the white gates which end the drive
going out of the estate, her pet donkey came running to the fence
and brayed that strange biblical trumpeting, such a common
sound in the fields of Ireland then. When she had been 'laid to
rest' beside the General in the family grave up in the windy little
churchyard at Aghabog Church, Tony and Judy came back to the
house and shut themselves up for a long time. 'A merciful, even
beautiful end . . . grief is largely self-indulgence. All the same the
parting is terribly painful and almost overwhelmingly mysterious
and solemn,' he wrote to a friend. And later, in reply to Xtopher's
letter of sympathy, he said: 'Really relief and happiness that she
is at rest, and no longer BLIND, outweighs any feelings of
sadness and loneliness.'

What was to become of Annagh-ma-Kerrig? There was no
time to go into all that before he flew to join the Stratford
company taking *Oedipus* to Edinburgh. The production at the
Assembly Hall was well enough received, but the most satisfactory response, for him, came from Sybil Thorndike:

I'm just a few minutes back from Edinburgh. I must write at
once to say that *Oedipus* exalted me—knocked me over—
exhilarated me more than anything I've seen in the theatre for
years—in fact I can't think of anything except perhaps Barker's
Winter's Tale that has had such an effect on me—and *Oedipus*
more than that even. For the first time in my life I've seen
something in the theatre which is as big as Picasso and Braque
and the great sculptors—the theatre to me has always lagged
behind about 50 years and had never expressed violently and
splendidly and *awe*fully the world now. That's why I've come
back in a state of exhaltation. You've done such a wonderful
thing—and the whole . . . Douglas (Oh! I never thought he
could be that big!)—Tanya—that company—all was deeply
significant—beautifully spoken—so full of sheer creation—
those amazingly musical sounds—Douglas's terribly moving
intakes of breath—the bird noise of the old white bald fellow—
and the masks—change of sound—I've never seen anything
like it—and I'm so moved . . . And Oh! . . . how I wish I were
young and could do something cataclysmic like that. Who
knows, I may do something Aweful before I conk out!!! Thank
you, thank you—I remember the first time I heard the Bach
Passion with full orchestra and chorus—I was 14—and I

thought I'd *die* from sheer thrill. I had something the same last night.

I'm filming with Marilyn and Larry!! Wouldn't it be awful if I was so affected by *Oedipus* that I broke the camera—no knowing!

This probably was his best work to date and devoted to what he considered to be 'the best constructed play in the world'. It was a play which satisfied his belief that, at the heart of the greatest drama, there lay rituals of the human spirit which could not be played out realistically. And because the development towards this sort of production of his took place largely abroad, his profundity has been greatly under-estimated in Britain, where his reputation tends still to be that of the clever and gimmicky director.

When I talked to her recently, Dame Sybil said that, when she had been approached to play Jocasta, ten years before, she just had not liked the play; found it distasteful. Now she found it a matter of awe. At this new level of artifice—played with masks, and moving in a more than natural way in its universal ritual—this production had none of the stage realism which Guthrie had taken exception to in the Vic production. The gouged and sightless eyes of Oedipus streaming theatrical blood, and therefore physically duplicating the more powerful description in the words of Sophocles, that had offended him. By contrast, in the Guthrie production, Oedipus re-entered in the same mask he had worn before but with his head veiled. The blindness and the blood were in the mind and imagination of the audience, which is a more disturbing place for them to be than sensationally objectified on stage.

With this *Oedipus* and the death of his mother, Guthrie had reached a crossroads in his career. It is not without significance that now he began to write his autobiography. The Stratford Festival triumph was undoubtedly the peak of his life's achievement. But he was a man who could not live without the challenge of 'the next thing'. At this crossroads, one of the ways forward was still towards a more than Shakespearean theatre playing true repertory. He took this way.

CHAPTER EIGHTEEN

THE U.S. REPERTORY CAMPAIGN
(1956–1963)

AFTER HIS mother's death, Guthrie concentrated the use of his natural gifts on two main purposes—one professional, one private: to found a new theatre for Repertory in the U.S.A., and to revitalize Annagh-ma-Kerrig and its bit of Irish homeland, for which he now had full responsibility.

The talents he was going to apply now come out clearly as these: the gift of directing players and the play, the gift of organizing people and projects, and the gift of the gab (a capacity for lecturing). For the next few years almost the whole of his professional life was to be addressed Westwards, with much trans-Atlantic shuttling by air, principally to New York, with the occasional guest visit to Stratters, Ont. He had no responsibility there now, with the succession handed firmly on to Michael Langham. The great tent's days were numbered and Skip Manley was no longer to be a colourful summer migrant. In 1957 Vincent Massey laid the foundation stone of a handsome permanent building, reflecting the shape of its canvas origin and designed by Robert Fairfield who had designed the tent. It rose above the original auditorium on the same site and was opened in time for the 1958 Festival.

Guthrie's U.S. Repertory ambitions had begun with *Six Characters in Search of an Author* and that first link with the Phoenix Theatre in New York. But it was through a high-level show-business fiasco that he was to start his association with one man of the adventurous trio which was to constitute the advance guard in the U.S. Repertory campaign. This man was Peter Zeisler, the Stage Director when Guthrie directed his disastrous *Candide* in New York. It was one of these occasions which proved the exception to the Broadway show-business rule, that provided you hire enough top-level talent and manage it well the result will be large bookings and high success. Lilian Hellman, Leonard Bernstein, Oliver Smith, Irene Sharaff, Richard Wilbur and

Tyrone Guthrie—it was just too much talent in the one place, and resulted in a production of many brilliant things which just did not add up. For Lilian Hellman, author of the musical, it was a bitter disappointment. For Leonard Bernstein, composer of the score, it was a further bright feather in his cap. For Tony Guthrie it was an exciting musico-dramatic experience and a lesson in the strains, pains and penalties of hit-and-miss Broadway. Peter Zeisler voiced to him his total despair of the conditions of the New York theatre. Guthrie admired the high technical skill of this small, dark, aseptic stage director. To get out of the New York squirrel's cage for a time, Guthrie advised the youngish Zeisler to apply for a Fulbright Grant and go away for a year to Europe. He applied, got it, and took off with his wife for Europe and its theatre scene. Guthrie went on to earn a few more dollars to help modernize Annagh-ma-Kerrig away from oil lamps towards 'the electricity'—and also to suffer again a lesson about New York theatre. The play was *The First Gentleman* by Norman Ginsbury—a comedy about George IV and his daughter. It had been a success in London. It was light, elegant, with a good deal of both wit and pathos. The problem was to find within the American scene the actor who could play the part of George IV (Robert Morley had played it brilliantly at home). Guthrie persuaded the producers that Walter Slezak was the man.

> I had seen him and admired his performance in an otherwise boring musical. He had gaiety, elegance, wit and he looked like 'Prinny' . . . Naively I failed to appreciate that speaking brief perfunctory lines in musical comedy is one thing, handling rhetoric and quick-fire lines in a comedy of style is quite another . . . He struggled gamely and with admirable good temper against a most frustrating situation.

Guthrie would have assumed that any actor of Slezak's standing would have had the training and experience to tackle this problem of style. But where would he get it, when there was no classical repertory theatre within which to train, and the professional schools were heavily 'Method' in their training? The production suffered and the playwright most of all.

> Agonies were undergone during a try-out tour. Wiseacres would come to New Haven, to Boston, to Philadelphia and prescribe this remedy and that; the unfortunate author was

persuaded to cut and re-write and really to harm the style of a stylish comedy. Everywhere the critics hailed the magnificent performance of Mr. Slezak doing wonders with a stodgy, verbose English play. It was an ironic situation from which bad business rather quickly delivered us.*

When Guthrie returned home from this disappointment; Peter Zeisler and his wife turned up and spent a happy two weeks of spring with Judy and him at Annagh-ma-Kerrig. Theatre, Repertory, and the U.S. were discussed while he directed Zeisler in how to wield an Irish cleaver in hacking away the undergrowth and the jungle of rhododendron bushes to give the old house a new look.

And in this year—1957—he again joined Hambleton, Houghton and their associates at the Phoenix Theatre for two productions. These were to give them new heart in their struggle for a sort of repertory theatre: Schiller's *Maria Stuart* (Irene Worth as Mary and Eva le Gallienne as Elizabeth) and a controversial production of that highly artificial play so dependent on its central female role, Carl Capek's *The Makropoulos Secret* in 'a new adaptation by Tyrone Guthrie'. He had absolutely the right actress for the central role, Eileen Herlie. One is not sure that he had the right adapter. It was the less successful production of the two but out of it came a renewed friendship with Eileen Herlie, who had played for him in the Old Vic during the war and had also beautifully contributed to the success of *The Matchmaker*.

Out of their friendship came his meeting with the third man who was to make up the important trio with him and Peter Zeisler. Oliver Rea was a rich impresario, with Irish blood in his veins. He shared the same dissatisfaction as Guthrie and Zeisler with the whole set-up of New York Theatre. It was to prove an important meeting. Ideas were taking shape while Guthrie spent more dollars, and still more sweat, on Annagh-ma-Kerrig.

During that summer my wife and I saw for ourselves the new Guthrie ménage at Annagh-ma-Kerrig; saw the power poles advancing across the little green fields to bring 'the Electricity', and savoured the Guthrie benevolent domestic dictatorship. Fanny Lubitsch of the Habimah Theatre staff was there to discuss *The Merchant of Venice*, the play he had chosen to do in his second visit to the Jewish homeland. And he behaved as if he were

* *A Life In The Theatre.*

running a kibbutz. The other guests of the house at the time were Tanya and Max Schaffner, a Jewish friend from New York. As we all trod the bog together of a morning and discussed the play, he made it quite clear that, as far as he was concerned, Shakespeare's Christians on the Rialto were a morally disreputable lot. Now, you cannot comfortably tramp the grounds and forests of Guthrie land in Tel-Aviv shoes. Gumboots are essential footwear. Among the reserve boots of the old house none fitted Fanny Lubitsch. So, 'We must get Fanny gumboots'. Then Guthrie Tyrannos decreed how—and in doing so revealed his homespun relationship to his Irish folk. One was not to spend money unnecessarily. One need only spend energy, use one's wits and employ local resources. After lunch the Guthrie Voice announced clearly, 'The Guthries and Forsyths will wash up; the Jews will rest; and the entire party thereafter will pick blackberries.' They were to be gathered and taken in to Newbliss, where they would be sold for the dyeing of cloth. And, from the proceeds, we would buy Fanny a pair of gumboots. This sort of gypsy approach to economics brings to mind how that tough little genius of backstage Stratford and the Phoenix too, Jack Merigold, came to Ireland to visit, was met at the station at Dundalk and on the way back to Annagh-ma-Kerrig was somewhat surprised to be given a basket of flowers. These had been picked by Judy, and when they stopped by a fishshop Jack Merigold was ordered to get out, go in, and barter the flowers for fish. Which, hesitantly, he did, and to his amazement found that he came out with fish for supper.

Next February, 1959, when Guthrie arrived at the Habimah he had a hero's welcome. Tanya, Judy and he shared a sunny Tel-Aviv flat; and he directed a not entirely satisfactory *Merchant of Venice*. It was in a Jewish translation too sedately literary to accord with his modern dress production (which turned Shylock into a sort of Rothschild). By March he was back in New York and was ready and keen to talk to Peter Zeisler and Oliver Rea. The three got together and over a discursive breakfast at the Plaza Hotel the whole tantalizing scene of U.S. Theatre was gone into again. If they all felt as vehemently fed up with it as they said, Guthrie wondered, should they not *do* something about it? The triple resources of the three were fairly impressive. Artistic direction from Guthrie; technical direction from Zeisler; financial and promotional management from Rea. The answer, obviously,

was Yes. Zeisler—bursting with informed enthusiasm from his
year in Europe—suggested right away an Anglo-American
scheme whereby a company formed by Guthrie and flying the flag
of his Anglo-American repute would do six months in London
(where it was cheaper to launch a play)—say at the Lyric,
Hammersmith—and then six months in New York at, say, the old
Phoenix and ... Guthrie did a verbal handclap and cut short what
was going to be a lengthy argument. For neither Rea nor he was
interested in becoming tied up with London or New York.
Guthrie had a better suggestion: that they should all three meet
again at Annagh-ma-Kerrig—'ideal place to talk—no interruptions—suggest July'. Peter Zeisler knew it and loved it. Oliver
Rea had Irish in his blood and forebears in Belfast. It was agreed.

In April, Tony Guthrie used the pages of the *New York Times
Magazine* to write a long article on 'REPERTORY THEATRE—
IDEAL OR DECEPTION?'. It was calculated to do three things:
make a great many actors and actresses—especially the younger—
love him for the hugely sympathetic analysis of their plight in
seeking work, suffering the brutalities of Broadway and finding
little of the company life and training they truly longed for;
establish profound doubts about New York as a scene for
repertory; convince the Countryside and *NYT* arts public that
Repertory in a theatre with a policy was the life of Theatre; and
that that life could be lived in the U.S.A. One statement shows the
width and humanity of his view in this manifesto; it refers to the
'solidarity' of a theatre company which has some continuity of
existence: 'I think it hardly possible to over-estimate the importance of this sense of solidarity, not for its purely artistic or
theatrical results but as an element in the spiritual life of those
who feel it.' Others have hammered the unique claims of 'the
live theatre' because of the 'live' occasion of performance; he was
hammering home something no film or TV project could claim,
the creation of that lively artistic 'family'—*the company*:

> To the members of a theatre company this loyalty, this sense of
> belonging to something collectively larger than the sum of its
> individuals, is one of the central points of their lives. This,
> more than any of the fine individual talents, more than the
> collective achievement of two distinguished organizations, was
> what impressed me about Habimah in Israel and the Swedish
> Theatre at Helsingfors.

Without this feeling our theatre, however glamorous, however efficiently organized, however heavily financed, is comparatively poor. It is weakened where it can least afford to be
weak—at the heart. It is deprived of an important ingredient
of the wherewithal to make what I consider its most important
contribution to society: the feeling of intimate companionship
between audience and stage.*

Here he was right back to his basic consideration—not just to
build theatres of a certain kind, open or thrust stage, or whatever,
but to establish the human and material circumstances of playing
by which this 'companionship' might be at its most vital.

Earlier in the year he had begun to show his exasperation with
the dogged Phoenix Theatre pair, Hambleton and Houghton, for
still not formulating a policy, nor creating a company. He
despaired of the whole atmosphere of New York and its enslavement to the gambler's fever, Success; even at the Phoenix,
which he loved.

Of that summer of their Summit Meeting at Annagh-ma-Kerrig
he describes in his book, *A New Theatre*, the enervating Irish mists
that wrapped around Annagh-ma-Kerrig when Peter Zeisler,
whom he now knew well, and Oliver Rea, whom he hardly knew
at all, came to thrash out what was to be their plan of attack on
theatrical U.S.A. Guthrie let Rea talk, encouraged by generous
portions of Irish whiskey. He found a natural liking for this
almost burly Irish-American business man with his quiet but
alert manner and good humour. He was not much more than half
Guthrie's age and he looked what he was—rather rich and very
durable: both recommendations to Guthrie for the job ahead.
Zeisler was a young man too. As senior man of the trio, Guthrie
then demolished and dismissed the London–New York plan.
Both cities had plenty of theatre, and mostly of the wrong kind.
He then played a card straight out of the pack of experiences he
held from Stratters, Ont. Their theatre and company should be
'provincial', should relate to another part of the map altogether
than New York or the big cities on the East Coast. It should
relate to a real community, not a metropolis. He would not discuss budget before they had all agreed on a policy. And before
the two Americans flew out, they had agreed that it should be a
regional—or provincial—theatre with a real *company*, a clear *policy*

* *New York Times Magazine*, April 26, 1959.

and a *repertory* of . . .? The Irish days were not long enough for all three to be certain of the last of these essentials—except that it would be a 'classical' repertoire and 'classical' should accommodate modern American masterpieces liable to become 'classics of our time'. What their indefatigable host meant by 'Rolling Rep' was a little lost in the Irish mist but it seemed to mean a number of different plays within one week and the opportunity to withdraw a flop 'in the dark of the night' and keep a successful play rolling for a sensible time.

There was just time for Tony to breathe deep, dream dreams on the theatre's physical design (soon to be shared with Tanya) see a revival of *The Three Estates* in Edinburgh and fly back to Brooklyn Heights again, to prepare for rehearsals of a new American play, *The Tenth Man* by Paddy Chayevsky. But before getting down to rehearsals on that, he, Oliver Rea and 'Pee Zee' had some consultations with that sympathetic 'senior statesman' of the New York Theatre, Brooks Atkinson—whose concern for American Theatre went well beyond his immediate concern as drama critic of the *New York Times*. They discussed with him potential regional cities which they should have a look at. A short-list was thrashed out. Oliver Rea, Tony and Judy Guthrie set off on a 'whistle-stop' tour. Zeisler was tied at the time to the New York scene, as stage director of *The Sound of Music*.

They moved around the U.S. map, and the word spread that Guthrie was out to establish a new theatre in whatever city he considered to be the best bidder—financially and in the amenities. They looked at Cleveland, Milwaukee, San Francisco, Detroit. But by then something had been happening spontaneously in a town not on their list, Minneapolis—and its twin city, St. Paul. This 'City of Lakes' stands astride the Mississippi in the Mid-West. Certain of its citizens concerned with a local ambition saw, in an Atkinson article in the *New York Times*, what Guthrie was after. They were after it too. *They* got after *him*.

The prime mover from Minneapolis was Professor Frank Whiting, director of Theatre in the large University of Minnesota, in Minneapolis. That this was a man of a like mind to Guthrie's is instanced by the fact that, several years before, when Tony Guthrie had tried to generate a scheme to take over a river-boat in New York and turn it into a theatre, Professor Whiting had done just that. His Mississippi stern-wheeler was still there, moored to the bank, and *was* a theatre, in which Frank Whiting's students performed plays. He was no more likely to get Guthrie now to accept the boat as his new theatre than Tom Patterson was likely to confine Guthrie to the Queens Park bandstand when he first visited Stratford. But that was not Frank Whiting's plan. He wanted a new theatre for the civic community to be built on the university campus. This was something, at the time, dear to Guthrie's heart: somehow to relate U.S. academic theatre to professional theatre and by doing so to keep the Young coming into the Theatre. In his feeling for theatre 'family' he wanted young people around him now. Minneapolis went on his list.

With this whistle-stop reconnaissance behind him and much to consider, he went ahead to direct *The Tenth Man*. It opened on November 5 in the Booth Theatre, New York, to a good press, except that two senior critics took exception to amounts of Guthrie 'horseplay' in the production. But it was a fine play and had a good success. The consultations with Rea, Zeisler and others went on and the choice of cities was finally narrowed down to three—Milwaukee, Detroit, Minneapolis.

One of the results of this survey of the nation was that he lectured Oliver Rea's children like a severe though loving uncle on having too much money—and the evils thereof. 'The trouble with you Americans is that you have no limitations—in space, money, population, food . . . What you need to do is draw a circle and work within its limitations.' In his commitment to America, that was just what he was trying to do. And he leaned towards Minneapolis because it was a large enough 'circle' of community to support the theatre he had in mind but small enough to have its own integrity—like Stratford, Ont. But Minneapolis would have to stretch itself to match Detroit for money. While the 'auction' went on, Minneapolis showed its faith in itself by forming a steering committee, headed by John Cowles, Jnr., a brilliantly practical, hard-headed and comparatively young president of the *Minneapolis Star and Tribune*.

The Guthries had to fly home. The choice of town was still at issue; but had to be decided by May of the coming year. Oliver Rea over in Ireland, to show one of his sons the community his paternal forebears came from, found Tony Guthrie in hospital in Belfast. He had sinus trouble (something that often, like his pestiferous knee, and his teeth, gave him a remarkably constant background of pain that nobody except Judy knew of). The patient talked himself out of the hospital for the day and insisted

on showing the Reas round Belfast. He walked out as he was, and
there were the American visitors trying hard to ignore the
amazed looks of the Irish at the neighbouring table during their
lunch. For at their table was, of course, the normally noticeable
great Guthrie, but right now he was a great big man with a big
nose up which immovable medical tubes were stuck.

Plans for 1960 went on. And, just as the year turned, Peter
Zeisler and Oliver Rea, in New York, heard shocking news. Tony
Guthrie had collapsed after his sinus operation and was lying
critically ill, in the Benn Hospital, Belfast. He had had a heart
attack, had pulled through, but would not be allowed to do anything for months. Actually, it had been touch and go; when he
was able to write to them, he kept the whole business of consultation going. But Rea and Zeisler now had to go off on their
own to make the second reconnaissance of the three cities the
choice had narrowed to: Minneapolis, Detroit, Milwaukee.

By February the patient was out. So were the snowdrops at
Annagh-ma-Kerrig. He made plans. Flying was forbidden. So he
booked a passage on a slow boat for New York, via Halifax. He
left Liverpool in the *Corinthia*. On the quay in New York on
March 18 an anxious Oliver Rea and Peter Zeisler met Guthrie.
He was in good spirits, had next to no luggage, and so was
hurried through customs to a warm apartment and lots of talk.
The next day he was off to Toronto by train to start casting
auditions for *H.M.S. Pinafore*.

Before his collapse Langham had asked him to do *King John* in
Stratford's new 'permanent' theatre. But he 'wasn't strong
enough'. He wanted to do something light—and something he
had often wanted to do—Gilbert and Sullivan. He got through
his auditions and was warmly welcomed by many anxious old
friends of the Stratters, Ont., days. He also interested Douglas
Campbell in his new theatre venture (knowing that Campbell
had been disappointed not to be his successor in Stratford). By
the end of the month he was on the *Ivernia* headed for England;
each voyage a convalescence but no time wasted and the work
going on.

While he was in England he became involved in advising on
the new theatre at Chichester (a direct product of the enthusiasm
of Evershed Martin—that township's 'Tom Patterson'—for the
Stratford Ontario theatre). And it is interesting that when
Evershed Martin asked him later if he, not Sir Laurence Olivier,

had been asked to take on the directorship at Chichester would he have accepted, he answered 'No'. He felt that America and Canada were going to be the most powerful countries in the world, but that they still needed cultural background and artistic development to give them the balance to rule wisely. If he could add his little contribution to this he felt it his duty to do so. It was a more than theatrical commitment to America. But it was now May and no decision yet taken between the three cities. This was when Minneapolis showed its mettle and chose to take the initiative.

The steering committee had gone ahead to find a site, and the necessary funds were now within reach. Peter Zeisler got a wire in New York: would he and Oliver Rea meet the steering committee if they came right now to New York? Of course. The resolute men of Minneapolis, lead by John Cowles, Jnr., got in the private plane of the *Minneapolis Star and Tribune* and flew straight to New York. There was a meeting, in the Century Club. It was tense with all the grim practicalities of Finance. They explained about the site—not on the university campus, not a remodelled theatre in town, but a new site adjacent to their civic gallery, the Walker Art Center. They explained about funds— now available in the region of $1,300,000. Would this sum do? Rea and Zeisler risked being tough show-business men. Could this be increased by a few hundred thousand if necessary? A cold and calculated 'Yes' came from John Cowles, Jnr. A calculated— and not cold at all—'Yes' was given by Rea and Zeisler. Minneapolis and St. Paul on the Mississippi—'The City of Lakes'— it was to be. Tony Guthrie took good long looks at his beloved lake with its Irish swans, and booked a passage for June on the *Queen Mary*.

In the middle of June, feeling a new man, he shared his satisfaction with Rea and Zeisler in New York then went on up to happy rehearsals of *Pinafore*, which opened to much laughter and applause in July, in Stratford's Avon Theatre—the town's original house. In Minneapolis, where he visited for a couple of days, 'the Tyrone Guthrie Theatre Foundation' was set up. A devoted lady secretary took up office in one of the corners of the jade and porcelain galleries of the Walker Art Center. Professor Rapson of the chair of Architecture at the university was briefed to produce designs for the new theatre. Tanya Moiseiwitsch and Douglas Campbell were brought in to hand on the accumulated experience of the functioning of the Stratford Festival Theatre.

Pinafore moved down into New York and, at the Phoenix, brought some brightness and box-office business to his old friends there. I had a play running across the street, so I saw and shared in that happiness. What was not so happy was that this distinguished heart patient went straight on to produce the new play of his old friend of Old Vic and Canada, Robertson Davies, *Love and Libel*. That he made a proper botch of it, all agreed. It was an unwise undertaking, to do a new play when the prognostication had been that he would not be fit enough to do one old one. Rob Davies had been of great assistance in all the Stratford ventures and Tony probably felt he owed it to him. But the play and the playwright, suffered.

He now went back to Minneapolis, to find that Rapson's design had costed out at several thousand dollars above the budget figure. Alterations he greatly regretted resulted, which in no way penalized the public at the foyer end but backstage took away a large slice of cubic footage and consigned future backstage workers to windowless rooms. As he pointed out, these people spent *all day* in the theatre, whereas the public came in only for part of the evening or afternoon. He was still thinking towards 'company', 'solidarity' and the welfare of his theatre family.

Back in New York, at the airport, on the way to his plane, he turned to Oliver Rea and let out something which had added to his preoccupation at this time. 'Something rather secret to tell you,' he said. 'Have been offered a knighthood. Don't think I should take it. The people of Minn. might be put off by grand title.' To which Oliver Rea said, as, surely, he expected him to: 'Take it! They'll *love* it.' Having almost died at the start of the year, he was able on its last day to read in the London *Times*, 'Mr. T. Guthrie (Knight)'. Sir Tyrone—and a new American theatre to be built which would bear his name—1961 started with an up-beat. It is noticeable, in these years, how little he had to do with England, and rumour has it that the pressures towards getting him that long-delayed honour came from across the sea, from Canada. Whatever Minn. might feel, Stratters, Ont. was not going to let their hero die unhonoured.

While adjusting to being Sir Tyrone Guthrie of the dwelling house and lands of Annagh-ma-Kerrig, etc., he spent more time at home and a little more looked to Ireland and its Drama Festivals. But planning for Minneapolis went on all the time. There was the whole of building, fund-raising and trying to keep the peace between a determined Tanya Moiseiwitsch and a stubborn Ralph Rapson, so that he might still achieve the desired design for stage and for auditorium. Once again, in 1961, he launched a summer production in Stratters, Ont., of Gilbert and Sullivan (*The Pirates of Penzance*) and once again he brought it to New York. In 1962 both *Pirates* and *Pinafore* went to London, and were completely successful in the West End. In fact, very ordinary success was attending him, to the degree that he found it profitable to found—with his old friend, George Chamberlain— his own company, the Wharton Production Company, and the Wharton Street house of the Chamberlains became his lodging whenever in London.

By the spring of 1962 the contractual agreement had been signed between Sir Tyrone Guthrie and the Tyrone Guthrie Theatre Foundation of Minnesota. Thereby he was designated 'Artistic Director' of the proposed 'Repertory Theatre Company'. Thirty consecutive weeks of each year would be given by him— and this would be for three years commencing 1962. For this service he would receive $400 per week with $160 living expenses, and the round trip air fare from Shannon, Ireland, to Minneapolis for himself and Lady Guthrie.

Tony had wondered if 'Sir Tyrone' would put a kind of royal proscenium arch between him and the folks in Minneapolis. In fact, with his capacity to play the outrageous eccentric, under any title, he need not have worried. It was Judy who was to be disturbed by being put under a sort of polite ostracism, the result of too much respect for the title 'Lady Guthrie'. But for the moment all was happy expectancy over the prospect of being much in what they called 'dear Minn.'.

In New York he went ahead to produce the second of the Paddy Chayefsky plays, *Gideon*, a rousing biblical piece he loved doing with two actors he thought highly of, Fredric March and Douglas Campbell. It settled down to a good run at the Plymouth and he went into various conferences with Campbell, Rea, Zeisler and Tanya—who were now all signed on with Minneapolis. By November 1961 there was a scale model of the theatre and its stage sitting on Oliver Rea's office desk. On November 20, Lady Guthrie and Sir Tyrone arrived on site at 8.00 a.m. It was a frozen Mid-Western morning, with the lakes solid with ice. The Guthrie 'naughty' journalism gives a vivid account:

To me was accorded the honour of . . . Turning the First Sod.
My tiny hand was frozen, and into it someone thrust a coal
shovel. I had hoped for a gold and platinum trowel with a
moving inscription on its mother-of-pearl handle. But in the
flurry of events this had been overlooked and at the eleventh
hour someone had produced the shovel from the furnace room
of the Walker Art Center . . . It was apparent that to turn even
an eggspoonful of earth would require a superhuman effort.
At the first attempt the shovel buckled pitifully. There was a
faint titter. I bent it back into shape and tried again. After
several attempts, red in the face and grunting heavily, I had
turned enough earth to bury a flea. An anonymous lady—I
shall love her for it always—scooped together the six or seven
grains and declared she would plant an acorn in them. At this
moment from behind our backs a giant bulldozer appeared,
with a roar . . .*

The business-like city meant business, and without delay the
building was begun.

It was steady progress from then on. Like the Stratford,
Ontario, project they had had their Point of Abandonment or
Point of No Return. This was when the academic architect's
plans had faced the board with a rise in budget not at all 'academic'
—another million dollars and more. But John Cowles, Jnr., had
set his hand to the plough and Minneapolis had the biblical
backbone not to look back.

1962 in America was mainly devoted to the recruitment of the
Company. The Guthries went back in November to blizzards in
Britain and Annagh-ma-Kerrig under snow. But one small event
there signified the continuity of the thrust forward of life in the
Irish community. Seamus McGorman, of the garden and grounds,
married his Mary. And maybe it is as well now to say who
Seamus was, since he would play quite a part in the Guthrie last
act. He was, to put it in traditional terms, the rugged faithful
steward of Sir Tyrone. He was the outside man who ran the
farm. He had come to Annagh-ma-Kerrig as the gardener's boy,
succeeded to the stewardship of Becky Daly's brother, in fear
and awe of Mister Tony, and now welcomed every day that the
master came home. Inside the house it was Bob Burns and *his*
Mary who were the servants—and 'lived in'. Seamus and his

* *A New Theatre*, Tyrone Guthrie. McGraw-Hill, 1964.

Mary lived under the same roof too, but further back than the kitchen quarters, where the stables gave on to the farm buildings. The old house therefore was exemplary in the sectarian harmony under its roof, for Bob and Mary Burns were Protestants and Seamus and his Mary were Catholics. And their baby was to be the first of a veritable tribe of ruddy-cheeked McGormans (to whom Sir Tyrone would, without fail, send coloured postcards from all his travels). Seamus now took over the job of driving not only the tractor but the house car. The less robust Bob was not fit enough for the job now. It was Seamus, therefore, who would mostly meet Sir Tyrone at airport and train, and in his thick Monaghan accent give him, as they drove home, a quick fire account of how everything local was going on.

There was a need now to sit by the log fire and plan Minneapolis. But there was more and more the other necessity: to think how to evolve some plan whereby the occupancy of this old house, and the squire-like obligation to give employment to the dependent Irish Folks around, would make economic sense. At the time of its inheritance he had worried about it openly, and Douglas Campbell—speaking straight out of *The Three Estates* like a Glasgow John of the Commonweal—had said, 'Och, give it away! It's not your problem. On with the good work.' True, the best work he could do was in Theatre, but to break with Annagh-ma-Kerrig was to sever roots he was not prepared to see cut off. Nor would Peggy have liked it. She and Hubert were managing to preserve and give some new vitality to the Butlers' big old house of Maidenhall, down in Kilkenny. And during the war and before, it was they who had slaved to keep the Irish jungle away from the bog garden and who got the Forestry Commission to lease the woods. They of course had a child like the McGormans. There was no class condescension in his attitude to the Irish servants and workers on the estate.

It was around now that fate, and a tendency towards folk industry (first seen in the blackberry picking), turned Guthrie Tyrannos of the Realm of Theatre, and Sir Tyrone of the House By The Lake, towards *Jam* and to the manufacture of same.

Shopping in the little local township of Newbliss—where the weeds now grew over the 'dead' railway station—he went into the shop-cum-bar to buy a bottle of whiskey; and he heard a man talking. He stopped, and he got into talk with this smallish, intent Irishman with the local accent. His name was Joe Martin. He had been born, and grown to manhood, in the locality. But he had been away in South Africa, on something to do with engineering. It was not long since he had come back home, because his mother or his father had died—or something. Things do not bother to be clear-cut in such talk. And in Monaghan there is a dreaming runs through logical statement. The talk had first caught the alert Guthrie ear, because the returned local boy was describing the depressed local scene; and from the same returned-from-abroad objective viewpoint as he himself had. Joe Martin was deploring that there was now no employment, no hope for the young in the community. Guthrie agreed. And, without the next generation having something to do which would hold it here, the place would die. They both agreed. It had happened elsewhere. It should not happen here. 'Come up to Annagh-ma-Kerrig. Come to supper. Think we should talk more of this, don't you?' So Joe Martin went to supper with Sir Tyrone and Lady Guthrie up in the big house which he had only seen from afar as a boy. Joe Martin was supping with the gentry.

The people in the village whispered a bit; and in the Annagh-ma-Kerrig kitchen too. 'What was Sir Tyrone thinking of?' 'What was Joe Martin on about?' and 'What is he up to now?' For Joe was known for dreams and schemes. Joe was up to his ears in quite genuine enthusiasm about sharing a social reformer's dream with Sir Tyrone; and Lady Guthrie was chipping in too. The reformation of this dream was no less than the Guthrie grand scheme to regenerate Newbliss; not quite in the Patterson way for Stratford, Ont., but to stimulate the surrounding farm community by the creation of a local folk industry; something which would give employment to the young and stop the general drift off the land, towards Belfast, Liverpool and England beyond. It was not that Sir Tyrone had right away any clear-cut scheme, but he was determined to *do* something—not just talk. Just talking had ruined Ireland before. If Joe Martin was free and ready to be employed, then they should meet again and start taking action. Joe left Annagh-ma-Kerrig very much Sir Tyrone's man, and dreaming and scheming like mad about Newbliss and a factory.

For Tony Guthrie's fertile mind it was not too many steps from bartered flowers from his garden and wild blackberries picked to furnish Fanny Lubitsch with rubber boots, to Fruit— to Jam—to homemade jam—to a home industry and the Irish Folk employed in some sort of local factory. If farmers could be persuaded to give their sons the orchards and some ground of their own to grow fruit locally for the jam? . . . would this not hold the new generation on the land? Experiments would have to be made—starting with stewpots in the kitchen while a site for the factory would have to . . . 'secra, secra' (as his letters said for 'etcetera').

While planning a repertory theatre and company for the U.S.A. he was therefore planning for Ireland an industry. He would have to go full out on the Minneapolis work soon. Next year would be the opening and need a lot more time than the contracted thirty weeks. He started right away on the jam. Judy did experiments. But it needed a greater scale of production than kitchen pans to test the whole thing. Joe and he found a derelict bakery. It had the ruined rudiments of a witch's cauldron amidst its weedy 'plant'. They both got down to it with their sleeves up; they were like sixteen-year-olds. The boiler would need repair. Joe went on the search to find engineers expert in that field. One day two well-dressed Irish gentlemen-craftsmen drove up in their motor to one side of the defunct bakery. They got out; took one glance at the big fellah, sweating the hell out of his guts among the ashes. Maybe they noted the grimy white shirt and a haircut that looked as if it had been done in the Belfast Barracks. But anyway they had a smoke and waited for 'Sir Tyrone Guthrie' to turn up. The beknighted bugger was nearly a half-hour late when they went around the other side to ask the big fellah muckin out the furnace where the hell did he think 'Sir Tyrone' had got to. One can imagine the shock as they discovered that he had just got to the end of shovelling out all the ashes.

And on the other side of the Atlantic it would need a supreme effort of imagination on the part of the keen, clean 1,200 women of Minnesota, now mustered to make their drive to raise funds for '*Sir* Tyrone Guthrie's new theatre', to believe that their English knight could be the unrecognizable mucker-out of a derelict bakery boiler. Yet they 'had their sleeves up' too. They christened themselves the Stagehands and provided a shining proof of Sir Tyrone's positive answer to that question he had posed way back in 1933 (in *Theatre Prospect*), 'Is Organization Necessary?' By next March 22,000 people had bought season tickets, giving them admission to the four productions of the first season—*Hamlet*, *The Miser* (Douglas Campbell directing), *The Three Sisters* and *Death of a Salesman* (again, Campbell not Guthrie directing).

The opening was now only four months away. The army of ladies sold tickets. The building went on. Peter Zeisler and Oliver Rea and the committees dealt with a welter of administrative problems. At the end of January Tony got back to the U.S. He had to leave Judy and Joe to take forward the Jam project. He had all sorts of public relations jobs to do before the arrival of the company in Minneapolis.

On one such public occasion, when he had been talking in Minneapolis about the recruitment of the company, he had the wind taken completely out of his sails (one of the few times in his life). He was in his 'best blue', standing up before a university and high school audience. In his talk he had said that there might be a necessity to depend greatly on Canada for recruitment of suitable players. A consciously American high school boy rose up at the back:

'Sir—why Canada?'

'Because there is now in Canada a very considerable number of actors and actresses who can speak Shakespearean dialogue and the speech of the classical repertoire. Next?'

But probably more out of jealous pride than bedevilment the boy persisted.

'Sir—do you mean that you want actors who'll speak affected, like you?'

There was only an awkward silence and on to the next question. Maybe the normal sharp riposte did not come because the boy was 'being personal'—or maybe because it did strike him that he had forgotten how even now at home, in Britain, Youth had an antipathy towards the sort of superior accent he had, and which reflected a class distinction. Even at Oxford now, students affected Birmingham and Liverpool accents more than BBC Oxbridge. After the lecture he did say, 'He's got a point, hasn't he?' He got his own back a year later, in his own book on *A New Theatre*: 'It must be remembered that in current American life it is considered not only unimportant but unacceptable to speak "well". It is thought to be un-American, undemocratic and unmanly.'*

Players from all over the American map did in fact come, literally in their hundreds, to the auditions in New York. This was a comforting sign that maybe it was not going to be as difficult as many had said to get players to commit themselves to the

* *A New Theatre*, Tyrone Guthrie. McGraw-Hill, 1964.

Mid-West and move away from the Broadway bright lights and Television. But it faced him with the old perplexity of the ineffectiveness of auditions. One actor told me that all Guthrie did was ask hundreds in quick succession two questions. 'Can you sing? What is your religious belief?' It is surely apocryphal. Although, in planning a classical repertoire, there is a lot of sense in both questions. It was probably the opening provocation to a conversational exchange. What he did was to give all who came an interview. From the interview came a short list who were auditioned more or less in the standard way, on stage. He was a pretty good spotter of players by then. Ken Ruta, for instance, he talked to for nearly half an hour. When he got him on stage he simply called to him: 'Say something loud and clear, boy!' ('A classical repertoire demands talent and demands intelligence. Beauty and sex appeal can to a great extent be achieved by artifice. What cannot be faked is vocal quality.')*

Voice he was after. And those who could *breathe*. One day at the theatre he told Paul Ballantyne to go outside and come back only when he could say one long speech in one breath. And, in fact, unless you have a trained pair of lungs, as under control as the bag of a bagpipe, you cannot keep the flow of the rhythmic and long sentences of Shakespeare, with their continuous line of thought.

The search for an American Hamlet was hard and long. It is surprising that he finally alighted on one who had never spoken verse on stage before, a young actor, George Grizzard. But he and Campbell had seen the young man play in *Who's Afraid of Virginia Woolf?* He was intelligent. He was witty. He was modest. He could suggest a prince. He would obviously give his eye teeth to have a shot at Hamlet, therefore—the one essential for Guthrie—he would *work*. At the heart of the company they had strength, experience and intelligence—as well as female beauty thrown in—with Hume Cronyn, his wife Jessica Tandy and Zoë Caldwell. One of the attractions to the players who came flocking was of course the whole raison d'être of Operation Repertory—the variety of parts they could play within the season.

The Company when formed would be thirty-five players strong, with twelve locals to be brought in and a few McKnight Scholars, who were mainly student apprentices to the technical

* Ibid.
10

and writing side of Theatre. These made, as he said, a much needed bridge between the academic and professional theatre.

With all things set at Minneapolis—and major confrontations reduced to a minor clash with the architect (on the multi-coloured seats in the auditorium and some architectural phantasy on the façade) he visited Leonid Kipnis in New York. This was for a final consultation—but not about Film. Kipnis was to be the translator for three great productions of Chekhov he was to do in Minneapolis, starting with *The Three Sisters* this first season. Annagh-ma-Kerrig, Chekhov and the Russian Kipnis family were one amalgam in his imagination now; and the Russian in Tanya Moiseiwitsch too was to enrich these productions. *And* they were family plays.

At this time he went with Douglas Campbell to see the latest offering of the Phoenix Theatre Company, now moved up-town to a smaller theatre. It was Arthur Kopit's *Oh Dad, Poor Dad, Mamma's Hung You in the Closet and I'm Feelin' So Sad*, directed by Jerome Robbins. The Phoenix was in the full flush of a successful long run. When his friend Hambleton, beaming with success, asked him how he liked the play, he said, 'Hated it.' Then, via an article in the house magazine that T. Edward Hambleton had courageously asked him for—on Policy—Guthrie publicly signed off after years of active support for the Phoenix:

> I, for one, cannot rally round a programme which veers from British veterans, like *Pirates of Penzance* or *The Dark Lady of the Sonnets* to modern Polish farce, culminating in a pseudo-psychic, quasi-crazy, ultra-umbilical entertainment, which has occupied the theatre for many months because it is popular. That seems to me to be nothing but a policy of commercial expediency and no more worthy of disinterested support than General Motors . . .

His particular hope of an American Repertory Theatre with an enduring policy now centred entirely on Minneapolis. In early April rehearsals began.

Tanya was there ahead of him. The final battle for the shape of the stage had been won by her. It was an irregular 'thrust' with an adjustable back wall which could swing away to let trucked scenic elements come through on to the stage. (Unlike Stratford it had no central architectural feature, like the famous pulpit-cum-balcony.) The design of the auditorium resulted in a theatre far

more matey and informal than the larger more severe amphitheatre of Stratford, Ontario. It was for one thing asymmetrical.
The seating on one side section swept steeply straight up from
stage to back wall, while for the rest of the house the seating was
divided into main seating and separate gallery. The upholstery of
the seats was unusual in that there were several separate colours
and the colours grouped irregularly. Guthrie had tried to keep
the colours to two or three. But the general effect is of a quite
restrained autumnal mosaic with bright patches. Altogether the
house has a welcoming and friendly informality within the
idiom of modern design, seats 1,437, and has none of its seats
more than fifty-two feet from the stage centre.

But, to work. There was no tin-hut rehearsal here. There was
an ample rehearsal room, and the theatre. *Hamlet* then *The Miser*
was to be the opening order. His *Hamlet* was to be in twentieth-
century dress. Not half of the audience in this theatre would have
seen a professional production of *any* Shakespeare play. They
might expect the stereotype Elizabethan costume but he explained
his rejection of this:

Perhaps it is impertinent, but as a director I feel it is my duty to
protect Shakespeare, and to try to protect all of us, from our
passionate addiction to Romance and a Stereotype.

Therefore it seemed a good idea to dress the characters in a
manner which accords with the text but does not necessarily
accord with the stereotype . . . Our final reason for producing
this particular *Hamlet* in modern dress was that we believed it
would better suit an American cast, less at home with 'period'
plays than British actors . . .

In addition to the rehearsals for the two opening plays, there
was a daily movement class conducted by Campbell. It was
part-dancing, part-gym, part-breathing . . . then there were
fencing classes . . . In addition, on most days, right after the
movement class, I used to rehearse the whole company for
twenty minutes or so in the choral speaking of the 118th
Psalm. This was partly to prepare it for the Service of Dedication which was to open the theatre, and partly to try to get us
all thinking along broadly similar lines, and talking a broadly
similar language, about the speaking of words. *

* *A New Theatre*, Tyrone Guthrie. McGraw-Hill, 1964.

I underline the above because here is Guthrie Tyrannos—the patriarchal figure with the whole 'family' or 'tribe' gathered together as one—with one voice.

> '. . . Let them now that fear the Lord say, that
> his mercy endureth forever! . . .
> The stone which the builders refused is become
> the headstone of the corner.
> This is the Lord's doing . . .'

Echoes of the Rev. Thomas Guthrie.

A Lutheran minister, a Jewish rabbi and a Catholic priest were on the platform for the Dedication . . . 'four trumpeters and the tympanist, who are the theatre's resident musicians, played pieces by Bach and Gretchaninov . . .'

Hamlet opened two nights later on a May evening. Lights glowed out from the elegant glass shell of the contemporary structure of the Guthrie Theatre into a warm, lazy evening breeze. Inside a celebrity audience found itself first caught up then trapped by a long Shakespeare tragedy. It went on for nearly four hours. The length and the weight of the evening militated against what they all most desired to do: celebrate—celebrate the fact that their theatre was open. But then this was not Festival. This was the start of a long-term repertory theatre—not just a summery seasonal affair. Walter Kerr of the *New York Herald Tribune* was at pains not to discourage:

> As of Tuesday evening, Mr. Guthrie, Mr. Grizzard, Minneapolis and an architect with holes in his façade all said, 'What have we got to lose, except money and our reputations?' And went for broke. They won't go broke. They'll probably go to heaven for their nerve, cheek, faith, recklessness, impracticality and wisdom, with no more than a month or two in purgatory for the sins they haven't bothered to avoid.

This was not very gratifying to all concerned, even if he went on to pick out 'typical Guthrie improvisations that work most wonderfully . . . such as a buzz of (onstage) spectators catching the implications of the play-within-a-play long before Claudius lets his nerves be shown . . . Jessica Tandy, as Gertrude . . . reporting Ophelia's death, and moving away from us all, a vanishing stalk of gray, as though she were going to say nothing more as long as she lived.'

In the *Boston Herald*, Elinor Hughes hailed the opening as 'a major event in American theater history', and was guardedly complimentary about George Grizzard.

Howard Taubman of the *New York Times* said that Grizzard 'played with shining intelligence'.

But they were far from 'rave' notices and in New York the production would have been dead and gone in a week. That, however, was the point. They were not in New York and this was not 'a production'. It was the first performance of a new company and theatre which was to grow, and would have to suffer growing pains. The critics were less tense about *The Miser*. But the company had to 'rise above' Claudia Cassidy and her *Sunday Tribune* notice out of Chicago: 'Sir Tyrone gave the crucial product a queasy start with a singularly cheapened *Hamlet*, and Mr. Campbell beat *The Miser* to a simpering froth of surface slapstick . . . When I say I was sharply disappointed, I mean precisely that . . .'

Five weeks later *The Three Sisters* opened—and to a rather different reception. Almost everyone with any judgment agreed that here was 'ensemble playing', here was a real company in play, here was what repertory was all about.

In the library it is possible to admire Chekhov's *Three Sisters* as an accurate, clinical study of provincial melancholy without caring too deeply about what happens . . . to its characters. . . . On the stage it is the task of the director to make us care for them—if possible to make us love them. The glory of Tyrone Guthrie's lovely production . . . is that we do . . . Guthrie's *Hamlet* moved with the rhythm of a fist relentlessly clenching and opening. His *Three Sisters* rises and falls like quiet, even breathing. It is compassionate and lovely and I hope that you will see it.

This being the *Minneapolis Morning Tribune*, one senses a bit of partisan pride; but one also senses that here was the greater informality, greater community 'companionship' of the new theatre beginning to pay off with 'the family play'. It was also the pay-off from the start of a love affair between Guthrie and the plays of Chekhov.

Finally, a critic greatly given to honest and constructive support but not to unprofessional partisanship, Brooks Atkinson, got the whole thing in perspective by waiting to see all four plays of the season and writing of 'Minneapolis's First Repertory Season':

Last May Guthrie inaugurated repertory with a resident company on a platform stage in a fresh, modern theatre 1,016 air miles from the economic insane asylum of Broadway.

Everyone interested in the theater as an art has talked wistfully about this sort of project for years. Thanks to the confidence and generosity of the people of Minneapolis, Guthrie and his two associates, Oliver Rea and Peter Zeisler, have made the first decisive step. During the summer they have provided Minneapolis audiences with four classics . . . the vigorous open stage in Minneapolis suits all four plays in the first season. It is ideal for Shakespeare. The open stage also suits *The Miser* which is a harlequinade. Although Chekhov wrote *The Three Sisters* for a proscenium, the delicate interior life of the play unfolds on an open stage where a profusion of props sufficiently defines the scenes. *Death of a Salesman* is the least successful of the productions. But the failure is less from a lack of scenery than from the incongruity of the brisk, skeletonized structure that supports a second-level playing area upstage. The style, not the stage is at fault.

Second, repertory. Everyone has long agreed that repertory develops the range and sensitivity of actors and also relieves them of the sterile monotony of playing one part for months. But, until the skills of the actors are developed over a period of years, the repertory system results in compromises. Although Hume Cronyn is perfectly cast as the irascible miser and is well cast as the doctor in *The Three Sisters* he lacks the stature and broken spirit of Willy Loman in *Death of a Salesman*. George Grizzard does not have the depth for Hamlet but his petulant army officer in *The Three Sisters* is admirable . . .

In Minneapolis the greatest success this year has been the audience. It has been not only consistently large but attentive and responsive . . . We will be lucky if New York audiences support all the Lincoln Center productions with as much hospitality and taste . . .

How splendid for 'the Stagehands' to read. And altogether—knowing the ups and downs and the great importance of most critics to the commerce of theatre and lack of importance to the art of theatre—how satisfactory to Guthrie. He knew, with Brooks Atkinson, that this was just a first step. He knew it would take five years to have such a repertory company in full maturity. But here it was proving the worth of its service to the community and justifying the courage and faith of so many of that community.

The University of Minnesota made Sir Tyrone, to his delight, a Professor of Speech and Drama. It was the start of a period when, in America, he did a lot of teaching of the young and enjoyed it. But it was now back with Judy to home; and to Joe and wherever he had got to with the Jam. *The Three Sisters* opened on June 18. On July 12, in capital letters in his diary, Guthrie was going to be able to write firmly, 'JAM MAKING BEGINS.'

CHAPTER NINETEEN

MONEY FOR JAM
(1963–1969)

IN THE now derelict station in Newbliss village, where Guthrie had first arrived as a small schoolboy on holiday, the little signal-box cabin still stood. But now it was transformed by more than a coat of paint. It didn't signal anything any more but under full steam was 'Irish Farmhouse Preserves Ltd. Directors: Sir Tyrone Guthrie. Joseph Martin (Managing)'. The signal box was the office. The view down the line was a bed of weeds where the rails had been. The printed brochure of the company was phrased to make appeal to an international market:

> In what was once Newbliss Station on the Great Northern Railway of Ireland (the single branch line has been closed for over a decade) the factory has been established. What was once the freight shed is now a huge kitchen, refrigeration plant and extensive packing and storage space have been added; and the waiting room is a Laboratory.

He had bought the Newbliss railway station. The experiments were over, the company formed, the capital found. Joe Martin and he had their factory and their employees, and jam-making had begun in earnest. In the promotional 'poem' which follows one can see the vision which led him on. The artist's picture on the front of it shows Annagh-ma-Kerrig standing above fields of fruit bushes which do not just stretch to a lake shore but right on to the shores of Ireland and the sea that stretches to America.

> It is all in the midst of fields of the most intense green, surrounded by great hedges of whitethorn and blackthorn and the ash trees, from which the village of Newbliss (so called by Scottish settlers in the early seventeenth century) derives its more ancient Celtic name—Lisdarragh, the Fort of the Ash Trees.
>   The jams and jellies are made of fresh fruit and beet-sugar, grown and manufactured in Ireland. All the fruit is locally

grown, with the exception of oranges imported from Malaga for the marmalade; no artificial colouring or flavouring is added, and no chemical preservatives whatsoever are added.

Later there was added when he looked beyond jam:

Also from Ireland's green pastures and meadows come the milk cream, butter and cheese, which have made Irish Dairy Produce world-famous. Vegetables for soups, wheat for flour, honey from the heather and clover, delicious prawns from the seas which wash our coasts—all the natural abundance, which, with careful cultivation and a temperate climate can, after centuries of neglect, begin to transform a wretchedly poor and unhappy island into prosperous contentment.

Tyrone Guthrie.

For the next few years the diary of his movements reads like that of either an airline pilot on the North Atlantic route or an Irish marketing executive whose beat was North America. Towards the end of these years it built up to such a frantic to and fro, that it promised to be the Death of a Salesman: 'Oct. 29th Minneapolis, Nov. 4th Concord, Mass., 8th Utah, Salt Lake City, 11th Texas, 12th Pittsburg, 14th Michigan, 16th San Antonio, Texas, 18th Indiana, 19th Illinois, 20th St. Louis, Mo., 21st Orange City, Iowa, 22nd Liberty, Mo., 23rd Meadville, Penn., 25th Minneapolis, 30th *Atreus* Canada, 1st Dec. Minneapolis, 8th New York, 14th Leave for Ireland.' He was into his late sixties, he was a salesman, he was selling. His two 'lines' were Regional Rep. and Irish jam; U.S. headquarters for the one, the Guthrie Theatre, Minneapolis, Minn., and U.K. headquarters for the other, the Newbliss Station Factory. And to get the second established he sold Theatre like mad—to make money for jam. He could write to Judy, who was now often alone at home: 'I am now box-office on the LECTURE CIRCUIT.' The gift of the gab came into full play. With his presence, intelligence, humanity and 'carrying voice', he could stand up anywhere and hold the attention of a crowd. And, when it came to saving the soul of Ireland through jam, financed by dollars from American academe, he was as unprincipled as Lilian Baylis in getting his hands on the cash for 'the work'.

Many, many thousands of dollars went straight to the signal cabin office, where they were not left long on the spike. The farmers were beginning to co-operate and to plant fruit for the future. Even the Rev. Mr. Lumley at Aghabog vicarage was

10*

turning in a nice line in luscious raspberries. Young people—of
all religious denominations and both political sides—were in the
factory boiling, bottling and labelling. Even by mid-1964 Guthrie
was boasting to friends in America, many of whom he had
persuaded to buy shares in the Company:

> The JAM is going great guns . . . rather too much so . . . straw-
> berries, raspberries, b.currants, all ripened at self-same moment.
> ENARMOUS quantity (and quality) . . . factory working day and
> night . . . 7 or 8 thousand pounds of jam in 24 hrs. 60 children
> sit (when fine) in open air at 3 long tables shredding currants . . .
> indoors 30 grown-ups, cooking, bottling, etc . . . my hands are
> mauve and I smell like semi-rancid strawberry . . .

All this may suggest that he was just exploiting the one 'line'—
Theatre—for the sake of the other—Jam. But, on the contrary,
his work as a director—and principally for the Minneapolis
company—deepened. It canalized in two directions—towards
Chekhov and towards the sort of theatre he had found in his
productions of *Oedipus*, whose subject matter was of the great
legends, the great stories running through the mythology of
man's belief. If this seems a sudden plunge into profundity from
jam and strawberry-stained hands, that was the man. One thing
common to these two directions was that in both he was going
more and more towards 'the family play', like *Uncle Vanya*, or *The
Oresteia*. But in this second year at Minneapolis, he produced
Henry V and *Volpone* in a company repertoire completed by *St.
Joan* and *The Glass Menagerie*. The main development for him,
however, had to do with the Young. He became for a season guest
director at the university and with the students he did his old
friend *Six Characters in Search of an Author*. He was as adventurous,
as 'naughty', as extravagant, as all the relief from commercial
pressures would allow. He wallowed in the richness of numbers he
could command in academic theatre where the question of a
company pay-bill did not apply. He loved them. He provoked
them. He joked with them; and he drove them tyrannically. They
all had such informative fun. What, seriously, it did for him was
to develop a real concern for the teaching processes then being
applied to the younger generation. It was this interest which led
him to become later on—in 1969—a resident professor of English
Literature in the Jesuit University of Detroit; where he became as
he said 'a timid novice in Academe'.

Two significant rows now happened at home. The first also had to do with University and the Young. In the previous year, he had not only been made a Professor of Speech and Drama at Minneapolis, he had been made Chancellor of Queen's University, Belfast. He took a real actor's delight in playing the part of Chancellor in his grand robes and academic headgear, but the serious satisfaction was that—very much to the governing body's surprise—he defeated the traditional candidate for the office, the current Duke of Abercorn, and that it was the student vote that gave Guthrie victory. Now, in October 1964, in a speech at City Hall he suggested, to students of Belfast and Dublin gathered there, that they should work for the abolition of 'the senseless line which separates our countries'. Now it is a reflection on Guthrie and discretion that one just does not call that bloodstained border 'senseless', or suggest that it is dispensable, without raising a row in Belfast. He was summoned to account by the university authorities. He argued his case and preserved his independence by eating his lunch not with them but, like a student, from the picnic basket in his car in the quad. But he only just preserved his position as Chancellor.

The second row was domestic and painful and had to do with the future of Annagh-ma-Kerrig. With the kind of dangerous life he was living, shuttling to and fro over the Atlantic and all over America, his will had to be thought about. As Oedipus Rex of the Newbliss Thebans, he saw that his family line terminated in him and the House of Guthrie was in this sense doomed. He began to see that perhaps the house *should* be given away—to the people— that the Irish folk who *had* a future should inherit the house and lands—the McGormans. Peggy was shocked; not because it was the McGormans, who were good people, but because the whole gesture seemed to be contrary to the expressed wishes of their mother who, in her will, had left Annagh-ma-Kerrig equally to Tony and Peggy. When he and Judy made it their home he had bought out Peggy's share but morally if not legally Peggy felt that it was her mother's wish that when Tony no longer had any interest in the property it should pass to her.

Tony and Judy came down to visit her at Maidenhall, where Hubert now grew fruit and vegetables for market and lived the old-fashioned life of a country scholar. He was working on a vast and sceptical book about the Irish Saints.* It had much to do

* *Ten Thousand Saints*, Hubert Butler, Wellbrook Press, 1974.

with genealogy and the continuity of inheritance was precious to
him. For that very reason he had founded the world-wide Butler
Society, whose centre was at Kilkenny Castle nearby. In the
gentle and homely atmosphere of Maidenhall, with cats and dogs
by log fire and his niece Julia present, Tony stubbornly re-
asserted his intention to give Annagh-ma-Kerrig and all its lands
to the McGormans after his and Judy's death. His attitude so
infuriated Julia—much of whose childhood had been spent there
—that she retorted 'Anyone would think that you hated us'. He
rounded on her. 'You *know* I adore your mother!'. Emotions got
rather out of control and Tony Guthrie invoked that clause in his
personal charter which says 'I always had enough sense to know
when to run out into the dark'. He did just that. He fled from
impassioned tears out into the night, put up in some hotel
bedroom in Kilkenny and did not go back; went in fact back to
Newbliss and then on to Belfast and Dublin on jam business with
Joe. For one to understand this, it has to be stressed that Peggy
and he were, all their lives, passionately attached to each other,
and that the violence of this sort of row was just one manifestation of that love. Worry about the eventual conditions of the
will went on and it went through some revision.

In 1965, the third year of Minneapolis, he went back to
Chekhov. This meant working again with Lola Kipnis in the very
Russian atmosphere of his Connecticut home. They were preparing together a new version of *The Cherry Orchard*. As they discussed the play the question of family, country property—cherry
trees—could not have been detached in Guthrie's imagination
from Annagh-ma-Kerrig, wills, property, jam. (At this time, with
the office in the hands of a good secretary, and during the off-season
for fruit, he got Joe Martin over to make American contacts.)

The Cherry Orchard opened in June. It was a triumph of co-
operation between Guthrie, Kipnis and Chekhov and also that
other 'natural' to the Russian family subject-matter, Tanya Moiseiwitsch. By all accounts it was rich in humanity, a great achievement in ensemble playing, completely at home in the theatre, and,
according to Peter Zeisler, as near 'a perfect production' as could
be. Guthrie in his maturity was warming to the family intimacy of
Chekhov which could be handled in the Guthrie Theatre in a way
never possible in the Old Vic, the Assembly Hall or the Stratford
Festival Theatre. He encouraged Kipnis to go on to prepare an
Uncle Vanya. His Russian colleague was showing signs of ill-

health but this was work he could do at home. Judy and he flew off from Minneapolis for Australia.

This was a second quick visit to the Antipodes and, though all visits tended now to have something to do with jam promotion, the main purpose was to go to Perth in Western Australia to advise the university there on the building of a new theatre. They were back in Minneapolis within two weeks—he having struggled through sinus pains and a blinding old-fashioned English cold to convince Professor Fred Alexander and his colleagues on the Australian campus to chuck out of the window all hopes of that horror, the all-purpose auditorium, and to 'go for broke', building a thrust-stage theatre with affinities to the Guthrie. This they eventually did, and called it the Octagon; to which Guthrie would one day return.

What he brought back now was that heavy cold and what he left behind was that heavy overcoat—dark, thick, indestructible, and weighing a ton; and, over more years than any coat deserved to survive, a familiar object to Guthrie friends. Then, in summery Minnesota, a young Australian actress turned up one day, diffidently lugging the great coat towards its awe-inspiring owner. This was Patricia Conolly. The grateful Guthrie took the girl to see *The Cherry Orchard*, which was playing, showed her over his theatre, said, 'Watched how you watched the play,' and made a mental note that resulted in her playing in *Uncle Vanya*, when it was ready.

But now, in 1965, he had completed his three-year contract with the Minnesota Repertory Theatre Company and on August 6, in his light-weight suit and looking like the jam executive departing on summer circuit (except for the characteristic Guthrie footwear of 'sneakers'), he had a sunny send-off from staff and company and flew home via Toronto and New York. Douglas Campbell was left as his successor at the Guthrie. Peter Zeisler stayed on. Oliver Rea had been uncertain if he should stay on. Guthrie's advice was typically forthright: 'No—not to stay. You are a strong business man and it is bad for a theatre to have a strong business person in power. Promise me that when I go, you will go two years later at most.' Rea went the next year.

Up till this time the Minnesota Theatre Company of the Guthrie Theatre had enjoyed all the cohesion in management of a 'family business' (with all the meaningful and immediate consultation and co-operation family businesses can provide, and with no doubt

who was head.) From this time on there were high achievements
'in the shop', but in 'the back shop and upstairs' things were
never so happy again. Essentially the actor, Campbell, and the
theatre technician, Zeisler, were neither of them the directorial
executives needed to fill the Guthrie 'sneakers'. And when
Campbell and Zeisler got into harness later to share the theatre's
direction—just as with the Old Vic 'troika'—these two highly
trained steeds pulled rather different ways.

Of course it was made very clear to Sir Tyrone, as he went, that
as a 'guest producer' he was *more* than welcome back—at any time.
Well, there was *Uncle Vanya* and there were other things brewing
which he very much wanted to bring to the boil at the Guthrie.
But right now it was back to Newbliss to keep the Jam on the boil.
And soon he was writing to say, 'Sold £6,000 worth since June.'
He was also, however, having to say that the 'grave difficulties
Oliver hints at' were nothing. They *were* something, and for the
moment that something might only have had to do with the
refrigerating plant breaking down around them and somebody
not being too particular about the state of the fruit before it got to
the boiler, but they were worrying.

However, Christmas was peaceful and 1966 started with a complete break away from all forms of worry. He and Judy flew off to
visit Xtopher in sunny Beirut, where Tony was able to see Professor Scaife's university and point out jokingly that he too had
reached professorial status. It was one of the great Guthrie train
journeys to come back overland from Constantinople, bearing
gifts from the East in the form of two baskets, the size of which
only the Guthries could have persuaded a Near-Eastern railway
official were their personal luggage.

After a nostalgic *Measure for Measure* at the Bristol Old Vic, he
made preparations for a year in which there was no production for
Minneapolis and almost all his energy went into the intensive
Jam-Lecture round in the U.S.A. And, though he said he saw
some sociological reasons for doing it, his production on Broadway of *Dinner at Eight* really came into the money-for-jam round
too. When interviewed by the press and asked why the king of
grass-roots repertory should do *Dinner at Eight* on Broadway, he
did not exactly improve the publicity by his reply, 'Nobody is
averse to making money.'

Then began the preparations for two deeply serious productions, both for Minneapolis: *Harper's Ferry* and *The House of*

Atreus. The first was a new play by Barrie Stavis. Right after the war Guthrie had been impressed by and tried to do his *Lamp at Midnight*, about Galileo. In 1960, while he was producing *Pinafore* in Ontario, Stavis had brought him the draft of what now was *Harper's Ferry*—a play about John Brown, who took to arms to try to liberate the American negro slaves. Guthrie recommended revisions, which were done, and in 1963, when the Minneapolis theatre started, he made the decision, in principle, that this was a fine play on a subject of national importance which his Minneapolis theatre should do. But not then. He wanted no new play until the company was established in the classics. Now, in the summer of 1966, Guthrie, Campbell and Stavis met and the decision was taken to do the play for 1967. He and Stavis set to work in a final session on a play which he had watched grow from the start. This work session almost wore the playwright down. And Barrie Stavis is not unknown for stamina. It would start at 9.30 a.m. in the Stavises' solid family apartment in up-town New York, and go on, without break, till 6.30 p.m. Tony would fire the gun to start by saying, 'Right! I'll read it out. You stop me, and comment.' Line by line, day by day, it went on till poor Stavis was crying out to his devoted wife, 'He doesn't even stop to go to the john! He gets brighter the later he gets and I get weaker and weaker, then, when I'm right low, he bursts into song!'

Guthrie left him to complete the revisions and also left him with the impression that Douglas Campbell should play John Brown; he would be willing to direct it. He did say Campbell might be too tied up as artistic director of the theatre, and another actor should be thought of. This was to be a cause of trouble in production. On Guthrie went to work with another playwright on the other big production for 1967, *The House of Atreus*.

The playwright-adapter of this work had been a young actor in the Minneapolis company, John Lewin—a somewhat scholarly man, who found he shared with Guthrie a deep interest in mythology, its psychology and symbolism. *The House of Atreus* was the title they chose for what was *The Oresteia* of Aeschylus, the trilogy of three short plays on the story of Orestes, that Hamlet-like son of the fate-ridden house of his grandfather Atreus. For Guthrie this great, Greek 'family drama' would give him the opportunity to develop the sort of theatre he had struck with *Oedipus*.

1967 promised to be an eventful year. He got ahead of all the theatre work by going on the money-for-jam lecture circuit from

January all through February. On February 18th he wrote to tell
Judy that his health was holding out and that he had 'now done 19
lectures and have either 20 or 21 to do . . . Please ask Joe to *make a
note of each cheque he gets*, so that we can check with lecture list
eventually . . . Quite enjoying it . . .' In fact he was enjoying, with
the wicked old relish, '. . . state college where fat spectacled boys
and pale, pale spectacled gals get degrees as Beauticians, Morti-
cians, Jazzicians, and—as Lutheran Pastors (Jesusicians?).'

He homed on Minneapolis in late spring and got down to the
production of *Harper's Ferry* which was due for June 3. *Atreus* was
not due till July. Thumbing through sketches and material for the
John Brown play, he found a photograph, from the publicity department, that would strangely evoke memories of Edinburgh and
the statue of the Rev. Dr. Thomas Guthrie, for there, on a stone
plinth, was a bronze statue of a man, and his arm was around the
shoulders of a 'ragged boy', but this boy was black and this man
was John Brown. Like Thomas Guthrie he was an orator who had
spoken Christian thunder. But he had also used a gun, in his
violent battle for the blacks at Harper's Ferry. And this right to
resort to violence was an issue that greatly exercised Guthrie
because it applied to Ireland and troubles again brewing there. He
had written to Stavis that, 'An important matter of principle was
at stake in J.B's trial, as well as the slavery . . . People simply
cannot be permitted to take the law into their own hands, however
convinced of the rightness of their cause.' It was a character, and a
play, he felt deeply about.

At rehearsals he was plagued with a painful swelling of the leg,
which, alarmingly, turned out to be phlebitis. Much directing had
to be done from a seat in the eighth row. And he ran into further
trouble too. Rather late in the preparations Stavis had been
informed that another actor, Ed Binns, was playing John Brown
—not Douglas Campbell. He was understandably hurt and it was
only rubbing salt in the wound for Guthrie to say that Campbell
was not only directing *The Shoemaker's Holiday* and playing
Simon Eyre in it, but in Guthrie's production of *Atreus* he was
playing both Clytemnestra *and* Pallas Athena. (As with the Greek
original, all the women in *Atreus*, other than some of the Chorus,
were to be played by masked male actors.) 'Think,' Guthrie said,
'what the comments would be if Dougie played the lead in *Harper's
Ferry* too. Think of the effect on the company.' One cannot but
sympathize with Stavis's cry, 'What about the effect on my play?'

Tanya Moiseiwitsch and Cecil Clarke with the model of the stage, Stratford, Ontario, 1953

With Tanya Moiseiwitsch in rehearsal, by the tent pole

Oedipus Rex. The Stratford Festival Company at the Edinburgh Festival, 1956. (Douglas Campbell as Oedipus, Donald Davis as Tiresias.) *Photo The Scotsman*

With T. Edward Hambleton in The Phoenix Theatre, New York, 1960. *Photo Henry Grossman*

Uncle Vanya, the Guthrie Theatre, Minneapolis, 1969 (Patricia Conolly as Yelena; Helen Carey as Sonia)

By the Newbliss Signal Cabin office of the jam factory

The House of Atreus, the Guthrie
Theatre, Minneapolis, 1967.
Agamemnon (Lee Richardson)
returns from the Trojan war with
Cassandra (Robin Gammell).
Photo Donald Getzug

The House of Atreus.
Orestes (Len Cariou)
suppliant
Photo Donald Getzug

Tony and Judith Guthrie

And after much rehearsal and just before opening, he bemoaned, 'With Ed Binns as John Brown, about one fifth of my play is going to come through.' Campbell, who was there, said, 'Aw, not as bad as that, Barrie.' 'Yaas,' said Guthrie. 'Quite agree. Barrie is right. On!' And on they went to a sad first night with a dispiriting response.

Guthrie got on with rehearsals for *Atreus*, but he was able to write to Barrie Stavis to assure him Binns was now fine, and his play running well, to good houses. Also he hoped he was recovering from the 'misplaced lacerations of the critics', and, please, not to go on voicing even his legitimate complaints outside 'the family', the company. Again the plea for solidarity. And both, whatever their failings, being big men, there was a reconciliation.

As for Campbell, he was nearly suffering martyrdom for the art of Theatre; rehearsing and preparing to play Pallas Athena in a sculpturally encrusted costume that was as much scenery as costume. The Guthrie-Moiseiwitsch inventions of costume were monumental in scale and not designed at all for the claustrophobe. But the result on the first night was extraordinary.

The House of Atreus was a phenomenon. It opened to an amazed, disturbed and—in the classical sense—an ecstatic audience. This was the full manifestation of the Master's art. It was something that had never quite happened like this before, in Minneapolis or anywhere. The response recalls the rapture of Sybil Thorndike about attending his *Oedipus Rex* in Edinburgh. (And it is interesting to note that she and her husband, Lewis, were there and sat in on rehearsals.) It produced the same 'awe', had the same artistic integrity, achieved the same touching, through contemporary idiom, of the ancient tap-roots. 'AESCHYLUS DRAWS PACKED HOUSES IN MINNEAPOLIS' was the headline in the *New York Times*, of October 18, 1967. Henry Popkin, their dramacritic, wrote:

I cannot say that the Tyrone Guthrie Theatre of Minneapolis and its director emeritus, Sir Tyrone himself, have done it again. This time Guthrie and his theatre have accomplished what has never been done before on this continent and seldom anywhere else outside Greece. They have made an artistic, popular and even an historical success out of the *Oresteia* of Aeschylus, which they choose to call *The House of Atreus* . . . it surpasses the achievement of last year's Greek Festival in Ypsilanti . . . Ypsilanti banked everything on the personality of its Clytemnestra, Dame Judith Anderson . . . Guthrie, on the other hand, far from relying on personalities, has disguised his actor's individuality by using masks, casting men as women . . . This policy was obviously directed against achieving any easy popularity; its result has been to sell out every night . . .

They [*the players*] are overshadowed in the first play by a giant, elaborately wrought gate and in the last by the giant figure of Athena, in whose arms the suppliant Orestes nestles like a small child . . .

ATHENA: And you, people of my city! For the good of all men a compact has been made between the power of Zeus and the power of Fate, between the light of the mind and the voices of the blood. Think of these things in silence.*

This was quite a moment, in Life and in Art, for this particular director. If the whole achievement of Stratford, Ontario, was the crown of Guthrie's career, this production was the peak of his artistic achievement.

But one cannot talk of Tony Guthrie's achievement without Judy Guthrie. This was an inseparable pair—one of the great theatrical partnerships—and at the heights he had now reached one must look at a certain disturbing depth to which it all was plunging her. She had been left a great deal on her own at Annagh-ma-Kerrig in these last years when he was busy abroad. When she did accompany him she was, inevitably, overshadowed by him. When alone, at what was always *his* family home there was . . . to quote Guthrie's own words, talking of Irish weather:

. . . day after day, clouds, like damp, dark-grey tulle, enveloped the house, the landscape, ourselves, in warm, soft, permeating vagueness.

This weather is the cause of Ireland's glories and her miseries. It is relaxing. It is conducive to gentle, melancholy meditation. It is supremely non-conducive to strenuous physical, mental or moral effort. It induces late rising—who wants to get out of a warm bed and put on damp underclothes in a damp, twilit bedroom? It induces long, lazy, philosophic or reminiscent talks over the ruins of breakfast. It induces anecdotage. It induces alcoholism . . .†

* *The House of Atreus, Aeschylus*, John Lewin, University of Minnesota Press.
† *A New Theatre*, Tyrone Guthrie. McGraw-Hill, 1964.

And this, by all circumstances, was being induced in Judy: no children, no satisfying achievement in her writing, no home that she could really make her own; and, when on the nomadic tours, no time to establish personal friendships. But, in Minneapolis, at the height of his achievement and in the depths of her isolation as 'Lady Guthrie' she found a friend—a woman friend, Ravina Gelfand, wife of the first publicity man the project had. And, in case all this sounds as if Judy was just trying to escape from the Guthrie tyranny, her answer to a close friend of mine, when Judy had been criticizing something Tony had done and the friend had said, 'Then don't you love him?' was 'But, my dear, I *adore* him.' And that did not change.

She had not the sort of intellect or artistry to understand what he now was pursuing in his work. It added to the isolation, that she was, emotionally, and deeply, affected by it. At a full-dress run-through of *The House of Atreus*, she suddenly rose from her seat, reached for Ravina Gelfand's arm and said, 'Vina, please— take me home. I'm too devastated by this . . . devastated.'

Dominic Argento wrote the music for this production. Tony greatly admired his musical gift; thought they might collaborate on something else. One day, as they all three—Argento, Judy and Tony—sat in the sun on a picnic bench out at the back of the theatre, Tony drew out from the picnic basket a dog-eared script. It was his libretto for some sort of Christmas opera. From the state of the script, Tony had been working at it for some time. He read it out aloud. It was set in a public place, with actors and actresses presenting some sort of Nativity. They built up a great tableau, high on the apex of which was the actress playing Mary. It seemed to Argento that it was in a piazza in Italy. Mary held in her arms a plaster Christ child. And at the climax of this great tableau the bambino slipped out of her hands and crashed to the ground, and was smashed to pieces. A lot of pigeons were then released, many banners held by the many players fell to reveal many crosses. It was all very spectacular. Argento noticed that Judy was weeping. 'What did you mean by that?' she said, to Tony, 'Read it again.' He did. That Judy was so emotional, could, of course, be attributed to the fact that she was drinking too much. She was smoking too much too. She had been in and out of hospital at Minneapolis with acute bronchitis.

One day the telephone purred in the pleasant suburban house of Lou Gelfand. Ravina answered. It was Lady Guthrie. 'Vina—why do they keep asking me to polite teas, lunches, dinner and never let me muck-in? Why am I never allowed to slice and butter the bread?' Vina Gelfand worried about her state nervously— because 'Lady Guthrie' was someone she still felt a little in awe of and she was a shy woman. But she telephoned back to the Guthrie lodging. Judy answered: 'Your call is an answer to a prayer. May I come over?' Vina said, 'Well, yes—but the house is in an awful ...' 'Please, may I?' 'Yes—I'll wash up and ...' 'No! Let *me* wash up! Let me come *now*!'

It began a rather beautiful, rather sad friendship. Vina Gelfand had just recovered from a serious illness. Judy Guthrie was dreadfully thin at the time. From her description, they must have looked, in a delicate way, like a couple of refined and deprived surviving squaws from a tribe which had all died from tuber-culosis. It was hot, Judy would come in a straight slip of a dress under which she would be wearing the ancient bathing costume which had seen much service in the Annagh-ma-Kerrig lake. Moving like a Sitwell female, she would walk with Vina Gelfand down the hundred yards or so to where huge willows grew at the edge of the suburban Cedar Lake. Judy christened it Loch Gelfand. They would go into the water where, on hot days, the musk rats would lie and soak with their snouts just above the surface. In that water the best fish were wall-eyed pike. And, while a sound came from the far side of the big lake like the thud of a repeating traffic accident (the freight trains shunting in the yards), there would be girlish laughter. She'd 'steal' Vina's 'ciggys' and smoke another of the interminable chain of cigarettes; and cough in a way that would bring back all Vina Gelfand's worry about her. 'Vina—Do you ever have anything you don't tell Lou?—that you think you should—and keep putting it off? Do you really like *Six Characters In Search of An Author*?' And, when Vina said to this last, 'Well, yes, I do.' Judy would say, 'Do you? I don't understand it at all. Explain it to me ...'

It became a wonderfully close and gentle friendship. I know of no other such female friend that Judy had—only Peggy Guthrie, but that was at its best when they were schoolgirls, and it was so competitive. Judy wrote to Vina later to remind her of one experience they shared which was unforgettable to her: 'the mustering of the birds'. All over the great willows by the lake and all the trees in all the gardens there had been a rush of bird sound. 'Vina—quick!' she had called 'Come and see this!' Vina Gelfand remembers that Judy was out on the high verandah pointing towards the lake: a massive, deafening congregation of blackbirds suddenly rose up and flew away, leaving silence. 'I wish Tony had been here to see,' Judy said. They were in fact not very romantic birds—grackles, a black bird like a largish starling.

When the Guthries went from Minneapolis, Tony wrote to Lou Gelfand to say how much he appreciated what Vina had done for Judy. He himself was well aware of the problem; but he was noticeably impatient of Judy now.

Back in Annagh-ma-Kerrig a BBC TV team headed by his friend and colleague John Gibson turned up to do a documentary on Sir Tyrone Guthrie, his way of life and the jam factory. And at this time Flora paid them a visit. Tony wrote to T. Hambleton in New York and mentioned that Judy had 'buggered up their shooting schedule by getting 11 wasp stings and having to be pumped full of penicillin'.

Again the question of the eventual fate of the house came up and he went over to London where he saw Lord Goodman, then Chairman of the Arts Council. This was about a scheme to hand over Annagh-ma-Kerrig, when they were gone, to the Arts Council of Ireland as an international retreat for writers and artists.* He went on up to Sheffield where Tanya was becoming involved in the designing of the new theatre there, the Crucible. After this, at the Old Vic—where Sir Laurence Olivier was now in charge of the National Theatre Company—he did a remarkably inept production of *Tartuffe*, with Sir John Gielgud as Orgon. Following close on this, he also directed *Volpone* at the New. He then flew off to the U.S.A. on another money-for-jam lecture tour, leaving Judy at home, as she was none too well. And despite the care of the good Irish folk there, this was again leaving her dangerously alone. The whole Jam project, which at first he must have conceived would be a home interest for her, was getting a little out of hand, for them both. He had left in a state of worry about the management of the Jam. His letters kept showing worry about her, too. He kept advising her to get up to Dr. Jack Smyth in Belfast, and to insist on 'nothing less than the truth' about her condition. But Belfast was beginning to be troubled again, in fact it was becoming a very troubled time over the whole landscape of his life. His old friend, George Chamberlain, was

* He had now ruled out from his will the gift of the house itself to the McGormans and had adopted the scheme which Hubert had suggested.

'done' (he had written when last in London), beyond medical help now with some insidious form of sclerosis. Then he wrote home from the U.S.A.—'not to worry'—but he himself had been overtaken by the 'same as in Phila . . . another little "vascular occlusion" '. Mortality was now very much in mind.

The one bright bit of the year was a production up in the Glasgow Citizen's Theatre of the play of his old, and late, friend James Bridie, *The Anatomist*; Dr. Knox played splendidly by Tom Fleming, assisted by two old survivors of the Scottish National Players, Jean Taylor-Smith and James Gibson. This production was a memorial to Duncan MacRae—an eccentric genius of an actor who played for him in *The Three Estates*. He wrote to Judy, 'The play went simply splendidly—one of those occasions when the actors and the audience conduct a love affair.' Because of his recent experience with students and the Young he emphasized the medical student element in the play and at one critical moment flooded the stage with the student following of Dr. Knox. From the U.S.—where students were about to flood the campuses in waves of protest—he wrote back to Judy to say, 'I am *quite* worried about Joe. He entirely evaded my queries.' There was a question about his replacing Tony 'on the Jam Factory board'.

When he got back to Ireland there was a surprising scene in the Signal box office. He had gone down to Newbliss, to the Jam Factory. He had gone up into the signal cabin, and assisted by the devoted lady secretary he had started to write out cheques to pay some of the bills obviously outstanding. At this point Joe came in and, with anger and a lot less than the deference due, he told Sir Tyrone more or less to get the hell out of there and leave the management to the manager. Tony rose silently, said nothing. Joe went out with a slam. He knew Joe was not well. He knew that Joe had gall bladder pain to put up with. And to the amazement of the secretary—who thought Joe's outburst outrageous—all he said was 'Joe was probably tired'. But he left the factory thoughtfully.

There was also trouble at the Guthrie Theatre. Where good friend and sometime host in Minneapolis, John Goetz, a fine lawyer and a literary man, had taken on the chairmanship and was wrestling with dissension between Campbell and Zeisler. Goetz wondered if Guthrie would come back and take charge. No, he wrote back, he had troubles enough to sort out at home.

It was at this time that the shocking news reached him that his great companion in Chekhov, Lola Kipnis, was desperately ill—

and probably dying—of cancer. He heard just after he had got back from directing a production of *Carmen* in Düsseldorf. He must have been tired and there was a critical annual general meeting due of Irish Farmhouse Preserves, but he cancelled all engagements and flew off to New York. He found the Kipnis family very changed—all the Russian ebullience gone and the state of his old friend distressing. He had a large malignant tumour of the lung, which even noticeably distorted the shirt on his chest. His appalled wife had not the nerve to nurse him; so Guthrie did, changed his clothes, did everything. He then coaxed Kipnis to work and—little by little each day—to get on with his translation of *Uncle Vanya*.

When he wrote back to Judy, anxious to know if there had been any of the angry scenes he said he anticipated at the Jam A.G.M., he also wrote: '*Uncle Vanya* with its muted, philosophic emotion is a very good companion for this time; and, tho' nothing has been said, I can see that Lola feels this . . .' He had been with Kipnis to the doctor. The doctor had been humane and honest; all he could do was keep him out of pain to some degree, but there was no stopping the disease. Tony Guthrie continued to bathe his friend, attend to his needs right down to those tasks one would do for a loved and incontinent child. On the big desperate occasions he was magnificent. '*No* idea when I can get away. I think, if Lola is able, we must finish *Vanya* . . . What a funny s A D interlude this is being—but not wholly sad—*by no means* gloomy, rather an *uplifting* contemplation . . . One *must* not think of it solely as an *end*. It's the end only of the very tiny little element of "reality" of which we are presently conscious . . . passing through nature to Eternity. Keep writing Love T.'

A great affection flowed between them now, in the letters. Tony and Lola got through Act Two; while in this bit of old Russia out on Long Island Sound, Sonia, Lola's wife, went about and for some strange Russian reason showed no emotion at all; just kept 'being busy'. His letters kept coming home, in the big bold hand on yellow legal, lined foolscap—some in pencil: 'I think I am being a help, if only by being a new element. The novelty will wear off and I shall become a bore. But I think by then Lola will be beyond human companionship.' But the attack of the disease seemed to slow down. And now Tony was seriously beginning to worry about Judy. The doctor had described her condition as 'psychic'. He wrote, 'Does he [*Dr. Smyth*] think you have been

DRINKING too much ?' Answers were not any more satisfactory than from Joe about Jam. He flew home.

It was quite obvious to everyone near her now that Judy was drinking too much. Whatever Seamus McGorman might report on the way home from the airport, it would not be his place, nor his habit, to speak personally about Lady Guthrie. And Mary Burns, in the house, who was very fond of 'Lady' would not say a word that would get her into trouble, but he could see for himself. The Jam too had its troubles. The trading loss was heavier than it should be. In full summer the factory was getting more fruit brought to it than it could use; some of it was stacked in the sun and rotting, while certain local growers who brought it in were complaining that they weren't getting paid. Tony felt that if he had encouraged them to grow the fruit for his jam then he was obliged to pay. With the unprofitable state the business was still in it was a sort of moral madness . . . Pay for rotten fruit we can't use? 'Yaas,' Tony insisted. The fruit was paid for. One just had to improve output in the factory and this year get out the special Christmas gift package in time for Christmas. There would on his part have to be more lectures, more fees. But—suddenly the news came—Lola was sinking.

He flew straight back to New York, on September 5. Somehow, together, Lola and he completed what he had been doing on the last act of *Uncle Vanya*. They had done the whole play. On September 12, Leonid Kipnis died. Judy flew out to be with Tony. At the funeral Tony gave a simple, quite unsentimental but rather moving speech of tribute to his friend; then helped his widow with all the legal arrangements. Barrie Stavis, who was there with his wife, tried to get Judy and him to come to them to rest. No, they wanted to be by themselves. Together, Judy and he went out to Coney Island—out of season. Even deserted, Coney Island is the height of seaside low vulgarity, but there Sir Tyrone and Lady Guthrie, these two giant and greatly dignified 'children', went bathing.

They flew off to Minneapolis. And for a few nights they took refuge in the lovely home of John and Margaret Goetz—in a room whose windows look across grass, across the lakeside road and across, where the large willows grow, to Cedar Lake, Judy's 'Loch Gelfand'. By simply pulling the blind from where he lay Tony could see the sun come up. And dawn over Cedar Lake is one of the sights of the City of Lakes. Through the bare tracery of the birch trees (the fall had then begun) the first manifestation of the sun is an apricot blush, spreading up into pale steel blue and giving an increased definition of all the trees and their tracery. The red segment appears on the far side of the lake, still capable of being looked at. Then, quite quickly, the complete disc has a glacial brilliance beginning to be intolerable to the eyes, and seems to spill over the rim of the disc, like white-hot molten metal. The sun's reflection on the surface of the water slowly affects the whole landscape. And now it would bring the Guthrie room into its total lighting effect, till, from being source of light, it becomes source of heat; warmth comes through the long glass windows. Then that lake-dweller, Guthrie, would have to face the day and the days ahead. Their considerate hosts in this immaculate house would, as always, be kindness itself to the guests. But at this time John Goetz would have to talk plans for next season, and another plan for the next month; which was why Guthrie was there. Success and local pride had urged the Guthrie Theatre to take their *House of Atreus* to New York. The plan was for Tony and Tanya to adjust the staging so that it could go into the Billy Rose Theatre. Perhaps it was because he was tired that Guthrie was persuaded to do something he had grave doubts about. But he did it. And there it was—in the first week in December 'MINNESOTA THEATRE COMPANY OF THE TYRONE GUTHRIE THEATRE, MINNEAPOLIS' up in lights—on Broadway. But it was what Tony had feared, a great mistake. The production did not suit the theatre; the audience did not suit the play. This was Repertory uprooted. The production limped on into Los Angeles, with not much better results.

All Guthrie was interested in now, was why the hell Joe had not got out the publicity material for the Christmas gift package of jam. Before getting back for Christmas, to find out why, and to have a much needed rest, he had to consult with Barrie Stavis, about his first production for 1969, *Lamp at Midnight*. Out of friendship he wanted to do this earlier play of Stavis's, as, with *Harper's Ferry* he felt he had not done his best for him. Casting was completed and arrangements were made for it to open in the early new year at Columbus, Ohio—with Morris Carnovsky playing Galileo. At New York's Kennedy Airport he sat down before boarding the plane and ran through all the major issues likely to be faced in rehearsal. It was obvious to Stavis, when he saw him go, that Tony's strength was low. He was due to be back in New York the day before rehearsals began, in January. But a few days before he was due to arrive a telephone call came through from Newbliss 3. Pneumonia. The doctor had forbidden him to travel. What action should be taken in New York? Barrie wanted to know. Tony said to go ahead—probably in a week's time he would be able to come. 'I'll call you in the middle of the week.' In his ancestral hall, where the sad stag with the cross between its horns looked down, Tony Guthrie rang off and went wearily back to bed. Barrie Stavis got the permission of his management to fill in for a week and to start rehearsals himself; on the basis of the discussions he had had with Sir Tyrone. After some days a rather flat cast were still asking, 'When—is Doctor Sir—Mr—Guthrie going to come?' Dear old Becky Daly had just died. It was proving to be a dreadful year for Tony Guthrie.

He arrived at the airport on January 4, looking haggard, and said he would take rehearsal next day. The Stavises refused to let him leave the apartment that day or the next. When he did leave, he asked if he could borrow a clean handkerchief and they went on to rehearsal. As they walked, Barrie noticed that the sole of his shoe had come loose from the upper and was flapping away on the cold sidewalk. Barrie insisted he get it repaired in a while-you-wait shoe-shine and boot-repair bar. But he would not have it. They charged too much. 'At home in Cootehill they'd do it for a whole dollar less.' Barrie knew that he had $7,500 coming to him as a director's fee. Was the man mad or just mean? Or was *every* dollar committed to the Jam? More concerned for others than himself, he made sure Barrie Stavis had a proportion of the fee to cover the rehearsals taken by Barrie before his arrival.

He struggled through his rehearsals. A good company responded splendidly. It is a fine play. Carnovsky was magnificent. It opened in Ohio to rave notices and the whole tour was a triumphal progress. But by now Tony was, as he said, 'incapable of any mental or physical exertion'. He flew back to Ireland two days after the opening and went to bed in the old house while the snow built up outside. Quilts of it lay on the larch forest by the lake and inside the house Mary Burns went to and fro up the big hall stairway with trays while he studied the score of *Peter Grimes*.

Two weeks later he was in New York again—this time with Judy. This should have been a delight—to do *Grimes* at the Met. This was the sort of New York event he *could* enjoy, opera on the grand scale and theatre of the category of 'lavish and luxurious goings-on', which were his own words for one aspect of what he considered to be a legitimate expectation from a paying public in any theatre.

The happiness of the occasion was wrecked by all the dangers for Judy in 'entertainment' by generous New Yorkers. Tony had now to keep an eye on her, not easy in the circumstances. She was hurried into hospital: too many 'ciggys' affecting lungs; too much of 'the hard stuff', as they call it in Ireland, 'the wicked stuff' as she herself now called it. But she was soon out. He was committed to going to Minneapolis now to get the company off to Los Angeles, with *The House of Atreus*. He packed Judy off home and from Minneapolis airport he sent off an anxious note: '*Please* make a point of seeing Jack Smyth at early opportunity. Tell him fully about the withdrawal symptoms; and follow his instructions *to the letter*—vitally important if you are not to slip into deadly alcoholic dependence. I don't know if you realise what danger you are in.' He must have known the risk in her being alone where dear and over-compassionate Irish servants would not stand in the way of the order for whiskey going through to a gentle local store-keeper to whom Lady Guthrie's commands were of course his to obey. The great man just seems like an irresponsible child, writing to a playmate, when he relates that, in Utah, he saw '. . . the oldest living thing on earth!—a juniper tree 10,000 years old!!'

When he got back home it was obvious now to those in the house 'back-stairs' that he was irritably impatient with 'Lady'. There was a strong streak of Presbyterian morality and almost military discipline deep in him that made him too intolerant of anybody who lacked 'self-control'. He organized things. The 'sweet aloes' were up and Tanya came over so that they could get down to a production he had promised to do for his Ulster Theatre friends in Belfast—*McCook's Corner* by George Shiels. Though here was another trouble on his horizon: Ireland's perennial 'Troubles'. This time it looked serious in Belfast. He wrote to John Goetz in Minneapolis. '. . . Quite uncomfortable' up there at rehearsals. '. . . Civil War a very real danger now . . .' He was advising Goetz, in his administrative troubles, to try to get Michael Langham—who had been long enough in Stratford, Ont.—to take on at Minneapolis. In May he got *McCook's Corner* on in Belfast, and he then for a time gave all his attention to the Irish situation.

John Boyd, a courageous Irishman who had been a friend of his ever since he produced a talk of Guthrie's on the Belfast BBC, was in charge of talks on TV. He had a discussion spot. He had hopes of getting the Rev. Ian Paisley—that champion of extreme Protestantism—on the screen. Boyd maintained that the only man around of the weight and scale to stand up to Paisley was Guthrie.

Guthrie did his survey of the explosive scene. As the Chancellor they had once chosen, he talked with the Belfast students; as a responsible church-going Christian he talked with the clergy; as landowner and factory director he talked with the farmers and people in industry. Then he drafted a script. John Boyd read it and he asked his BBC boss if he could do a solo on Guthrie—he so believed in what he had to say. But this would break all the rules on BBC policy in Belfast; so he and Guthrie went to Dublin and recorded it there. When it was done, the BBC in Belfast decided to send it out on the TV screen.

This was even stronger stuff than the public speech he had made to the students which almost lost him the Chancellorship. It was like the desperate fireside to fireside 'family' talk by a president to his people in time of crisis. But there was nothing cosy about it. It was more like King Oedipus in the mask of tragedy speaking to his Thebans about their plague. It was not the admonition of a disinterested English knight, but a deeply Irish heart-cry, and his position was more that of the dying Mercutio, than Oedipus—'a plague on both your houses'—rise above it—for God's sake 'catch yourselves on!' He used this Belfast phrase for 'get a grip of yourselves' and he was speaking to the people he knew in his own factory and lands, to the students, to the citizens who had been children when he was 'Uncle Will' to 2BE. And it was on them, not 'the authorities', political or sectarian, he put the responsibility.

It went out on July 15, 1969. It stirred people. It was received with relief by all those who had longed for someone, above all partisanship and above all fear, to speak out. But to too many he was just the big man from the big house of Anglo-Irish origin and it was an appeal in vain. By August 15, the wave of city bombings had begun and great areas of Belfast were burning.

In Annagh-ma-Kerrig, Judy was holding her own. He started shuttling back and forth by car to Dublin, keeping his promise to produce a play on Dean Swift. This was by a neighbour and TV writer, Eugene McCabe, who with his family had been very good to Judy. Added to all the troubles were those of the Jam, about which his business advisers were beginning to put pressure on him to sort out. What he had called to his Irish colleague, Brian Friel 'the most important production of my life'—The Jam—was underrehearsed, miscast and beginning to be misdirected. He flew off to Minneapolis to do something close to his heart—his production of the Lola Kipnis *Uncle Vanya*; and he took Judy with him.

In Minneapolis, there was a sort of 'other side of despair' contentment about these summery days on the edge of autumn; all rather Old Russian. Michael Langham made a visit, and found the Guthries one sunny Sunday in their passé but sedate apartment house (Oak Grove, which they—in the prevailing mood—called Oak Grave). Over the ruins of breakfast, Tony was trying to coach a young actor on how to speak Chekhovian speeches. The maestro was dressed in an ancient wool dressing-gown with braid round the edges (probably bought along with the bacon in Cootehill). This was over his flannel pyjamas, and he now started 'organizing' the Sunday, while preparing to shave. 'Actors and directors to cut sandwiches for picnic meal; Tanya to read aloud Letters of Chekhov; Judy to tend window box plants.' All was delightfully 'family' and very relaxed.

Rehearsals of *Vanya* were a delight—again the play and the mood had this strong 'family' atmosphere. Patricia Conolly, 'the girl from Australia with my coat', had been engaged and Guthrie cast her as Yelena. It was in trying now to get her to give a non-romantic interpretation of Yelena's excitement over the doctor in the play, that Guthrie made the admission to her, 'I have always been rather prim and shy about sexual matters.' Of the original Minneapolis 'family' of players there were enough to make a genuine ensemble, used to playing together. Tanya—with a strong sense of the production being 'special', in its link with Kipnis and that Russian family—had worked hard and sensitively to get the atmosphere in costume, props and stage furnishings of the old Russian country house.

The work done—for 'the work' for Tony was rehearsal—Judy and he had a rather excessively carefree meal with the family of Dr. Arthur Ballet (with whom Tony had been working on a book to do with Myth and Ritual). The Guthrie party arrived almost late at the theatre on the first night. On this occasion the wine had flowed for all. They could have faced the event stone cold sober—it was itself so heart-warming. He wrote of it to Barrie Stavis:

'Very sorry you couldn't make it to *Vanya*; sorrier for the reason it went well—haven't seen any press but wd. be surprised if it were bad, the audience laughed nicely and came out in the end in a gratifying mist of tears, wiping their eyeglasses and blowing their noses.'

He need not have worried about the press. 'Guthrie, Chekhov Score Again With Sensitive Staging of *Uncle Vanya*'. 'Guthrie's *Vanya* Predictably Excellent.' '*Uncle Vanya* Shows Old Master's Hand.'

Finally, Peter Altman of the *Minneapolis Star*: 'There is nothing particularly surprising about the Minnesota Theatre Company's production . . . It simply is outstanding theatre: sensitive, intelligent, varied, human, totally convincing and compelling drama . . . Guthrie's direction is invisible. He has not tried any of his famed showmanship, his vaunted razzle-dazzle, this time. He must have known it was not needed . . .'

Before they would let him go, the Stagehands—that great, and female, part of the Minneapolis success, entertained and honoured him and Judy at a Ye Olde Russian Buffet in a lovely country club. There was a finality about this *Vanya* visit to 'dear Minn.'.

Jim Wallace—a mature student—was after Guthrie before they let him go, to know, 'What do you plan to do now, Sir Tyrone?' Well, he was wanted in Australia. He wanted to do *Harper's Ferry* properly and there was a scheme to produce a drama spectacular in a valley by Salzburg. But, no, wouldn't be able to do that. 'Have some breakfast, my boy. Eggs?' But Wallace must have persisted, for he got the puzzling reply: 'We're going back to Ireland for the gathering up.'

Wallace: 'Gathering up?'

Judy Guthrie: 'We're going to die, dear boy.'

The 'gathering up' is a term used by Russian peasants. It is used by Leo Tolstoy. It was used by his wife, Sonia, describing the last actions of the dying Leo's hands; it was what Norah Guthrie did when she got rid of junk in the green house and house before she died. But it was not said in any gloom by Judy or Tony. There was a lot of 'gathering up' to do back there and they were both very openly discussing mortality and wills and the disposal of property.

This was in mid-December, just before they flew back home. On the last day of December Tony was in the Benn Hospital, Belfast, having suffered a second, and severe, heart attack. It was not certain that he would live.

CHAPTER TWENTY

TRIP TO THE ANTIPODES
(1970)

THEY HAD returned home to what he announced was 'the first ever Christmas à deux'. He said it was a cosy one at Annagh-ma-Kerrig. But it was the un-cosy big issues of life and death that he was interested in now, and the 'gathering up' was begun without much delay. He wrote from his own fireside that he was 'reading the Bible from cover to cover'. Yet it had looked as if he would not get too far on beyond Genesis, because 'breathlessness' set in. Seamus got out the car and they got him through the snow to Belfast and into hospital; and for a time the Guthrie lifelong indebtedness to tents was limited to the oxygen tent. What he called his 'dicky ticker' continued to beat.

But they got him back to the old house, to what looked as if it must be enforced 'retirement' for the rest of his life. And, on the surface, his life *did* begin to look like that of a retired gentleman: positively no exertion allowed; goodbye to gardening and hacking away at the rhododendrons; late rising and slow walks to the lake; and all of Mary Burns' rich Irish cuisine reduced to variations on boiled white fish.

The state of the Jam he had to leave very much to Joe and to the accountants. The state of Ireland was one of desperation but beyond him now. He kept to the house, began cataloguing the books in his library and made a start on the book he had been asked for, on Acting. But in a way this was all a bit of an act. He might not be going to die but he certainly was not going to retire.

Peggy and Hubert were under invitation to make one of their visits, the promised high point of which was to be a musical evening with the 'Gram'. One could excuse Peggy if she nursed hopes that at last his medical state had forced him right out of the realm of Theatre (which had been such a hateful separator over all these years). Certainly the signs seemed to be that he was settling down, and, with only Irish miles between, there was the pleasing prospect that they would now see a lot more of each other. After all, he loved her deeply. Whatever the arguments, there was no argument about that. He was even preparing to spend time in tracing the family tree right back to the roots from which Tyrone Power had sprung, not so many miles away from Kilkenny. Changed days. No more international shuttling to and fro.

So it seemed. But, in fact, something was going on under the surface of this convalescent calm not at all in accordance with either the doctor's orders or Peggy's wishes. He had brought it up before; but that was prior to the heart attack, which surely altered everything. It was about producing plays in Australia. Even then she was against it; because he had said he was suffering from 'breathlessness'. The reply was typical:

> I'm sorry you take such a sniffy tone about Antipodean trip . . .
> But don't you think it *vastly* preferable to go pop in an
> Australian aeroplane, with a herculean crimson stewardess in
> strident attendance, rather than make a perhaps more dignified
> departure in one's own centrally-heated and flower-decked
> death chamber? And as to the disposal of the Remains . . . I'm
> not the *least* averse to the idea of lying toothless on a slab under
> the mocking gaze of Australian med stoodents.

He could not resist provoking her. However, the trip to the Antipodes was surely now in the past. But when she and Hubert visited in April 1970, there was another house guest and his wife at Annagh-ma-Kerrig; an American. It was John Lewin from Minneapolis—who had done the translation of *The House of Atreus*. He was working with Tony on a new translation of one of the plays Tony was going to do on the Australian trip. Yes— it was on. It was all fixed up for Tony to go in August, and the play John Lewin was working on now was *Oedipus Rex*. The other one was a very suitable title for 'gathering up'—*All's Well That Ends Well*.

This must have seemed more like suicide than 'gathering up'. He had told her in that letter that '. . . the heart is much enlarged— due to strain—and might, if further strained, go pop . . .' The one concession he had made to medical advice was that they would go by boat, not by plane. For, of course, Judy was going with him. And here there was one other reason for the trip—the traditional treatment in his father's day for the alcoholic of a well-to-do family was a long sea voyage. And Judy loved ships and the sea.

John Lewin reported a rather grim dinner at Annagh-ma-Kerrig. With the same wicked brotherly provocation, Tony directed the table conversation to the subject of Death. The Lewins looked uncomfortably to the cutlery as pale Mary Burns came quietly, taking to table a full tray and leaving to cross the stone-flagged hall with an empty one. The sad stag's head stared down, glassy-eyed, as she went to the kitchen. Talking of Death, they were. Not only this, after she had come and gone with the coffee, Tony got the Gram going. And he subjected Peggy and the company to three versions of Verdi's *Requiem*. Finally John Lewin recollects his own shock at Tony's comment as he put on another record, 'And here is a piano piece by a young pianist of great talent, who—died of cancer.' But this, obviously, was directed at Judy—smoking like a chimney; and coughing—always coughing now. The music would drown it, but he was continuing to be noticeably impatient with Judy.

At the week-end another American visitor turned up—Mildred Stock, author and theatre historian. Like John Lewin she had come to work, too; with the same sort of invitation—'ideal place to work—no interruptions'. Her interest in the original Tyrone Power, the actor, had developed at the same time as Tony Guthrie became interested in his family tree and his own origins.

Mildred Stock had done much conscientious work on Tyrone Power's origins and had once before come to Annagh-ma-Kerrig on an invitation, only to find that as she arrived Sir Tyrone was off; flying to the deathbed of Lola Kipnis. She arrived now—found the house full of people and left in two days with understandable exasperation and the comment of, 'All this way for a house-party!' This discourteous result would be something deplored by Tony Guthrie and have something to do with the fact that Lady Guthrie had times of confusion about diaries and engagements, etc. When the other guests left, the Lewins stayed on and the work on the new *Oedipus* continued while Tony completed a promised period of 'convalescence'.

There were two evenings after dinner that the Lewins could never forget, if only for the fact that in both of them they saw Guthrie shed a tear. On both occasions the 'entertainment' after dinner was Tony Guthrie reading aloud.

On the first evening he was to try out on the Lewins some items he might include in a personal anthology programme he had to do for his old friend John Boyd at the Belfast BBC. One item he was not at all certain he should include. It might be reckoned too sentimental, but he loved the poem: Keats' 'Ode to a Nightingale'.

He proposed to read it, and the setting could hardly be more designed for sentiment, if not sentimentality. Beyond the drawing-room windows, which rose up tall above the broad window seats, the spring sun was doing its dying arc which ended in the dark trees; their shadows fell across the now rather unkempt garden, where the flowers had been 'not for you to pick'. He had to use reading glasses now, so he bowed to the page a bit. But rather beautifully—and with a clarity too meaningful to be sentimental in its delivery—he read through the whole ode—until the verse beginning:

> *Thou* wast not born for death, immortal bird!
> No hungry generations tread *thee* down.

The American guests looked up from cold coffee to a very warmly emotional man—

> The voice I hear this passing night was heard
> in ancient days by emperor and clown:
> Perhaps the self-same song that found a path
> Through the sad heart of Ruth, when sick for home—
> She stood in tears amid the alien corn.

It came clearly out; but it was a line the reader had great difficulty in getting beyond. Lewin saw the tears. Tony stopped; put Keats aside, 'No. Very undigny,' and mentally struck that item off the 'suitable' list. Yet about a week later, he read Keats' 'Ode to a Nightingale', clear as a bell, over the air. He was not going to be done out of his true loves by a bit of uncontrolled sentiment.

He now got down to the big play on the big issue: Oedipus and 'this question of my origins'. It led to the other reading. It came out of a discussion on the need for any formal speech. 'No need to make the speech hieratic', he said. Then, he added, '*But* with the Chorus, Yeats is smashing,' and he upped and read the passage after Oedipus has gone into the palace with his cry of—'O light of the sun never let your rays strike me again!'—and did not come out till he was blinded by his own hand.

CHORUS: What can the shadow-like generations of man attain
            But build up a dazzling mockery of delight
            that under their touch dissolves again.
            Oedipus seemed blessed, but there is no man blessed
              among men.
            Oedipus overcame the woman-breasted Fate;
            he seemed like a strong tower against Death
            and first among the fortunate;
            he sat upon the ancient throne of Thebes,
            and all men called him great.
            But, looking for a marriage bed, he found the bed of
              his birth,
            tilled the field his father had tilled,
            cast seed into the same abounding earth;
            entered through the door that had sent him wailing
              forth.
            Begetter and begot as one! How could that be
              hid?
            What darkness cover up that marriage bed?
            Time watches, he is eagle-eyed,
            And all the works of man are known, and every soul is
              tried.
            Would you had never come to Thebes, nor to this
              house.
            Nor riddled with the woman-breasted Fate . . .*

(Lewin says his voice began to falter)

        . . . beaten off Death and succoured us,
        that I had never raised . . . this song . . . heartbroken . . .

(And melodramatic though it may seem, the voice actually broke
here)
        . . . heartbroken Oedipus!

To someone who has never come across the terrific emotional
energy that goes with being one of the great masters of any
art, his tears will seem sheer bathos. They are in fact inevitable
in the mechanics of genius, should a crack come in the dam
that holds the head of power. And, in his mother's house at

* *Oedipus The King*, W. B. Yeats trans. Collected Plays, Macmillan, 1934.

this time, a lot of cracks were appearing in the fabric of his own life.

'In his mother's house' was a disturbingly meaningful place for Lewin to be working, for his obsession at that time was a book by Joseph Rheingold called *The Mother Anxiety and Death*—and he read passages from it to Tony. The gist of this somewhat involved psychological work is that it throws the onus of 'crime' against the child (the casting out of Oedipus on to Mount Kythaeron) on the mother, not the father; the motive for her action being that she loves the father more than she loves the son. This put a new emphasis for Tony Guthrie on the moment in the play of Oedipus's shocked realization, '*Her own child*?'—to be cast out and left to die with pierced feet on barren Kythaeron.

Lewin is convinced that his fourth time of directing this play was to be, for Guthrie, 'a deeply personal and valedictory state-ment'—'if spared'. This was a recurrent phrase in Guthrie letters now, 'IF SPARED'. But he was gaining strength and he went on to face another strangely disturbing bit of research into the character of Oedipus. And—in his obsession with Identity and that character—into his own character too.

In these spring days at Annagh-ma-Kerrig he was daily reading from the book by Abraham Velokovsky called *Oedipus and Akhnaton*. Like Oedipus, Akhnaton had 'swollen legs or feet'. Oedi having the same root as Oedema=swelling and 'Pous' in ancient Egypt meaning either legs or feet. And the argument of this persuasive book is that the story of Oedipus is founded not on Greek folklore but on Egyptian history; that the Thebes of the legend is not the city in Greece of that name but the Royal and Ancient capital of all Egypt, Thebes on the Nile, near Gizeh. This would mean that the story (on which Sophocles based his play) was the story of Akhnaton, royal son of Ty, the Queen of Egypt whose husband, Amenhotep III, banished Akhnaton as a child to Northern Syria (to a culture which practised royal incest). When he returned to Thebes he 'destroyed' his father, established his own sun-kingdom, married the beautiful near-relation, Nefertiti, and had a child by his own mother.

'If spared' to Sydney this production was to reveal a revised Oedipus—a sun god and messianic figure, like Akhnaton of Egypt.

With the jobs on the script done and the Lewins gone, he was amazingly recovered in strength and spirit and by the end of

April was writing to John Sumner with the old zest about the
other play, *All's Well That Ends Well*. Sumner is the artistic
director of the Melbourne Theatre Company: 'I have been giving
some thought to the scenic arrangements of "All's Well" . . .'
and there followed a packed five-page letter which is greatly
revealing in the detailed way he directed—almost dictated—the
design side of these productions; in which he could not depend
on—nor dominate—Tanya:

Scene 18 is supposed to be Roussillon, but we'll play it in
Trophy set with elegant gilt chairs scattered around and foot-
men holding eight-foot candelabra—real candles if possible.

Wings and Borders should look like leaves for Roussillon
and widow's house—long strips, like weeping willow leaves in
muslin and organdie; borders ditto.

Trophy scene should mask in with flags. I suggest these should
be mounted on little wheeled carts and be pushed on, in front
of the leaf-wings and leaf-borders. Flagpoles should have fancy
finials in metal, and should go up to as high as 16 feet.

The clothes are going to be quite sombre and I suggest that
the flags should be predominantly black and gold, with a little
crimson and salmon pink—NO green. They should appear to
be heavily embroidered in gold thread. This, I think, can
almost all be done with paint, with just a little 3-D where it
shows most.

like very low prams.
Soldiers can pull them into
position—3 or 4, as re-
quired and maybe a very
high one at the back.

Scene 7 D of Florence should, if practicable, endeavour to run
up a flagpole. He is a very incompetent personage and screws
up the whole business. I thought perhaps the flag might be
attached to a sort of arrangement they use in airports for people
to get on and off the planes. Whatever we use must be able to
be very easily set and struck.

The platform should be about four or five feet from the ground and flagpole as high as practicable.

Hope all this is reasonably clear and within your resources. And, as I said above, it's suggestion ONLY and I will welcome counter-suggestion.

The tone of the letter may suggest that great visiting director was prepared to spend company's money like sand. Not at all. He had, in fact, put it to John Sumner that *All's Well* could either be done in jeans, jumpers and a bare stage, or else in the grand style and in some period, if not Elizabethan, at least akin to the social norms of an essentially romantic play. Sumner chose the grand style and proceeded to book the biggest theatre in Melbourne—the 1,600-seater Princess (not the company's normal 400-seater, the Russell Street Theatre).

Farewells were made at Annagh-ma-Kerrig with the McGormans, the Burnses, the McGoldricks and all. And not a few of them thought these farewells were final ones. But though the 'dicky ticker' was ticking quicker than medically advisable, if he was going to reach seventy and the Antipodes too, they were both in high spirits and utterly relieved to be finally on the train at London's Victoria, and on the move again.

The Guthrie minimal baggage for foreign travel was there with them and they were on their way—May 29, 1970—with his diary marked up one month away as 'Strylia!'; and with their baggage labelled FLORENCE.

They were to join their ship at Genoa, but were to visit Xtopher *en route*. Christopher Scaife was now the retired 'Professore'—living in a villa of his own where the great hills of Tuscany rose up out of the Valley of the Arno. It might be the last chance to see this key figure in his life; against whom he, over and over again, measured the passage of time and his own progress.

It would be a bit like the visit to the oracle. An oracle who knew the Nile and all Akhnaton's territory too; geographical and psychological.

Xtopher met them at Florence. In a car as small as Tom Patterson's, he drove them towards the mountains and the vineyards that seem to carpet the whole area. The villa, 'Paternina', sat among its own patch of vineyards just below the road to Rome out of Arezzo. In essence it was a small farm where Professore Scaife stayed in great simplicity, assisted by his two faithful Tuscan 'dailies', Aurelio and his wife, Gina. He made his own bread, own wine; fed his own pigs from the windfall acorns from his own oaks. If this was the end of 'Xtopher', certainly it was all's well for him.

They had three blissful spring days and at least one evening's after-dinner entertainment which was for them most memorable. With the evening chill off the mountains, their now benign host put a match to the stack of sapless old vine twigs and oak branches. The fire sat on a plinth of renaissance brick a foot from the floor and under a great plaster canopy—very Elizabethan Italianate, very *All's Well*. A scene to evoke for Tony the words of the Clown in the play: 'I am a woodland fellow, sir, that always loved a great fire'. It was not the time to reconsider why he cut out the Clown from both his productions of *All's Well* and that he thereby cut out these lines:

'I think I shall ne'er have the blessing of God till I have issue o' my body; for they say barns (bairns) are blessings.'

At Paternina all three were in a state of great contentment and Christopher had a Shakespearean present for the travellers. It was given them on the one bit of sophisticated equipment in the old villa, a tape-recorder. It was a tape he had made of himself singing his own settings for some of the songs of Shakespeare. Tony couldn't resist putting sincerity before charity, and said he did not find the settings original. Then, like visiting royalty, he presented his, grander, gift: a tape he had managed to get Lola Kipnis's widow, Sonia, to obtain—of Alexander Kipnis singing 'The Erl King'. But it was a grand reunion—very Shakespearean in atmosphere and with no resort to argument with the oracle on Oedipus.

From the Italian liner at Genoa they both wrote him with sincere gratitude. 'Paternina' and he had been wonderful. At least for this he had been 'spared'. So far so good. They went below to find a gorgeous bouquet of flowers for

Sir Tyrone and Lady Guthrie,
Cabin 63, First Class,
GALILEO GALILEI.

That punctilious antipodean, John Sumner, had cabled this greeting. And knowing what flowers meant to the two, it must have been a very affecting gesture. On a Mediterranean misted with summer heat, they passed, somewhere north or south of Elba, a sea-misted island that Tony was convinced must be the magical island of Shakespeare's *The Tempest*. It was a lovely farewell to Italy.

For Judy, to be able to soak in the sun, swim, see people, read a book (they were reading Charlotte Brontë), all this, and the sea, was sheer happiness. For him, the rest, regular routine—including doses of his Irish doctor's heart medicine—all this was splendid for the health. But, as we know, ships became a prison for this restless man. When the *Galileo* headed out into the Southern Atlantic there was a long voyage ahead of him. Perhaps the name *Galileo* on the lifeboats and notepaper made him think of *Lamp at Midnight* and the Barrie Stavis play, because he read the text of a lecture on John Brown that Stavis had sent him. And as they steamed into the open ocean he read John Brown's statements at his trial:

> Had I interfered in the manner which I admit . . . had I so interfered in behalf of the rich, the powerful, the intelligent, the so-called great, or in behalf of any of their friends, either father, mother, brother, sister, wife or children, or any of that class, and suffered and sacrificed what I have in this inter-ference, it would have been all right . . . Every man in this court would have deemed it an act worthy of reward rather than punishment.

The Guthrie social-reforming soul was stirred. He wrote a letter to Barrie Stavis, to be posted at the first port of call, which congratulated him on the essay and spoke with some impatience of his fellow First Class passengers: '. . . mostly rich Australians and elderly, some Italians and Spanish, *very* few Inglese. The Tourist passengers are younger and more interesting.'

And it was with the Tourist passengers that something really interesting to him happened on the voyage. He escaped from the elegant confines of First Class accommodation and made a daily trip to Tourist territory to teach a class in Elementary English.

Working within a scheme organized by the Australian Government for non-English-speaking immigrants, he taught a class of about forty Italians, 'of widely differing degrees of knowledge in the language . . . an uphill fight'—and not quite what the doctor ordered in strain. But, assisted by 'a little book . . . that is what is called Lavishly Illustrated . . . I hope to have them counting *fluently* up to 20 and knowing the days of the week; and 20 or 30 words like knife, fork, spoon, cup; and a few useful phrases like "How much does this cost?" ' Good works on behalf of the underprivileged. He loved it.

Perhaps it was this pedantic reversion to exact English that made him unkindly caustic about the Aussie accent: '. . . more irrityting than I'd remembered. It's all sow minee and dyntee and prisee; especially coming out of the mouths of such whopping great bruisers, myle and feemyle!' But he was shortly to fall in love—hook, line and sinker—with this friendly large-scale land and its large-scale people.

Last port of call before Australia was Durban on the eastern side of Africa and here Tony got off an aerogramme to John Sumner in Melbourne. The *Galileo Galilei* would call at Melbourne for a day, *en route* to Sydney. The ship would not sail till late afternoon. Could one chat *All's Well* production plans, see company and what was playing in his theatre? Obviously he was chafing to get off and get on, having been a seaborne prisoner for just twenty days. His aerogramme finished with, 'Send word to Cabin 63 and a file and a rope ladder (you can bake them into a little loaf and smuggle in as Food Parcel) and be waiting in a fast car with forged number plates!'

Nine days later (June 29), when they had traversed the Indian Ocean to touch Antipodean territory, there was a letter waiting for them, at Fremantle. No file, no rope ladder, but firm assurance that arrangements in Melbourne were being made. Fremantle, being the port for Perth, they were able to see the newly-built theatre on the university campus—the Octagon. Another, and vital, reminder of his 1965 visit was their table companion at a luncheon reception—Professor Fred Alexander. They had been 'spared' to reach the Antipodes and impatiently they got aboard ship again to press on to Melbourne. Two days out of Fremantle they received this cable on the high seas:

CONOLLY AND I WILL PICK YOU BOTH UP AT SHIP

11*

2.00 PM STOP SUGGESTED PROGRAMME STOP PRESS
CONFERENCE STOP MEETING SOME STAFF STOP
5.15 PM THEATRE PERFORMANCE STOP DINNER STOP
LOOKING FORWARD TO SEEING YOU BOTH
                —JOHN SUMNER

'Conolly' was Patricia Conolly. He had stubbornly persuaded
John Sumner that she was now an actress in the first rank of
talent and that she should have the opportunity to come back
home and enjoy due acclaim from her own people. (No doubt
there was a wily Guthrie ploy at work too; for the girl to be able
to see again her own family and friends at no personal expense.)
He wanted her for Helena in *All's Well*. He also wanted her for
Jocasta in *Oedipus*, but she had thought this too much. When she
turned this down, he had written to say who the startling alternative might be—another, and famous, Australian, Robert
Helpmann. (It was now to be played by the Australian actress,
Ruth Cracknell.)

After the meeting on the ship at Melbourne, John Sumner took
Tony and Judy off to a press reception. Sumner was delighted to
see how well both looked, for—knowing Tony's condition—it
was to be a constant concern of his to see that he was not over-
taxed. To a friendly and curious press, Sir Tyrone was politely
defensive. It was almost a non-event till one journalist asked him
about this Jam business. Momentarily he lit up and gave the
Australians the whole spiel of the huge importance of the Newbliss factory to the soul of Ireland. He then met Sumner's staff at
the theatre and saw a production of Ibsen's *A Doll's House* in
which Patricia Conolly played Norah in the theatre and with the
company which had given her a start in her career. It was very
satisfactory. He was impressed by the efficiency and courtesy of
Sumner's theatre and company.

After dinner with the Sumners, they thanked them specially for
the flowers at Genoa—'the last precious campanula lasted till
Durban'—then sailed out of Melbourne Bay, late in the evening,
to make for Sydney further up the east coast, a day's journey
away. All the restless anticipation normal to the last day of any
voyage took over. Bags were packed; and little cubes and sachets
of shipping line sugar were packed too, as if there was still a
war on.

The famous great bridge, the notorious great opera house, the friendly Robert Quentin, their host, were all there to greet them. They settled in. Rehearsals of *Oedipus* were still weeks away. He got a letter off to 'Paternina':

> ... We are ensconced in a flat which only can be described as Magniff. It's the first floor of an old country house owned by the Austn. Natl. Trust. It's on a small peninsula sticking out into the harbour, with water on three sides ... *Marvellous* views in all directions ... battle ships anchor at the bottom of our lawn ... I'm loving the get-up of *King Oedipus* ... a distinctly good and madly keen company.

But then comes a bit of architectural discouragement. '... We have to do it in a hall so hideous, so *un*-intimate, so impractibly planned and acoustically so reverbrant that I can't see it being A Success. But one must Rise Above all that ...'

What he was rising above here was the large new Clancy Auditorium of the University of New South Wales, more or less just finished on time for this notable occasion. In one sense, he could blame himself for the choice of theatre. Robert Quentin had offered him, back in 1969, '*either* a small new playhouse seating 330' or 'a 999-seater (with a shelf-like stage 22 ft. deep and 50 ft. wide). This is a modern multi-purpose university auditorium with foul acoustics ...' Quentin had said. 'We would much prefer for your production to be staged in the small theatre ... in which stage to audience communication is excellent.' To which Sir T. had replied:

> *Oedipus/Syd*: I don't think this sounds a good idea for a small house. The stage doesn't need to be big; but a capacity of 330 is very small and the play doesn't, I think, 'do' as an 'intimate' offering; it must be monumental. Naturally, I'm not wild about the alternative ... Scaling it down to a tiny house looks like no confidence ... Isn't there a City Hall or a concert auditorium?

By November there was what Robert Quentin hailed as 'Good news—the Clancy Auditorium is definitely available'. A new building, no scaling down. He sent Guthrie a ground plan, and reported enthusiastically, 'On revisiting the half-completed building I feel more than ever convinced that it would be an excellent place in which to stage *Oedipus*'.

So that was it, he had more or less asked for it, and the dismay expressed when he had seen and begun to use it, came too late in the day to be a basis for change. It was galling, when this was to be the definitive *Oedipus*, for he could not hope to be 'spared' for another. But Sydney was a bit of all right, with lovely days in that lovely house. He kept in touch with Christopher: 'Sydney is changing at incredible speed . . . It still looks like a rose red suburb half as old as Croydon, which has been absurdly brought into being on a sub-tropical creek.'

He was at *work*—therefore happy. 'Oedipus/Syd', the big event, was on the boil. All the old alchemy was brought into play. Shirt sleeves were up and sneakers on. Despite sun-tan he looked much, much older to Jean Wilhelm, who had worked with him in Minneapolis and now was one of the staff of this Australian university. Two days before their ship had reached Australia Judy and he had quietly celebrated his seventieth birthday. She was now in strength, and though the cough went on and too many cigarettes were still being smoked, she was a great support to him now. She saw to it that the prescription was renewed and he continued to take their Irish doctor's heart medicine. From her seat, in the rehearsal hall or the awkward auditorium, she kept watch and kept the picnic thermos full and at the ready.

In the TV documentary made of this production one can see clearly how *much* he had to give and how they lapped it up, and how the things by which he swept them along were authority and sympathy. He had this deep familiarity with any player which was based upon the simple belief, that humanly we are all one. It may have started as such, but it was not now an outside authority that he exercised.

He had an imaginative designer working for him—Yoshi Tosa, a Japanese. His work was more showy than Tanya's but there was that in his work which served Tony in the new idea of the worshipper of the Sun to whom blindness would be the ultimate penalty to pay. Jean Wilhelm wrote: 'I would describe this costume [*of Oedipus*] as Universal with Egyptian overtones', and she describes his first entry as,

> . . . to a steadily growing roar of sound culminated in a huge CRASH on gongs—Whereupon the Mob flung itself, beseeching, upon the ground. From a dense cloud of smoke there suddenly emerged, twelve feet tall, it seemed, Oedipus himself: blazing forth, a Champion in massive golden headgear; a proud and mighty God.

He convinced the players, daunted by the formal masks and costumes, that the 'you' of their personalities would come through but that it would be on a greater scale. He told them that this play was not so much about what we knew as 'the Oedipus Complex' but about Identity. 'Who was my father? Who was *your* father. Who am I?'—the question we all must ask. *And* that the very important fact to Oedipus was not so much the hidden wish to kill his father but *the discovery that it was his mother who gave him away*. He impressed them that almost everything in the play had a symbolic meaning—but not to play that meaning, not to push that at the audience. 'We must *know*—they must *feel*.' They loved him as the wise old sage. Then like a youngster in passion he screamed at the young actor 'delivering the speech' which describes Oedipus's discovery of his mother/wife's suicide. 'No! No!! No!!!—no *meaning*!—You're not meaning it—are you?' No, he wasn't, he agreed. And Guthrie played it there and then—passionately, impressively—no extravagant 'hamming' now. How Oedipus hammered on the bronze doors, hammered till they broke open and PAUSE!—for then he saw his wife—mother—hanging, hanged—How all the vicious vengeance drained out of him; how he ran forward, embraced the beloved body, eased it to the ground; and—in doing so— found on her dress the brooches he had once unpinned in passion, and now he took them and with their pins struck and struck again at his own eyes till his whole face was covered with the dark rain from his eyeless sockets. And all this conveyed by the power of the Spoken Word and the poetry of Sophocles. This was no old man's, tired, end-of-career, production.

But he did now suddenly tire and have rests. In such a pause in rehearsal, the TV interviewer tried to get out of him why he had done this play so often. 'It's the best constructed play in the world,' he said. But the interviewer was after something more personal: 'What is its significance to *you*?' Guthrie's reply was: 'It has a theme that has puzzled—still puzzles me—Job's problem —Why does a good man like Oedipus get torn apart, like a fly by a wanton child—wings, legs—And God lets it happen.'

The interviewer went on, to the subject of incest, and got this from Guthrie: 'Don't really understand why in the modern Western world there is such a taboo on it. Don't advocate it. Still —in Ancient Egypt—in the royal family—they practised it for generations and continued to produce remarkably interesting

people. Don't know why.' And the interviewer questioned the
fact of the modern taboo. To which he replied, 'Oh, yes. If some
public figure in Double Bay [*Sydney*] were known to be "living
in sin" with his mother there'd be a frightful hullabaloo. Think
what we do to homosexuals, which is not very creditable.'*

He got back to the rehearsal of the Chorus, and drilled and
conducted them from chanting into singing. And it was not just
in the musical element that he said there was Music. The play had
a 'music' of its own. And sometimes in rehearsal he would not
look at what was being run through on stage—in fact he would
close his eyes and just listen; then the hand-clap and the rhythm,
tempo, tone would be adjusted.

The work was done and the first night came.

As at Stratford in Ontario, many Australians—and many
already friends or colleagues of Guthrie—came huge distances to
the Clancy Auditorium; among them John Sumner, with his
wife, from Melbourne. He says that when the lights went down
in the house and the Chorus of Theban citizens slowly invaded
that theatre, with great smokey torches flickering, they moved
like creatures who had a total coherence, all belonging to the one
perplexed and questing community. And 'it made my spine
prickle as seldom before in any theatre'. Dr. Wilhelm's description
adds to this.

> The production was invested with *light*. From the very begin-
> ning, when a great horde of plague-stricken Thebans staggered,
> limped, were carried through the aisles to the stage, accom-
> panied by the flickering of flame in braziers held aloft, by
> incense and branch-waving, an audience became mysteriously
> aware that this light was like nothing ever sensed before . . .

Then the steadily growing sounds that grew to become a great
roar and the CRASH of gongs and the entrance of Oedipus—
golden as a sun-king . . . The 'deeply personal and valedictory
religious' event, foreseen by John Lewin in Annagh-ma-Kerrig
as Tony's intent, began to take place.

Then came the Philistines—in the form of the first night press
(the production was presented by the Old Tote Theatre
Company):

* *I Think I Just Wanted To Hide In The Theatre*, 1970, quoted by courtesy of The
Australian Broadcasting Commission TV.

The Old Tote's production . . . is an astonishing, disconcerting affair. It starts with a crowd of Disneyish dwarfs dressed up like miserable peasants in an Hiroshige print . . . Tyrone Guthrie, an imaginative, inventive man, has been out for a walk in a dank, stony place, and he has overturned a big flat stone. His *Oedipus* is the result, an insect play . . . the whole lot of them seeming blind, groping about dopily, hoping that the stone lid will be put back on top of their world . . . Yoshi Tosha's superb dehumanising costumes . . . but it's not a tragedy, and it's not about people.

Was this to be the reward for coming all the way to the Antipodes to do what he had been, literally, dying to do? But no, the Philistines were defeated, the play ran and grew to resounding critical acclamation.

GUTHRIE'S OEDIPUS FULFILS ALL HOPES
The production will set a standard by which others will be measured. See it!

Sir Tyrone's production is a deliberate search after a spiritual truth . . .

His chorus, hugely masked and stiffly robed, are half domestic animals, half children, in the trust of the king, their father. The principals are giant statues of the gods, marked by age and compassion, and they move inside their huge theatrical armour not with a show of physical strength, but with a gentle spiritual power.

. . . most radical of all in this new adaptation is the end of the play, in which the author leads Oedipus in to a Christian New Testament of Oedipus at Colonus. Opening his eyes to the truth at last, the king blinds himself with the brooches from the body of the dead Jocasta. But here it is Jocasta whose suffering is physical; it is her cries which echo round the Theban Palace. Oedipus' blindness and exile are not self-imposed in anger or revenge at the gods' injustice, but accepted gladly by a king whose strength increases with the weight of the sins of the world: whose journey into darkness had begun long before and will go on and on, and carry with it its own light.

The 'valedictory statement' had been achieved and he was still 'spared', and on his way to the 'next thing'—*All's Well*—Melbourne; travelling through spectacular natural scenery, with Judy, baggage and a large dog in a little car, driven by Dr. Jean Wilhelm.

In Melbourne, friendly city of tramcars, it was to be quite a different manner of event—a glowing, warm, and romantic one. One recollects how he said in Minneapolis that he felt he had a duty to rescue Shakespeare from the 'stereotype' and 'Romance'. This production was set in the style he had indicated in that letter to Melbourne from Ireland and dressed, as he explained in his programme note,

> in the style of 1850. If we dressed it as a modern, realistic piece —certain ideas, upon which the story depends, would be belied: one must, for example, accept the notion that the King is God's earthly representative, to whom is owed unqualified obedience and awe: also that war is the chief and most respectable of manly sports.
>
>   We shall therefore try to present the play as occurring in an era as near as possible to our own, but in which its given attitudes to war and royalty were still generally accepted. It is not entirely caprice which has made us elect the period of *Jane Eyre* and *Villette*.

He read chunks of *Villette* and *Jane Eyre* with and to Patricia Conolly—read some in what he considered to be a Derbyshire accent and had great fun—all in preparation for her to play one of 'Shakespeare's great female creations'. His programme note stresses this:

> Shakespeare has peopled his Romance with characters with whose humanity he was deeply concerned.
>
>   His central character, Helena, is a person of powerful intelligence and driving will, whose sex makes it almost impossible to achieve ambitions which, had she been a young man would have been generally respected and well within her grasp. Nineteenth-century critics regarded her as an Unpleasant Person, and for this reason, though she is one of Shakespeare's great female creations, the play has been rarely produced.

Melbourne was fun, right from the moment John Sumner asked him, 'By the way, what would you like the company to call you? Tony?—or Doctor Guthrie?—or Sir Tyrone?' 'Oh—Sir

Tyrone will do.' He swore all to silence about the fact that he had 'written in a new scene' to *All's Well*. (It was only some extra dialogue to go along with a bit of business as Bertrand 'reviewed his troops'.) For all the solemnity and profundity of *Oedipus* and his own 'one foot in the grave' situation, he was still full of Irish devilment.

One day a very young member of the cast was sitting on the fringe of the stage action. He was staring at what was going on in a state of blank inattention to what was being said, when Sir Tyrone came silently across from his rear. Like a great deer-stalker he came up behind the boy, who felt a sudden pressure on his arm, and turned: 'Your face, dear boy, is registering what in common parlance is called "fuck-all!" ' As one actor there said, rehearsal was 'like a dangerous game. He had a general concept—which he never departed from. But within it he took every freedom—*and* gave you it too. He wouldn't tell you directly what he wanted you to do: just give you a clue to the answer; for, he wanted the answe o come from *you*. And *his* excitement when you found it for y)r rself was genuine pleasure.'

Suddenly there were days of acute anxiety for John Sumner. 'John', he said one day. 'Do you have a good heart specialist here?' And when Tony went off to see the heart specialist he made John Sumner swear he would not tell Judy.

The specialist's report to Sumner was of the nature of 'Well . . . not good at all. But he knows his condition and no doubt you know him.' Nothing they could say would persuade the great man into the petty condition of 'taking it easy'. He had already defied the doctor's orders by flying over to New Zealand and back before rehearsals, because he had promised them there that he would visit if they bore part of his transit fare out from Britain, and had so saved a bit of expense for Sumner and Quentin. A promise was a promise.

They were ready to open. He reminded his cast: 'The most exciting sound in the theatre is the intake of breath of an actor about to deliver a great speech.' On the first night they breathed deeply. On to the stage came the requested eight-feet candelabra (hand-held) and with live candles too. Beyond the first few flickering moments of the play—as Shakespeare's words were breathed out brilliantly—nobody worried but the Fire Department. Typical of the press on this happy occasion was: 'Every-thing about the production is stunning, scores of candles burn brightly, and there is a military musical comedy air about it all, enhanced by the gentle humour Sir Tyrone has managed to inject everywhere possible . . . though one misses the character of the Clown . . .'*

On the eve of departure from Melbourne there was a great party on stage, when Tony was presented, by John Sumner, on behalf of the Company, with two huge books of Australian paintings. He made an affectionate and witty farewell speech. In it he mentioned that Lady Guthrie and he would now be travelling rapidly east by train, to Perth. To this, someone was unwise enough to interpose the correction, 'Sir, east? You will be going west, won't you?' 'Well . . .' came the retort, '. . . it's a *very* long train journey. And if one travels far enough west, isn't one eventually going east? Shan't be put down.'

It was now Antipodean spring, the main work was done; and both were delighted and surprised by the profusion of wild-flowers they could see on the open ground by the side of the Permanent Way.

Friendliness again met them in Perth. Professor Alexander and his wife noted the signs of strain, the toll taken by two major productions. But these final four weeks were to be spent mainly alone, mainly at leisure, and on the sunlit campus of the University of Western Australia, with its handsome buildings, shady trees and vistas of the blue sea lapping its southernmost extremity. The beach was not five minutes from their college apartment.

One of the handsome buildings, not much more than a year old, was the Octagon Theatre, whose builders he had persuaded five years before to adopt the thrust stage and the raked audi-torium. His only professional commitment while in Perth was to direct a series of public readings in the Octagon. But when he was gone, and in the summer when the university vacation was on, both of these productions—*Oedipus* and *All's Well*, were—thanks to Professor Alexandra—to be staged, with great success, in the Octagon. Jean Wilhelm, who directed *Oedipus* in his absence, was to see how much more effective the production was in this Guthrie-type theatre.

Before they drove out of Perth to the port of Fremantle, to board ship, and sail for home, there was a memorable and relaxed evening in the Alexanders' flat. They were there because there was a TV set there. The programme that the Australian Broad-

* *The Stage*, Oct. 1970.

casting Company had made of the rehearsals and performance of *Oedipus* was being screened, and he wanted to check they had done nothing foolish and that he had said nothing silly. It was titled on the little screen, 'I Think I Just Wanted To Hide In The Theatre'. Well, he could remember saying that, when he was asked why in the first place he wanted to be an actor. He watched himself and the interviewer on the screen:

INTERVIEWER*: Were you a good actor?

GUTHRIE: I think I was, and am, quite a good actor but with some limitations in the parts I can play.

INTERVIEWER: What parts can you play?

GUTHRIE: Oh—mad emperors ninety years old and blind seers.

INTERVIEWER: Was it because you were frustrated in being an actor that you became a director?

GUTHRIE: Yes.

INTERVIEWER: Ego?

GUTHRIE: I don't think so. But there's no doubt that for the power crazy it is an attractive position to be in . . . but . . . I wanted to mould, shape the whole play rather than any one part.*

The film showed this happening with *Oedipus*, his consultations with players, designer, etc.—the whole 'moulding, shaping' process. And it was in fact a remarkably fine piece of work: a skilful record of great work done.

As they made for Fremantle and the great white ship the *Canberra*, John Sumner, in Melbourne, was faced with a crisis. He had been determined to cable them a bouquet of Australian flowers as a bon voyage gift from the company, but the *Canberra* was sailing on a public holiday when the service did not operate. So he called in the Navy. He telephoned an old wartime mate who was now in charge of a container-ship depot in Fremantle. Could he somehow get flowers to the ship before she sailed? When Sir Tyrone and Lady Guthrie were shown into their sumptuous cabin, beautiful 'Strylian' flowers were there to brighten their voyage home. They were sorry to go.

* *I Think I Just Wanted To Hide In The Theatre*, Australian Broadcasting Commission TV, 1970. Interviewer, Richard Oxenburgh.

CHAPTER TWENTY-ONE

ALL'S WELL THAT ENDS WELL
(*1971*)

IT WAS winter at home. On their way through London from Southampton they saw a relieved Peggy. At least he had been spared. They reached Annagh-ma-Kerrig. Tanya followed over to spend Christmas with them. When she got as far as the frozen stone steps at the front door, Tony came out in his tweeds and homespun sweater and said urgently, 'You must go. You *must* go!' Tanya looked startled. 'To "Strylia"—you must go.' After all, it was her mother's country. They took her in by the fire and raved about it.

Between sunny Australia and the grim problems to be faced in the New Year, over the Jam and what to do about the making of wills, Christmas was a blessed interval.

Tanya was there not just for the festivity but to work. At least that was what Tony intended. Now that the heart had held out he was determined to pursue his policy of dying in harness. Brian Friel, the Irish writer—whose short stories he admired enormously—wanted him to direct his new play, *Cass Maguire*, and he wanted to. His old friend Joan Cross wanted him to direct *The Barber of Seville* for her struggling Phoenix Opera Company; he wanted to do that for her. Colin George, director of the new Sheffield Crucible Theatre (designed by Tanya and inspired by Stratford and Minneapolis), wanted him to reproduce *The House of Atreus* there; and of course he wanted to. But Tanya had little belief that any of these projects would see completion. She was under no illusion about the strain that he was suffering now—and especially from the Jam.

Ironically, the Irish Farmhouse Preserves Ltd., was showing the first hope of making a small profit. But if there was to be any success ahead the shareholders would have to be angels of patience and Joe and he would have to show a Herculean capacity to expand sales. And he was tired and Joe did not seem to be able to cope. At any other time it might make a funny

Irish story that because some mouldy fruit had got in a consign-
ment of Irish Farmhouse Jam which was on its way to the
U.S.A. it was rumoured to have blown itself up in mid-Atlantic.
'Not funny at all', when Joe was complaining he had to scour the
country in a truck trying to find lids for the jars, which he
maintained the big companies were all buying up just to see that
he got none. And complaints were coming in about the quality of
the jam itself. A storekeeper in a local town was heard to say
'The marmalade's the best of it. *Irish* Farmhouse, preserve us—
who grows oranges in Monaghan!' Was not the idea to keep the
boys on the farms, fruit-farming? There was more than local
loose talk. There was the Irish government. It had invested a fair
number of thousands in the company and they were anxious about
how it was all being run. Also, good friends in the U.S.A. had
paid money for jam they had yet to see.

From now on he became a somewhat distracted man. And, at
this unfortunate time, the Arts Council in Belfast made an
approach to him. Ulster was to celebrate fifty years of its
existence. They proposed to put on a two-play Festival. Sir
Tyrone made a counter-proposal: that they should spend a considerable amount more on something less evanescent; the building of a theatre, that might in the end be a national theatre of
Ireland; and that it should be in Derry. He eventually got
Stormont's interest in such a large and daring politico-
cultural gesture. But, by the time Sir Tyrone had turned down
several sites suggested in the city by its council architects, and
said it must be at least fifteen miles outside the city ('the future of
Theatre no longer lies in towns,' he had said), the promoters of
the scheme were beginning to doubt if he knew his Ireland as well
as he knew his Canada and Australia. The theatre project came to
nothing.

Early in January 1971, there were critical meetings with the
accountants. The whole business of Finance and the Jam had to
be given a cold hard look. Meantime he was given an opportunity
of the sort of public reading he loved to do. At the Ulster Hall in
Belfast he spoke the narration for Honegger's *King David*—with
the Ulster Orchestra and the Ulster Singers. He loved stories
anyway. And this story he loved greatly; of the shepherd boy
who stood up to Goliath and slew the giant, became the man
David, struggled with Saul, and was crowned King; then came
his latter days which lead, in the oratorio, to his 'Song of

Penitence'. There was a mood of penitence in Tony now too. Maybe his own life's cycle was over. But, if it ended now—with his will not finalized, because of doubts about the fate of Annaghma-Kerrig, the Jam concern in difficulties, and Judy liable to slip back, and (as all the Irish folk around knew) no wish to live on should he go… It was a bad time. (Seamus had heard Sir Tyrone lecturing 'Lady' on the sin of suicide). On the 15th there was a shock: he received a courteous but deeply concerned letter from the head of the Bank in Dublin. Irish Farmhouse Preserves Ltd. was overdrawn by something more than £100,000.

He saw his solicitors, then went away to Sheffield to honour a promise to visit the new Crucible Theatre. There he got the story of how Colin George's hope of doing *The House of Atreus* had been defeated by matters of finance too.

From this point onwards it seems as if he began to play 'Last Scenes From The Life Of . . .' He re-visited his old school. Since leaving Wellington he had never gone back, nor had he spoken too kindly of it or the Public School system. But without the tough discipline Wellington put in his soul, the economies it taught him and the disavowal of triviality Vaughan passed on to him, Guthrie rehearsals would never have been half as vital. And now he had received an invitation to go and talk to the college's dramatic society which, as a preparation for possessing a new theatre, had changed its name from the earthy Elizabethan one of The Gravediggers to The Tyrone Guthrie Society. He said he preferred the old name, but he accepted the honour. He set off to return by the old route, by train, to the little local station of Crowthorne because, as he said, he wanted to 'retrace the whole Via Dolorosa of Going Back to School' (which had many times begun from where he would board the first train by the signal cabin at Newbliss Station).

There was the sleet of January slithering across the railway carriage windows when he got to Crowthorne, yet he was determined not to cheat. He would therefore walk from the station and by the footpath; where once every step further had shrunk the young heart, as he went towards the world of 'dorm'. However he was met at the station by two courteous but resolute men. Irresolution is no part of Wellington education. One of them— the ways of God being mysterious to men—was Ronald Horner who taught the college Drama and was a Belfast man, schooled in the old Lyric Theatre there. Horner and Michael Curtis (of

History and Drama) saw that the great man was bare-headed, carried a small, worn leather bag and had the collar of his big dark overcoat turned up against the January sleet. With all due respect for his wishes to walk, this Wellington old boy was seventy-plus and breathless. They firmly conveyed him to College by car.

He was surprised to find it physically little changed. Inside its Edwardian complex of brick and stone buildings he did find changes, later reported by letter:

> . . . in this last year only four boys went into the Army and Young fellows with Clapham accents and *hair to shoulders* were MODELLING in Clay—rotten little cissies!

After several whiskies and a sustaining dinner in a staff dining-room he said to the nervous Horner, as he passed water in neigh-bouring urinal, 'What in Heaven's name am I going to talk to them about?'

HORNER: Lilian Baylis stories?

SIR T: Forgotten them all.

HORNER: *Oh, Calcutta?*

SIR T: Haven't seen it.

Maybe the setting of the scene was influencing the drift of the dialogue.

HORNER: *Hair?*

SIR T: *Have* seen. Hate it. But *not* an unreasonable start to the proceedings.

He buttoned up and prepared for battle.

With the military backcloth behind him of a large, long oil-painting showing the Duke of Wellington on his charger, point-ing imperiously over the roaring field of Waterloo, he sat on the edge of a table and faced his young audience. They sat around him in the same relation the audience had been to *Hamlet* in the Elsinore ballroom. This was Wellington's elegant Edwardian 'Great School' and these—still well-scrubbed if long-haired —schoolboys didn't have a clue what the big bullet-headed old boy would say: '*Hair?*' he said (which was *the* new thing in London then)—

> . . . deliberately aimed at shocking the Surbiton housewifes, and has been performed in New York no less than a decade ago, with precisely the same reactions . . . plot childish . . . tunes infantile . . . singing positively painful to listen to. Besides, there is nothing original about dangling pricks over

footlights. The houses for that sort of things are well established, and everyone knows where to find them; and it certainly
is not in the West End theatre!*

Shocked silence while he went on and laid into another of their
current sacred cows—'*Far from the Madding Crowd*?—the film?—
a trivialized travesty of what Hardy intended'—(loud outcry) . . .
And having troubled the waters to a wicked degree, then came the
thundering angelic message.

He spoke of the great plays—the great family plays where all
humanity met by a common hearth. 'There is a singing quality
about all great plays,' he said—challenging plays which made
Hair pathetic by comparison, plays which 'gave to every man,
woman and child a cosmic location' and knocked for six that
comfy sense of planned location in a high-rise flatlet, before the
goggle box: *Hamlet*, *Oedipus*, *The Three Sisters*, *Death of a Salesman*
. . . and in all he reinforced the value of the great relationships
within Family. Between father, son, mother, daughter. Death
to the Superficial in Theatre! and 'always work from the centre
out—the heart of the matter is what matters. Read Conrad—
Nostromo?—what a book!' Read Jane Austen if you must, but
only for a study of superficial style. The interchange was fast and
furious: 'Amateur and Professional?—always mingled them . . .'
It was a feast of advice. Then—he was suddenly very tired. And
the evening came to an end. And there was no time for going up
the bare stairs in his old house, the Hardinge, to see 'the dorm',
where his name was still on his cubicle walls, on a list which
looked as old as the Tyrone Power playbills at Annagh-ma-
Kerrig.

In the morning he was to be taken to the station, but this time
the guest insisted—he would walk. This time it was the 'Going
Home From School' and he wanted to do it step by step. He did
not accept the faithful Mr. Curtis's company beyond the open
boundaries of 'The Turf' and the purlieus of 'Grubbies'—the
tuck shop, where the trees began. It was reportedly a haunting
figure: the great man in his big dark coat, little, much-travelled
bag in hand, taking the worn footpath to the station; a figure as
seemingly lonely as Willy Loman on a last, and rural, round as
salesman.

Well—he had sold the boys the best goods he knew—at little

* *Wellington College Magazine*, 1971.

cost to them, but not a little to him in terms of his limited energy, and limited time. And now, on the train from school to his birthplace—Tunbridge Wells. This was a sad sort of geriatric round of ageing relatives. Except for his own state of heart and breath, it might have made him feel, young by comparison. It meant visiting Lansdown Road—Number 5—now a gentle grey-stone nursing home-cum-old folks hotel. There is no record that he looked at or into Number 2—'Peacemeal'. One hopes not. The Bretherton red-brick edifice was beginning to suffer from its piecemeal architectural plan. It and the garden were showing the sad signs of disuse and decay which now necessitate, be-yond straggly bushes and street litter in the short drive, the notice—'DANGER, PLEASE KEEP OUT'. Bohemian ways were never meant to lead to this sort of decay. His birthplace, in Church Road, had of course long since yielded ground to strip-lit offices of Insurance and other businesses. The General's 'Kilmore' was still monumentally solid behind its Ionic portico of stone, and was about to become a school for secretaries. Only Warwick Lodge remained and remains almost unchanged: a well-kept, 'tastefully conceived' sort of architectural monument to suburban Success. The Opera House, where both Tony and Judy, separately, sang, in their first encounters with Gilbert and Sullivan, was still there; amateur opera still just keeping it out of total capitulation to the cultural pressures of a bingo-seduced society.

On to London, and the geriatry continued when he again saw George Chamberlain, lovingly attended to by faithful Prevost but beyond rational communication.

There was one lively encounter with one of his many disciples and spiritual sons—John Gibson, of Ballymena, who had worked with him in Edinburgh and, as TV director, had done a beautiful piece of TV documentary on him in the BBC series 'One Pair of Eyes'. But it was again a sort of last visit on this final tour and was devoted to setting straight the affairs of his Wharton Pro-ductions Company (in which Gibson was a director along with George Chamberlain and Aubrey Blackburn, Tony's London agent). The meeting also dealt with the matter he had to get straight now—the will and the eventual fate of Annagh-ma-Kerrig.

He returned home and tried to get a decision on this matter before Xtopher should arrive for a final visit. His idea now was that the house should become a house of reconciliation for the young of both sides of the border. But he had been unable to extract any decision from the Irish Youth Hostel Association. While they were alive he was prepared for Judy and himself to occupy one room, with the use of the public rooms. While the house was full of hikers? 'Ya-as.' Maybe the Youth Hostel Association thought it embarrassingly selfless, for still no decision came and he settled down to a heart-warming return of the hospitality Xtopher had given them in Tuscany, to the accompaniment of Verdi on the gramophone. It was spring again and by March he had drafted a revised will offering the house, on his and Judy's death, to either the Irish Arts Council or Queen's University, in that order.

He now had a touch of bronchitis and was suffering formidable heart symptoms. It was not the time to face all the strain of a meeting of the creditors of Irish Farmhouse Preserves—even less to fly off to London to make the first of two public statements deeply related to his own beliefs, before his heart should 'go pop'. But he flew.

With the sands of time very much running out now, he faced the TV cameras in the Greek galleries of the British Museum. In the interests of popular education, Thames TV were making a series of such programmes. This one was on the Greeks and its sub-title was 'The God-Haunted'. He was commentator and he faced the camera in his 'best blue' as immaculately dressed as any traditional Hardinge head boy ready for church parade. As he came across the gallery the signs of his medical state were a certain pushing forward rather than stepping, as if the legs were slightly perilous support for the giant torso. And though the Voice was a model of clarity, 'the most exciting sound in Theatre', the intake of breath was definitely bronchial:

> My name is Tyrone Guthrie. I am not an expert on Greek history . . . we shall look at things together, not as experts, but as ordinary people . . . We might think of the Greek heritage as Democracy and all that, but the dominant theme of Greek Art is God and Man . . . and one principal reason why Greek society made so pre-eminent a contribution to human development was because it was so [*pause*] god-conscious. We have lost this . . . We are so smug that we tend to look down upon the religion of the classical Greeks as ignorant superstition . . .

And with his big back to the Elgin Marbles he went on: '. . . in the midst of all this profusion of deity no one ever felt very far away from divine protection, divine supervision and, indeed, divine vengeance. This head . . .' And here he stood beside the bronze bust of a head of Sophocles, that favourite playwright of his and author of *Oedipus Tyrranos*. This was not the plumpish patrician head of the Lateran portrait but the keener older Sophocles, whose nose is not unlike the Guthrie nose and whose open mouth and furrowed brow seemed like Guthrie's in heroic archetype.

> . . . on the evidence of his works he was a man of powerful intellect and sensitive feeling . . . Such a person would hardly be given to vulgar superstition or to the unthinking devotion which satisfies very simple and uneducated people. How may we suppose that such a man as Sophocles accepted the conventional religion of his time? If we may judge from the evidence of his tragedies, with considerable scepticism . . .
> . . . similar to that highly intelligent and educated men of much later date . . . We must never regard ourselves as . . . [of]
> . . . being superior to the past . . . Our human life is short . . . but the Great Gods are immortal, for ever vital, for ever young, for ever dangerous, for ever wise and benevolent and therefore beautiful. *

Here, in the script which he used, there is a significant revision. Referring to the sacrificial procession of the animals of the Parthenon frieze he added, in his own hand, 'the most celebrated heifers in the world's history' and 'if you are going to be famous in this world, really famous, it almost seems as if you have to be a victim'.

He got back to Annagh-ma-Kerrig and within ten days he was down in Dublin and, in Powers Hotel, facing one of the most sickening defeats in his whole life—the meeting of 'The Jam's' creditors. Beyond that painful experience, by which he, the Irish government and many good friends could say goodbye to a lot of money, and also to a great and essentially philanthropic hope, he drove up to Belfast to get something else off his, now labouring chest: 'Thoughts on Holy Week'. Palm Sunday was four days away and the Belfast BBC recorded this talk in Studio 5—so different to when he had first talked to the Irish people through the big box microphone in 2BE.

* Thames TV Documentary, *The Greeks*, April 1971.

Perhaps I should make my position clear . . . As the years have gone on, I have become more and more sceptical about many Christian assumptions. I find there is hardly a phrase in the Creed, which I can say with conviction . . . One must not confuse scepticism with irreverence; nor Un-belief with Disbelief. I, for one, do not *dis*-believe the Gospels . . . the inspiration, to me, lies in the fact that a *Man* achieved this degree of courage and dedication. This I understand. God in man's flesh is a concept which I cannot grasp—it seems only self-contradictory. Rightly we reverence Him. Wrongly we allow reverence to obscure any realistic view of what kind of man this Jesus of Nazareth really was. If you visit Nazareth . . . *

—and he went back to those sun-baked days when he had time off from the Habimah production of *The Merchant of Venice*; he told how, like the stable at Bethlehem, the carpenter's shop was really a very humble dwelling, and how in following the official guide up the rickety steps out of the stable, he found himself in 'a splendid church erected on top of it all', where the centrepiece was 'a large, electrically spotlit, painting . . . of about 1880, depicting a European bourgeois conception of the carpenter's shop, totally at odds with the earthy dark, candle-lit place we had just visited . . .' Finally, he said,

At the end of all, the idea which, for me, emerges most strongly from the Drama of Holy Week is the idea of Victory arising out of apparent Defeat. I do not think that I believe, literally, in the Physical Resurrection of Jesus at Easter . . . It is one of those Mysteries which cannot, I suppose, be understood literally. It must be apprehended by a combination of intelligence and feeling, in which feeling must predominate. What feeling? The hope, the intense longing that Death should not be an end? that, when life is over, we shall, in some manner not specifically known, be reunited with the Holy Trinity, with the Company of the Blessed and with our own parents, children and friends who have preceded us into Bliss and Glory?

I do not dis-believe this; but I do not believe it . . . I don't passionately *want* to believe in such eternal life, in casting golden crowns upon the glassy sea or ten thousand times ten thousand in sparkling raiment. Well—who wants *that*? But I can, and do wholeheartedly and reverently, embrace . . . the

* *Thoughts on Holy Week*—Belfast BBC, Radio, 5 April 1971.

Resurrection of Jesus Christ . . . as symbol. It figures Victory
arising from Defeat; spring after winter; the violet fertilised by
the bones in the grave from which it springs . . .*

This said and put on record, he recrossed the border that he
did not believe in; faithful Seamus met the train and drove him
back from Dundalk—never at a speed good for the heart—like a
racing driver at practice on his own domestic circuit, of straight
roads, twisting lanes and forest sections, till the Annagh-ma-
Kerrig lake driveway slowed their arrival.

At least, in his mind, things had now simplified themselves to
Judy and the Jam. Whatever happened, Judy would have the
house and all the care of the Burnses and the McGormans. She
had ample money of her own, and they—his Irish Folk—he had
provided for. The Jam?—well, this was Thursday and on Sunday
Joe was due to come over and see him. It was not a meeting he
looked forward to.

In the house he was reminded that there would be guests for
this Palm Sunday week-end including Colin George of the Crucible
Theatre, Sheffield, and John Goetz and his wife of the Guthrie
Theatre, Minneapolis.

Observant lawyer that he was, John Goetz soon became aware
of how distracted their host was; also how distressingly ready he
was to snap at Judy. They were not unaware of Judy's drinking
problem, but apart from dismaying rumours about the Jam among
friends in Minneapolis, they had no means of being aware of the
kind of crisis state Tony was in. What they were all aware of was
spring at Annagh-ma-Kerrig. Hosts of golden daffodils were
between them and the wild-swan lake. And on the Saturday
morning the Goetzes and the Guthries picked armfuls of daffodils.
These Judy was to sell in Cootehill. After lunch the men chopped
down rhododendrons. After tea came rest and after dinner more
Verdi Requiems. After that, readings of Brian Friel's short stories
by Tony. Next day, Palm Sunday, there was no church-going.
Tony was restless and fractious with Judy who, the night before,
had taken an indiscreet number of nips at 'the wicked stuff'
(possibly in retreat from that eternal Requiem). 'A man is coming,'
Tony said. He had to see him privately. He was grim and as
nervous and lost in thought as in the hour before a first rehearsal.

The guests all set off for a walk. As John Goetz left the front

* Ibid.

steps, up came a car with two children and a dog, and a man driving. The man got out and left the children and the dog in the car, looking out over the daffodils to the lake. The man, Joe Martin, went up the front steps and into the house.

After the walk, John Goetz, returning to the house, saw the man drive off in his car. When he went in, only Judy was to be seen. 'Unpleasant visit,' she remarked as they got ready for lunch. At lunch Tony appeared, looking very shocked and strained. The conversation was boring and dull, an unheard of thing at a Guthrie table. Next day, John and Margaret Goetz left, a little mystified and not at all happy at the state in which they were leaving their great friend.

I have no revelations to make about that meeting. Only the two men know what went on between them. One could not and one did not talk about it when I was in the position to ask questions. What I do know is that the bigger of the two men—in whatever contest that went on—came out white and shaken, and that it was at a time when both men knew that any emotional crisis could have been the end of Sir Tyrone Guthrie. What I also know, is that for a time Joe Martin and he had truly shared the same social dream, and that Tony had not only poured much of his money into the Jam Factory but had, over the years, resolutely championed Joe against adverse opinion, in the typical way he had of championing the underdog or those who seemed simply less fortunate than he.

Things in Ireland have a way of twisting themselves into mysterious sorts of Celtic knots nobody can untie. There is no evidence that Joe was more than native and natural and right out of his depth in a bog where gold was supposed to be. And how could Sir Tyrone run a Jam Factory and be so much in absentia?— any more than at one time Sir Laurence could run the Old Vic so. Tony Guthrie was a man always willing to admit where he had gone wrong, and to 'Rise Above' and go on. But this was so far beyond rising above that from this shock he began to show a quite uncharacteristic detachment.

Tanya had been wrong that all the productions he was planning would come to nothing. One did happen. He now flew to London —to Peggy's despair—to start rehearsals for *The Barber of Seville* and thus to honour his promise to Joan Cross 'if spared'. And as if determined to give Death a good run for his money, he replied to correspondence with T. Edward Hambleton that, yes, within the year, God willing, he would direct a play for the Phoenix. Which play? He said, 'Oedipus Rex'.

From London he wrote to a distraught Peggy, who had heard from him about some extraordinary revisions of his will.

> I can't think why I was such a *goat* as to open the topic again. It only seems to lead to total misunderstanding and rather pointlessly distressing recriminations. Our spirits move on such a similar course (wave length?) that the irritable differences due to many years of extremely diff. environment, experience and companionship, are the more painful. Let's try not to wound one another . . .*

He wrote to Colin George on April 16, 'The high spirits of the *Barber of Seville* are KILLING me . . .' And again on April 30, 'The unrelenting high spirits of *Barber of S.* are killing me, I've literally lost my voice . . .' But he got through rehearsals.

And before they left Wharton Street and London for Brighton, Judy wrote to me saying they would love to come to Old Place, our home, in Sussex, for two or three days after the production opened in Brighton. Tony offered my wife, Louise, and myself their first night seats, as they would not want to sit in them in any case. At dress rehearsal Tanya reported that Tony's voice was just getting beyond a whisper. She was naturally very concerned about his state. On the first night—Wednesday, May 5—we met them at the Old Ship Hotel before the play. Gin and tonics were sipped and they led off for the theatre—on foot, of course—a fine evening after one of a series of glorious May days. He dismissed Judy's concern that it was uphill all the way to the Theatre Royal from the sea front. The performance went well and it was well received.

Tanya's mother was there. Judy and Tony met her as she came from one of the side boxes. She said to Tony, 'How do you do it? What's your secret?' 'What secret?' he said. 'To look fifty,' she said, 'when you are seventy.' His reply was enigmatic and, on thinking it over, disturbing: 'Come to Annagh-ma-Kerrig in a few days time and I'll tell you.' Then he turned back and said, as an afterthought to her, '*Do* look after Tanya.' And he went on, to see the singers. There was nothing wrong with Tanya's health and it may be hindsight and hasty deduction but 'in a few days at Annagh-ma-Kerrig' it would be his mother's birthday.

---

* Peggy was still hurt that there was no real consultation with her on the disposal of the old house, its lands and family treasures.

Next day we drove down the twelve miles, over the South Downs, to bring them both to Old Place to stay for a couple of days. Dame Flora lives near the Brighton sea front, not ten minutes walk from the Old Ship Hotel. It seems she had made a visit to see them both; an unextraordinary and friendly call. As she walked away at the end of it she turned and he was standing, in this detachment he now had, watching her go. We brought Judy and him home. I had not for years been able to get to Annagh-ma-Kerrig or make any real contact with him and we both looked forward to giving them a bit of rest and peace.

I noticed that he went about our old house like an animal (royal stag is the image) with his nose in the air—detached, yes—because he seemed to be alert for signs: not internal, external. 'No'—he did not want notable neighbours in to meet—just wanted us to themselves. But all right, the director, Peter Potter, was coming over to dinner because I was involved with him in a rather urgent bit of casting for a TV play of mine. This was the first coincidence and something that he pricked up his ears about: *The Last Journey* was the play and it was about how Leo Tolstoy chose to die (as Tolstoy said, 'How the peasants die'). Round the table we discussed who could play Tolstoy. Another coincidence: the TV company were negotiating then with his Stratford Oedipus, James Mason. He was deeply concerned about the whole play: and of course I now know why. Tolstoy's decision to make that last train journey against all advice including his doctor's; the painful business in the family about his will and the fate of the family home and property; and Tolstoy's wife Sonya's mental illness and attempted suicide. His own statement in his book, 'At least I had the sense to know when to run out into the dark.' The ageing Tolstoy—suffering from heart symptoms too—got up and left his family home in the middle of the night . . . and died in a wayside station. It all must have been strangely relevant to him. Next day we walked the hedgerow path of a field of barley. He in fact seemed more fit for it than Judy, whose cough was nearly continuous. He asked me what else I had on the stocks.

Two plays came up for discussion, *Everyman*—a new version entitled *Everyman and Every Woman Too*, which I had been revising since doing it with a group of American students. He wanted to read this; did so on the spot and said he 'would like to have a crack at it in New Zealand'—if spared. The other play was *Defiant*

Island a play about Henry Christophe of Haiti, the first black king of the New World, who so drove his people towards the realization of his dream of kingdom that they turned on him (Henry Tyrannos) and he killed himself. This he read partly, said 'very impressed', and asked if he might take it home with him.

Everyman came up for discussion again. The whole subject of the play being the process of dying, I might have been more worried if his own discussion of it had not been so lively and without a hint of gloom. He took me up on the matter of Everyman's scourging—the penance. 'Let the scourge fall. Let the scourge fall!' Why had not I cut that? Penitence he could see as a good and necessary thing, but Penance—flagellation?—was it not just a mawkish sort of masochism? I said I didn't think Medieval Man thought so and I felt that it was, within the concepts of the play, a necessary stage in the process of redemption and, for Everyman, his way of identifying with, and knowing, in fact, not by argument, the suffering of Christ. He nodded, dropped the argument, and moved on to other things.

The next day, Saturday, I had to go up to London. I took early morning tea up to their room. Judy was not there. To my query, he answered, 'She's coughing her lungs out in the bathroom.'

I went off to town. After breakfast they insisted, as always, in helping wash up, then when Louise was alone in the kitchen Tony came back in. He had a medicine bottle in his hands. As he got to the sink, Judy got to the kitchen door. And the following dialogue was played out:

TONY: Louise—may I pour this down the sink?

Louise saw the medicine bottle but had no cause to be more than curious at being asked.

LOUISE: Well—if you want to . . .

JUDY: (who had *every* cause for being alarmed) But, that's the medicine the Doctor gave you for your heart.

TONY: (not turning). Louise—may I pour this down the sink?

JUDY: The doctor said you had to go on taking it.

TONY: (totally ignoring her) Louise—may I pour it down the sink?

LOUISE: (who shared with Tony a considerable mutual respect, but whose sensitivity made her always a little in awe of him) If you feel you should. But . . .

Tony poured his heart medicine down the sink and set the bottle aside.

JUDY: (to Louise) I think divorce at this stage would be a little
    painful, don't you?

That night they spent with their old friends the Foxes, in
Cuckfield, just a mile from us. Robin Fox had not long since died
of cancer and his wife, Angela, welcomed the chance to talk with
Tony who had known Robin well. When we went to pick him and
Judy up next day, he was speaking to Edward Fox in the garden
in the sun. We drove them on up to Gatwick Airport. There was
little conversation of any consequence and Tony seemed very
detached. At the airport they insisted that it was both unnecessary
and foolish to wait on till they were allowed through the departure
gate. He did not argue. He just wandered away. When we looked
back Judy was sitting by their bags. He was standing tall against
the glass walls of the airport, his feet in blue and white gym shoes,
moving little. He was staring out at the sky beyond the runways.
It was Sunday, May 9.

Within the week we had a thank-you letter from Judy for their
stay with us, saying they had arrived 'feeling ninety years old and
left feeling twenty years younger.' In it she mentioned something
uncharacteristic of Tony. He was showing great impatience about
answering his mail; and he was being 'naughty' in doing an
awful lot of forbidden stooping and gardening. The next Sunday,
I flew from Gatwick Airport to be with Judy at his funeral.

Tony Guthrie was dead. After several days of wilful work
outside—and much of it weeding his mother's garden—he had
got up on the morning of her birthday, May 15 (a day he never
forgot in any year) and he had come down to the morning room,
which looks to the flower garden, leaving Judy to follow. He sat
down to start answering his mail, and he died. Seamus (called by
Judy, who had discovered him sitting there 'with a smile on his
lips') said, 'Yes. He's gone.' It was a nice bit of timing—well-
directed, surely?—to die on his mother's birthday. The setting
was proper too—on the chair where his back leaned was an
engraved zinc plate set in the wood: 'Presented to Reverend
Thomas Guthrie by a few of the female servants of his congregation in token of their affectionate regard'. But the Guthrie
male line was finished. Mary Burns came anxiously through.
And 'Lady' turned to her and said, 'I'm afraid it's all over now.
Pray for him. Pray for me. Pray for us all.' Seamus said in his
gentle rough way, 'Now wasn't it a good thing he was at home',

and he noted that the one letter Sir Tyrone had opened was certainly not the cause of death. It was a rebate on the rates.

It took as many strong, soberly dressed friends and Irish neighbours to get the big man's coffin down the front door steps to the hearse as it took guardsmen to get Churchill down the steps of St. Paul's. But this was a very simple country affair. And we walked behind the hearse in the rain and shower of a soft May day, winding down and uphill to little Aghabog Chapel on its windy green hill and its graveyard where his mother lay, and all the Moorheads and Powers ahead of him. The little chapel was packed, and by all denominations, all factions; and for a time the little chapel was a true house of reconciliation.

There were deeply personal shocks felt all over the world and in the Stratford Theatre in Canada and the Guthrie Theatre in the U.S.A. special services were held. But the 'big day' of celebration of his life—and it was celebration and in no way a mourning of his loss—was a month later in 'the actors' church', St. Paul's, Covent Garden, where all his theatre friends gathered to give tribute to his spirit. And it was in his spirit that singing from many of the former Sadler's Wells chorus 'lifted the roof', and gusts of affectionate laughter swept through what is normally a too solemn occasion.

When I met Seamus McGorman, on arrival in Ireland for the funeral, he said in his deep Irish brogue, 'Aye, James, a great tree has fallen.' As we all walked into St. Paul's it was noticeable that a tree that had stood for many years by its door had fallen down.

Sir Alec Guinness began his prepared address to us all assembled in the actors' church, 'A great tree has fallen'. In his splendid tribute to a very great colleague and friend he went on to say these things:

There are some names—not many—which when they crop up over a dinner table, on a walk, or round a fire, immediately seem to take charge of the conversation. Guthrie has been pre-eminently such a name for over thirty-five or forty years; giving rise to a wealth of anecdote, laughter, admiration, love and speculation. The strength of his personality has been a vitalising influence on all who knew him. And will continue to be so.

He was, I suppose our own, original, home-grown 'enfant terrible' of the theatre; galvanising, delighting and shocking a whole generation of performers and spectators, long before more recent 'terrible children' were born or thought of. And he showed no signs, even at the age of seventy, of relinquishing his provocative activities . . .

But he was not only a great man of the theatre, he was great in himself. Extremely witty—sometimes devastatingly so; generous with money and time to a fault; interested in all men and loving most; I think the clue to his greatness lies in the fact that he was never 'all things to all men' but, on the contrary, always totally himself to all men. He never cut his cloth, or trimmed his sails, to suit other personalities, but gave wholly himself. A man of the greatest integrity . . .

He had great personal humility—and rather hoped for it in others. And riding above all else was his laughter—rich, ironic, kind and memorable. . . .

Rehearsals were always immensely lively, with never a slack or unconcentrated moment. I can hear his fingers snapping up and down the stalls—a sure sign that he was going to call out 'Faster, faster!' He was a demon for speed in speech . . . Personally I don't think I got through any production with him without a bicker somewhere along the line. But he was always the one who made the gesture of reconciliation—usually by some extravagantly absurd and funny statement. But once we had a row which, through my fault, reached proportions whereby we were non-speakers for two days. It all had to do with the severed head of Hastings in *Richard III*. Tony's gesture of reconciliation was to give me, very solemnly, a small brown paper bag of rather squashed cherries . . .

He was a firm advocate of de-centralisation—in almost everything. The present crop of civic theatres, springing up throughout the country, are a direct result, I feel, of his spade-work and the voicing of his ideas over the past twenty years . . . He gave of his energy and, rather exasperatingly, took too little care of his health. His wife said that if the Ladies Guild of Timbuctoo wrote, suggesting he might give a talk over tea, he would consult his diary and then write back, 'Delighted. Can fit you in nicely on Thursday, on my way from Minneapolis to Belfast.' . . .

. . . A great and giving man. Our hearts go out to Judy.

IN MEMORIAM, JUDITH GUTHRIE

'I'M AFRAID it's all over now,' said Judy Guthrie, and his death meant just that for her. As Mary Burns said, 'She didn't want to live on.' She was nobility and courage itself at the services. And, she bore up well through the summer, but when she had the hardness of bearing the long nights of the winter and the darker days, things predictable happened between her and 'the wicked stuff'. Mary Burns tried to help and Seamus gave stalwart support and Freddie Bennett, who had played so often in Guthrie productions at the Vic, crossed the water and tried to break the loneliness and act as a sort of male nurse and secretary. But she had to face the full purgatory of what Tony had feared. Only through the good ministrations of St. Patrick's Hospital in Dublin was she prevented from drinking herself to a death she had reason to welcome. And while breaking the grip of 'the wicked stuff' they diagnosed inoperative cancer of the lung. She came home to a short period at Annagh-ma-Kerrig of quite remarkable peace. The purgatorial Dublin days were over, when visitors were figures come into her own nightmare and even Tanya she turned away as an unrecognizeable stranger. Now she was lucid, clear-eyed, calm as the lake, rather beautiful; and still deep as a gypsy monarch in her own intent. She rather enjoyed having her cousin, Mary Quinlan, read the holy book to her. But when the Bishop, of Clogher and beyond, arrived and he appeared to be bringing up institutional reinforcements to save her soul—she didn't like it, didn't like it at all. He brought her a poem, clearly touching on Death and the Beyond—'don't understand it,' she said to him. He read the 23rd Psalm with its reference to 'the valley of the shadow of death'. When he had gone, 'Don't like implications,' she said to Mary Quinlan. 'Give me the scissors.' When she had the scissors, she repeated, 'Don't like implications.' And, acting not unlike that intelligent and independent little girl over-governed by the Guthrie governesses, she cut the poem up into little bits.

Her condition worsened. She began to drift. But in one lucid period she asked that Eugene McCabe be sent for. She had something special to say. Eugene, the good neighbour and playwright, sat with pencil poised. It was to be a sort of Testament of Gratitude, but it drifted out of her control. Eugene wrote it all down:

Dear McCabes,

Where do we go from here? [*Then something about the diesel engine, which beat outside like a heart throb, pumping the water up from the lake*] ... The house is beautiful ... and the fields ... and the lake and the animals . . . all lovely, and that's enough, more than enough . . . I don't think any more. Perhaps there's hope. Is there anything? . . . I'm not afraid [*and she patted the cushion she held in her lap*]. I don't think there's anything in here. No ... nothing. I'm very tired . . .

She kept drifting off during the next days. Then came more quiet Bible readings from Mary Quinlan; to which she suddenly said, 'Don't want this clap-trap. Want to be entertained ... Music . . .' Music? Mary Quinlan did a thing that took them both back to Tunbridge Wells Opera House, where she had seen and heard her tall and beautiful cousin sing, and seen her dance, tambourine in hand. In a Cootehill shop she dug up a copy of *The Gondoliers* and she played it on the Gram. Gilbert and Sullivan took over in the spacious old house again.

She slept. When she wakened, 'Don't laugh, Mary,' she said. 'Dreamt I danced before God.' Not many days later on July 25, 1972, she died.

It had been a wonderful life—but not an easy one—to be linked by love to Tyrone Guthrie.

A VERY IRISH SORT OF WILL

THE THEN gentle incumbent of Aghabog Church called it 'a cross will'. No, it was not a 'cross will', it was a will conceived in distraction. And those who thought his devoted partner in life was insufficiently provided for, did not know, as he did, that Lady Judy had plenty of provision in her own private means. Despite the Jam Factory neither died poor. However, when it is taking years for those legally skilled to find out just how much Sir Tyrone's estate amounted to, I doubt if he knew in those last months how much he had left.

The main intent of the will was to safeguard the future of Annagh-ma-Kerrig, with whatever money was left. Beyond the Youth Hostel hope—of which Tony had despaired perhaps too soon (on the week of his death he received the Association's official acceptance of his plans)—beyond that hope, the intention of the will was really quite clear, and very Tolstoyan. It was Chekhovian, too. The time of the great landed families was gone; the Cherry Orchard must pass to the robust steward. Seamus McGorman was to have all the lands of Annagh-ma-Kerrig, Knockcor, Grappagh, etc., along with that part of 'my dwelling of Annagh-ma-Kerrig' which he now occupied at the back. The forests, now under lease to the Forestry Commission, would revert to the family McGorman in its future generations. The family of Guthrie and the Power line were doomed to termination.

On Judy's death the house was to be offered to the Irish Minister of Finance (as the Ministry with responsibilities to the Arts Council of Ireland). The gift was to be subject to its being used as 'a place of retreat for artists and other like persons . . . so as to enable them to do or facilitate them in doing creative work.*
. . .' If the Minister of Finance in Dublin did not accept the gift

---

* He had now fully accepted this idea which Hubert, in his concern to keep the house from ruin, suggested to him. Peggy and he felt that Seamus would simply find the big house a burden which he could not afford to maintain.

with these conditions attached, it was to pass to Queen's University, Belfast, absolutely. But the Minister did accept the gift of the house. Mary Burns, and her husband stayed as custodians while endless negotiations went on. And they still go on, as Annagh-ma-Kerrig stands, somewhat desolate, though well cared for, while it waits for its day of creative peace; and so does all Ireland.

LIST OF
THEATRICAL PRODUCTIONS

1924   *The Triumph of Death* (Scaife)   Barn Theatre, Oxted, England

1924–1926   Various Radio Productions   Belfast BBC, Ireland
including:
Iphigenia in Tauris (Euripides/Murray)
The Land of Heart's Desire (Yeats)
Good Friday (Masefield)
A Night in a Victorian Drawing Room (Guthrie)

1926–1928   Various Stage Productions
as Producer for the Scottish National Players   Scotland
including:
The Glen is Mine (Brandane)
C'est la Guerre (Graham)
Britain's Daughter (Bottomley)

1929–1930   Various Productions as Artistic Director of the Anmer Hall Company
at the Festival Theatre, Cambridge, England
including:
Six Characters in Search of an Author (Pirandello)
Iphigenia in Tauris (Euripides/Murray)
The Rivals (Sheridan)
The Machine Wreckers (Toller)
Rosmersholm (Ibsen)
The Merry Wives of Windsor (Shakespeare)
Dandy Dick (Pinero)
Le Malade Imaginaire (Molière)
The Cherry Orchard (Chekhov)
Warren Hastings (Feuchtwanger)

1930   Radio Series for the Canadian National Railways
The Romance of Canada   Montreal

1931–1932   Various Stage Productions as Artistic Director of the Anmer Hall
Company at the new Westminster Theatre, London
including:
The Anatomist (Bridie)
Six Characters in Search of an Author
Love's Labours Lost (Shakespeare)
Follow Me (Guthrie)

1932   *Dangerous Corner* (Priestley) at the Lyric Theatre, London

1933   *Lady Audley's Secret* (Hazlewood)   Arts Theatre, London
Count Albany (Carswell)   Arts Theatre, London
The Lake (Massingham)   Arts Theatre, London and The Westminster
Theatre, London
Richard II (Shakespeare)   The Memorial Theatre, Stratford-upon-Avon

1933–1934   As Producer to The Old Vic Theatre, London
Twelfth Night   Old Vic Theatre, London

12*

1933–1934 *Henry VIII* Old Vic Theatre, London
    Measure for Measure Old Vic Theatre, London
    The Tempest Old Vic Theatre, London
    Macbeth Old Vic Theatre, London
    The Cherry Orchard (Chekhov) Old Vic Theatre, London
    The Importance of Being Earnest (Wilde) Old Vic Theatre, London
    Love for Love (Congreve) Old Vic Theatre, London

 1934 *Sweet Aloes* (Carey) Wyndham's Theatre, London
    Mary Read (Bridie) His Majesty's Theatre, London
    Viceroy Sarah (Ginsbury) Arts Theatre, London

 1935 *Hervey House* (Cowle, Avery, Lawrence) His Majesty's Theatre, London
    Viceroy Sarah Whitehall Theatre, London
    Mrs. Nobby Clarke (Macdonald) The Comedy Theatre, London

 1936 *Call it a Day* (Smith) Morosco Theatre, New York
    Sweet Aloes (Carey) The National Theatre, Washington and New York
    The Dance of Death (Auden) The Westminster Theatre, London

1936–1937 As Producer at The Old Vic Theatre, London:
    Love's Labours Lost Old Vic Theatre, London
    The Country Wife (Wycherley) Old Vic Theatre, London
    Hamlet Old Vic Theatre, London
    Twelfth Night Old Vic Theatre, London
    Henry V Old Vic Theatre, London

 1937 *Love and How to Cure it* (Wilder) The Globe Theatre, London
    Paganini (Knepler and Jenbach, adapted by A. P. Herbert)
    The Lyceum Theatre, London
    The School for Scandal (Sheridan) The Queen's Theatre, London

1937–1938 As Producer at The Old Vic Theatre, London
    Pygmalion (Shaw) Old Vic Theatre, London
    Measure for Measure Old Vic Theatre, London
    Richard III Old Vic Theatre, London
    A Midsummer Night's Dream Old Vic Theatre, London
    Othello Old Vic Theatre, London

 1938 *Goodness How Sad* (Morley) The Vaudeville Theatre, London

1938–1939 As Producer at The Old Vic Theatre, London
    Trelawney of the Wells (Pinero) Old Vic Theatre, London
    Hamlet Old Vic Theatre, London
    A Midsummer Night's Dream Old Vic Theatre, London
    She Stoops to Conquer (Goldsmith) Old Vic Theatre, London
    An Enemy of the People (Ibsen) Old Vic Theatre, London
    The Taming of the Shrew Old Vic Theatre, London
    The Good Natured Man (Goldsmith) Opera House, Buxton, and Streatham Hill Theatre, London

 1941 *King John* (Joint production with Lewis Casson) Old Vic Theatre, London
    The Cherry Orchard (Chekhov) The New Theatre, London

 1943 *La Traviata*—The Sadler's Wells Opera Company on tour
    Abraham Lincoln (Drinkwater) The Playhouse, London
    The Russians (Simonov) The Playhouse, London

 1944 *The Last of Mrs. Cheyney* (Lonsdale) The Savoy Theatre, London
    Guilty (Zola's *Thérèse Raquin* adapted Boutall) Lyric Theatre, Hammersmith, London
    Hamlet (Joint Production with Michael Benthall) The New Theatre, London

1944 *Uneasy Laughter* (*He Who Gets Slapped*), (Andreyev, adapted Judith Guthrie) The Playhouse, Liverpool
   Peer Gynt (Ibsen) The New Theatre, London
1945 *The Alchemist* (Jonson) The Playhouse, Liverpool
1946 *He Who Gets Slapped* (Andreyev adapted Guthrie) The Booth Theatre, New York
   Cyrano de Bergerac (Rostand/Hooker) The New Theatre, London
1947 *Oedipus Rex* (Sophocles) The Habimah Theatre, Tel-Aviv
   He Who Gets Slapped The Duchess Theatre, London
   Peter Grimes (Britten) Royal Opera House, Covent Garden, London
   La Traviata Royal Opera House, Covent Garden, London
1948 *Oedipus Rex* (Habimah Production) Broadway Theatre, New York
   Oedipus Rex The Svenska Theatre, Helsinki
   The Three Estates (Lyndsay) The Assembly Hall, Edinburgh
   The Beggars Opera (Gay/Britten) Holland Tour, Holland, and The Sadlers Wells Theatre, London
1949 *Henry VIII* The Memorial Theatre, Stratford-upon-Avon
   The Three Estates The Assembly Hall, Edinburgh
   The Gentle Shepherd (Ramsay) The Royal High School Hall, Edinburgh
   The Taming of the Shrew Svenska Theatre, Helsinki
   Carmen The Sadler's Wells Theatre, London
1950 *The Miser* The New Theatre, London
   Hamlet The Gate Theatre, Dublin
   Henry VIII The Memorial Theatre, Stratford-upon-Avon
   The Barber of Seville The Sadler's Wells Theatre, London
   Falstaff The Sadler's Wells Theatre, London
   The Queen's Comedy (Bridie) The Assembly Hall, Edinburgh
   The Atom Doctor (Linklater) The Assembly Hall, Edinburgh
   Top of the Ladder (Guthrie) St. James's Theatre, London
1951 *The Three Estates* (Joint production with Moultrie Kelsall) The Assembly Hall, Edinburgh
   The Passing Day (Shiels) The Lyric Theatre, Hammersmith, London
   The Sham Prince (Shadwell/Loudan) The Lyric Theatre, Hammersmith, London
   Danger Men at Work (Stewart) The Lyric Theatre, Hammersmith, London
1951–1952 As Artistic Director of The Old Vic
   Tamburlaine (Marlowe) The Old Vic Theatre, London
   A Midsummer Night's Dream The Old Vic Theatre, London
   Timon of Athens The Old Vic Theatre, London
   Carmen The Metropolitan Opera House, New York
1952 *The Highland Fair* The Assembly Hall, Edinburgh
1953 *Henry VIII* The Old Vic Theatre, London
   As Artistic Director, The Shakespeare Festival Theatre, Stratford, Ontario
   Richard III The Festival Theatre, Stratford, Ontario
   All's Well That Ends Well The Festival Theatre, Stratford, Ontario
1953 *The Highland Fair* The Assembly Hall, Edinburgh
1954 *Pen Don* (Williams) The Natural History Museum, Swansea
   Taming of the Shrew The Festival Theatre, Stratford, Ontario
   Oedipus Rex (Sophocles/Yeats) The Festival Theatre, Stratford, Ont.
   The Matchmaker (Wilder) Edinburgh Festival, Edinburgh, and The Haymarket Theatre, London
1955 *The Bishop's Bonfire* (O'Casey) The Gaiety Theatre, Dublin

1955	*The Merchant of Venice* Festival Theatre, Stratford, Ontario
	Oedipus Rex Festival Theatre, Stratford, Ontario
	A Life in the Sun (Wilder) The Assembly Hall, Edinburgh
	Six Characters in Search of an Author (Pirandello) The Phoenix Theatre, New York
	The Matchmaker The Royale Theatre, New York
1956	*Troilus and Cressida* The Old Vic, London, and The Winter Garden Theatre, New York
	Tamburlaine Toronto, and The Winter Garden Theatre, New York
	Oedipus Rex The Assembly Hall, Edinburgh
	Candide (Hellman/Bernstein) The Martin Beck Theatre, New York
1957	*La Traviata* The Metropolitan Opera House, New York
	The First Gentleman (Ginsbury) The Belasco Theatre, New York
	Twelfth Night The Festival Theatre, Stratford, Ontario
	Maria Stuart (Schiller) The Phoenix Theatre, New York
	The Makropoulos Secret (Capek) The Phoenix Theatre, New York
1958	*The Bonefire* (McLarnon) The Opera House, Belfast, and The Lyric Theatre, Edinburgh
1959	*The Merchant of Venice* The Habimah Theatre, Tel-Aviv
	All's Well That Ends Well The Memorial Theatre, Stratford-upon-Avon
1959	*The Three Estates* The Assembly Hall, Edinburgh
	The Tenth Man (Chayefsky) The Booth Theatre, New York
1960	*HMS Pinafore* Avon Theatre, Stratford, Ontario, and The Phoenix Theatre, New York
	Love and Libel (Davies) The Martin Beck Theatre, New York
	The Pirates of Penzance The Avon Theatre, Stratford, Ontario, and Phoenix Theatre, New York
	Gideon (Chayefsky) The Plymouth Theatre, New York
1962	*A Time to Laugh* (Crean) Theatre Royal, Brighton
	The Pirates of Penzance Her Majesty's Theatre, London
	HMS Pinafore Her Majesty's Theatre, London
	The Alchemist Old Vic Theatre, London
1963	As Artistic Director of the Minnesota Theatre Company.
	Hamlet The Guthrie Theatre, Minneapolis
	Three Sisters The Guthrie Theatre, Minneapolis
	Coriolanus The Playhouse, Nottingham
1964	Henry V The Guthrie Theatre, Minneapolis
	Volpone The Guthrie Theatre, Minneapolis
	Six Characters in Search of an Author Scott Hall, University of Minnesota, Minneapolis
1965	*Richard III* The Guthrie Theatre, Minneapolis
	The Cherry Orchard The Guthrie Theatre, Minneapolis
1966	*Measure for Measure* Theatre Royal, Bristol
	Dinner at Eight Alvin Theatre, New York
1967	*Carmen* Metropolitan Opera House, New York
	Harper's Ferry (Stavis) The Guthrie Theatre, Minneapolis
	The House of Atreus (Aeschylus/Lewin) The Guthrie Theatre, Minneapolis
	Tartuffe Old Vic Theatre, London
	Peter Grimes Metropolitan Opera House, New York
1968	*Volpone* The New Theatre, London
	The Anatomist The Citizens' Theatre, Glasgow
	Carmen The Opera House, Dusseldorf

1968   *The House of Atreus* Billy Rose Theatre, New York, and Mark Taper
        Forum, Los Angeles
1969   *Lamp at Midnight* (Stavis) Mershon Auditorium, Columbus, Ohio,
        and US tour
        Peter Grimes The Metropolitan Opera House, New York
        McCook's Corner The Opera House, Belfast, and The Abbey Theatre,
        Dublin
        Swift (McCabe) The Abbey Theatre, Dublin
        Uncle Vanya The Guthrie Theatre, Minneapolis
1970   *Oedipus the King* (Sophocles/Lewin) The Clancy Auditorium, Sydney,
        Australia
        All's Well That Ends Well The Princess Theatre, Melbourne
1971   *The Barber of Seville* Theatre Royal, Brighton

TYRONE GUTHRIE'S
HONOURS AND AWARDS

1923   BA Oxford (History)
1931   MA Oxford
1948   Fellow of The Royal Society of Arts.
1950   Hon. Lld. St. Andrew's University, Scotland.
1954   Hon. D.Litt. University of Western Ontario.
1955   The Antoinette Perry Award of The American Theatre Wing for his direction of *The Matchmaker*.
1961   Knighthood.
1963   Elected Chancellor of Queen's University, Belfast.
1964   Hon. Lld. Queen's University, Belfast.
      Hon. Fellow of St. John's College, Oxford.
      Hon. D.Litt. The Citadel, Military College of South Carolina.
      Distinguished Service Award, Minneapolis Chamber of Commerce.
      Hon. D.Litt. Trinity College, Dublin.
      Hon. Lld. Queen's University, Kingston, Ontario.
      Hon. Dr. of Fine Arts. Ripon College, Wisconsin.
      Hon. D.Litt. Franklyn and Marshall University, Penn. U.S.A.
1965   Hon. Lld. University of Aberdeen, Scotland.
1967   Hon. D.Litt. Wartburg College, Connecticut.
      Citation of The American Educational Theatre Association for Distinguished Service to the Theatre.

PUBLISHED WORKS

Squirrel's Cage
The Flowers Are Not For You To Pick } (Radio Plays) 1931,
Matrimonial News }   Cobden and Sanderson.
Theatre Prospect   1932   Wishart & Co., London.
Top Of The Ladder   1950   Plays of the Year, Paul Elek.
A Life In The Theatre 1959   Hamish Hamilton, London.
A New Theatre   1964   McGraw-Hill, New York.
In Various Directions 1966   Michael Joseph.
3 Volumes on The Shakespeare Festival Theatre, Stratford, Ontario
  Renown at Stratford (with Robertson Davies and Grant MacDonald) 1953
  Twice Have The Trumpets Sounded (with Robertson Davies and Grant MacDonald)
    1954
  Thrice The Brinded Cat Hath Mew'd (with Robertson Davies) 1955, Clarke, Irwin &
    Co., Toronto.
  Tyrone Guthrie On Acting 1971, Studio Vista, London.

INDEX

Abbey Theatre, Dublin: Influence on Scottish National Players, 71, 72, 194

Abercorn, Duke of, 287

Abraham Lincoln (Drinkwater), 185

Actor, Guthrie as: child, 4; school, 7; University, 44; Oxford Playhouse, 46, 49; Scottish National Players, 76; radio, 72; film, 160; own estimation, 327

Adams, Bridges, 36, 45

Adrian, Max, 171

Agate, James, 123

Aghabog, Tragedy at, 37; Family Chapel, 109, 258, 343

Ainley, Henry, 74, 111, 112

Albery, Bronson, 157, 184

Alchemist, The (Jonson), 194, 251

Alexander, Professor Fred, 289, 317, 326

All's Well That Ends Well, 237, 241, 245, 308, 313, 314, 318, 324

Altman, Peter, 306

Anatomist, The (Bridie), 106, 107, 111, 298

Anderson, Judith, 160; Dame Judith, 294

Anderson, Molly, 47

Annagh-ma-Kerrig (the Guthrie family home, Monaghan, Ireland): childhood influence, 8–12, 16; moves with Monaghan into Irish Free State, 37; week-end retreat from Belfast BBC, 58, 64; parents move to, 74, 75; sister Peggy's marriage at, 92; Guthrie's marriage and celebrations at, 107–109; Guinness *Hamlet* rehearsals at, 166; Christmas at, 201; call from Stratford, Ont. at, 222; mother's death at, 257–258; becomes Guthrie's own home and responsibility, 260, 262–263; Guthrie, Zeisler, Rea discussions at, 265–266; economics of lead to jam factory plan, 272–275; crisis over future of, 287, 288; life and work at, 307–314; the will and its future, 347, 348; Sir Tyrone's death at, 342; Lady Judith's death at, 346

Argento, Dominic, 295

Arlen, Stephen, 215, 216

Arms and the Man (Shaw), 188

Arts Council, The, 184, 215

Arts Council of Ireland, 297

Arts Council of Northern Ireland, 329

Arts Theatre, The, 125, 139

Arts Theatre, Cambridge (see also under Cambridge), 206

Arundell, Dennis, 130

Assembly Hall, Edinburgh (see also under Edinburgh), 204

As You Like It, 150, 153, 157

Atkinson, Brooks, 255, 266, 281, 283

Auden, W. H., 143

Australia: Guthrie radio plays broadcast, 103; first visit on national theatre survey, 200; new theatre visit Perth, 289; Sydney *Oedipus*, Melbourne

Australia—*cont.*
   All's Well, Perth Octagon Theatre, see Chapter Twenty.
Ayont the Hill (Simpson), 72

Bach B Minor Mass, 43
Badel, Alan, 219, 232
Ballantine, Paul, 277
Ballet, Dr. Arthur, 305
Barber of Seville, 36, 211, 328, 338; last Guthrie production, Theatre Royal Brighton, 339
Barker, Granville, 95
Barrie, J. M., *Peter Pan*, 5, 36, 45, 46
Bates, Michael, 235
Baylis, Lilian: 115; visit to Westminster Theatre, 117; interviewing Guthrie, 117–119; letter engaging Guthrie, 123–125; 127, 128; the Laughton engagement, 129–136; second Guthrie engagement, 144–147; 151, 152, 154, 155; on National Theatre, 157, 158; Elsinore visit, 158–160; death of, 160–163
Beaumont, Hugh ('Binkie'), 140, 141, 142, 187, 193, 249
BBC Belfast: 2BE, 51–67; 335, 336
BBC London: 2LO, 50, 82; 193
Bees on the Boat Deck (Priestley), 149
Beggar's Opera, The, (Britten/John Gay), 207
Belfast: 1924–1926 Chapter Four; 297, 303; BBC TV, 304; Festival of the Arts 1951, 213; Guthrie in hospital in, 267, 268, 306
Bell, Mr. Alfred, 227, 238; Mrs. Dama, 227
Bellamy, Cecil, 51

Ben Greet Company, 48, 102
Ben Greet, Sir Philip, 151
Bennett, Arnold, 46
Bennett, Freddie, 150, 345
Bennett, Vivienne, 116
Benthall, Michael, 186, 198, 221
Bernstein, Leonard, 260, 261
Bing, Rudolf, 218
Binns, Ed., 292, 293
Birmingham Repertory Theatre, 81, 149, 188
Bitter Sweet (Coward), 81
Blackburn, Aubrey, 333
Blake, Mervyn, 247
Bloom, Claire, 232
Blow Your Own Trumpet (Ustinov), 185
Bolton, Guy, 51
Bonham-Carter, Lady Violet, 216
Booth Theatre, New York, 195
Boswell, James, 209
Bourgeois Gentilhomme, Le (Molière), 43
Boyd, John, 303, 304, 310
Bradley, A. C., 133
Brandane, John, 73
Bretherton Family: Gordon, 7; Nellie, 7; Martin, 5, 7, 32, 33; Judith (Judy), 6, 7, 25, 80, 82, 87, 88, 90, 92, 94, 95, 98, 107, 108 (and see under Guthrie, Judith)
Bridges, Robert, 46
Bridie, James (Dr. Osborne Mavor), 94, 102, 105, 107, 112, 123, 133, 140, 203, 204, 205, 224, 231, 298
Bristol Old Vic, 207, 290
Britain's Daughter (Bottomley), 72
Britten, Benjamin, 143, 200, 207
Broadway, 99; first production on, 142; 261, 282, 290
Brothers Karamazov, The (Dostoyevsky/Guinness), 197

Bronowski, Jacob, 88

Brook, Peter, 197

Brown, Ivor, 122

Brown, Tom, 249

Buchan, Mrs. John, 44

Buchanan, Meg, 107, 111

Burnley: (and see under Old Vic Company); Old Victoria Theatre, 181; lodgings etc., 182, 183

Burns, Bob and Mary, 234, 272, 273

Burns, Mary, 300, 302, 307, 309, 342, 345

Burrell, John, 188, 193, 198, 202, 207

Butler, Hubert and Peggy (brother-in-law and sister): Hubert, 35, 58, 59, 73, 82; marriage, 92; 94, 96, 98, 108, 114, 131, 150, 172, 184, 273, 287, 288, 307, 347; Peggy (Susan Margaret), marriage, 92; 96, 98, 114, 139, 150, 172, 173, 234, 252, 273, 287, 288, 307, 308, 309, 328, 339, 347; Julia Mary Synolda, daughter of, 150, 287, 288

Butler Society, 287

Buxton: Theatre Festival, 166, 170; Opera House, 170; in war time, 171

Caldwell, Zoë, 277

Call It a Day (Dodie Smith), 142

Campbell, Douglas, 205, 235, 243, 244, 257, 268, 269, 271, 273, 275, 277, 278, 279, 281, 289, 290, 291, 292, 293, 298

Cambridge: Chapter Seven; and University Amateur Dramatic Club, 83; Festival Theatre, 83, 116, 207

Canada: First visit as radio producer for Canadian National Railways, Chapter Eight, and 94, 95, 97; second visit and talk of tent theatre, 196; Coulter/Scott Lincolns Inn talk, 214; 215, 217, 220, and Chapter Sixteen (Stratford, Ontario story), 248–252; also see Stratford, Ontario 260, 268; *HMS Pinafore*, 269; *The Pirates of Penzance*, 271, 276; National Theatre, 214, 252

Candide (Hellman/Bernstein), 257, 260

Caplan, Rupert, 102, 106, 229, 235

Carey, Joyce, 140

Carmen (Bizet): Sadlers Wells, 208; New York Met., 218; Düsseldorf, 299

Carnovsky, Morris, 301

Cass Maguire (Friel), 328

Cassidy, Claudia, 281

Casson, John, 171, 175

Casson, Lewis, 168, 169, 173, 175, 178, 180, 181, 187, 293

C.E.M.A. (Council for the Encouragement of Music and the Arts), 181, 184

C'est La Guerre (Graham), 72, 92

Chamberlain, George, 143, 144, 161, 162, 163, 173, 176, 187, 188, 190, 191, 197, 216, 271, 297, 333

Chamberlain, Annette (see also Prevost), 176, 188, 190

Chekhov, 120, 278; Guthrie love of family plays of, 281, 286, 288, 305

Cherry Orchard, The (Chekhov), 129, 131, 184, 207, 288; at Minneapolis, 289

Chicago and the Stratford tent, 236, 238, 239

Chichester Festival Theatre, 268, 269

Church, Esmé, 141, 153, 168, 211

Clark, Mrs. Nobby (Macdonald/ Lennox), 141

Clarke, Cecil, 233, 234, 236, 237, 238, 239, 242, 244, 248, 249, 250

Clewlow, Frank, 69

Clunes, Alec, 150

Coates, Wells, 131

Collingwood, Lawrance, 176

Comedy Theatre, The, 141

Compagnie des Quinze, 121, 148, 197

Company of Four, 193, 197

Coney Island, 300

Compton, Fay, 142

Conolly, Patricia, 289, 305, 318, 324

Constant Nymph, The (Kennedy/ Dean), 63

Cooke, Alistair, 88

Cooper, Gladys, 142

Copeau, Jacques, 85, 121

Copley, Peter, 130; father's letter, 137, 138

Corrigan, Mickie, 170, 212

Cottrell, Cherry, 155

Coulter, John, 214, 215, 217, 220, 221, 223

Count Albany (Caswell), 125

Country Wife, The (Wycherley), 146, 147, 150, 152, 153

Covent Garden, 13, 199, 200

Cowan, James, 231

Coward, Noel, 36

Cowl, Jane, 141, 142

Cowles, John Jnr., 267, 269, 272

Craig, Gordon, 85

Critic, The (Sheridan), 193, 194

Cronyn, Hume, 277, 282

Cross, Joan, 176, 187, 190, 191, 200, 328, 338

Crucible Theatre, The, Sheffield, 297, 328, 330

Cummings, Constance, 171

Cundall, Jacqueline, 237

Curtis, Michael, 330, 332

Cyrano de Bergerac (Rostand), 197, 198, 199

Daly, Beckie, 5, 8, 9, 109, 211, 272, 302

Dance of Death, The (Auden), 143

Danger, Men At Work (Stewart), 214

Dangerous Corner (Priestley), 115

Darlington, W. A., 156

Davies, Robertson, 196, 215, 228; and Brenda, 230; 270

Dean, Basil, 63

Dear Brutus (Barrie), 27

Death of a Salesman (Miller), 282

Defiant Island (Forsyth), 341

Denham, Reginald, 59

Denison, Merrill, 95, 99, 100, 102, 106

Desire Under the Elms (O'Neill), 104

Detroit, 268; Guthrie teaching at University of, 286

Devine, George, 148, 197, 215, 217

Devlin, J. G., 214

Diffen, Ray, 233

Dinner at Eight (Kaufman/Ferber), 290

Dix, Dorothy, 155

Donat, Robert, 85, 88, 92, 93, 128, 129, 140, 141, 142, 167, 171

Doone, Rupert, 143

Duchêne, Jacques (Michel Saint-Denis), 193

Dunning, Ethel, 162

Eckstein, Dr. Gus, 201

Eddison, Robert, 88, 107, 111, 116, 125

Edinburgh: Father's home town, 5, 68; Great-grandfather's statue, 17; *The Anatomist*, 111; International Festival of Music and Art 1948 and first Assembly Hall production of *The Three Estates*, see Chapter Fifteen, 203–206; also Festival Edinburgh, 211, 220, 222, 232, 234, 249, 252, 257, 258

Education: early, 5–8; Public School, see Chapter Two; Oxford, see Chapter Three

Elgar, Edward, 46

Emmy or A Passenger to London (Guthrie), 73

Empson, William, 88

Enemy of the People, An (Ibsen), 167, 169

England, Mr. (Canadian National Railways), 94

Esher, Lord, 207, 215, 217

Esmond, Jill, 149

Evans, Edith, 139, 146, 150, 153, 157

Evans, Nancy, 207

Everyman, 340, 341

Fagan, James B., 44–49

Fairfield, Robert, 236, 260

Falstaff (Verdi), 211

Fata Morgana, 59, 60

Fatal Brand, The (Townsend), 93

Faust (Sadlers Wells Opera Production), 173

Faustus, Dr. (Marlowe), 207

Festival of Britain 1951, 213, 216

Films, Guthrie involvement with, 139–140, 160

Fire Over England (Film), 141, 149

First Gentleman, The (Ginsbury), 261

First Mrs. Frazer, The (St. J. Ervine), 81

Fleming, Tom, 298

Flowers Are Not For You To Pick, The, Radio Play (Guthrie), 90–92, 99, 103

Flu Epidemic (Wellington 1918), 29–30

Folk Art, 40, 44, 51, 55, 57

Follow Me (Guthrie), 113, 117, 122

Forster, E. M., 59

Forsyth, James, 153, 178, 179, 180, 190, 198, 219, 340, 341

Forsyth, Louise, 341, 342

Fox, Robin, 342; Angela, 342; Edward, 342

Francis, Alfred, 213, 216, 222

Frazer, Sir James, 212

Freeman, Norman, 245

Friel, Brian, 305, 328

Freud, 154, 212

Gaffney, Oliver, 236, 241, 245

Galsworthy, John, 36, 46

Garcia, Gustave, 32

Garrick Jubilee Rotunda 1769, 209

Gelfand, Lou, 295, 296, 297

Gelfand, Ravina, 295, 296

George, Colin, 328, 337, 339

Gibson, James, 298

Gibson, John, 211, 297, 333

Gideon (Chayevsky), 271

Gielgud, John, 2, 48, 63, 129, 147, 149, 154, 163, 166, 167, 173, 189

Gielgud, Sir John, 297

Gielgud, Mrs. Kate, 2, 132

Gielgud, Val, 48, 49, 90

Gingold, Hermione, 183

Ginsbury, Norman, 139, 168, 188, 261

Glasgow: Chapter Five; and 66,

Glasgow—*cont.*
  122; Citizens Theatre, 202, 205, 298
Glass Menagerie, The (Tennessee Williams), 286
Glen Is Mine, The (Brandane), 72
Globe Theatre, The, 157
Goetz, John, 298, 303; John and Margaret, 300, 301, 337, 338
Gooch, Lady, 165
Good Friday (Masefield), Oratorio of, 105
Goodman, Lord, 297
Good Natured Man, The (Goldsmith), 170, 196
Goodness, How Sad (Morley), 168
Goolden, Richard, 47, 116, 130
Gordon, Ruth, 146, 147, 150, 152, 153, 195, 249
Goring, Marius, 130, 133, 148
Graham, David Morland, 93, 107, 111, 122, 128
Graham, William, 204
Graves, Robert, 35
Gray, Terence, 85
Greene, Graham, 38
Grizzard, George, 277, 280, 281, 282
Guinness, Alec, 131, 147; Saint-Denis teaching, 148; Gielgud start, 149; Old Vic and Guthrie direction, 150, 151, 152, 156, 163; Gielgud and Queen's Theatre, 166; Guthrie Hamlet, 166, 167–8; Old Vic Europe and Asia Minor Tour, 169; War, 170, 178, 182; Old Vic at the New Theatre, 197, 199, 201, 207; Stratford, Ont., 230, 231, 232, 236, 240, 241, 243, 245, 247
Guinness, Sir Alec, 343, 344
Guthrie, Judith (Judy) née Bretherton—Wife: Marriage at Annagh-ma-Kerrig, 107–109;

Lincoln's Inn, 110–116; 122, 123, 125; Old Vic first period, 131, 137; 140; New York, 142; Old Vic second period, 150, 151, 153, 163, 166, 168, 170; War-time and Burnley, 177, 182; first play, 184; return to Lincoln's Inn, 192, 193; second play, New York, 195; Tel-Aviv, 200; 202; Stratford-upon-Avon, 208–210; 214, 215, 232, 234; Stratford, Ont., 243, 246, 249; New York, 253, 254, 267
Guthrie, Lady Judith (Judy): Minneapolis, 271, 274–276; Annagh-ma-Kerrig, 287, 288; 290; Minneapolis, 294–297; 302–306; 309; Australia, 316, 318, 320, 324, 325; Annagh-ma-Kerrig, 330, 337; Brighton and Old Place, 341, 342; Annagh-ma-Kerrig and In Memoriam, 342, 345, 346
Guthrie, Norah—Mother (see also Power): Tunbridge Wells, 1, 2, 3; marriage, 4; 7; War work at Tunbridge Wells, 25, 26; 42, 60, 63, 78, 79, 80; move to Annagh-ma-Kerrig, 83, 87, 96; Tony's marriage, 108; question of children, 109; blindness and the big cards, 201; 234, 252; death, 257; 258, 306
Guthrie, Dr. Thomas Clement—Father: 1, 2, 4, 5, 16, 26, 30, 31; fatal illness, 74, 75, 77; death, 78
Guthrie, Rev. Dr. Thomas, DD—Great-grandfather: 17, 18, 204
Guthrie, Rev. David, Grandfather, 18
Guthrie, Susan Margaret (Peggy)—Sister (see also Butler): 2, 3, 6,

7, 11, 25, 26, 37, 59, 60, 62, 79, 82; marriage, 92

Habimah Theatre, Tel-Aviv: *Oedipus*, 199, 200; *The Merchant of Venice*, 262, 263; 264

Hall, Amelia, 235

Hall, Anmer (A. B. Horne): 73; Cambridge Festival Theatre, 83–86, 88, 94, 95; The Westminster, 103, 106, 107, 111–114, 122, 123; 126

Hambleton, T. Edward, 252–256, 262, 265, 278, 297, 338

Hamlet: first encounter with, 23; Old Vic productions of: Olivier, 149, 150, Freudian approach Hamlet/Oedipus, 154–157, Elsinore staging of, 158–159; Guinness, 166–168; Helpman, 186–187. Scaife, Westminster Theatre, 159; Ronald Ibbs, Dublin, 210; 219, 232, 233; Grizzard Theatre, Minneapolis, 275, 277, 279–282

Hardy, Betty, 122

Hardy, Thomas, 46

Harper's Ferry (Stavis), Minneapolis, 290–292, 301, 306

Harrison, Rex, 143

Hauser, Frank, 255

Hayes, John, 249

Haymarket Theatre, The, 13, 252

Heartbreak House (Shaw), 46, 49

Hellman, Lillian, 260, 261

Helpman, Robert, 164, 186, 318

Helsinki: *Oedipus*, 202; *The Taming Of The Shrew*, 208; 264

Henry IV, Part I, O.U.D.S. Production, Guthrie as Glendower, 44

Henry V: Old Vic, Olivier, 150, 157; Old Vic European Tour, 168; Minneapolis, 286

Henry VIII: 74; Old Vic, Laughton, 129, 132; Stratford-upon-Avon, 208; Old Vic Coronation Production, 234, 239

Henry VIII, The Private Life of, (Film), 132

Herlie, Eileen, 262

Hervey House (Cowl), 141

He Who Gets Slapped (Andreyev adapted Judith Guthrie), 193

Highland Fair, The (Mitchell), 221

His Majesty's Theatre, 142

Hollywood, 257

Holmes-Gore, Dorothy, 122

Horner, Ronald, 330, 331

Horniman, Mrs. Annie, 69

Houghton, Norris, 252, 254, 255, 256, 262, 265

House of Atreus, The (The Oresteia): Minneapolis production, 290–295; on Broadway, 301; Los Angeles, 303; Crucible Theatre plan, 328, 330

Hughes, Elinor, 281

Hughes, Richard, 54

Hunt, Hugh, 207, 215, 217, 221

Hurry, Leslie, 218, 256

Hurstleigh School, Tunbridge Wells, 6

Hutchinson, Harry, 111

Hyland, Frances, 248

Hyson, Dorothy, 208

Ibsen, 2; *Rosmersholm* 'my favourite play', 92; *An Enemy of the People*, 169

I Have Been Here Before (Priestley), 168

Importance of Being Earnest, The (Wilde), 49, 129, 133

Iolanthe (Gilbert and Sullivan), 36

Iphigenia in Taurus (Euripedes), 64, 87, 88

Ireland: childhood influence, 8–11; Home Rule for, 19; 'The

Ireland—*cont.*
Troubles', 37, 56, 297, 303, 304; Twelfth of July, 65
Irish Farmhouse Preserves Ltd., 284, 328, 330, 334
Irish Literary Theatre, 67, 78
Jackson, Sir Barry, 81, 208
Jam Factory, The, Newbliss, Monaghan (See also Irish Farmhouse Preserves Ltd.): Idea for, 273–275; 283, and Chapter Nineteen pp 284–286, 288, 298, 300, 307, 328–330, 334, 335, 337–338
Jeans, Ursula, 130, 133
Job, Ninette de Valois Ballet, 163
John, Evan, 85, 86, 88, 94, 107, 108, 116, 150
Jones, Dr. Ernest, 154–156, 165
Jones, Dr. Tom (Pilgrim Trust), 181
Journey's End (Sherriff), 81
Joyce, James, 212

Kanin, Garson, 249
Kelsall, Moultrie, 205
Kemp, Robert, 203, 204, 206
Kempson, Rachel, 150
Kennedy, Daisy (Mrs. Moisei-witsch/Drinkwater), 194, 339
Kerr, Walter, 280
Keynes, Maynard, 88, 187
King David (Honegger), 329
King John, 184
Kipnis, Alexander, 256, 315
Kipnis, Leonid ('Lola'), 256, 257, 278, 288, 298–300, 305, 309
Kirk, Hannah, (Grandmother), 18
Knighthood, 270
Komisarjevsky, Theodore, 121
Korda, Alexander, 141
Kraus, Otakar, 207
Krish, Felix, 194

Lady Audley's Secret, (Hazlewood), 90, 125
Lake, The (Massingham), 125
Lambert, Constant, 176
Lamp at Midnight (Stavis), 290, 301
Lanchester, Elsa (Mrs. Charles Laughton), 129, 131, 135, 160
Land of Heart's Desire, The (Yeats), 49, 64, 65
Landstone, Charles, 216
Lang, Matheson, 129
Langham, Michael, 175, 219, 252, 256, 257, 260, 268, 303, 305
Last Journey, The (Forsyth), 340
Laughton, Charles, 81; at Old Vic, 129–136; 158, 160
Lawrence, D. H., 34, 98
Lawrence, Gertrude, 142
Le 14 Juillet (Romain Rolland), 145
Le Gallienne, Eva, 262
Leigh, Vivien, 159, 164, 168, 183, 184, 207, 211
Leighton, Margaret, 188, 199
Lewin, John, 291, 308, 309–312
Libel, 169
Lincoln Center, New York, 282
Liverpool, 215, 268; Festival Society, 213, 216; Old Vic Company, 186, 194, 251
Love and Libel (Davies), 270
Livesey, Roger, 130, 133
Lincoln's Inn, 23; Old Buildings (Guthries' flat): 109–111, 115, 168; War damage, 177, 193; Coulter visit, 214; Patterson visit, 233; Showalter call, 240; moved from to Annagh-ma-Kerrig, 260
London Group Theatre, 142
London Theatre Studio, 148, 188
Lopokova, Lydia, 187
Lorne, Tommy, 74

Love And How To Cure It (Wilder), 157

Love For Love (Congreve), 49, 129, 133

Love's Labours Lost, 116, 150, 151, 152

Lubitsch, Fanny, 262, 263

Lyric Theatre, Hammersmith, 197, 214

Lytton, Henry, 3

Lytton, Lord, 163, 169, 186

MacArthur, Molly (Designer), 51, 111, 140, 141

Macbeth, 81, 129, 133, 160, 161, 162, 163, 180

MacDonald, Murray, 170

MacEwan, Mollie, 206

Machine Wreckers, The (Toller), 87, 89

Mackay, Fulton, 205

MacKemmie, Glen, 69, 70

Macliammoir, Michael, 57

MacOwan, Michael, 159

MacRae, Duncan, 298

Madame Butterfly (Puccini), 173

Madison Square Gardens, New York, 13, 15

Magee, Patrick, 214

Maidenhall, Kilkenny, 150, 273, 287

Makropoulous Secret, The (Capek), 256, 262

Man and Superman (Shaw), 168

Man of Destiny, The (Shaw), 49

Manley, Skip, 242, 247, 250, 260

March, Frederic, 271

Maria Stuart (Schiller), 256, 262

Marre, Albert, 252, 253

Marriage (Gogol), 87, 88

Martin, Leslie Evershed, 268

Martin, Joseph, 273–274, 284, 298, 329, 337–338

Masefield, John, 35, 46

Mason, Elliot, 71, 73, 77, 80, 92, 122, 125

Mason, James, 130, 248, 250, 340

Massey, The Rt. Hon. Vincent, Governor General of Canada, 235, 245, 260

Master Builder, The (Ibsen), 49

Mary Read (Bridie), 140–141

Matchmaker, The (Wilder), 249, 252, 253, 257, 262

Mauretania, S.S., 97, 240

McCabe, Eugene, 304, 346

McClelland, Alan, 214

McCook's Corner (Shiels), 303

McGorman, Seamus and Mary, 272–273

McGorman, Seamus, 287, 300, 342, 343, 345

McKnight Scholars, 277

Measure for Measure: 87, 88; Old Vic, 129, 133; Stratford, Ont., 248, 250; Bristol Old Vic, 290

Melbourne, Australia: Melbourne Theatre Company, 313; Princess Theatre and Russell Street Theatre, 314, 318, 324–326

Merchant of Venice, The: Gielgud Production, 166; 184; Stratford, Ont., 255; Israel 262, 263

Merigold, Jack, 263

Merrick, David, 252, 253, 254

Merry Wives of Windsor, The, Cambridge, 87, 88

Messel, Oliver, 147, 153, 164

Metropolitan Opera House, New York, 218, 302

Midsummer Night's Dream, A, Old Vic, 164, 218; 219

Miller, Gilbert, 147

Mills, John, 213

Milne, A. A., 46

Milne, Lennox, 75, 205, 206

Milton, Ernest, 116, 129, 150, 151

Milwaukee, 267, 268

Minneapolis and St. Paul, Guthrie Foundation and Theatre: Choice of, for repertory theatre, 266–269; Company and productions, 270–283, 286, 288–297, 305, 306; Minnesota Repertory Company, 289; on Broadway, 301; The Stage-hands, 275, 306; Minneapolis Star and Tribune, 267–269; University of Minnesota, 266, 283

Mirandolina (Goldoni), 49

Miser, The (Molière), 279, 281, 282

Mitchison, Mrs. Naomi, 113

Moiseiwitsch, Benno, 194, 233

Moiseiwitsch, Tanya: Old Vic, Liverpool and London, 193, 194, 199; Covent Garden, 200; Cambridge, 207; Stratford-upon-Avon, 209; Lyric Hammersmith, 214; Stratford, Ontario, 230, 233, 234, 236, 237, 239–241, 249, 250; Habimah, Israel, 263; Minneapolis, 269, 271, 278, 288, 293; Sheffield, 297; Belfast and Dublin, 303, 304; Minneapolis, 305; Annagh-ma-Kerrig, 328; Brighton, 339

Monna Vanna (Maeterlinck), 49

Montreal: Chapter Eight and 95, 196, 235, 241, 249, 257

Montreal Repertory Company, 101, 102

Moody, John, 122, 176, 215, 216

Moore, Dora Mavor: first Guthrie visit to Canada, 95, 102; Stratford, Ont., 220, 221, 222, 224, 226, 229, 231, 235, 237, 239

Moore, Henry, 143

Moore, Mavor (son of Mrs. Dora), 224, 229

Moore, Tia, 2, 5, 9

Moorhead, Martha (see also Power)—Grandmother, 15, 16

Morley, Robert, 168, 261

Murray, Gilbert, 46

National Theatre: Oxford Playhouse manifesto, 45; Scottish National Players, 69; Granville Barker, 95; *Theatre Prospect*, 119–120; Baylis on, 157; 165, 181, 184, 186, 187; South Bank site, 197; Government action, 202; 207, 211; foundation stone, 215, 217; National Theatre Company, 297; for Ireland, 329

Neilsen, Flora, 207

New English Opera Group, 207

New Theatre, The, 157; Old Vic Company wartime London home and office, 186; the great seasons at, 188; Olivier *Oedipus* at, 192, 194; *Cyrano* at, 198–199; 207, 216; *Volpone* at, 297

New Theatre, Oxford, 219

Newton, Robert, 155

New York, 99; first Broadway production, 142; *He Who Gets Slapped*, 193, 195; *Carmen*, 218; rehearsing Pirandello, 254–255; Repertory at The Phoenix, 264, 265

New Zealand, 325

Ney, Marie, 141, 171

Night in a Mid-Victorian Drawing-Room, *A*—Radio Play (Guthrie), 62

Niven, David, 171

Noah (Obey), 147

Northern Ireland Festival Company, 1951, 214

No Trifling With Love (de Musset), 49

Oedipus Rex (Sophocles): Guthrie
as Tiresias (O.U.D.S.), 49; 55;
Ernest Jones on *Oedipus* and
Hamlet, 154; Olivier/Saint-
Denis, 192–195; Habimah, 199,
200; Helsinki, 202; Stratford,
Ont., 245, 250, 251; film of,
256, 257; Edinburgh, 258, 259;
286; Sydney, Australia, 308–
312, 319, 320; rehearsal and
TV interview, 321–323, 326–
327
Oedipus and Akhnaton (Velokov-
sky), 312
*Oh Dad, Poor Dad, Mamma's
Hung You in the Closet and I'm
Feelin' So Sad* (Kopit), 278
Old Vic (see also Baylis): Guthrie
first engagement, 117–119, 123,
139 and Chapter Ten; Laugh-
ton engagement, 129–130; re-
hearsals, 130–131; Laughton-
Robson season, 131–134; Baylis/
Laughton battle, 134–136;
Guthrie second engagement
Chapter Twelve, Ruth Gordon
Country Wife, 146; 147, 152,
153; Edith Evans *As You Like
It*, 153; Olivier *Hamlet*, 149,
154–156; Elsinore, 158–159;
Saint-Denis/Olivier *Macbeth*
and death of Baylis, 160–163;
Olivier-Richardson *Othello*, 164,
165; Guinness *Hamlet*, 166–
168; Guthrie Director Vic and
Wells, 169; War and Buxton
Season, 170; the Ballet and the
Blitzkrieg, 173–174; Sadlers
Wells and Blitz, 175–177; Old
Vic Theatre bombed, Burnley
Old Vic HQ, 181–184; return
to London, 185; post-war
plans, 186–188; Olivier,
Richardson, Burrell 'Trium-

virate', success at The New,
188–189; Peace, and Guthrie
resignation, 190; *Peter Grimes*
and farewell to Sadlers Wells,
191–192; *Cyrano*, 198–199;
organisational troubles, 201;
the 'Triumvirate' sacked, 202;
Guthrie recalled, 215; the Old
Vic Centre closed, 197; Guthrie
reorganisation, 216, 217, 221
Old Tote Theatre Company,
Australia, 322
Olivier, Laurence, 81, 146; Old
Vic season, 149, 150, 151;
Hamlet, 154; *Henry V*, 157;
Elsinore, 158; *Macbeth*, 160,
161; *Othello*, 164, 165; Holly-
wood, 168, 171; Burnley visit,
183; Old Vic *Peer Gynt*, *Arms
and the Man*, *Richard III*, *Uncle
Vanya*, 188, 189; Oedipus and
Mr. Puff, 192–195; *Lear*, 197;
Hamlet film, 198; Knighthood,
201
Olivier, Sir Laurence, Old Vic
Australian tour and *School for
Scandal*, 207; *Top of the Ladder*,
211; New York, 224; director
National Theatre Company at
Old Vic, 297
One Pair of Eyes BBC TV Docu-
mentary, 333
Opera: writing own, 182; British
opera hopes, 187; Sadlers Wells,
190, 191; New English Opera
Group, 207
Oresteia, The (Aeschylus), 286
O'Rourke, J. A., 111
Othello, 164, 165, 184
Other Heart, The (Forsyth), 219
O.U.D.S. (Oxford University
Dramatic Society), 36, 43, 44
Oxford Players, 45
Oxford Playhouse: Fagan's old

Oxford Playhouse—*cont.*
  Red Barn, 45, 46; modern
  theatre, 194
Oxted (Surrey) Barn Theatre, 51

Passing Day, The (Shiels), 214
Patterson, Tom, 222–229, 231–
  233, 235, 236, 247
Pears, Peter, 200, 207
Pearson, Hesketh, 88
Peer Gynt (Ibsen, adapted Gins-
  bury), 188, 215
Pegler, Miss ('Peglerino'), 7, 25
Pen Don (Emlyn Williams), 248,
  249
Perth Mutual Insurance Company,
  Stratford, Ont., 241
Peter Grimes (Britten), 191, 200,
  302
Phoenix Opera Company, 328
Phoenix Theatre, New York, 252,
  253, 255, 256, 260, 262, 265, 278
Pilgrim, Miss, 134
Pilgrim Trust, The, 130, 181
Pinafore, HMS (Gilbert and Sulli-
  van), 268, 269; Phoenix Theatre,
  270
Pinero, Arthur, 46
Piper, John, 143
Pirates of Penzance, The, Phoenix
  Theatre, 271
Pitlochry Theatre, 232
Playfair, Nigel, 46
Plummer, Christopher, 257
Popkin, Henry, 293
Power family, The: Power,
  Tyrone, (Great-grandfather),
  12–15, 308, 309; Power, Gen.
  Sir William, K.C.B. (Grand-
  father), 4, 15, 16; Power,
  Martha, née Moorhead (Grand-
  mother), 15, 16; Power, Norah
  (Mother), see Guthrie; Power,
  Ann, 4; Power, Susan (Aunt

Sue), 4, 19, 25, 83, 175; Power,
  Frederick, 15; Power, Tyrone
  the film star, (Cousin), 15;
  'Power, Tyrone' (Guthrie's
  nom de plume), 62
Potter, Peter, 340
SS *President*, 12, 14
Pretenders, The (Ibsen), 36
Prevost, Annette (see also Cham-
  berlain), 116, 117, 127, 130,
  131, 135, 159–163, 173
Priestley, J. B., 115
Princesses Elizabeth and Margaret,
  164
Princess's Theatre (Glasgow Citi-
  zens Theatre), 74
Private Life of Henry VIII (film), 129

Quartermain, Leon, 130
Quayle, Anthony: The West-
  minster, 116; Old Vic Company,
  168, 171; Stratford-upon-Avon,
  208, 210; *Tamburlaine*, New
  York, 256
Queen Bee (Judith Guthrie), 184
Queen's Comedy, The (Bridie), 211
Queen's Theatre, The, 143, 160,
  161, 166
Queen's University, Belfast,
  Chancellor of, 287
Quentin, Robert, 319
Quinlan, Mary, 345, 346

Radio: see Chapter Four, Belfast
  and 'The Wireless'; The 'radio
  craze' 1920s, 55; Guthrie's
  'microphone plays', 81–82, 90–
  92; Canada, 100, 101, 103
Rae, Kenneth, 43, 44, 103, 104,
  114, 197
Ramsdell, Roger, 211
Rank, J. Arthur (Canada), 231
Rank, J. Arthur (London), 232,
  233

Rapson, Professor Ralph, 269, 270, 271

Rea, Oliver: New York, 262, 263, 264; Annagh-ma-Kerrig, 265, 266; Minneapolis, 267, 268, 269, 270, 271, 276, 282, 289

Redgrave, Michael, 88, 150, 153, 163

Rees, Llewellyn, 215, 217

Reinhardt, Max, 253

Return of The Prodigal, The (Hankin), 49

Rhesus, The (Euripedes), 37

Richard III: Olivier, 188, 189, 207; Guinness, 233, 237, 245

Richardson, Ralph, 149; *A Midsummer Night's Dream*, 164; *Othello*, 165; 171, 183; *Peer Gynt* and the seasons at The New, 188, 193; *Cyrano*, 198, 199; Knighthood, 201

Richardson, Sir Ralph, 202, 215

Rivals, The (Sheridan), 49, 87, 88, 167, 168

Robson, Flora: Oxford Players, 46, 48, 49; Oxted, 51; *Fata Morgana*, 59, 60; *Iphigenia*, Belfast BBC, 64; 72; Cambridge Festival Theatre, 84–95; 104; The Westminster, 107; *The Anatomist*, 111–115; 125; Laughton-Robson Old Vic season, 128, 129; 131–135; films, 139; *Mary Read*, 140, 141; Hollywood, 171; *Thérèse Raquin*, 186; C.B.E., 218; Annagh-ma-Kerrig, 297; Brighton, 340

Rogers, Paul, 219

Romance of Canada, The, see Chapter Eight, and 95; 224

Rosmersholm (Ibsen), 87, 88, 92, 93

Royal Ballet of Covent Garden, 190

Royal Society of Arts, The, 218

Royal Warwickshire Regiment, 210

Royalty Theatre, Glasgow, 71

Russians, The (Simonov), 185

Ruta, Ken, 277

Rutherford, Margaret, 142

Rylands, George, 88

Sadlers Wells Theatre: Baylis and, 118, 127, 135; Guthrie policy, 145; Wartime HQ Vic-Wells Organisation, 173, 176, 177; Post-war reopening, 191; Opera, 173, 176, 191, 208; Ballet, 156, 164, 173, 174

Saint-Denis, Michel: Compagnie des Quinze, 121, 147; London Theatre Studio, 148, 149; Old Vic *Witch of Edmonton*, 153, 154; *Macbeth*, 160–163; 'Jacques Duchêne', 193; Olivier *Oedipus*, 193, 194; Old Vic Centre, 197; C.B.E., 201; closure of School and end of Centre, 215–217

Saint Joan (Shaw), 74, 286

St. Andrew's University, 225

St. John's College, Oxford, 31, 34–35

St. James's Theatre, 211

Salaman, Merula, 166, 168

Schaffner, Max, 263

Scaife, Christopher: Oxford friendship, 38–42; folk art punt trip, 43–44; 48, 51; Belfast, 55, 63; Glasgow, 73–74; 79; Cambridge, 83; 104; Annagh-ma-Kerrig, 107–108, 137, 334; Westminster *Hamlet*, 158, 159; Beirut, 290; Arezzo, 314–315; and as correspondent throughout

Scaife, Gillian, 51, 63, 73, 83, 85, 107, 112, 158

Scaife, Isobel, 116, 150

School for Scandal, The (Sheridan), 160, 161, 163, 207

Scott, Herbert ('Bertie'), 56, 57, 140, 141, 214; death of, 215

Scottish National Players, 66, see Chapter Five, and 80, 86, 92, 205, 298

Sea Symphony (Vaughan Williams), 43

Seyler, Athene, 130, 131

Shakespeare Memorial Theatre, Stratford-upon-Avon, 208, 209

Shakespeare, Ontario, Town of, 231

Sham Prince, The (Shadwell/ Loudan), 214

Sharaff, Irene, 260

Shaw, George Bernard, 36, 46, 47

Shaw, Glen Byam, Old Vic Centre, 197, 215, 217

She Stoops To Conquer (Goldsmith), 169

Showalter, Dr. Harrison, 223, 230, 236, 238, 239

Short Story (Morley), 143

Silver Tassie, The (O'Casey), 81

Six Character in Search of an Author (Pirandello): Cambridge, 86, 87, 88; Westminster, 114; Phoenix, New York, 234, 252, 255, 260; University of Minnesota, 286; 296

Slann, Miss Mabel, 5

Sleeping Princess, The (Ballet), 182

Slezak, Walter, 261, 262

Sligo (Ireland) Drama Festival, 82

Smith, Dr. Jack, 297

Smith, Oliver, 252, 260

Sofaer Abraham, 116

Sophocles, 251, 335 (and see *Oedipus*)

Speaight, Robert, 51

Squirrel's Cage, The (Guthrie), 81, 99, 103

Stavis, Barrie, 291, 293, 300–302, 305, 316

Steen, Mr. (Cambridge Theatre electrician), 85, 87

Stevens, Risë, 218

Stevens, Roger, 256

Stock, Mildred, 309

Stratford-upon-Avon, 208, 245

Stratford, Ontario, Shakespearean Festival and Theatre: Chapter Sixteen, and Coulter/Scott/ Guthrie meeting, 214; 217, 220, 248, 256, 260, 268, 269

Streatham Hill Theatre, 173

Sullivan, Francis L., 155

Sumner, John, 313, 314, 318, 325, 327

Swansea Amateur Dramatic Society, 248

Sweeny Agonistes (Eliot), 143

Sweet Aloes (Carey), 140, 142

Sydney, Australia, 312, 318–323

Tamburlaine (Marlowe), 218, 256

Taming of the Shrew, The, 169, 208, 248, 250

Tandy, Jessica, 157, 277, 280

Tartuffe (Molière/Wilbur), 297

Tatlock, Halbert, 69

Taubman, Howard, 281

Taylor-Smith, Jean, 69, 205, 206, 298

Tempest, Marie, 81, 143, 144

Tempest, The, 129, 133, 175

Templegrove School, Eastbourne, 6

Tenth Man, The (Chayevsky), 266, 267

Terry, Ellen, 4

Thames TV., Documentary *The Greeks*, 334, 335

Theatre Guild, New York, 142, 192, 195

Théâtre Populaire, Paris, 145

Theatre Prospect (Guthrie), 117–121

Thérèse Raquin (Zola) adapted as *Guilty* (Boutall), 186

Thorndike, Sybil: *St. Joan*, 74; *Short Story*, 143; Baylis' death, 163; Wartime *Macbeth*, 178; *Peer Gynt*, 188; *Oedipus*, 192, 258, 259; 293

Thorpe-Davis, Cedric, 206

Three Estates, The (Lindsay), 203, 266, 298

Three Sisters, The (Chekhov), Minneapolis, 275, 278, 281, 283

Timon of Athens, 218

Tobias and the Angel (Bridie), 87, 94

Tolstoy, 306, 340; link with Mavor family, 225

Tomelty, Joseph, 214

Top of the Ladder (Guthrie), 211–213

Toone, Geoffrey, 114

Toronto, 101, 102, 224, 226, 229, 235, 237, 268

Toronto Arts and Letters Club, 214

Tosa, Yoshi, 320

Toscanini, Arturo, 219, 255

Trains, lifelong love of, 101

Traviata, La (Verdi), 191, 200

Trelawny of the Wells (Pinero), 166, 168

Triumph of Death, The (Scaife), 51

Triumvirate, The, (Old Vic Directors 1944–49): Burrell/Olivier/ Richardson, 188–194, 197, 198, 202, 207

Tunbridge Wells: Guthrie childhood, Chapter One; Battle of Britain, 175; return to, 333

Tunbridge Wells Operatic Society, 42

Twelfth Night, 54, 102, 129, 131, 150, 157, 181

Uncle Vanya (Chekhov): Burrell production Old Vic, 188; 194; Guthrie Minneapolis, 288, 289, 299, 305, 306

Under the Sycamore Tree (Spewack), 232

Urquhart, Molly, 205

Valk, Frederick, 184

de Valois, Ninette, 156, 164, 173, 182, 190

Vaughan, Dr. William Wyamar (Headmaster Wellington College), 23

Vessel Of Wrath (Laughton-Guthrie film), 160

Viceroy Sarah (Ginsbury), 139, 169

Victoria Theatre, Burnley, 177

Volpone (Molière), 286, 297

Wager, Michael, 253, 254

Walker Art Center, Minneapolis, 269

Wallace, Jim, 306

Warre, Michael, 199

Warren Hastings (Feuchtwanger), 93

Way of the World, The (Congreve), 207

Weir, Austin, 94, 99, 106

Weir of Hermiston, The (Stevenson), 72

Wellington College, 19; Chapter Two; and 330–332

Westminster Theatre, The, See Chapter, Nine, and 142, 143, 159

Wharton Production Company, 271, 333

White, Joan, 116, 122

White Peacock, The (Lawrence), 98

Whiting, Professor Frank, 266, 267
Who's Afraid of Virginia Woolf (Albee), 277
Wilbur, Richard, 260
Wilhelm, Jean, 320, 322, 324, 326
Will, The, 347, 348
Williams, Emlyn, 48, 249
Williams, Miss Evelyn, 124, 130, 159, 162, 163, 173, 176, 181, 187, 190, 212
Williams, Harcourt, 116, 149
Wilson, A. P., 69
Wilson, Dr. Claude, 5
Wilson, Dover, 152
Windsor Hotel, Stratford, Ont., 227
Witch of Edmonton, The (Dekker), 150, 153
Wolfit, Donald, 218

Woodburn, James, 122
Worby, Miss ('Bunty'), 79, 80, 82, 83, 95, 96, 234
Worth, Irene, 219, 233, 243, 262
Wright, Basil, 88
Wyndham's Theatre, 140
Wynyard, Diana, 210

Yeoman of the Guard, The (Gilbert and Sullivan), 3
Y.M.C.A.: Montreal, 100; Toronto, 226
Young Vic Company, The, 197, 201, 216, 217 (See also under Old Vic)

Zeisler, Peter, 260, 262–264; Annagh-ma-Kerrig meeting 265–266; 267–269; Minneapolis, 271, 276, 282, 289, 290, 298